COMPUTER-ORIENTED APPROACHES TO PATTERN RECOGNITION

This is Volume 83 in
MATHEMATICS IN SCIENCE AND ENGINEERING
A series of monographs and textbooks
Edited by RICHARD BELLMAN, *University of Southern California*

The complete listing of books in this series is available from the Publisher
upon request.

COMPUTER-ORIENTED APPROACHES TO PATTERN RECOGNITION

WILLIAM S. MEISEL

Technology Service Corporation
Santa Monica, California

ALSO

Electrical Engineering and Computer Science
University of Southern California
Los Angeles, California

1972

 A C A D E M I C P R E S S   New York   San Francisco   London
A Subsidiary of Harcourt Brace Jovanovich, Publishers

ACADEMIC PRESS, INC.
111 Fifth Avenue, New York, New York 10003

United Kingdom Edition published by
ACADEMIC PRESS, INC. (LONDON) LTD.
24/28 Oval Road, London NW1

LIBRARY OF CONGRESS CATALOG CARD NUMBER: 72-77852

Second Printing, 1974

PRINTED IN THE UNITED STATES OF AMERICA

For Joyce and Joshua

CONTENTS

Preface   xi

Chapter I **BASIC CONCEPTS AND METHODS IN MATHEMATICAL
           PATTERN RECOGNITION**

1.1   What Is Pattern Recognition?   1
1.2   Computer-Oriented Approaches to Pattern Recognition   4
1.3   Examples of Pattern Recognition Applications   4
1.4   The Pattern Recognition Process   5
1.5   Basic Concepts in Pattern Classification   9
1.6   Basic Concepts in Feature Selection   24
1.7   Direct and Indirect Methods   28
1.8   Parametric and Nonparametric Methods   28
1.9   Some Simple Pattern Classification Algorithms   29
1.10 Overview   32
      Exercises   33
      Selected Bibliography   35

Chapter II **THE STATISTICAL FORMULATION AND PARAMETRIC
            METHODS**

2.1   Introduction   38
2.2   Statistical Decision Theory   39
2.3   Histograms   41
2.4   Parametric Methods   42
2.5   Conclusion   44
      Exercises   44
      Selected Bibliography   46

Chapter III INTRODUCTION TO OPTIMIZATION TECHNIQUES

3.1	Indirect Methods	47
3.2	Direct Methods	48
3.3	Linear Programming	50
3.4	A Localized Random Search Technique	51
	Exercises	53
	Selected Bibliography	54

Chapter IV LINEAR DISCRIMINANT FUNCTIONS AND EXTENSIONS

4.1	Introduction	55
4.2	Mathematical Preliminaries	56
4.3	Linear Discriminant Functions	58
4.4	Specifying the Loss Function	59
4.5	Minimizing the Approximate Risk	64
4.6	An Alternate Cost Function	65
4.7	The N-Class Problem	72
4.8	Solution by Linear Programming	76
4.9	Extension to General Φ Functions	77
4.10	Threshold Elements in the Realization of Linear Discriminant Functions	78
	Exercises	80
	Selected Bibliography	82

Chapter V INDIRECT APPROXIMATION OF PROBABILITY DENSITIES

5.1	Introduction	85
5.2	Integral-Square Approximation	85
5.3	Least-Mean-Square Approximation	88
5.4	Weighted Mean-Square Approximation	91
5.5	Relation to Linear Discriminant and Φ-Function Techniques	92
5.6	Extensions	94
5.7	Summary	95
	Exercises	95
	Selected Bibliography	97

Chapter VI DIRECT CONSTRUCTION OF PROBABILITY DENSITIES: POTENTIAL FUNCTIONS (PARZEN ESTIMATORS)

6.1	Introduction	98
6.2	An Alternate Interpretation	103
6.3	Generality of Potential Function Methods	104
6.4	Choosing the Form of Potential Function	105
6.5	Choosing Size and Shape Parameters	107
6.6	Efficient Decision Rules Based on Potential Function Methods	108
6.7	Generalized Potential Functions	114

6.8 Conclusion   116
      Exercises   117
      Selected Bibliography   118

Chapter VII PIECEWISE LINEAR DISCRIMINANT FUNCTIONS

7.1 Introduction   120
7.2 Implicit Subclasses   121
7.3 Perceptrons and Layered Networks   124
7.4 Indirect Approaches to Deriving Piecewise Linear Discriminant Functions   128
7.5 Piecewise Linear Decision Boundaries by Linear Programming   131
7.6 Limiting the Class of Acceptable Boundaries   133
7.7 Conclusion   134
      Exercises   135
      Selected Bibliography   136

Chapter VIII CLUSTER ANALYSIS AND UNSUPERVISED LEARNING

8.1 Introduction   138
8.2 Describing the Subregions   140
8.3 Cluster Analysis as Decomposition of Probability Densities   143
8.4 Mode Seeking on Probability Estimates   144
8.5 Iterative Adjustment of Clusters   145
8.6 Adaptive Sample Set Construction   146
8.7 Graph-Theoretic Methods   148
8.8 Indirect Methods in Clustering   152
8.9 Unsupervised and Decision-Directed Learning   155
8.10 Clustering as Data Analysis   157
8.11 Cluster Analysis and Pattern Classification   157
      Exercises   157
      Selected Bibliography   158

Chapter IX FEATURE SELECTION

9.1 Introduction   162
9.2 Direct Methods   166
9.3 Indirect Methods: Parameterized Transformations   169
9.4 Measures of Quality: Interset and Intraset Distances   179
9.5 Measures of Quality Utilizing Probability Estimates   183
9.6 Measures of Quality: The Preservation of Structure   190
9.7 Indirect Methods: Other Measures of Quality   191
9.8 Custom Orthonormal Transformations   193
9.9 Choosing n of m Features   199
9.10 Conclusion   205
      Exercises   206
      Selected Bibliography   208

Chapter X   SPECIAL TOPICS

10.1   Introduction   214
10.2   Binary Variables   214
10.3   Sequential Feature Selection   215
10.4   Structural, Linguistic, and Heuristic Analysis of Patterns   216
10.5   Asymptotic Convergence and Stochastic Approximation   219
10.6   Nonstationary Pattern Recognition   220
       Exercises   222
       Selected Bibliography   223

Appendix A   A SET OF ORTHONORMAL POLYNOMIALS

                                                                                   228

Appendix B   EFFICIENT REPRESENTATION AND APPROXIMATION OF MULTIVARIATE FUNCTIONS

B.1   Introduction   230
B.2   Continuous Piecewise Linear Form Approximations   233
B.3   Composed Functions   241
      Selected Bibliography   244

Index   247

PREFACE

The terminology "pattern recognition" has been applied to a wide body of work. The intent of this book is not to encompass all the work done under this label, but to cover a coherent body of selected material in relative detail. The orientation of the material covered is as follows:

(1) The author does not attempt to explain or model pattern recognition in humans, although many methods discussed arose from such origins.

(2) Methods which can be used in practical problems are emphasized; largely theoretical results are not discussed in detail and are often simply referenced.

(3) Heavy emphasis is placed on methods which are independent of the specific application for which they are utilized. This orientation does not imply that the choice of methods is independent of the application, but that the methods themselves can be discussed as independent tools.

(4) Another emphasis is on computer-oriented methods, rather than device-oriented methods in the design of pattern recognition systems. The decreasing cost of computation and computers and the availability of inexpensive minicomputers as hardware components led to an orientation toward the use of the general-purpose computer rather than special-purpose devices, particularly in the design phase. However, discussions of threshold-element realizations are included because of their historical importance and present practical value in some systems.

This book is based upon notes for a two-semester graduate-level course developed by the author as part of the Electrical Engineering and Computer Science curriculum at the University of Southern California. Portions of the book have been used as notes for a short course on computer-oriented methods in pattern recognition. The author has been lucky to be able to have tested many of the methods on practical problems at Technology Service Corporation in Santa Monica, California.

This book can be used as a text for a one-semester senior or graduate-level course in pattern recognition without supplement and as a basic text for a two-semester course with support from the instructor or supplementary textbooks. It is suitable as well for self-study.

Prerequisites include a knowledge of basic concepts in probability. Most of the mathematical foundation required is covered in short introductory chapters. Because most methods are interpreted both intuitively and in more formal terms, the book can provide a useful reference for a number of courses in engineering, computer science, operations research, management science, and biomedical engineering.

Because of the complex interrelationships and wide dispersion of pattern recognition literature, it is often difficult to isolate the source of a particular idea. A definitive historical bibliography has not been attempted. The author extends his apologies to anyone who was inadvertently slighted or whose work has been overlooked.

The author wishes to express his appreciation to Dr. David C. Collins for his criticism of the text in general and his contributions to Chapter IV in particular; the technical quality and clarity of the book was considerably improved by his recommendations. Some of the research reported in this work was supported in part by the National Aeronautics and Space Administration under Grant NGL-05-018-044 and by the Air Force Office of Scientific Research under Contract F44620-71-C-0093.

CHAPTER I

BASIC CONCEPTS AND METHODS IN MATHEMATICAL PATTERN RECOGNITION

*Pity the man who requires a lifetime to
learn the pattern of his own heartbeat.*

1.1 WHAT IS PATTERN RECOGNITION?

In their widest sense, patterns are the means by which we interpret the
world. A child learns to distinguish the visual patterns of mother and father,
the aural patterns of speech and music, the tactile patterns of cold and warmth,
patterns of the senses. As he grows older, he refines the detail of his pattern
recognition; he may be able to distinguish a symphony by Beethoven from a
symphony by Bach, or a painting by Renoir from a painting by Rembrandt.
He abstracts his sensory discrimination to indirect patterns; a mathematician
detects patterns in mathematics (an "elegant" proof), a social scientist finds
patterns in the data he analyzes. Some patterns have a physical manifestation
—typed characters on a sheet of paper, the electromagnetic signals of a radar
return. Other patterns have only an abstract existence, e.g., patterns in social
or economic data.

What is the pattern recognition process? When a human glances at a
printed page and recognizes character after character without hesitation,
he is using fixed rules which he learned from experience. He has long since
refined the discrimination of "o" from "a" in a standard type font to a
fixed decision rule. He certainly could not explain that rule, but it clearly
exists.

He developed this ability from experience. At some point in time, he was
repeatedly exposed to samples of the character "a" and samples of the

1

character "o" and told which they were. From examination of these "labeled" samples, he developed a decision rule.

There are thus two aspects to pattern recognition—developing a decision rule and using it. The actual *recognition* occurs in the use of the rule; the *pattern* is defined in the learning process by the labeled samples. In mathematical pattern recognition, we want a decision rule which can classify examples of patterns quickly. We may usually proceed with more leisure in learning the pattern, that is, in deriving the decision rule.

The pattern is defined by the labeled samples of that pattern. Samples are presented as examples of one class of patterns (e.g., the letter "o") or another (e.g., the letter "a"). The representation "o" in the present context is a character of the alphabet; in another context, it is a "circle" rather than a "square." There is no way of discriminating the character from the geometric figure except by stating what we wish to decide, by defining the pattern classes.

A pattern recognition problem thus begins with class definitions and labeled samples of those classes in some workable representation. The problem is solved when a decision rule is derived which assigns a unique label to new patterns.

Mathematical pattern recognition provides a formal structure for solving problems of the sort described. When those problems can be posed within this structure and when an adequate number of labeled samples of the classes are available, the results can be dramatic. However, the techniques of mathematical pattern recognition are simply a collection of numerical algorithms for solving very particular problems posed in very particular ways. Any success in their application depends on careful formulation by the user and an understanding of the assumptions involved in their use. Because of the rather miraculous feats of sensory pattern recognition performed by humans, there is a tendency to expect automatic results from computer-based pattern recognition. As in any other practical problem, a great deal of thought in preparation of the data and in selection and implementation of methods is required; quick "feasibility studies" in computer-based pattern recognition usually produce quick inconclusive results.

Numerical methods in mathematical pattern recognition are based on relatively simple concepts; they depend for their success not upon sophistication relative to the human, but upon the computer's ability to store and process large numbers of samples in an exact manner and upon the computer's ability to work in high dimensions. The human can do very sophisticated things in three dimensions or less, but begins to falter when dealing with higher dimensions; thus, when faced with a mass of data, the human often rushes to represent that data visually through a handful of two-dimensional charts and graphs. The approaches described in this book can be used to extract relationships among many variables not easily represented visually.

The concepts and algorithms of mathematical pattern recognition have other applications that, on the surface, do not fit the basic description. These other uses include the following, most of which are discussed in greater detail in the body of the text.

(1) *The analysis of multivariate data.* One can extract qualitative as well as quantitative conclusions from high-dimensional data; the detection of complex relationships among samples in pattern classification could be considered a highly generalized correlation analysis.

(2) *Continuously labeled variables.* A sample may be labeled with a continuous number rather than with a small, finite set of class labels. The objective would then be to determine an appropriate continuous value for an unlabeled sample.

(3) *Determining "natural" pattern classes.* In some problems, one may wish to *determine* natural pattern classes rather than to *assign* them. For example, one might ask how many distinguishable classes of abnormal heart action can be determined from electrocardiograms.

(4) *Specification of a multivariate probability density from samples of that distribution.* Many pattern classification algorithms are equivalent to the construction of a probability density from which the observed samples could have arisen.

(5) *Measurement selection.* One may rank proposed measurements or indicators by their usefulness in separating pattern classes.

(6) *Visual representation of high-dimensional data.* High-dimensional data may be represented in two or three dimensions in a manner which preserves as much as possible of the local structure of that data, as we do in a two-dimensional map of the three-dimensional world.

(7) *Data reduction.* In order to communicate a printed message, one need not transmit a high-resolution picture of each character, but only the class membership of that character (e.g., "a" as 1, "b" as 2, "c" as 3, ...). In many realistic situations, the amount of *relevant* information in a large amount of data is very small; pattern recognition algorithms can extract a reduced set of numbers representing essential information.

(8) *Artificial intelligence.* The process of abstracting the classification of an unknown sample from samples of known classification is similar to some types of learning in humans; in fact, devices designated "learning machines" have been built by realizing in hardware some of the pattern recognition algorithms we will study [29]. One can argue that a computer displaying creativity in its own media could be designed using variations of pattern recognition and numerical analysis algorithms as elements of a more complex superstructure [26].

1.2   COMPUTER-ORIENTED APPROACHES TO PATTERN RECOGNITION

The author has generally assumed throughout that the derivation of the decision rule from labeled samples, the analysis phase of a pattern recognition problem, will be performed on a general-purpose digital computer. The decision rule, once derived, will be implemented in a manner which is application-dependent, but is often on a general-purpose computer as well.

The decision rule may be quite simple and efficient once derived, while the derivation may require considerable effort. The cost of computation in that phase may be high, judged absolutely, but is most often low, judged relative to the cost of collecting and preparing data and of implementing the entire pattern recognition system. The emphasis on getting the most information from laboriously collected data will most often make the use of a general-purpose computer the rational choice in the analysis phase. This assumption of a computer-based effort is a viewpoint rather than a limitation of this book; many of the algorithms for deriving decision rules can be performed with special-purpose hardware.

A partial consequence of this point of view is an orientation toward practical rather than theoretical aspects of the ideas discussed. Geometrical and statistical arguments will lead to a variety of numerical procedures, each with its own advantages and disadvantages. These procedures, when their underlying concepts and limitations are understood, become versatile tools for solving difficult problems.

1.3   EXAMPLES OF PATTERN RECOGNITION APPLICATIONS

It is worthwhile to mention briefly some concrete examples of pattern recognition problems, making no attempt at an exhaustive list.

Visual pattern recognition problems include the following:

(1)   character recognition, where the object is to identify the membership of specimens of a given alphabet;

(2)   fingerprint classification;

(3)   reconnaissance photos, where one might be satisfied if a machine could reject a large proportion of the photos of no interest;

(4)   the identification of natural resources from satellites or planes; and

(5)   cell tissue analysis, where the classes might be "healthy," "unhealthy," and "indeterminate," or where one might care to identify chromosomes.

Auditory pattern recognition includes word identification, speaker identification, and detection of incipient failure of machinery or aircraft by engine vibration analysis.

Engineering applications include radar or sonar signature analysis, where one might attempt, for example, to identify types of aircraft by their radar returns. Another promising application is in the derivation of performance functions in process control [33]; often the direct measures of performance can only be measured off-line and must be related to quantities measurable on-line.

Seismic data yield a rich source of pattern classification problems. One might discriminate underground atomic blasts from earthquakes, or human footsteps from those of water buffalo.

Biomedical applications include electrocardiogram and vectorcardiogram analysis, electroencephalogram analysis, and diagnosis based on laboratory tests and physical measurements.

Another general area of application is in prediction of the future behavior of a system. For example, in economics one might collect a number of economic time series and attempt to distinguish the three classes of data preceding "inflation in the next quarter at an annual rate above 4%," "inflation in the next quarter at an annual rate between 4% and 0%," and "inflation in the next quarter at an annual rate below 0%"; the labeled samples would of course be based on previous history for which we know the outcome. In operations research, we may be interested in sales or demand forecasting. One might propose endless applications such as weather or smog forecasting.

In general, any system which can be considered a "black box" described by input–output data, where the output is a class label and exemplar data are available, is a candidate for pattern recognition algorithms. Some of the concepts and techniques to be proposed can be used in more general data analysis applications, as was outlined in Section 1.1.

On the other hand, an apparent application may dissolve because of (1) too few labeled samples, (2) the lack of a distinguishable pattern in the data available, or (3) the availability of a better way to solve the problem.

1.4   THE PATTERN RECOGNITION PROCESS

The two stages of pattern recognition, deriving the decision rule and using it, can be performed concurrently or sequentially. In Fig. 1.1a, the sequential procedure is diagrammed; all the labeled pattern samples are collected and the best decision rule based on those samples is derived. That decision rule is used without change to classify unlabeled samples.

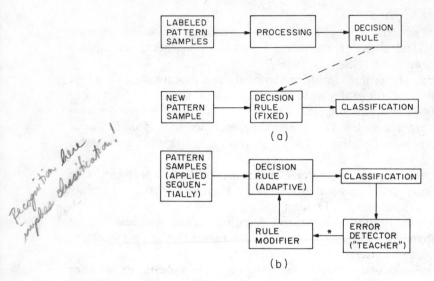

FIG. 1.1 Recognition strategies: (a) learning before recognition; (b) learning and recognition concurrently.

Figure 1.1b indicates the case where the decision rule is modified as it is used. In this case, a sample is presented and classified; an error detector (a "teacher") indicates whether the classification is correct, and the decision rule is left unchanged or modified as appropriate. The reader may have remarked that there is no need for a decision rule if the error detector can and does classify perfectly every sample which appears. If the error detector is removed at some point in time and the decision rule used thereafter without change, the procedure is effectively sequential and adequately represented by Fig. 1.1a. The concurrent procedure, Fig. 1.1b, is meaningfully different from the sequential procedure only if there is a time delay at the point marked by an asterisk. Then the decision rule classifies a sample upon presentation; the correct classification is not available without a delay. In economic forecasting (or any other sort of forecasting), for example, the accuracy of the forecast is available at some point in the future and can be used to adjust the decision rule at that time. This feedback procedure is a type of learning, since the performance of the system presumably improves with time. It should be noted, however, that the distinction between the two types of procedures represented in Fig. 1 blurs if one considers the "learning" procedure simply a repeated application of the sequential procedure; that is, we use a decision rule without modification until enough new labeled samples are available to justify rederiving the decision rule. If 1000 samples went into deriving the decision rule at some point in time, the derivation procedure would have to be very efficient to justify deriving a modified rule each time one additional sample was available. On the other hand, if the system from which we take the samples varies with time, a procedure which modifies the decision rule frequently, giving more weight to recent samples, is justified.

The process necessary in deriving the decision rule in a practical pattern recognition problem is indicated diagrammatically in Fig. 1.2. The system from which given patterns arise is characterized completely only by its physical embodiment. We characterize that embodiment numerically by some set of measurements. We shall refer to the raw data describing the system as the *measurement space*; that is, a sample of a pattern is represented by specific

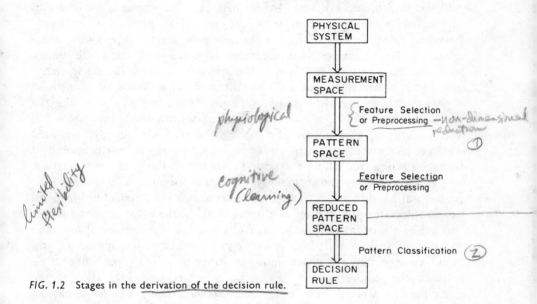

FIG. 1.2 Stages in the derivation of the decision rule.

values of all the measurements, corresponding to a point in the measurement space. The pattern classification algorithms we will study should be applied in a *pattern space* which (a) is finite-dimensional, (b) is of relatively low dimension, and (c) contains sufficient information to satisfactorily perform the classification. The pattern space may be identical with the measurement space, or several stages of intermediate processing may be necessary.

Feature selection (or *preprocessing*) is the process by which a sample in the measurement space is described by a finite and usually smaller set of numbers called *features*, say $x_1, x_2, \ldots, x_n$, which become components of the pattern space. A point in measurement space is transformed by the intermediate processing into a point $\mathbf{x} = (x_1, x_2, \ldots, x_n)$ in pattern space. Finally, we must develop, on the basis of a finite set of labeled samples, a *decision rule* with which we can classify a point in the pattern space corresponding to an unlabeled sample. The process of deriving the decision rule is called *pattern classification*. The two major areas of pattern recognition are feature selection and pattern classification procedures.

An example will serve to make this process more concrete. Consider the recognition of handprinted characters of the alphabet. The physical system is the group of humans generating the characters, along with their writing utensils, or, equivalently, the physical results of their efforts. A given character can be transformed into a set of measurements through, for example, a grid of photocells or a television camera. These two methods yield distinctly different measurement spaces. In the first case, we obtain a finite set of measurements, equal in number to the number of photocells, each proportional to the intensity of the light falling on the corresponding photocell. In the latter case, we obtain a continuous function of time as the camera scans the character; this results in a infinite-dimensional measurement space. The former measurement space is finite-dimensional, and thus may constitute a pattern space. The latter requires preprocessing, e.g., by sampling the scanning process periodically to reduce it to a finite number of measurements. The pattern spaces obtained directly by the methods already suggested would be likely to be of dimension too high for economical classification, and feature selection would be necessary. To transform the given pattern space into a space of lower dimensionality, one might use one's knowledge of the problem at hand to extract pertinent information; in the character recognition problem, features of a reduced space could be the number of grid points covered by the character, the number of crossings of a horizontal line, and so on. Each feature must be a scalar; e.g., x_1 might be the number of grid points covered. Since a given character serves to assign some value to all features, the feature vector $\mathbf{x} = (x_1, x_2, \ldots x_n)$ is a representation of the particular character. As in Fig. 1.3, each *sample* becomes a *point* in pattern space once the features are defined. The decision rule is derived from the set of labeled samples by pattern classification algorithms.

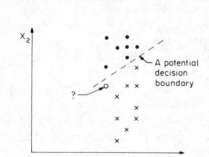

FIG. 1.3 A two-dimensional pattern space with samples: ● samples of class S_1; × samples of class S_2; ○ unknown pattern.

1.5 BASIC CONCEPTS IN PATTERN CLASSIFICATION

Let us begin this section by restating the abstract pattern classification problem more formally.

A pattern is described by a finite number of scalar variables called *features*: $x_1, x_2, \ldots, x_n$. A particular pattern is a point $\mathbf{x} = (x_1, x_2, \ldots, x_n)$ in an n-dimensional *pattern space* X encompassing the region in which patterns can occur. There are a finite number of *pattern classes* $S_1, S_2, \ldots, S_N$ into which we wish to classify points of the pattern space. (As shorthand, class S_i is often referred to as "class *i*.") These classes are unknown, except for a finite number of *labeled samples* of each class:

$$\mathbf{y}_1^{(i)}, \mathbf{y}_2^{(i)}, \ldots, \mathbf{y}_{M_i}^{(i)} \in S_i, \qquad i = 1, 2, \ldots, N,$$

where each $\mathbf{y}_j^{(i)}$ is a point of the pattern space

$$\mathbf{y}_j^{(i)} = (y_{j1}^{(i)}, y_{j2}^{(i)}, \ldots, y_{jn}^{(i)}).$$

[handwritten: $J = 1, \cdots, M$] *[handwritten: features (poor notation x's instead)]*

The geometrical concepts involved in pattern classification are deceptively simple. Consider, for example, a two-dimensional pattern space as illustrated in Fig. 1.3. There are two pattern classes, S_1 and S_2. We are given the labeled samples shown. The problem is then to classify an unknown point, such as the one indicated, into one of the two classes.

One way to do so is by determining a *decision boundary*, as indicated, separating the classes. Our *decision rule* is then to assign any point falling on one side of the boundary to class S_1 and those falling on the other side to class S_2. The unlabeled point would be classified as a member of class S_2. This simple diagram is worth the reader's pausing; it contains the essential geometrical concepts of pattern classification. In particular, it illustrates the assumed correspondence of closeness of two samples in pattern space to similarity of the patterns which they represent.

In two dimensions we can define a good decision boundary quite readily, and no real problem exists. But in higher dimensions we cannot visualize the sample distribution, and therein lies the motivation for our study.

1.5.1 Qualifications

There are some misleading simplifications in the geometrical viewpoint. The pattern space is artificially constructed, and the implications of a representation such as Fig. 1.3 should not be extended too far. Hidden problems occur in four areas: (1) normalization, (2) distance measures, (3) dimensionality, and (4) complex sample distributions.

① NORMALIZATION

Our usual concepts of distance may bear no relation to the problem. One feature may be measured in units different from another; in economics, the gross national product is measured in billions of dollars while the Federal Reserve discount rate is a percentage. In such a system, direct use of the Euclidean distance is pointless; that is, if x_1 is measured in billions and x_2 in fractions, then

$$(x_1{}^2 + x_2{}^2)^{1/2} \approx (x_1{}^2)^{1/2},$$

and the latter feature has negligible effect on the distance measure.

Thus, for our geometrical concepts to hold, explicit or implicit normalization of the features is a necessity. We will suggest two methods of explicit normalization; both have the effect of "squaring up" the space. Define

$$a_k = \max\{y_{1k}^{(i)}, y_{2k}^{(i)}, \ldots, y_{M_ik}^{(i)}; \quad i = 1, 2, \ldots, N\}$$

$$-\min\{y_{1k}^{(i)}, \ldots, y_{M_ik}^{(i)}; \quad i = 1, 2, \ldots, N\}, \tag{1.1}$$

$k = 1, 2, \ldots, n$; that is, let a_k be the range of the kth feature of the sample points over *all* sample points. The normalized variables are then x_k/a_k. This method considers only the extreme values; an alternative approach is to use the variances of the features

$$\sigma_k{}^2 = \frac{1}{M_1 + \cdots + M_N} \sum_{i=1}^{N} \sum_{j=1}^{M_i} (y_{jk}^{(i)} - \bar{y}_k)^2, \qquad k = 1, 2, \ldots, n, \tag{1.2}$$

where

$$\bar{y}_k = \frac{1}{M_1 + \cdots + M_N} \sum_{i=1}^{N} \sum_{j=1}^{M_i} y_{jk}^{(i)}.$$

The normalized variables are then x_k/σ_k. Sebestyen has shown that this latter normalization is optimum in a certain sense [35]; see Exercises 1.1 and 1.2.

Figure 1.4 indicates the effect of normalization by the range of each feature. Simple normalization is necessary for algorithms which have no self-normalizing quality and often speeds numerical convergence of those which do.

It should be emphasized that such a preliminary normalization by no means yields a pattern space where distances between samples correspond accurately to similarity of the physical patterns. This point will be discussed further.

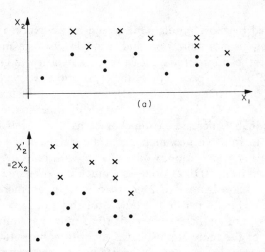

FIG. 1.4 The effect of scale changes: (a) unnormalized samples; (b) normalized samples.

(by range normalization)

② DISTANCE MEASURES

Presuming that the features are normalized, we can speak meaningfully of distance in the pattern space. But we need not choose the conventional Euclidean distance

$$d_1(\mathbf{x}, \mathbf{y}) = \left[\sum_{i=1}^{n} (x_i - y_i)^2 \right]^{1/2}. \qquad (1.3)$$

$x = (x_1, y_1)$
$y = (x_2, y_2)$
dimension here 1 & 2
$d = \sqrt{(x_1 - x_2)^2 + (y_1 - y_2)^2}$

Any *distance function* $d(\mathbf{x}, \mathbf{y})$ satisfying

Minimality $\quad d(\mathbf{x}, \mathbf{x}) = 0, \qquad d(\mathbf{x}, \mathbf{y}) > 0 \quad$ for $\mathbf{x} \neq \mathbf{y}$,

Symmetry $\quad d(\mathbf{x}, \mathbf{y}) = d(\mathbf{y}, \mathbf{x}), \qquad$ and $\quad d(\mathbf{x}, \mathbf{y}) + d(\mathbf{y}, \mathbf{z}) \geq d(\mathbf{x}, \mathbf{z}). \qquad (1.4)$

Triangle Inequality $\qquad$ *see Tversky + Rev. 4/77*

will have all the usual qualities of a distance. For example, it is considerably more efficient to compute

$$d_2(\mathbf{x}, \mathbf{y}) = \sum_{i=1}^{n} |x_i - y_i| \qquad \text{City Block} \qquad (1.5)$$

on a digital computer. On the other hand, the Euclidean distance is often more convenient to use in analytic studies since it has a derivative at all points.

Distance is a crucial concept in pattern recognition; we assume, roughly, that the closer a point is to another point, the more similar are the patterns represented by those points. One would hence expect that in many applications, a single normalization and a single distance measure might not be adequate; the appropriate measure of similarity might vary for different regions of pattern space. For example, suppose we were trying to determine the state of alertness of a driver from several measurements, and suppose that one of the features was the length of time at the wheel. That feature would probably increase in importance as a determinant of alertness as it increased in value; hence, its appropriate weight in the distance function, its appropriate normalization, would change with its value. An increase of time at the wheel from 20 to 21 hours is a much larger change in terms of alertness than an increase from 1 to 2 hours. Similarly, an increase in vehicle speed from 10 to 30 miles per hour would probably not force a significant increase in alertness, but an increase from 65 to 85 miles per hour certainly would.

Many of the more sophisticated algorithms in pattern recognition minimize the importance of any predetermined normalization and, in effect, vary the normalization throughout the space. When an algorithm is very sensitive to initial normalization, it is critically important to recognize this shortcoming.

DIMENSIONALITY

One can visualize the problem of pattern classification quite easily in two or three dimensions. We have noted the distortions involved in this visualization. It is important here to point out another pitfall.

Suppose in a one-dimensional space we have two sample points in a unit interval (Fig. 1.5a). If they were evenly distributed, we would have one for each half-unit interval. In two dimensions, if we have four sample points for the unit square (the square one unit in length on each side), we would have one sample point for each half-unit square (Fig. 1.5b). Three dimensions

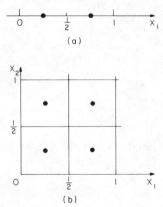

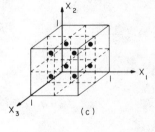

FIG. 1.5 The curse of dimensionality: (a) one dimension, two samples; (b) two dimensions, four samples; (c) three dimensions, eight samples.

and eight sample points again gives us one sample point for each half-unit cube within the unit cube (Fig. 1.5c). The obvious extension is that, in an n-dimensional cube, if we have 2^n evenly distributed points, we have one point for each half-unit cube. Certainly in the one-, two-, and three-dimensional cases we feel that such a situation represents a very sparse set of samples. We could hardly be confident that there was an overabundance of information upon which to base a decision. But the logical extension is that in a ten-dimensional space, 2^{10} sample points (1024 points) would be similarly unsettling. The problems compound dramatically with dimensionality. The number 2^{20} is over one million. This is the "curse of dimensionality," an apt phrase suggested by Richard Bellman [3].

Does this mean that in a practical high-dimensional problem we must have an immense number of sample points to obtain a satisfactory answer? The answer is that we often do if we use techniques carelessly extrapolated from geometrical concepts, for we have difficulty in imagining the size of high-dimensional spaces. We are interested in considering problems in which the number of samples is limited, and we must therefore use methods which will extract as much information as possible from what is most often, relative to the size of the space, a small sample.

The problem however, takes a slightly different form in many practical cases. That is, we may have a small number of samples clustered in small regions of the space, so that in these regions we have a fairly dense sample; but, consequently, much of the space must be empty of sample points. One might visualize widely separated sets of clusters, strings, or sheets of sample points from a geometrical point of view; we must keep in mind that we are likely to have either a very sparsely populated space or sample points occurring in only a very small proportion of the volume of the pattern space.

Let us examine the relationship between sample size and dimensionality further from a statistical point of view. Foley and co-workers have provided a convincing demonstration of the pitfalls inherent in using a small ratio M/n of sample size to number of features, where M is here the number of samples per class [9, 34]. Ten 21-dimensional samples of each class were generated from identical probability densities uniform over the same region (i.e., the position of occurrence of the samples was completely random within the pattern space). A linear transformation into two dimensions, designed to separate the classes optimally, was applied; the result is indicated in Fig. 1.6a. The classes are obviously separated easily despite the fact that they represent nothing but random noise! If M/n is increased substantially, samples from the same distribution, displayed by an optimum linear transformation, appear as in Fig. 1.6b; the true nature of the distributions is more obvious. Foley describes both experimental and theoretical results which suggest that a value of M/n of at least 3 to 5 is advisable to prevent an apparently significant

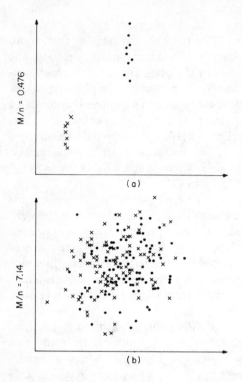

(a)

(b)

FIG. 1.6 Required sample size vs. dimensionality (from [9, 34]): (a) 21 dimensions, 10 samples/class, $M/n = .476$ (overprints not indicated); (b) 14 dimensions, 100 samples/class, $M/n = 7.14$ (overprints not indicated).

classification of an identical distribution. (The theoretically achievable accuracy on an infinite sample set is 50%; even with M/n between 3 and 5, Foley was obtaining 60 to 70% accuracy in classifying the samples used to generate the decision rule.)

The discussion to this point has emphasized the need for a substantial sample size because of the dangers inherent in ignoring this problem. This does not mean that one is precluded from applying pattern recognition algorithms to problems where the patterns are initially specified as high-dimensional vectors. Consider, for example, a hypothetical situation. Suppose the designer is presented with 100 labeled two-dimensional samples from each of two classes and suppose a linear hyperplane exists which separates the samples with 100% accuracy. Since M/n is 50, the designer may be confident that he could achieve a high accuracy on unlabeled samples. But let us introduce a villian; a prankster modifies the samples before the designer can analyze them. He adds 98 features to each sample, chosen from a source of random noise. The designer is presented with only 100 one hundred-dimensional samples per class; M/n is only 1. If he proceeds (with a resigned sigh) to obtain a perfect separating hyperplane by methods such as described in Chapter IV, it must intersect the original two-dimensional plane in a two-dimensional hyperplane which separates the two-dimensional samples with 100% accuracy. Since the problem is intrinsically two-dimensional, the derived decision rule should achieve high accuracy on unlabeled samples, to the surprised delight of the designer. This scenario suggests that the n used in M/n should in some sense be the *intrinsic dimensionality*. The fact that the problem is *posed* in terms of n variables is insufficient information to determine sample requirements.

In the best of all possible worlds, the optimum one hundred-dimensional hyperplane would have zero coefficients for the 98 fake variables; i.e., they would be effectively ignored, and the designer would realize they were useless and drop them. Foley's results suggest however, that because M/n is small, the 98 variables would appear to contain information, and the coefficients would, in general, be nonzero. We are thus restricted in a limited sense by M/n with n the dimensionality of the given samples; if M/n is small, we may be unable to extract the intrinsic dimensionality. We can verify the usefulness of the resulting decision rule on an independent test set, but it may be impossible to discover the intrinsic utility of a given feature.

The concept of intrinsic dimensionality is reinforced by some further theoretical work. Suppose we had a fixed sample size M. If the dimensionality n were less than the intrinsic dimensionality, information should be missing, and achieving maximum accuracy should not be possible. If n is greater than the intrinsic dimensionality, the possibility of a degradation in the performance of decision rules obtained by algorithms which are sensitive to sparseness of the samples may occur. Hence there may be an optimum value of M/n in some cases. Theoretical work by Hughes [13] and Abend *et al.* [1] shows, with certain assumptions, that there is in most cases an optimum M/n for the *average* pattern recognition problem. Kanal and Chandrasekaran [17] present a good discussion of this work; Allais [2] and Ullman [37] have reported related results. Section 1.6 and Chapter IX contain further discussion of intrinsic dimensionality and feature selection algorithms.

In summary, the geometrical impact of dimensionality consideration is expectation of a sparsity of labeled samples which our algorithms must be able to tolerate; the statistical impact is a requirement on sample size for validity of the results irrespective of the algorithm.

COMPLEX SAMPLE DISTRIBUTIONS

Samples are not always distributed in distinct contiguous clusters by class (i.e., unimodal distributions) as in Fig. 1.3. A given class may form more than one group in space (i.e., a *multimodal* distribution), as in Fig. 1.7a; an obvious example could arise from the fact that both "A" and "a" are in the class corresponding the first letter of our alphabet. A given class may

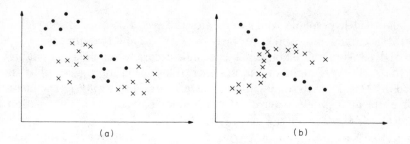

FIG. 1.7 Sample distributions: (a) multimodal; (b) sheets.

further form a sheet in pattern space rather than a cluster, as in Fig. 1.7b; it is conceivable, for example, that samples of two classes could fall on two concentric spheres of different radii. In higher dimensions the possibilities for complexity of the sheets increase.

There is a physical reason for expecting sheets rather than clusters in many applications. Suppose there is a physical law, albeit unknown, describing the members of a given class. Further suppose the location of a sample in pattern space is fully determined through m parameters in that law. If our pattern space is of dimension n, with $n > m$, the samples must ideally lie on a surface of dimension m in n-space. (Practically speaking, because of measurement error, etc., they would lie *near* the ideal surface.)

The point to be drawn from this discussion is that many practical problems will require complex decision rules; algorithms based on a mental image of two well-behaved clusters of sample points may fail.

1.5.2 Decision Boundaries and Discriminant Functions

How should we specify decision boundaries? We might do so by an equation of the boundary surface, e.g.,

$$g(\mathbf{x}) = 0. \tag{1.6}$$

For example, a linear hyperplane (the extension of the line of Fig. 1.3 to n-space) might, in a particular case, take the form

$$2x_1 + 3x_2 - 4x_3 - x_4 + 1 = 0. \tag{1.7}$$

How do we determine the resulting classification of a particular sample $\mathbf{y} = (y_1, y_2, \ldots, y_n)$? If the sample is on one side of the boundary, it is in class S_1; if on the other side, in class S_2. (If it is *on* the boundary, we must classify it arbitrarily.) Since the very meaning of Eq. (1.6) is that the boundary is the locus of all points $\mathbf{x}$ such that $g(\mathbf{x}) = 0$, $\mathbf{y}$ is on the boundary if $g(\mathbf{y}) = 0$. If $g(\mathbf{x})$ is a continuous function, then all points $\mathbf{x}$ such that $g(\mathbf{x}) > 0$ are on the opposite side of the boundary from all points $\mathbf{x}$ such that $g(\mathbf{x}) < 0$. [Since $g(\mathbf{x})$ is continuous, we must cross the boundary at $g(\mathbf{x}) = 0$ to get from the positive region to the negative region.] We thus define a *decision rule* $c(\mathbf{x})$ which tells us the classification of a point $\mathbf{x}$:

$$c(\mathbf{x}) = \begin{cases} 1 & \text{if} \quad g(\mathbf{x}) \geq 0, \\ 2 & \text{if} \quad g(\mathbf{x}) < 0, \end{cases} \tag{1.8}$$

where the 1 and 2 refer to classes S_1 and S_2, respectively. Using the example of Eq. (1.7), $\mathbf{y} = (1, 1, 1, 1)$ gives $g(\mathbf{y}) = 1 > 0$, and $\mathbf{y}$ is classified a member of class S_1 by the decision rule of (1.8).

Suppose, however, that we have more than two classes of samples. The boundary might be as in Fig. 1.8, a three-class problem. We may consider

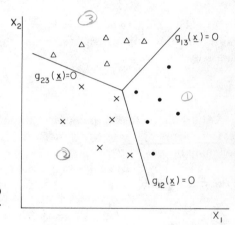

FIG. 1.8 Three-class boundaries: ● class 1; × class 2; △ class 3. Underscored symbols are vectors.

that we have three boundaries: between classes 1 and 2, between classes 1 and 3, and between classes 2 and 3. In general, for N classes, we would have $N(N - 1)/2$ boundaries. Suppose these boundaries have equations

$$g_{12}(\mathbf{x}) = 0, \qquad g_{13}(\mathbf{x}) = 0, \qquad g_{23}(\mathbf{x}) = 0, \tag{1.9}$$

where g_{ij} is the boundary between classes i and j. Our decision rule could then take the form

$$c(\mathbf{x}) = \begin{cases} 1 & \text{if} \quad g_{12}(\mathbf{x}) \geq 0 \quad \text{and} \quad g_{13}(\mathbf{x}) \geq 0, \\ 2 & \text{if} \quad g_{12}(\mathbf{x}) < 0 \quad \text{and} \quad g_{23}(\mathbf{x}) \geq 0, \\ 3 & \text{if} \quad g_{13}(\mathbf{x}) < 0 \quad \text{and} \quad g_{23}(\mathbf{x}) < 0. \end{cases} \tag{1.10}$$

This is an unwieldy way of specifying the decision rule; with 10 classes, there would be 45 functions to work with. Fortunately, there is an alternative approach. Suppose we define N *discriminant functions*, one for each class: $\rho_1(\mathbf{x})$, $\rho_2(\mathbf{x})$, ..., $\rho_N(\mathbf{x})$. The decision rule could be to classify $\mathbf{y}$ in class i if $\rho_i(\mathbf{y})$ has the largest value of all the discriminant functions when all are evaluated at $\mathbf{y}$; i.e., let

$$c(\mathbf{x}) = i \quad \text{if} \quad \rho_i(\mathbf{x}) > \rho_j(\mathbf{x}) \quad \text{for all} \quad j \neq i. \tag{1.11}$$

(Once again, ambiguity exists when $\rho_i(\mathbf{x}) = \rho_j(\mathbf{x})$ for $i \neq j$; this may be resolved by arbitrarily assigning $\mathbf{x}$ to the class labeled with the smallest integer.) The boundary between classes i and j is clearly the locus of points where $\rho_i(\mathbf{x}) = \rho_j(\mathbf{x})$; hence, the boundary functions of Eq. (1.9) are given by

$$g_{ij}(\mathbf{x}) = \rho_i(\mathbf{x}) - \rho_j(\mathbf{x}). \tag{1.12}$$

In particular, in the two-class problem, we may work efficiently with Eq. (1.8) or use two discriminant functions, in which case the two approaches are related by

$$g(\mathbf{x}) = \rho_1(\mathbf{x}) - \rho_2(\mathbf{x}). \tag{1.13}$$

A third alternative is to convert an N-class problem into a series of two-class problems by *successive dichotomy*, by successively splitting the classes remaining into two groups.

If we began with eight classes, we could solve the following three problems in the order given:

(1) Find a decision boundary separating classes 1 through 4 from classes 5 through 8.

(2) Using samples of classes 1 through 4 alone, find a decision boundary separating classes 1 and 2 from classes 3 and 4. Using samples of classes 5 through 8, find a decision boundary separating classes 5 and 6 from classes 7 and 8.

(3) Find decision boundaries separating each of the groups of two remaining.

As complex as this may seem, only $N - 1$ functions need be derived for an N-class problem. Referring to Fig. 1.9, we can display the decision procedure as a tree structure; each of the seven nodes corresponds to a decision function. Further, in the eight-class problem approached as described above (Fig. 1.9a), only three functions need be evaluated to reach a decision on a

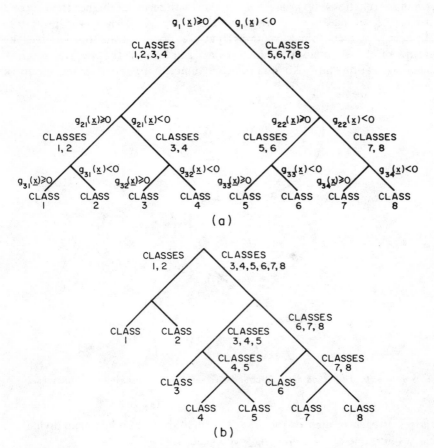

FIG. 1.9 Successive dichotomies in an eight-class problem: two possible trees. Underscored symbols are vectors.

given sample, versus eight functions if discriminant functions are used. Only seven functions need be derived for the series of dichotomies of Fig. 1.9b as well, but it may be necessary to evaluate four functions to determine class membership. On the other hand, if classes 1 and 2 occur much more frequently than the other classes, we need evaluate only two functions to reach a decision most of the time.

However, the decision boundaries resulting from successive dichotomies may be less satisfactory than those resulting from the use of discriminant functions, given that each has the same level of complexity. Consider Fig. 1.10: The solid-line decision boundary can be generated by quadratic discriminant functions, bivariate polynomials with terms no higher than second order; the samples shown are separated perfectly. Because the procedure of successive dichotomies requires that we first separate the samples by groups of classes, quadratic functions at each level of the tree can produce exact separation only if a quadratic is sufficient to separate the group of

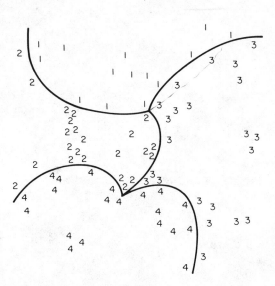

FIG. 1.10 Four-class decision boundaries generated by discriminant functions.

classes at each branch of the tree. The first-level boundary can divide the classes into one of the following seven groups:

$$\{1\} \{2, 3, 4\} \qquad \{1, 2\} \{3, 4\}$$
$$\{2\} \{1, 3, 4\} \qquad \{1, 3\} \{2, 4\}$$
$$\{3\} \{1, 2, 4\} \qquad \{1, 4\} \{2, 3\}$$
$$\{4\} \{1, 2, 3\}$$

Quadratic functions can separate the samples perfectly only if the first-level function separates one of the groups perfectly and only if this process can be repeated at every level. This is a more severe restriction than that imposed by quadratic discriminant functions; it cannot be met in Fig. 1.10.

To summarize, when successive dichotomies are employed, one must take care to choose the decision tree for (1) efficient utilization of the resulting decision rule, and (2) effective separation of sample points [23].

1.5.3 Probability Densities

The preceding discussion presented discriminant functions simply as a convenient way to specify class boundaries; this is often all that can be said about them. But, in some cases, they take on a deeper significance: The value of the discriminant function for a given sample can indicate the *degree* of class membership. For such a *characteristic* discriminant function, the larger the value of $\rho_i(\mathbf{x})$ at a point $\mathbf{x}$, the more likely it is that that point is in class i. Figure 1.11 illustrates this condition. This approach emphasizes the

FIG. 1.11 Characteristic discriminant functions for a one-dimensional pattern space: $\times$ class 1; ● class 2.

fact that most pattern classes are "fuzzy sets" [40]; that, in reality, class membership is not always obvious. If you have a friend with indifferent handwriting, you can probably testify to the fact that classifying a particular letter as "o" rather than as "a" can be a purely arbitrary decision. In such a case, a sample has a degree of membership in several classes, and we call it a member of the class to which it has the greatest degree of membership; that is, $\mathbf{x}$ is in class i if $\rho_i(\mathbf{x}) > \rho_j(\mathbf{x})$ for $j \neq i$. This is the decision rule in Eq. (1.12) motivated on different grounds.

If $\rho_i(\mathbf{x})$ is appropriately normalized, it may be viewed as a multivariate probability density for class i, and the samples of class i may be viewed as samples arising from the distribution described by that probability density. A probability density evaluated at a point $\mathbf{x}$ describes the probability of a sample's occurring in a small region about that point when multiplied by the volume of that region.

Figure 1.12 illustrates a bivariate (two-dimensional) probability density function and a set of samples that might have resulted from it. (From the opposite point of view, we might say that the density function "fits" the samples well.)

Because probability theory is such a well-developed tool, pattern recognition work is often phrased in those terms. Almost all the methods we shall discuss have both an intuitive and a more formal probabilistic interpretation. Chapter II is devoted to a more extensive elaboration of the probabilistic formulation.

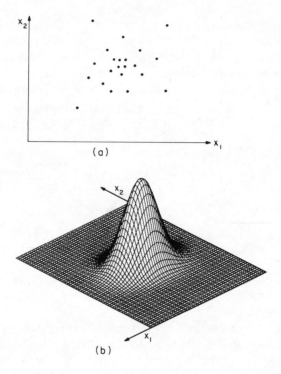

(a)

(b)

FIG. 1.12 A two-dimensional pattern space: (a) samples; (b) a probability density function describing the sample distribution.

1.5.4 Design Sets and Test Sets

In applying pattern recognition algorithms, one generally assumes that most of the information about the nature of the system is contained in the labeled samples; hence, the most practical validation of a decision rule is to apply it to a set of labeled samples and note the results. The percentage of mis-classified samples in this *test set* would hopefully be a meaningful estimate of the error rate to be expected in applying that decision rule to unlabeled samples. If 10 out of 1000 labeled samples were classified incorrectly, we could hope for a 1 % error rate (99 % accuracy) in practice.

Some care is necessary in applying this test. If the *design set*† (the labeled samples used in deriving the decision rule) is used as the test set, the results may be invalid. The nearest neighbor algorithm (Section 1.9.1) will always give 100 % accuracy when applied to the design set. Meisel [25] has shown that there exist continuously differentiable discriminant functions which

† Sometimes *training set, learning set.*

achieve 100% accuracy on the design set independent of the nature of that set. (It is assumed in both cases that there are no identical samples from different classes.) In general, one must divide the labeled samples into a design set and an independent test set. There are at least two approaches to independent testing:

(1) Divide the set of labeled samples into two disjoint sets. Derive the decision rule from the design set; estimate its accuracy using the test set.

(2) Remove one sample from the M total samples and use the remaining samples to derive a decision rule; test it on the isolated sample. Repeat the process M times, removing each sample, deriving a decision rule from the rest, and classifying the isolated sample. The error rate on the isolated samples is a good estimate of the performance of the decision rules [17, 21].

Let us consider the first procedure. It is painful to sacrifice scarce samples from the design set for the test set; yet, if the test set has too few samples, it yields an inaccurate estimate of performance. What is the minimum number of samples we need devote to the test set? Highleyman [11] studied this problem in some detail, and relates the number of samples required for a given confidence in the calculated error rate to the value of the actual (unknown) error rate and total number of samples. Kanal and Chandrasekaran [17] suggest that Highleyman's results be used with care, since they are accurate only for small error rates and probably only for large samples sizes. If the number of test samples is in the hundreds, one should expect only a rough estimate of the probability of error; this may be sufficient, however, as a feasibility test. Having obtained an estimate of the probability of error by the use of a test set, the designer may wish to take full advantage of a limited number of samples by deriving the final decision rule using *all* the samples. It is a reasonable assumption that the probability of error on unlabeled samples will not be degraded (and will probably be improved) by this procedure.

The second approach, successively withholding one sample, has the advantage of allowing the decision rule to be based on all except one sample and allowing a test size set effectively equal to the total number of samples, but requires deriving M decision rules. Further, one must choose the final decision rule from among the M rules generated; there are no good guides to this choice.

If one argues that the many decision rules generated by the latter procedure should be essentially identical (since any two design sets differ by only two samples), one is led to conclude that those decision rules are essentially identical to one obtained by using *all* the samples (since the design set consisting of all samples differs from each of the other design sets by only *one* sample). Hence, under such conditions, one should obtain a nearly identical estimate of the error rate by using the full set of samples as both design and test set as one would by the calculation of M decision rules. The conditions under which it may be meaningful to use the design set as the test set are thus when (1) the decision rule resulting from the pattern recognition algorithms used is insensitive to the deletion of single samples, and (2) the total number of samples is large enough relative to the dimensionality to avoid the problem discussed in Section 1.5.1. [Condition (2) also helps assure that condition (1) holds.]

How many samples *of each class* should be used in the design set? Hughes [14] concludes in the two-class case that fewer samples should be taken of the more probable class than is indicated by the relative probability of occurrence of that class (the *a priori* probability), but that the probability of error is insensitive to nonoptimal sample partitions. It is common practice to use a number of samples of a given class in the design set in proportion to their occurrence in the total sample set.

1.6 BASIC CONCEPTS IN FEATURE SELECTION

Feature selection can be a multistage process, as was indicated in Fig. 1.2; there may be several stages in the reduction of a measurement space to a space suitable for the application of pattern classification algorithms. Often these steps require an intimate knowledge of the particular application. There are, however, many feature selection methods which can be discussed *abstractly*, those which may be applied in general perhaps to aid the application of knowledge particular to the problem, but without explicit restriction to a given problem. For example, we will not here discuss feature selection concepts particular to visual pattern recognition.

What do we wish of the final set of features, the set which forms the pattern space? We might list four general requirements.

1 LOW DIMENSIONALITY

The features defining the pattern space must be relatively few in number. This is necessary both to make the algorithms meaningful and computationally feasible. We have noted that the curse of dimensionality implies that the number of sample points should, as a rule of thumb, increase exponentially with dimensionality. Pattern classification algorithms increase at least linearly, and usually much faster, in cost with dimensionality. If it is necessary to apply classification algorithms directly to a high-dimensional space, one must take great care to note the difficulties inherent in such a situation; in such cases, it will seldom be reasonable to use sophisticated methods, and simpler methods should be tried first.

(2) SUFFICIENT INFORMATION

The final features which we use must retain sufficient information to allow recognition of the patterns desired. One might wonder if it is possible to extract from a representation in a 1000-dimensional measurement space, e.g., the outputs of a 25 × 40 matrix of photocells, a set of numbers, say ten, which contains sufficient information for the recognition desired. If there exists a solution to the recognition problem, however, that fact constitutes a proof of the fact that a single "feature" is sufficient to represent all of the *relevant* information in the measurement space. For, the overall objective of the entire project is to classify the pattern represented by those 1000 numbers as a member of one of N classes. We might then visualize the recognition process as the transformation of the measurement space into real line; more particularly, each sample is mapped to one of the integers $1, 2, \ldots, N$, denoting class membership. Hence, all the information desired from the system is contained in a one-dimensional space. Representing the information by a small set of numbers is thus clearly possible if the problem has a satisfactory solution at all. Like most existence proofs, however, this argument does not make the problem of feature selection any easier.

As a side note, we might add that the information which we are interested in retaining is seldom the combinatorial or probabilistic definition of information [18]. Instead, we are not interested in the retention of "pure" information, but in the retention of relevant information. Approaches to the measurement of goal-defined information have received some attention [18, 41], and one might hope that further development along these lines could result in a more formal statement of the requirement discussed.

(3) GEOMETRICAL CONSISTENCY   *What about Venn diagrams vs 3-dim. structure?*

There is a basic geometrical assumption in the use of almost all pattern classification algorithms. We assume that a small distance between two points in pattern space corresponds to a small difference in the actual patterns *in terms of the quality to be recognized*. This statement contains two points: (1) different patterns must be distinguishable; and (2) differences which are irrelevant to the quality to be recognized (e.g., the position in the alphabet) need not be reflected in the pattern space. Figure 1.13 illustrates this point. In Fig. 1.13a, note that the A's are transformed into points in feature space near one another and the letter B is distinguishable by distance in pattern space. In Fig. 1.13b, the A's are transformed into points close to one another despite the fact that they appear in radically different forms in terms of rotation and size in the physical pattern; the characteristic to be recognized is not relevant to size or rotation. Of course, irrelevant differences *may* be reflected

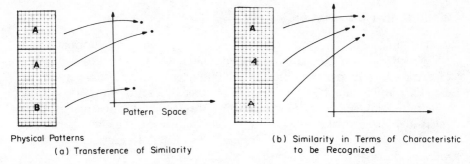

Physical Patterns
(a) Transference of Similarity

(b) Similarity in Terms of Characteristic to be Recognized

FIG. 1.13 Distance as a measure of similarity: (a) dissimilarity between classes; (b) similarity within a class.

in pattern space; this is acceptable as long as pattern classes are distinguishable.

④ Consistency of Features throughout the Samples

A point which is often overlooked in feature selection is that each feature must be expressed consistently over all patterns. A feature is intended to allow comparison of one aspect of different patterns, and must be suited to this purpose. This point is a difficult one to express without recourse to an example. If the present income of an individual is one of the features of a system designed to recognize the suitability of a person for a particular job, one must ask the question whether one can compare the incomes of individuals living in different parts of the country directly. A person living in one portion of the country may be much better off in terms of standard of living than an individual living elsewhere with a considerably higher income. Hence, perhaps the correct feature should be a ratio of the individual's income to regional average income. Similarly, comparing income in 1949 directly with income in 1969 is meaningless unless those incomes are adjusted to a constant dollar.

Another obvious but conceptually important example of this latter problem occurs in the use of time as a feature. Formally, in a process which one suspected was nonstationary over time, one could include time as one of the features. Because of the apparently inexorable flow of time, however, a given value of the feature "time" would never occur in future samples, making it meaningless to compare those samples with historical samples. Any feature which essentially increases monotonically with time, such as the gross national product of the United States, is similarly unsuitable for use as a feature; however, related features, such as the percentage change in the gross national product over a year, can reasonably be compared to historical data. On the other hand, a time-related feature which does *not* increase monotonically with time, but which repeats itself, such as do the seasons of the year, is a possible feature.

 Possible approaches to feature selection include the following:

(a)   One may attempt to define features by an intuitive understanding of the system in question. One may simply choose a small number of features which can be calculated from the measurement space and which supposedly satisfy the above four conditions; pattern classification algorithms are then applied to samples expressed in terms of these features.

(b)   One may define a large number of features postulated relevant to *Multivariate Prin Comp.* the quality to be recognized in the system, and quantitatively rank these features, using the sample points, to obtain a reduced set of " best " features.

(c)   One may find the best of a class of transformations upon the measurement space, e.g., the best linear transformation. This, of course, requires defining a measure of the utility of a set of features in separating the classes.

(d)   In cases where the measurement space is essentially infinite-dimensional, that is, essentially consists of functions of one or two variables (such as photographs or electrocardiograms), these infinite-dimensional functions can be approximated by an orthogonal expansion with a finite number of terms; the coefficients of the expansion of a particular sample would constitute a point in pattern space; i.e., the coefficients become the features. In a Fourier expansion of a signal, the ith feature might be the coefficient of the ith term. *Karhunen–Loeve.*

Of course, combinations and variations of these approaches are possible. One might, for example, take the coefficients of a two-dimensional Fourier expansion of a two-dimensional image and attempt to choose a reduced set of coefficients " best " for classification.

It should be emphasized that the division between pattern classification and feature selection is largely artificial. Pattern classification is a form of feature selection, since, in the two-class case, it transforms the measurement space into a one-dimensional pattern space by the transformation

$$x' = \rho_1(\mathbf{x}) - \rho_2(\mathbf{x}).$$

On the other hand, feature selection is a form of pattern classification, since, if we transform the problem into one or two dimensions, the decision boundary may be specified by inspection. Nevertheless, the distinction is a useful tool because (1) the computational feasibility of most pattern classification algorithms is restricted to relatively low dimension; (2) practical sample sizes restrict the dimensionality of the space for which the concepts upon which these algorithms are based are valid; and (3) a degree of normalization of the raw measurements is often necessary for accurate derivation of the decision boundary. Further, the two-stage process will often result in a more computationally efficient decision rule.

Advanced techniques in feature selection are discussed in Chapter IX, largely because the discussion employs approaches developed in the intervening chapters on pattern classification methods. The location of the chapter is not intended to suggest that feature selection is of secondary importance; indeed, many workers in the field consider feature selection the most critical stage of the recognition process. In many applications, however, strong features can be designed through knowledge of the system, keeping in mind the four principles just outlined; there is hence no logical difficulty in proceeding as if we have an acceptable set of features.

1.7 DIRECT AND INDIRECT METHODS

In both pattern classification and feature selection, we can proceed by two basic routes:

(1) we can directly construct features or a decision boundary using a procedure which we have reason to believe will provide good results because of the nature of the construction itself; or

(2) we can define a cost function which we believe, if optimized, would provide good features or a good decision boundary.

The first approach is a *direct* method; the second, an *indirect* method. The first puts the burden on choosing a meaningful constructive algorithm; the second requires the definition of the qualities of " best " features or a " best " decision boundary.

In an indirect algorithm, a great deal of effort may be necessary to obtain the optimum of the cost function among a set of parameterized decision rules or transformations, but the result is determined as soon as the cost function and parameterized family are chosen; that result is only as valid as those choices. Indirect methods provide an " optimal " solution, but this is false security if our definition of optimality was poor.

Both approaches have their advantages and disadvantages; we shall discuss these as we encounter them.

1.8 PARAMETRIC AND NONPARAMETRIC METHODS

Pattern recognition algorithms are often classed as *parametric* or *nonparametric*. A parametric approach to pattern classification defines the discriminant function by a class of probability densities defined by a relatively small number of parameters. In fact, almost all parametric methods in both pattern classification and feature selection assume that each pattern class arises from a multivariate Gaussian (normal) distribution, where the parameters are the mean and covariances (as further discussed in Chapter II).

Nonparametric methods, despite the label, often use parameterized discriminant functions, e.g., the coefficients of a multivariate polynomial of some degree. The intended implication of the term is that no conventional form of probability distribution is assumed. Most of the methods in this text are nonparametric.

1.9 SOME SIMPLE PATTERN CLASSIFICATION ALGORITHMS

We discuss in this section two direct pattern classification algorithms based on the concept of the equivalence of closeness in pattern space and pattern similarity.

1.9.1 Nearest Neighbor Classification

The geometrical interpretation discussed in Section 1.4 suggests the following decision rule: classify a point as a member of the class to which its nearest neighbor belongs. This procedure is *nearest neighbor* pattern classification [8]. If membership is decided by a majority vote of the k nearest neighbors, we call the procedure, naturally enough, a *k-nearest neighbor* decision rule. Such an algorithm is capable of generating quite complex class boundaries. Figure 1.14 indicates its power. It has, however, important shortcomings in assumptions and implementation.

It assumes that the distance between points is a legitimate measure of the similarity of the patterns they represent. We have already discussed the dangers of this assumption. Further, the k-nearest neighbor algorithm weights

see p 12.

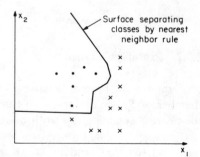

FIG. 1.14 Nearest neighbor classification: class 1; × class 2.

equally all *k*-nearest neighbors, no matter what their relative distance from the point in question. On the other hand, the nearest neighbor algorithm can be criticized for making poor use of all the information available. When one begins modifying the algorithm to overcome these objections, it loses its simple character and begins to resemble other methods to be discussed in this volume. In implementation, nearest neighbor pattern classification requires storage of all the sample points and computation of the distance from all to a point in question. In summary, use of this method must be preceded by careful normalization of pattern space and choice of distance, and is best for small numbers of samples of reasonably low dimension. Several authors discuss the theoretical validity of this approach from a probabilistic viewpoint [5, 6, 31].

We have viewed nearest neighbor pattern classification in terms of the boundaries between classes. It could as well be viewed in terms of discriminant functions. For, if we define

$$\rho_i(\mathbf{x}) = -d(\mathbf{x}, \mathbf{y}_k^{(i)})$$

Smaller the distance, the larger neg. value of ρ

for $\mathbf{y}_k^{(i)}$ the closest sample point of class *i* to *x*, where $d(\mathbf{x}, \mathbf{y})$ is a distance function, the nearest neighbor rule is equivalent to placing a point **z** in class *i* if

largest → closest

see p. 18

$$\rho_i(\mathbf{z}) > \rho_j(\mathbf{z}) \qquad \text{for} \quad j \neq i.$$

Figure 1.15 illustrates such a discriminant function for a one-dimensional example.

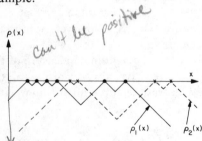

Can't be positive

FIG. 1.15 Discriminant functions constructed by the nearest neighbor rule.

1.9.2 Prototype Classification

Suppose we have a "perfect" example $\mathbf{m}_i$ of each class S_i, and every member of S_i is a distortion of that prototype. A simple rule, equivalent to the nearest neighbor rule with one sample of each class, is to assign a point to the class to whose prototype it is closer; that is, decide **x** is in S_i if $d(\mathbf{m}_i, \mathbf{x}) < d(\mathbf{m}_j, \mathbf{x})$ for $j \neq i$ (and make an arbitrary assignment if the distances are equal). Thus, this approach is equivalent to choosing discriminant functions

$$\rho_i(\mathbf{x}) = -d(\mathbf{m}_i, \mathbf{x})$$

for each class S_i.

If the Euclidean distance is used, linear discriminant functions will suffice; for,

$$d(\mathbf{m}_i, \mathbf{x}) < d(\mathbf{m}_j, \mathbf{x})$$

if and only if

$$\sum_{k=1}^{n} (x_k - m_{ik})^2 < \sum_{k=1}^{n} (x_k - m_{jk})^2,$$

where $\mathbf{m}_i = (m_{i1}, m_{i2}, \ldots, m_{in})$. Rewriting this inequality, we have

$$\sum_{k=1}^{n} x_k{}^2 - 2 \sum_{k=1}^{n} x_k m_{ik} + \sum_{k=1}^{n} m_{ik}^2 < \sum_{k=1}^{n} x_k{}^2 - 2 \sum_{k=1}^{n} x_k m_{jk} + \sum_{k=1}^{n} m_{jk}^2.$$

We thus see that $\sum_{k=1}^{n} x_k{}^2$ can be canceled, and linear discriminant functions

$$\rho_i(\mathbf{x}) = \sum_{k=1}^{n} x_k m_{ik} - \tfrac{1}{2} \sum_{k=1}^{n} m_{ik}^2 \qquad (1.14)$$

will suffice. In particular cases, this corresponds to the concept of a " matched filter " used in communication theory.

Clearly, this latter method is less powerful, but simpler, than the nearest neighbor approach. In fact, one might obtain a prototype for a given class by calculating the mean of a set of samples of that class; this last approach uses very little of the information contained in the samples. The concepts and formulas derived here can be employed in generating piecewise linear discriminants and will be so used in Chapter VII.

Simple approaches can be used to obtain initial guesses at optimum hyperplanes for use in indirect methods such as those to be described in Chapters IV and V. For example, suppose we consider the two-classes case and assume that $\mathbf{m}_1$ and $\mathbf{m}_2$ in Eq. (1.14) are the means of samples of classes 1 and 2:

$$\mathbf{m} = \frac{1}{M_i} \sum_{j=1}^{M_i} \mathbf{y}_j^{(i)}. \qquad (1.15)$$

Then, the decision boundary between the two classes is $\rho_1(\mathbf{x}) = \rho_2(\mathbf{x})$; that is, from Eq. (1.14), the linear hyperplane

$$\sum_{k=1}^{n} x_k(m_{1k} - m_{2k}) - \tfrac{1}{2} \sum_{k=1}^{n} (m_{1k}^2 - m_{2k}^2) = 0, \qquad (1.16a)$$

or, in vector notation,

$$(\mathbf{m}_1 - \mathbf{m}_2) \cdot \mathbf{x} - \tfrac{1}{2}(\|\mathbf{m}_1\|^2 - \|\mathbf{m}_2\|^2) = 0. \qquad (1.16b)$$

This is an easily computed decision function; it is the hyperplane bisecting the line between the means of the two classes.

1.10 OVERVIEW

The reader should not assume that the importance of a subject or chapter in this text is proportional to its length. In particular, in the later chapters, it will often be possible to describe important and difficult methods quite briefly by referring to previous work. At the same time, the author has repeated some ideas to ease the plight of the reader who may wish to use this text as a reference.

Chapter II discusses the statistical formulation of the pattern recognition problem, which provides a theoretical framework for the results as well as important basic concepts. This book however, tends to emphasize the intuitive basis of methods and to minimize the statistical background required of the reader.

Further groundwork is provided in Chapter III, where the fundamentals of optimization techniques required for the remainder of the text are provided.

Chapters IV and V discuss closely related indirect pattern classification methods, where the decision boundaries or discriminant functions are linear or in which the unknown parameters appear linearly (e.g., higher-order polynomials). Several cost functions defining the optimality of a given decision rule are described and compared.

An important class of direct pattern classification methods, potential function (Parzen estimator) methods, is the subject of Chapter VI. These techniques allow the construction of probability densities corresponding to a distribution of samples and allow the direct application of many statistical concepts. The relation of some potential function methods to the indirect methods discussed in Chapter V is noted.

A powerful family of decision rules is based upon the use of piecewise linear decision boundaries and/or discriminant functions (Chapter VII). The indirect methods discussed are computationally difficult, although limiting the generality of the decision rule by means discussed improves their feasibility; most methods proposed are hence direct methods. The perceptron (or layered network) realization of such decision rules is presented.

This chapter formulated the pattern recognition problem in conventional form. There are several variations which Ho and Agrawala [12] categorized by the type of knowledge available about the samples:

(1)   the functional form from which the probability densities arise, i.e., a specific family of parameterized distributions;

(2)   the exact parameters of the distribution;

(3)   labeled samples; and

(4)   unlabeled samples (unknown classification).

Combinations of these four types of knowledge define a wide set of variations on the basic theme. (Some combinations are, of course, contradictory or present an impossible problem.)

If both (1) and (2) are known, the probability densities defining the classes are fully defined, and the problem is nearer to pure statistics than pattern recognition. The results of statistical decision theory outlined in Chapter II are applicable to this case. If only (1) and (3) are known, it remains to identify the parameters from the labeled samples. Such parametric methods are briefly discussed in Chapter II as well.

The bulk of this text describes the most common problem, where only labeled samples are provided.

When the samples are unlabeled, the problem is one of identifying natural clusters or modes of the probability densities from which the samples arise. This problem is the subject of Chapter VIII; there the emphasis is on the situation where only (4) rather than (1) and (4) is available.

Chapter IX deals extensively with advanced techniques in feature selection, drawing from concepts developed in pattern classification.

The final chapter, Chapter X, deals with a few special topics which can be briefly related to the work of previous chapters.

The methods suggested are tools that must be applied with care to particular applications. This text can only describe the capabilities and limitations of those tools; the reader must judge their suitability in the specific case. Some applications will require a great deal of cleverness on the reader's part in order to formulate them so that the techniques described herein can be utilized; other applications will require originality in choosing combinations of algorithms to achieve the desired ends. The reader's education in pattern recognition can only begin with this volume.

EXERCISES

1.1.   Let $Y = \{\mathbf{y}_1, \mathbf{y}_2, \ldots, \mathbf{y}_M\}$ be the set of all sample points. Find normalization factors $w_1, w_2, \ldots, w_n$ for features $x_1, x_2, \ldots, x_n$ such that the mean-square Euclidean distance between the normalized sample points $\bar{\mathbf{y}}_i$,

1. Use partial derivatives
We
2. Set equal to 0

$$Q = \frac{1}{M(M-1)} \sum_{i=1}^{M} \sum_{j=1}^{M} d^2(\bar{\mathbf{y}}_i, \bar{\mathbf{y}}_j)$$

$$= \frac{1}{M(M-1)} \sum_{i=1}^{M} \sum_{j=1}^{M} \sum_{k=1}^{n} w_k^2 (y_{ik} - y_{jk})^2,$$

is minimized, subject to the constraint that

$$\sum_{i=1}^{n} w_i = 1.$$

(Hint: Use the method of Lagrange multipliers.)

$\lambda \left(\sum w_k - 1 \right) = 0$
[Solve for w]

1.2. Repeat Exercise 1.1 with the substitute constraint

$$\prod_{i=1}^{n} w_i = 1.$$

(This says that the volume of a unit cube is not affected by the normalization.)

see p. II

1.3. Show that the function of Eq. (1.5) satisfies Eq. (1.4).

1.4. Find a distribution of sample points of two classes in a two-dimensional pattern space such that a change of scale for one of the features will result in a change of classification of a particular test point using the nearest neighbor rule. $\rightarrow$ *collapsing of one scale*

1.5. Note that a discriminant function representing nearest neighbor classification can be drawn looking at only the members of the given class (as in Fig. 1.15). Can this be done for k-nearest neighbor classification (restrict yourself to the case of $k > 1$, k odd, 2 classes)? How may such a discriminant be constructed? Give a one-dimensional example.

majority — step function transition

1.6. Given the following pattern recognition problem: Taking the set of diagrams of two perfect circles drawn in a 1-unit square, classify them into the classes of "intersecting circles" and "nonintersecting circles."

Same

   (a)   Suppose you are given a set of samples of both classes of diagrams and are asked to use these samples to define the class boundaries. What set of features would you choose (e.g., circumference of circle 1, radius of circle 2)?

   (b)   Derive, if possible, the exact equation of the surface separating the classes in pattern space in terms of the features you have chosen.

$(d - \sum r)$

1.7. State briefly a possible pattern recognition problem. For the stated problem, indicate how, by poor choice of features, one might violate each of the four principles cited for choice of features.

1.8. (a) For what reasons might you choose successive dichotomy rather than N discriminant functions in an N class pattern classification problem, and vice versa?   *cost factor (p.18) N-1 functions*
   (b) Why might you choose one dichotomization over another? *of binary decision*
   (c) If $p_1 = 0.4$, $p_2 = 0.3$, and $p_3 = 0.3$ (p_i is the *a priori* probability of class i), what is the best dichotomization to minimize the average number of evaluations of decision boundaries?

1.9. Show that the number of unique decision trees that may be used for successive dichotomy in an n-class problem is given iteratively by†

$$d(n) = \sum_{j=1}^{n/2} \binom{n}{j} d(n-j)\, d(j) - \frac{1}{2} Q_n \binom{n}{n/2} d^2(n/2),$$

where

$$Q_n \triangleq \begin{cases} 1, & n \text{ even,} \\ 0, & n \text{ odd,} \end{cases}$$

with $d(1) = d(2) = 1$. The notation $\{x\}$ is the integer part of x; the notation $\binom{n}{j}$ is the binomial coefficient.

SELECTED BIBLIOGRAPHY

1. Abend, K., Chandrasekaran, B., and Harley, T. J., Comments on the Mean Accuracy of Statistical Pattern Recognizers, *IEEE Trans. Information Theory* **15**, 420–423 (1969).
2. Allais, D. C., Selection of Measurements for Prediction, Stanford Electron. Labs., Stanford, California, SEL-64-115, 1964.
3. Bellman, R. E., "Adaptive Control Processes," Princeton Univ. Press, Princeton, New Jersey, 1961.
4. Bellman, R. E., Kalaba, R. E., and Zadeh, L. A., Abstraction and Pattern Classification, *J. Math. Anal. Appl.* **13**, 1–7 (1966).
5. Cover, T. M., Rates of Convergence for Nearest Neighbor Classification, *Proc. 1st Ann. Conf. Systems Theory, Hawaii*, January 1968.
6. Cover, T. M., and Hart, P. E., Nearest Neighbor Pattern Classification, *IEEE Trans. Information Theory* **13**, 21–26 (1967).
7. Estes, S. E., Measurement Selection for Linear Discriminants Used in Pattern Classification, IBM Res. Rept., San Jose Res. Labs., San Jose, California, RJ-331, 1965.
8. Fix, E., and Hodges, J. L., Jr., Discriminatory Analysis, Nonparametric Discrimination: Consistency Properties, Univ. of California, Project 21-49-004, Rept. 4, 1951.
9. Foley, D., The Probability of Error on the Design Set as a Function of the Sample Size and Feature Size, Ph.D. dissertation, Syracuse University, June 1971. Available as Rome Air Development Center Rep. RADC-TR-71-171.
10. Fu, K. S., "Sequential Methods in Pattern Recognition and Machine Learning," Academic Press, New York, 1969.

† This result was derived by Lee W. Martin.

11. Highleyman, W. H., The Design and Analysis of Pattern Recognition Experiments, *Bell Sys. Tech. J.* **41**, 723–744 (1962).
12. Ho, Y.-C. and Agrawala, A. K., On Pattern Classification Algorithms, Introduction and Survey, *Proc. IEEE* **56**, 836–862 (1968).
13. Hughes, G. F., On the Mean Accuracy of Statistical Pattern Recognizers, *IEEE Trans. Information Theory* **14**, 55–63 (1968).
14. Hughes, G. F., Number of Pattern Classifier Design Samples per Class, *IEEE Trans. Information Theory* **15**, 615–618 (1969).
15. Kanal, L. N. (ed.), " Pattern Recognition," Thompson, Washington, D.C.,
16. Kanal, L. N., and Abend, K., Adaptive Modeling of Likelihood Classification—I, Philco–Ford Corp., Blue Bell, Pennsylvania, Tech. Rep. No. RADC-TR-66-190, 1966; also Vol. II (with T. J. Harley, Jr.), RADC-TR-68-118, 1968.
17. Kanal, L. N., and Chandrasekaran, B., On Dimensionality and Sample Size in Statistical Pattern Classification, *Proc. NEC Conf., 1968*, pp. 2–7 (to be published in " Pattern Recognition ").
18. Kolmogorov, A. N., Three Approaches to the Quantitative Definition of Information, *Problemy Peredači Informacii* **1**, 3–11 (1965) (*English transl.: Problems of Information Transmission*).
19. Krishnaiah, P. R. (ed.), " Multivariate Analysis," Academic Press, New York, 1966.
20. Krishnaiah, P. R. (ed.), " Multivariate Analysis II," Academic Press, New York, 1969.
21. Lachenbruch, R. A., and Mickey, M. R., Estimation of Error Rates in Discriminant Analysis, *Technometrics* **10**, 715–725 (1968).
22. Marill, T., and Green, D. M., On the Effectiveness of Receptors in Pattern Recognition Systems, *IEEE Trans. Information Theory* **9**, 11–17 (1963).
23. Martin, L. W., and Meisel, W. S., Successive Dichotomies in Pattern Recognition (to be published).
24. Mason, C. J. W., Pattern Recognition Bibliography, *IEEE Sys. Science and Cybernetics Group Newsletter*, February, October, and December 1970.
25. Meisel, W. S., Potential Functions in Mathematical Pattern Recognition, *IEEE Trans. Comput.* **18**, 911–918 (1969).
26. Meisel, W. S., On the Design of a Self-Programming Computer, presented at *Ann. Conf. Amer. Soc. Cybernetics, Washington, D.C., October 1968.*
27. Mendel, J. M., and Fu, K. S. (eds.), "Adaptive, Learning, and Pattern Recognition Systems," Academic Press, New York, 1970.
28. Nagy, G., State of the Art in Pattern Recognition, *Proc. IEEE*, **56**, 836–861 (1968).
29. Nilsson, N. J., " Learning Machines," McGraw-Hill, New York, 1965.
30. Page, J., Recognition of Patterns in Jet Engine Vibration Signals, *Digest 1st Ann. IEEE Computer Conf., September 1967*, pp. 102–105.
31. Peterson, D. W., Some Convergence Properties of a Nearest Neighbor Decision Rule, *IEEE Trans. Information Theory* **16**, 26–31 (1970).
32. Richardson, J. M., Theory of Property Filtering in Pattern Recognition, Hughes Aircraft Res. Labs., Malibu, California, Tech. Rept. No. RADC-TR-66-531, 1966.
33. Russo, F. A., and Valek, R. J., Process Performance Computer for Adaptive Control Systems, *IEEE Trans. Comput.* **17**, 1027–1036 (1968).
34. Sammon, J. D., Foley, D., and Proctor, A., Considerations of Dimensionality versus Sample Size, *IEEE Symp. Adaptive Processes, Austin, Texas, December 1970.*
35. Sebestyen, G., " Decision-Making Processes in Pattern Recognition," Macmillan, New York, 1962.
36. Tou, J. T. (ed.), " Computer and Information Sciences—II," Academic Press, New York, 1967.

37. Ullman, J. R., Experiments with the *N*-Tuple Method of Pattern Recognition, *IEEE Trans. Comput.* **18**, 1135–1137 (1969).

38. Watanabe, S., "Knowing and Guessing," Wiley, New York, 1969.

39. Watanabe, S. (ed.), "Methodologies of Pattern Recognition," Academic Press, New York, 1969.

40. Zadeh, L. A., Fuzzy Sets, *Information and Control* **8**, 338–353 (1965).

41. Zunde, P., Information Measurement and Value, presented at *Ann. Mtg. Amer. Soc. Cybernetics, Gaithersburg, Maryland, October 1969.*

CHAPTER II

THE STATISTICAL FORMULATION
AND PARAMETRIC METHODS

2.1 INTRODUCTION

It has been noted that discriminant functions in the classification problem may be viewed as probability densities describing the occurrence of the sample points of each class; that is, we may imagine that the sample points of class S_i occur according to a probability density $p_i(\mathbf{x})$, and that the problem of pattern classification may be considered the approximation of $p_i(\mathbf{x})$. Note that $p_i(\mathbf{x})$ is the conditional probability that $\mathbf{x}$ will occur, given that $\mathbf{x}$ is a member of class S_i, i.e.,

$$p_i(\mathbf{x}) \equiv p(\mathbf{x} \mid i).$$

Other relevant statistics are the *a priori* probabilities p_i, the probabilities that a sample of class S_i will occur. If the number of samples in each class is representative of the process being measured and there are M_i members in class S_i, then a reasonable approximation is

$$p_i = M_i/(M_1 + M_2 + \cdots + M_N) \tag{2.1}$$

presuming N classes. It should be noted that there are many cases where Eq. (2.1) is not reasonable. Consider the character recognition problem. One might collect an equal number of handwritten samples of each character for study, but this does not imply that in an application, the probability of occurrence of each character is the same.

For the bulk of this chapter, we will make the hopeful assumption that

$p_i(\mathbf{x})$ and p_i, $i = 1, 2, \ldots, N$, are known. Statistical decision theory will not tell us how to obtain these statistics, but the optimal way to treat them once we have them. The chapter will conclude with a brief discussion of *parametric methods*, methods where we assume a form of probability distribution determined by parameters with simple interpretations and estimate these parameters using the sample points.

2.2   STATISTICAL DECISION THEORY

Statistical decision theory will tell us, given the appropriate probability densities and a point $\mathbf{x}$ in our pattern space, the optimal decision rule to minimize a mathematically defined risk. We wish to define a decision function $c(\mathbf{x})$, the value of which is the best choice of class to which to assign $\mathbf{x}$. The *risk R* is defined as the expected value of a loss function, that is,

$$R = E_i E_{\mathbf{x}} \{L[c(\mathbf{x}), i]\}, \tag{2.2}$$

where $L(c, i)$ is the loss associated with choosing class c when the correct class is i, and E_y indicates the expected value with respect to the distribution of y [see Eq. (2.4)]. The loss function must be defined by the mathematician; it is not defined by the theory. For example, one loss function might be the following:

$$L(c, i) = \begin{cases} -h_i & \text{for} \quad c = i, \\ 0 & \text{for} \quad c \neq i, \end{cases} \tag{2.3}$$

where $h_i > 0$. This loss function simply says that we assign a negative loss, i.e., a positive gain, to a correct decision and no loss to an erroneous decision. (In other words, the loss is greater for an erroneous decision than for a correct decision.) The constants h_i can all be the same or they may be different to indicate the relative importance of guessing correctly one class rather than another. We will discuss some alternate loss functions at a later point.

The expected value in Eq. (2.2) is an average over all the classes and over all the pattern spaces; that is,

$$R = \sum_{i=1}^{N} \int_X L[c(\mathbf{x}), i] p(i, \mathbf{x}) \, dX, \tag{2.4}$$

where the integral is over the entire pattern space X, and $p(i, \mathbf{x}) = p_i \, p_i(\mathbf{x})$ is the joint probability density of the point $\mathbf{x}$ occurring and being a member of class S_i. We may proceed somewhat further without choosing a particular loss function. We do so by writing

$$R = \int_X \left[\sum_{i=1}^{N} L[c(\mathbf{x}), i] p(i, \mathbf{x}) \right] dX. \tag{2.5}$$

We note that minimizing the expression in brackets in the above equation for each **x** will minimize the risk; that is, given **x**, we should minimize the function $F(c)$ over $c = 1, 2, \ldots, N$, where

$$F(c) = \sum_{i=1}^{N} L(c, i) p(i, \mathbf{x}) = \sum_{i=1}^{N} L(c, i) p_i \, p_i(\mathbf{x}). \qquad (2.6)$$

It is at this point that we must choose a loss function to proceed. The loss function of Eq. (2.3) yields

$$F(1) = -h_1 p_1 p_1(\mathbf{x})$$
$$\vdots \qquad\qquad\qquad (2.7)$$
$$F(N) = -h_N p_N p_N(\mathbf{x}).$$

We note that the decision function which minimizes F is the following:

$$c(\mathbf{x}) = i \quad \text{if} \quad h_i \, p_i \, p_i(\mathbf{x}) \geq h_k \, p_k \, p_k(\mathbf{x}) \quad \text{for all} \quad k \neq i. \qquad (2.8)$$

(This does not yield a unique decision if the inequality becomes an equality, but we may make an arbitrary decision at such boundaries.)

Note that our decision boundary, the locus of points for which the equality holds in (2.8), would remain unchanged if both sides of the inequality in (2.8) were operated on by a monotonic function. A monotonic function of a probability is often denoted a *likelihood*. Further, if there are two classes, instead of comparing two functions as in (2.8), we may use the *likelihood ratio*

$$\Omega(\mathbf{x}) = p_1 p_1(\mathbf{x}) / p_2 p_2(\mathbf{x}). \qquad (2.9)$$

If then,

$$\Omega(\mathbf{x}) \geq h_2/h_1, \qquad (2.10)$$

we categorize **x** as belonging to class 1. 2

Let us consider another loss function of some importance:

$$L(c, i) = \begin{cases} K_1, & c = 1, \; i = 2, \\ K_2, & c = 2, \; i = 1, \\ 0, & c = i, \end{cases} \qquad (2.11)$$

where we have two classes and K_1 and K_2 are positive constants, K_1 representing what might be called the penalty for false alarm and K_2 representing what might be called the penalty for no alarm. In general, K_1 will be less than K_2. One might imagine the situation of a system for warning against enemy air attack in which class 1 represents the class of enemy aircraft and class 2, friendly aircraft. If the system indicates incorrectly that a friendly aircraft is an enemy aircraft, that is a false alarm—the case $c = 1$, $i = 2$. If there is indeed an enemy aircraft and it is classified a friendly aircraft and no alarm occurs, the result could be a disaster. That is, we pay a larger penalty for no alarm than we do in the case of the false alarm which requires some attention but may avert obliteration of the decision maker. An analysis as before yields the decision function

$$c(\mathbf{x}) = \begin{cases} 1 & \text{if } K_2 \, p_1 p_1(\mathbf{x}) \geq K_1 p_2 \, p_2(\mathbf{x}), \\ 2 & \text{otherwise.} \end{cases} \qquad (2.12)$$

As a concrete example of the application of decision theory, let us consider a coin identification problem. We have located some rare coins, but many of the faces of the coins have been worn smooth and we cannot tell one type of coin from another. However, some of the coins are identifiable. Table 2.1

TABLE 2.1 Coin identification example[a]

$h_1 = 2 \qquad h_2 = 1$

Weight x	Coin type 1	Coin type 2	Decision $c(x)$
$1 \leq x < 2$	0.05	0.30	2
$2 \leq x < 3$	0.15	0.20	2
$3 \leq x < 4$	0.15	0.05	1
$4 \leq x < 5$	0.05	0.05	?
	$p_1 = 0.40$	$p_2 = 0.60$	

[a] Table entries are $P(x, i)$, point probabilities, rather than probability densities.

indicates how the 2 types of coins are distributed by weight. For example, 5% of the coins that are identifiable are of type 1 and weigh between 1 and 2 grams, 20% are of type 2 and weigh between 2 and 3 grams, and so on. The *a priori* probabilities are .40 for class 1 and .60 for class 2. If we adopt the loss function in Eq. (2.3) with $h_i = 1$ for all i, then the optimum decision one would make in classifying an unidentifiable coin purely by weight is given in the decision column of Table 2.1. Note that if a coin weighs 4 to 5 grams there is no optimum decision since the two probabilities are equal.

2.3 HISTOGRAMS

The classical method by which one constructs the probability density from a set of samples is by means of a histogram. Table 2.1 is the result of such a method. Generally, this approach consists of the following, using a one-dimensional space as an example: The line in which samples occur is divided into intervals. The probability of a sample occurring in each interval is considered to be the number of sample points in that interval divided by the total number of sample points. The probability density is the probability divided by the length of the interval. Clearly, as the number of sample points approaches infinity and the interval length approaches zero, one would expect to obtain the true probability density. The problem in higher-dimensional spaces is the "curse of dimensionality." Quite obviously, dividing a 10-dimensional unit cube into one-half-unit cubes provides a relatively coarse approximation to the density. And yet, if we have only one sample in each such interval, we would need over a thousand sample points, as previously noted, and statistically meaningful results would require many more.

Thus, a histogram is seldom practical in high-dimensional spaces. Potential function methods (Chapter VI), however, can be regarded as an extension of the histogram concept, as we shall see.

2.4 PARAMETRIC METHODS

An important probability distribution is the Gaussian or normal distribution. It is†

$$p(\mathbf{x}) = \frac{1}{(2\pi)^{n/2} |C|^{1/2}} \exp[-\tfrac{1}{2}(\mathbf{x} - \mathbf{m}) C^{-1}(\mathbf{x} - \mathbf{m})'], \qquad (2.13)$$

where C is a positive definite matrix with elements c_{ij}. In Eq. (2.13) C and $\mathbf{m}$ are arbitrary; that is, the Gaussian distribution in Eq. (2.13) represents probability density for any C and $\mathbf{m}$. A one-dimensional Gaussian distribution is sketched in Fig. 2.1.

The mean and covariance of a density $p(\mathbf{x})$ are defined as

$$\mathbf{m} = \int_X \mathbf{x} p(\mathbf{x}) \, dX \qquad \text{and} \qquad \sigma_{ij} = \int_X (x_i - m_i)(x_j - m_j) p(\mathbf{x}) \, dX, \quad (2.14)$$

where

$$\mathbf{x} = (x_1, \ldots, x_n) \qquad \text{and} \qquad \mathbf{m} = (m_1, m_2, \ldots, m_n);$$

or, more briefly,

$$\mathbf{m} = E\{\mathbf{x}\} \qquad \text{and} \qquad \sigma_{ij} = E\{(x_i - m_i)(x_j - m_j)\},$$

where $E\{\cdot\}$ denotes the expected value. By substituting (2.13) into (2.14), we find that $\mathbf{m}$ is indeed the mean of the distribution and C the covariance matrix: $c_{ij} = \sigma_{ij}$. Since we may estimate the covariance and the mean of the

---

† We use $\mathbf{x}'$ to indicate the transpose of the row vector $\mathbf{x}$.

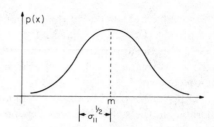

FIG. 2.1. Gaussian probability density function.

distribution from sample points occurring according to that distribution by the equations

$$\mathbf{m} \approx \frac{1}{M} \sum_{j=1}^{M} \mathbf{y}_j, \tag{2.15a}$$

deviations

Covariance $\quad \sigma_{ij} \approx \dfrac{1}{M} \displaystyle\sum_{k=1}^{M} (y_{ki} - m_i)(y_{kj} - m_j), \tag{2.15b}$

the parameters determining the Gaussian distribution are easily estimated.

One parametric approach to pattern classification is to assume that the samples occur by a Gaussian distribution; the parameters of that distribution are then easily estimated by Eqs. (2.15).

One can as well calculate the mean and variance in an iterative manner or update an estimate of those parameters. If $m_i(M)$ and $\sigma_{i,j}(M)$ are the mean and covariance estimated by the first M samples [as in Eqs. (2.15)], we note

$$\sigma_{ij}(M) = \frac{1}{M} \sum_{k=1}^{M} y_{ki} y_{kj} - m_i(M)m_j(M) \tag{2.16}$$

by expanding the product in (2.15b) and define

$$s_{ij}(M) = \frac{1}{M} \sum_{k=1}^{M} y_{ki} y_{kj}.$$

We now note that

$$m_i(M+1) = \frac{1}{M+1} (Mm_i(M) + y_{M+1,\, i}), \tag{2.17a}$$

$$s_{ij}(M+1) = \frac{1}{M+1} (Ms_{ij}(M) + y_{M+1,\, i}\, y_{M+1,\, j}), \tag{2.17b}$$

and

$$\sigma_{ij}(M+1) = s_{ij}(M+1) - m_i(M+1)m_j(M+1); \tag{2.17c}$$

Eqs. (2.17) provide us with an iterative algorithm for calculation of the parameters, given successive samples.

Once having calculated the parameters, we have the distribution specified completely. That is, we have $p_i(\mathbf{x})$ of Eq. (2.8). We are given h_i, assuming Eq. (2.3) is the appropriate loss function, and the p_i, the *a priori* probabilities can be estimated, perhaps by Eq. (2.1). Thus, our decision function is completely specified.

Other methods to be discussed in later sections could be called parametric methods in the sense that they depend upon determining a set of parameters describing the distribution. However, in the sense that the parameters do not arise from familiar families of probability densities, we shall adopt the conventional usage and not denote these as parametric methods. Further, the preceding methods often describe a distribution in terms of a much smaller number of parameters than methods to be considered later.

2.5 CONCLUSION

This chapter is intended to impart to the reader some comfort with a statistical framework for pattern recognition techniques. The important basic concepts are the concept of risk [Eq. (2.4)], the nature of the resulting decision rule [Eq. (2.8)], and the use of a priori probabilities where appropriate. The value h_i of a correct decision for class i becomes a justification in Eq. (2.8) for adjusting the constant factors to reflect the relative importance of different classes. We have not discussed criteria other than the risk (average loss); however, other criteria such as Neyman–Pearson and minimax also result in comparison of the probability densities [10]. We have also limited discussion at this point to formulation of the classical pattern classification problem; Ho and Agrawala [10] include in their survey statistical formulations of the many variations of the basic problem.

This chapter has not done justice to the rich field of parametric methods, in part because of the limitations of those methods, but largely because of the difficulty in presenting the statistical preliminaries necessary for an adequate discussion.

EXERCISES

2.1. Let the loss function for two classes be

$$L(c, i) = \begin{cases} -K_1, & c = i, \\ K_2, & c \neq i, \end{cases}$$

probabilities only make the diff.

where $K_1 > 0$, $K_2 > 0$. Derive the decision function $\hat{c}(\mathbf{x})$ which minimizes the loss. Explain the effect of the choice of K_1 and K_2.

2.2. For the coin identification example given in Table 2.1, what is the recognition rule if $h_1 = 2$, $h_2 = 1$? What is the minimum risk?

2.3. Given the loss function

$$L(c, i) = \begin{cases} -1, & c = i, \\ 0, & c \neq i, \end{cases}$$

and the probability law for a one-dimensional pattern space

$$p(i, x) = \begin{cases} (6\pi)^{-1} \exp(-x^2/2), & i = 1, \\ (6\pi)^{-1} \exp[-(x - 2)^2/2], & i = 2, \\ (6\pi)^{-1} \exp[-(x + 1)^2/2], & i = 3. \end{cases}$$

Find $c(x)$.

2.4. Show that the decision function minimizing the loss function of Eq. (2.3) with $h_i = 1$ is the same as that obtained for

$$L^*(c, i) = \begin{cases} 1, & c \neq i, \\ 0, & c = i, \end{cases}$$

with N pattern classes.

2.5. Let

$$Y_1 = \{(0, 0), (0, 1), (1, 1)\}$$
$$Y_2 = \{(-1, 0), (-1, -1), (-\tfrac{1}{2}, -\tfrac{1}{2}), (0, -1)\}.$$

Given that $p_1(\mathbf{x})$ and $p_2(\mathbf{x})$ are bivariate Gaussian distributions:

(a) Give expressions for $p_1(\mathbf{x})$ and $p_2(\mathbf{x})$ by estimating the parameters from the sample points.

(b) Assuming that the number of samples in each class is indicative of the a priori probabilities p_1 and p_2, find the equation of the optimum separating surface [minimizing the expected loss given in Eq. (2.3) with $h_1 = h_2 = 1$]. Sketch it and the sample points.

(c) If two more points occur, $(0, \tfrac{1}{2})$ in Y_1 and $(-1, -\tfrac{1}{2})$ in Y_2, what is then the optimum separating surface? Sketch it and the sample points.

2.6. Prove that the optimum separating surface [for the loss function in Eq. (2.3) with $h_1 = h_2$ and equally likely probabilities of occurrence of classes $(p_1 = p_2)$] is linear if the two classes arise from multivariate Gaussian distributions with equal covariance matrices.

SELECTED BIBLIOGRAPHY

1. Abramson, N., and Braverman, D., Learning to Recognize Patterns in a Random Environment, *IRE Trans. Information Theory* **8**, 558–563 (1962).
2. Anderson, T. W., "Introduction to Multivariate Statistical Analysis," Wiley, New York, 1958.
3. Anderson, T. W., and Bahadur, R., Classification into Two Multivariate Normal Distributions with Different Covariance Matrices, *Ann. Math. Statist.* **33**, 422–431 (1962).
4. Blackwell, D., and Girshick, M. A., "Theory of Games and Statistical Decisions," Wiley, New York, 1954.
5. Chow, C. K., An Optimum Character Recognition System Using Decision Functions, *IRE Trans. Electron. Comput.* **6**, 247–254 (1957).
6. Cooper, D. B., and Cooper, P. W., Nonsupervised Adaptive Signal Detection and Pattern Recognition, *Information and Control* **7**, 416–444 (1964).
7. Cooper, P. W., The Hypersphere in Pattern Recognition, *Information and Control* **5**, 324–346 (1962).
8. Cooper, P. W., A Note on an Adaptive Hypersphere Decision Boundary, *IEEE Trans. Electron. Comput.* **15**, 948–949 (1966).
9. Day, N. E., Linear and Quadratic Discrimination in Pattern Recognition, *IEEE Trans. Information Theory* **14**, 419–420 (1969).
10. Ho, Y.-C., and Agrawala, A. K., On Pattern Classification Algorithms, Introduction and Survey, *Proc. IEEE* **56**, 836–862 (1968).
11. Hocking, R. R., and Smith, W. B., Estimation of Parameters in the Multivariate Normal Distribution with Missing Observations, *Amer. Statist. Assoc.* **63**, 159–173 (1968).
12. Kanal, L. N., and Randall, N. C., Recognition System Design by Statistical Analysis, *Proc. 19th Nat. Conf. Assoc. Computing Machinery, August 1964*, Publication P-64.
13. Kaplan, K. R., and Sklansky, J., Analysis of Markov Chain Models of Adaptive Processes, Aerospace Medical Res. Labs., AMRL-TR-65-3, 1965.
14. Keehn, D. G., A Note on Learning for Gaussian Properties, *IEEE Trans. Information Theory* **11**, 126–132 (1965).
15. Minsky, M., Steps toward Artificial Intelligence, *in* "Artificial Intelligence," (IEEE Publication S-142), Institute of Electrical and Electronics Engineers, pp. 107–128. New York, 1963.
16. Nilsson, N. J., "Learning Machines," Chap. 3, McGraw-Hill, New York, 1965.

CHAPTER III

INTRODUCTION
TO OPTIMIZATION TECHNIQUES

(See Chap. 9)

In our study we will have need to refer to several basic optimization techniques. This chapter will outline some approaches to optimization. The reader is referred to the works in the bibliography for greater detail.

3.1 INDIRECT METHODS

Suppose we wish to find an extremum (a maximum or minimum) of $F(\mathbf{x})$, where $\mathbf{x} = (x_1, x_2, \ldots, x_n)$. A necessary condition for an extremum $\tilde{\mathbf{x}}$ is that

$$\nabla F(\tilde{\mathbf{x}}) = 0, \qquad (3.1)$$

that is, that the gradient of F evaluated at $\tilde{\mathbf{x}}$ be 0. The gradient of F is

$$\nabla F = (\partial F/\partial x_1, \partial F/\partial x_2, \ldots, \partial F/\partial x_n). \qquad (3.2)$$

1st partials

Equation (3.1) gives a set of n equations in n unknowns (which may or may not be linear). There are many numerical methods for solving both linear and nonlinear sets of equations [2, 4]; the nonlinear methods are often equivalent to using direct methods immediately. Solution of Eq. (3.1) gives a candidate or candidates for an extremum; a solution may be a maximum, minimum, or point of inflection and must be tested by examination of the second partial derivatives or by investigating nearby points.

3.2 DIRECT METHODS

Direct methods are based upon a search for an extremum. The search may be completely random; we may simply evaluate $F(\mathbf{x})$ at a large number of randomly generated points, assuming the maximum is close to the one of those points which gives the smallest value for $F(\mathbf{x})$ (for minimization).

Gradient techniques use more information about the local character of the function. One starts at some initial guess, $\mathbf{x}^{(1)}$, of the optimum, and attempts to improve this guess successively by making the next estimate $\mathbf{x}^{(i+1)}$ such that $F(\mathbf{x}^{(i+1)})$ is less than $F(\mathbf{x}^{(i)})$ (for minimization). In gradient techniques, the choice is made so that it tends to decrease (or increase) F as quickly as possible.

Suppose $\mathbf{x}^{(i+1)} = \mathbf{x}^{(i)} + \Delta\mathbf{x}$ for $\Delta\mathbf{x}$ of small magnitude, where $\Delta\mathbf{x} = (\Delta x_1, \Delta x_2, \ldots, \Delta x_n)$. Then

$$F(\mathbf{x}^{(i+1)}) = F(\mathbf{x}^{(i)} + \Delta\mathbf{x})$$

$$\approx F(\mathbf{x}^{(i)}) + \sum_{j=1}^{n} \left.\frac{\partial F}{\partial x_j}\right|_{\mathbf{x}^{(i)}} (\Delta x_j),$$

using Taylor's expansion. It follows that the change in $F(\mathbf{x})$ is

$$\Delta F(\mathbf{x}^{(i)}) \equiv F(\mathbf{x}^{(i+1)}) - F(\mathbf{x}^{(i)})$$

$$\approx \sum_{j=1}^{n} \left.\frac{\partial F}{\partial x_j}\right|_{\mathbf{x}^{(i)}} (\Delta x_j). \tag{3.3}$$

Noting Eq. (3.2), we can write this more simply as[†]

$$\Delta F(\mathbf{x}^{(i)}) \approx \nabla F \cdot \Delta\mathbf{x}. \tag{3.4}$$

We are looking for the direction of $\Delta\mathbf{x}$ which will maximize (or minimize) ΔF for $\Delta\mathbf{x}$ of constant length. Since the Schwarz inequality

$$-\|\mathbf{x}\|\,\|\mathbf{y}\| \leq \mathbf{x} \cdot \mathbf{y} \leq \|\mathbf{x}\|\,\|\mathbf{y}\| \tag{3.5}$$

implies by Eq. (3.4) that

$$-\|\nabla F\|\,\|\Delta\mathbf{x}\| \leq \nabla F \cdot \Delta\mathbf{x} \leq \|\nabla F\|\,\|\Delta\mathbf{x}\|; \tag{3.6}$$

ΔF will be maximized (minimized) for $\Delta\mathbf{x}$ such that the right-hand (left-hand) inequality holds. This is the case for

$$\Delta\mathbf{x} = \pm K\,\nabla F, \tag{3.7}$$

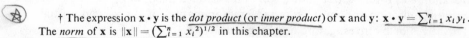

[†] The expression $\mathbf{x} \cdot \mathbf{y}$ is the *dot product (or inner product)* of $\mathbf{x}$ and $\mathbf{y}$: $\mathbf{x} \cdot \mathbf{y} = \sum_{i=1}^{n} x_i y_i$. The *norm* of $\mathbf{x}$ is $\|\mathbf{x}\| = \left(\sum_{i=1}^{n} x_i^2\right)^{1/2}$ in this chapter.

where, for K positive, the positive sign is for maximization and the negative sign for minimization. This yields the general form of the gradient technique: Given an initial guess $\mathbf{x}^{(1)}$,

$$\mathbf{x}^{(i+1)} = \mathbf{x}^{(i)} \pm \varepsilon_i \, \nabla F\,(\mathbf{x}^{(i)}), \qquad i = 1, 2, 3, \ldots, \tag{3.8}$$

where ε_i is a positive constant that may be different for each iteration, and the sign is fixed throughout the procedure. Several possible choices of ε_i are :

$$\varepsilon_i = \varepsilon, \qquad \text{a constant,} \tag{3.9}$$

$$\varepsilon_i = \varepsilon/\|\nabla F\,(\mathbf{x}^{(i)})\|, \tag{3.10}$$

as gradient gets smaller it is weighted more

$$\varepsilon_i = 1/i, \tag{3.11}$$

slow convergence

and

$$\varepsilon_i = \varepsilon \Bigg/ \left\|\frac{\partial^2 F\,(\mathbf{x}^{(i)})}{\partial x^2}\right\| \tag{3.12}$$

2nd derivative

if we define

$$\frac{\partial^2 F}{\partial x^2} = \left(\frac{\partial^2 F}{\partial x_1{}^2}, \frac{\partial^2 F}{\partial x_2{}^2}, \ldots, \frac{\partial^2 F}{\partial x_n{}^2}\right).$$

Combinations of these and other methods can often be used to advantage. More sophisticated approaches vary the step size as a function of the rate of convergence [3]. A common intuitive interpretation of the gradient technique is that it corresponds (for maximization) to climbing a hill by taking each step in the direction of steepest rise.

Generally speaking, there is a trade-off between speed of convergence and stability of convergence. The smaller the magnitude of ε_i, the slower the convergence; but if ε_i is too large, the algorithm may never converge.

The choice of Eq. (3.11) yields particularly slow convergence, but it will yield convergence in most cases. This is the case because of the divergence of the harmonic series

$$\sum_{i=1}^{\infty} 1/i = \infty. \tag{3.13}$$

If

$$\sum_{i=1}^{\infty} \varepsilon_i = \alpha < \infty, \tag{3.14}$$

the algorithm may converge to a point which is not an extremum. For example, suppose ∇F to be a nonzero constant vector $\mathbf{K}$ over a large region; then

$$\mathbf{x}^{(M)} = \sum_{i=1}^{M-1} \varepsilon_j \nabla F(\mathbf{x}^{(i)}) + \mathbf{x}^{(1)} = \mathbf{K} \sum_{i=1}^{M-1} \varepsilon_i + \mathbf{x}^{(1)}$$

and

$$\mathbf{x}^{(m)} \to \mathbf{K}\alpha + \mathbf{x}^{(1)}$$

as $M \to \infty$ if $\mathbf{x}^{(i)}$ never leaves the region of constant gradient. Since the minimum cannot occur in this region, ε_i should not be chosen to form a convergent series.

Although Eq. (3.11) converges too slowly to be the best choice when ∇F can be calculated accurately, it converges despite random noise in the estimation of ∇F (if the mean of such noise is zero), and is often chosen in such cases. This is a loosely stated result from the area of stochastic approximation [1, 6].

Equation (3.10) yields an algorithm in which each successive iteration is changed by an increment of constant magnitude ε in the direction of the gradient. Equation (3.12) decreases the step size in proportion to the curvature of the function at $\mathbf{x}^{(i)}$.

 As we may readily visualize by the hill-climbing analogy, we may obtain a *local maximum* rather than a *global maximum* by the gradient technique. We would thus prefer to minimize functions with no stationary points (points where $\nabla F = 0$) other than the global optimum.

We would further prefer functions whose derivatives were continuous; otherwise the functions may exhibit "edges" which frustrate rapid convergence.

3.3 LINEAR PROGRAMMING

Optimization with constraints yields another wide class of methods. We will be particularly interested in inequality constraints. Linear programming provides a method of minimizing a linear cost function with variables constrained by linear inequalities [4, 5].

The usual form of the problem solved by linear programming algorithms is the following: Find a solution $z_1, z_2, \ldots, z_n \geq 0$ which minimizes $\sum_{i=1}^{n} c_i z_i$ subject to the constraints that $\sum_{i=1}^{n} a_{ij} z_i \geq b_j$ for $j = 1, 2, \ldots, m$. If a problem is posed in this form, with m and n sufficiently small, a linear programming algorithm will either give a solution or indicate that none exists.

The *dual problem* in linear programming is a formulation of the problem which transposes the matrix of elements a_{ij} to result in a problem where the roles of m and n are reversed but the solution of which can be used to obtain the solution of the original problem. This transposition is often of value because it is the number of constraints m which largely determines the computational cost of the procedure.

3.4   A LOCALIZED RANDOM SEARCH TECHNIQUE

The following algorithm will find a local minimum of a continuous function without requiring an analytic expression for the gradient, and is presented as an example of this type of algorithm.

Let $\mathbf{x}^{(i)}$ be the ith guess of the minimum of $F(\mathbf{x})$. We wish to generate a sequence $\mathbf{x}^{(0)}, \mathbf{x}^{(1)}, \ldots, \mathbf{x}^{(i)}, \ldots$, such that $F(\mathbf{x}^{(0)}) > F(\mathbf{x}^{(1)}) > \cdots > F(\mathbf{x}^{(i)}) > \cdots$. We do so by first choosing an initial guess $\mathbf{x}^{(0)}$ by intuition. The procedure is then as follows:

(1) Calculate $\Delta\mathbf{x} = (\Delta x_1, \Delta x_2, \ldots, \Delta x_n)$ by taking n samples from the probability density of Fig. 3.1a, by means to be described.

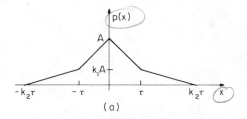

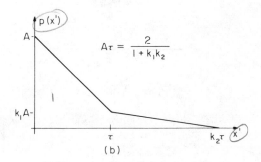

FIG. 3.1   Generating random numbers: (a) probability density function desired; (b) one-sided density function.

(2) Set $\mathbf{x}_{\text{TEST}} = \mathbf{x}^* + \Delta\mathbf{x}$, where $\mathbf{x}^* = \mathbf{x}^{(i)}$, the last calculated member of the sequence $\{\mathbf{x}^{(i)}\}$ (and $\mathbf{x}^* = \mathbf{x}^{(0)}$ initially).

(3) If (for minimization) $F(\mathbf{x}_{\text{TEST}}) < F(\mathbf{x}^*)$, then $\mathbf{x}^*$ is set to $\mathbf{x}_{\text{TEST}}$ (i.e., $\mathbf{x}^{(i+1)} = \mathbf{x}_{\text{TEST}}$) and the procedure continues from step (1).

(4) If $F(\mathbf{x}_{\text{TEST}}) \geq F(\mathbf{x}^*)$, then $\mathbf{x}'_{\text{TEST}} = \mathbf{x}^* - \Delta\mathbf{x}$ is similarly tested. If $F(\mathbf{x}'_{\text{TEST}}) < F(\mathbf{x}^*)$, $\mathbf{x}^*$ is set to $\mathbf{x}'_{\text{TEST}}$ (i.e., $\mathbf{x}^{(i+1)} = \mathbf{x}'_{\text{TEST}}$), and the procedure continues from step (1). (The theory is that, if a step in one direction is "uphill," a step in an opposite direction is likely to be "downhill.")

(5) If $F(\mathbf{x}'_{TEST}) \geq F(\mathbf{x}^*)$, $\mathbf{x}^*$ remains unchanged and step (1) is initiated.

why

The width parameter τ in the distribution should in general shrink as the solution is approached; it may in fact be different for each component of $\mathbf{x}$. We will see that τ appears *only multiplicatively* in the equations generating the samples of the distributions and may easily be imposed after the random number is generated.

Constraints are easily handled by testing each $\mathbf{x}$ before using it. Reasonable stopping rules can be devised based on the number of successes in the last N tries and on the step size for successful tries.

The overall process is diagrammed in Fig. 3.2.

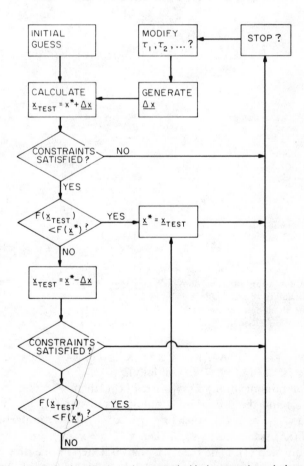

FIG. 3.2   Flow chart for localized random search. Underscored symbols are vectors.

GENERATING RANDOM SAMPLES OF THE GIVEN DISTRIBUTION

Let z be a random number uniformly distributed in [0, 1]. Then x' has the distribution in Fig. 3.1b if

$$x' = \begin{cases} \tau(1 - k_1)^{-1}[1 - (K_6 z)^{1/2}], & z \le z_0, \\ \tau\{k_2 - [K_5(1 - z)]^{1/2}\}, & z > z_0, \end{cases} \tag{3.15}$$

where

$$z_0 = 1 - k_1(k_2 - 1)/(1 + k_1 k_2),$$
$$K_5 = (k_2 - 1)(1 + k_1 k_2)/k_1, \quad \text{and}$$
$$K_6 = (1 - k_1)(1 + k_1 k_2).$$

If z' is a random number which takes the values 1 and -1 with equal probability, then $x = z'x'$ has the distribution in Fig. 3.1a, as desired.

EXERCISES

3.1. One value of x which minimizes $F(x) = (2 - x^2)^2$ is clearly $x = \sqrt{2}$. Starting with $x^{(1)} = 1.5$ and using the gradient technique

$$x^{(i+1)} = x^{(i)} - \varepsilon_i \, \nabla F(x^{(i)}) \qquad i = 1, 2, \ldots,$$

give five iterations each for

(a) $\varepsilon_i = 0.1/i$,   (b) $\varepsilon_i = 0.1$,   (c) $\varepsilon_i = 1$.

Explain any unusual results.

3.2. Use the gradient technique to find the minimum of $F(x) = |2 - x^2|$. Do five iterations with $\varepsilon_i = 0.5$ and $x^{(1)} = 1.5$.

3.3. Using the gradient technique with ε_i as in Eq. (3.10) with $\varepsilon = 1$: do five iterations toward finding the minimum of

$$F(\mathbf{w}) = \tfrac{1}{4} \sum_{i=1}^{4} \left(\sum_{j=1}^{3} w_j y_{ij} - 1 \right)^2,$$

where

$$\mathbf{y}_1 = (y_{11}, y_{12}, y_{13}) = (0, 1, 1), \qquad \mathbf{y}_2 = (1, 0, -1),$$
$$\mathbf{y}_3 = (1, 1, 1), \qquad \mathbf{y}_4 = (2, 0, -1).$$

3.4. Derive Eq. (3.15).

SELECTED BIBLIOGRAPHY

1. Dvoretzky, A., On Stochastic Approximation, *in Proc. 3rd Berkeley Symp. Math. Stat. Prob.* (J. Neyman, ed.), pp. 95–104, Univ. of California Press, Berkeley, 1965.
2. Isaacson, E., and Keller, H. B., "Analysis of Numerical Methods," Wiley, New York, 1966.
3. McMurty, G. J., Adaptive Optimization Procedures, *in* "Adaptive, Learning, and Pattern Recognition Systems" (J. M. Mendel and K. S. Fu, eds.), Academic Press, New York, 1970.
4. Ralston, A., and Wilf, H. S. (eds), "Mathematical Methods for Digital Computers," Wiley, New York, 1960.
5. Simonnard, M., "Linear Programming," Prentice-Hall, Englewood Cliffs, New Jersey, 1966.
6. Wilde, D. J., "Optimum Seeking Methods," Prentice-Hall, Englewood Cliffs, New Jersey, 1964.
7. Wilde, D. J., and Beightler, C. S., "Foundations of Optimization," Prentice-Hall, Englewood Cliffs, New Jersey, 1967.

CHAPTER IV

LINEAR DISCRIMINANT FUNCTIONS AND EXTENSIONS

4.1 INTRODUCTION

Risk was defined as expected loss [Eq. (2.2)]. The risk is given by Eq. (2.4), which can be rewritten as

$$R = \sum_{i=1}^{N} p_i \int_X L[c(\mathbf{x}), i] p_i(\mathbf{x}) \, dX. \tag{4.1}$$

Since $p_i(\mathbf{x})$ is unknown, the risk cannot be evaluated directly. But, noting that the integral represents the expectation with respect to the distribution of the ith pattern class, we can obtain an *approximate risk* $\tilde{R}$ by replacing the expectation by the average

$$\tilde{R} = \sum_{i=1}^{N} \frac{p_i}{M_i} \sum_{j=1}^{M_i} L[c(\mathbf{y}_j^{(i)}), i], \tag{4.2}$$

where the samples of class i are $\mathbf{y}_1^{(i)}, \mathbf{y}_2^{(i)}, \ldots, \mathbf{y}_{M_i}^{(i)}$. If we assume $p_i = M_i/(M_1 + M_2 + \cdots + M_N)$, we get a somewhat simpler expression:

$$\tilde{R} = \frac{1}{M} \sum_{i=1}^{N} \sum_{j=1}^{M_i} L[c(\mathbf{y}_j^{(i)}), i], \tag{4.3}$$

where $M = M_1 + \cdots + M_N$. Appropriately interpreted, this expression is equivalent to the "mean error" of Koford and Groner [26]. Equation (4.3) is a reasonable criterion in itself—the average loss over the labeled samples.

Thus, once we have specified the loss function, we have a well-specified minimization problem. In order to apply the methods of Chapter III, we shall express the decision function $c(\mathbf{x})$ in terms of a finite number of parameters and optimize these parameters. This involves choosing a particular form for $c(\mathbf{x})$; we thus are minimizing the approximate risk $\tilde{R}$ only over a restricted set of decision functions. If the optimum decision function is not adequately approximated by some member of that restricted set, we cannot hope for a useful solution without expanding the set.

Although the remainder of this chapter will be devoted to linear discriminant functions, a final section will show that the methods discussed can be applied directly to a much larger class of discriminant functions which includes general multivariate polynomials. The methods of this chapter can thus yield quite complex decision functions.

4.2 MATHEMATICAL PRELIMINARIES

It will be well to review some notational and geometrical ideas before we proceed.

The *dot product* (or *inner product*) of two n-dimensional vectors $\mathbf{x}$ and $\mathbf{y}$ is

$$\mathbf{x} \cdot \mathbf{y} = \sum_{i=1}^{n} x_i y_i,$$

where $\mathbf{x} = (x_1, x_2, \ldots, x_n)$ and $\mathbf{y} = (y_1, y_2, \ldots, y_n)$. The *length* (or *norm*) of $\mathbf{y}$, denoted by $\|\mathbf{y}\|$, will be the *Euclidean norm*

$\|y\|^2 = SS$

$$\|\mathbf{y}\| = \left(\sum_{i=1}^{n} y_i^2 \right)^{1/2}$$

unless otherwise noted. In two dimensions, $\mathbf{x} \cdot \mathbf{y} = \|\mathbf{x}\| \|\mathbf{y}\| \cos \theta$, where θ is the angle between the two vectors. Because most two-dimensional geometrical concepts are valid in higher dimensions, we will often use geometrical arguments, expecting that the reader will understand that these arguments can be translated into a more rigorous derivation. For example, since $|\cos \theta| \leq 1$,

$$|\mathbf{x} \cdot \mathbf{y}| \leq \|\mathbf{x}\| \|\mathbf{y}\|$$

in two dimensions. This can be proved to hold in higher dimensions as well.

 A *hyperplane* in n-space is the n-dimensional analog of a line in 2-space or a plane in 3-space. A hyperplane is the locus of points satisfying the equation

$$w_1 x_1 + w_2 x_2 + \cdots + w_n x_n + w_{n+1} = 0, \tag{4.4}$$

intercept

where the coefficients w_i determine the hyperplane. It will be convenient to define *weight vectors*

$$\mathbf{w} = (w_1, w_2, \ldots, w_n, w_{n+1})$$

and

$$\boldsymbol{\omega} = (w_1, w_2, \ldots, w_n).$$

We can then write Eq. (3.1) as

4.4 ?

$$\boldsymbol{\omega} \cdot \mathbf{x} + w_{n+1} = 0 \qquad \text{gradient} = 0 \tag{4.5}$$

or

$$\mathbf{w} \cdot \mathbf{x} = 0 \tag{4.6}$$

if we interpret $\mathbf{x}$ as $\mathbf{x} = (x_1, x_2, \ldots, x_n)$ in the first case and $\mathbf{x} = (x_1, x_2, \ldots, x_n, 1)$, an *augmented vector*, in the second case. Rather than introduce different notations for the two, we will distinguish them by context.

The distance from the hyperplane represented by Eq. (4.5) to the origin is given by

$$\text{distance to origin} = |w_{n+1}| / \|\boldsymbol{\omega}\|. \tag{4.7}$$

The normal (perpendicular) distance from a point $\mathbf{y}$ to this hyperplane in n-dimensional sample space is

$$\text{distance from } \mathbf{y} \text{ to hyperplane} = |\boldsymbol{\omega} \cdot \mathbf{y} + w_{n+1}| / \|\boldsymbol{\omega}\| = |\mathbf{w} \cdot \mathbf{y}| / \|\boldsymbol{\omega}\|. \tag{4.8}$$

It will often be helpful to consider the $(n + 1)$-dimensional *augmented sample space* as in Eq. (4.6). In this space, the hyperplane will always pass through the origin [by Eq. (4.7)]. In this augmented space, as indicated in Figs. 4.1 and 4.2, we may draw the vector $\mathbf{w}$ since it is of the same dimen-

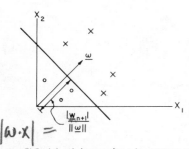

$|\boldsymbol{\omega} \cdot \mathbf{x}| = \dfrac{|w_{n+1}|}{\|\boldsymbol{\omega}\|}$

FIG. 4.1 A hyperplane in pattern space ($n = 2$): × sample class 1; ○ sample class 2. Underscored symbols are vectors.

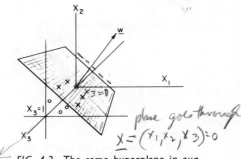

plane goes through

$X = (Y_1, X_2, X_3) = 0$

FIG. 4.2 The same hyperplane in augmented pattern space. Underscored symbols are vectors.

sion as **x**. But, since **w** · **x** = 0 for every point **x** on the hyperplane, **w** is perpendicular (orthogonal) to the hyperplane. The hyperplane divides the space into two regions; since **w** · **x** = 0 only at points on the hyperplane, **w** · **x** > 0 for points **x** on one side of the hyperplane, and **w** · **x** < 0 on the other. That the positive side is the side into which **w** points is easily shown: the point **w** is on that side, and **w** · **w** = $\|\mathbf{w}\|^2 > 0$.

There is a duality between the augmented sample space and *weight space*, the space of weight vectors **w**. A point in weight space corresponds to a hyperplane in augmented sample space and vice versa.

4.3 LINEAR DISCRIMINANT FUNCTIONS

If we have sets of samples $\mathscr{Y}_1, \mathscr{Y}_2, \ldots, \mathscr{Y}_N$ from N classes, we can look for a set of linear discriminant functions

$$\rho_i(\mathbf{x}) = \mathbf{w}_i \cdot \mathbf{x}, \qquad i = 1, 2, \ldots, N, \tag{4.9}$$

which best separate the classes. That is, for $N > 2$, we specify the decision function in terms of N weight vectors $\mathbf{w}_1, \mathbf{w}_2, \ldots, \mathbf{w}_N$, where

$$c(\mathbf{x}) = k \qquad \text{if} \quad \mathbf{w}_k \cdot \mathbf{x} \geq \mathbf{w}_j \cdot \mathbf{x} \qquad \text{for} \quad j = 1, \ldots, N,$$

and we choose the smallest index k if two or more weight vectors satisfy the above relationship.

For the case of $N = 2$, we can simplify the notation considerably by considering one hyperplane and thus one weight vector rather than two discriminant functions and two weight vectors; the decision function

$$c(\mathbf{x}) = \begin{cases} 1 & \text{if} \quad \mathbf{w}_1 \cdot \mathbf{x} \geq \mathbf{w}_2 \cdot \mathbf{x}, \\ 2 & \text{if} \quad \mathbf{w}_2 \cdot \mathbf{x} > \mathbf{w}_1 \cdot \mathbf{x}, \end{cases} \tag{4.10a}$$

is equivalent to specifying $c(\mathbf{x})$ as

$$c(\mathbf{x}) = \begin{cases} 1 & \text{if} \quad \mathbf{w} \cdot \mathbf{x} \geq 0, \\ 2 & \text{if} \quad \mathbf{w} \cdot \mathbf{x} < 0, \end{cases} \tag{4.10b}$$

where the hyperplane **w** is the difference between $\mathbf{w}_1$ and $\mathbf{w}_2$:

$$\mathbf{w} = \mathbf{w}_1 - \mathbf{w}_2. \qquad (2 \text{ dimensional case}) \tag{4.10c}$$

To be specific, we would like to find a hyperplane **w** · **x** = 0 in n-dimensional sample space such that

$$\mathbf{w} \cdot \mathbf{y} > 0 \qquad \text{for} \quad \mathbf{y} \in \mathscr{Y}_1 \qquad \text{and} \qquad \mathbf{w} \cdot \mathbf{y} < 0 \qquad \text{for} \quad \mathbf{y} \in \mathscr{Y}_2. \tag{4.11}$$

(If it is possible to find a solution with, say, $\mathbf{w} \cdot \mathbf{y} \geq 0$ for $\mathbf{y} \in \mathscr{Y}_1$ and $\mathbf{w} \cdot \mathbf{y} < 0$ for $\mathbf{y} \in \mathscr{Y}_2$, it is possible to find a solution without the equality.) A form equivalent to (4.11) is

$$\mathbf{w} \cdot \mathbf{y} \geq d \quad \text{for} \quad \mathbf{y} \in \mathscr{Y}_1, \quad \mathbf{w} \cdot \mathbf{y} \leq -d \quad \text{for} \quad \mathbf{y} \in \mathscr{Y}_2 \quad (4.12)$$

for a given positive constant d, as the reader may verify. Clearly, Eq. (4.11) is equivalent to

$$\mathbf{w} \cdot \mathbf{y} > 0 \quad \text{for} \quad \mathbf{y} \in \mathscr{Y}_1, \quad \mathbf{w} \cdot (-\mathbf{y}) > 0 \quad \text{for} \quad \mathbf{y} \in \mathscr{Y}_2;$$

if we form the set $\mathscr{Y}$ consisting of elements of $\mathscr{Y}_1$ and negatives of elements of $\mathscr{Y}_2$, Eq. (4.11) becomes simply

$$\boxed{\mathbf{w} \cdot \mathbf{y} > 0} \quad \text{for} \quad \mathbf{y} \in \mathscr{Y}, \quad (4.13a)$$

and (4.12) becomes

$$\mathbf{w} \cdot \mathbf{y} \geq d \quad \text{for} \quad \mathbf{y} \in \mathscr{Y}. \quad (4.13b)$$

4.4 SPECIFYING THE LOSS FUNCTION

The algorithms of this chapter are derived by a simple procedure: we first choose a loss function through geometrical arguments. The loss function will involve $c(\mathbf{x})$ which in turn is specified by the as yet unspecified parameters $\mathbf{w}$. We insert the loss function in Eq. (4.2) or (4.3), and minimize $\tilde{R}$ with respect to the parameters $\mathbf{w}$. This chapter will be concerned with such indirect methods. The *cost function* to be minimized is $\tilde{R}$, the overall measure of separability of the classes; it is specified by choosing the *loss function* $L[c(\mathbf{y}), i]$, the loss associated with the classification of a particular sample $\mathbf{y}$.

The choice of overall cost function to be minimized is critical. No matter how efficient or elegant the algorithm for minimization, the result is determined by the cost function; if it does not meaningfully express the "goodness" of a solution, any effort utilizing that cost function is merely an exercise. Thus, the primary consideration in choosing a cost function is its relevance.

The appropriateness of the cost function, however, must be balanced against the difficulty of optimizing it. Since the dimensionality of practical problems will often force us to use direct optimization techniques, such as the gradient technique, we would prefer the cost function to have a continuous derivative. To avoid the problem of getting stuck at local minima, we would prefer a cost function with only one minimum or one in which all the minima were equal. A further desirable characteristic of the cost function is con-vexity: a function is *convex* in a given region if any straight line within that

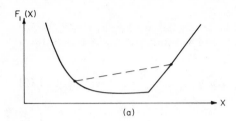

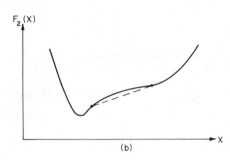

FIG. 4.3 Convexity: (a) a convex function; (b) a nonconvex function.

region with endpoints on the function lies entirely on or above the function (see Fig. 4.3). If the cost function is convex, the gradient technique generally converges to the minimum more quickly than otherwise.

Perhaps the most natural cost function would be the number of samples misclassified. This function, however, has several faults:

(1) It does not have a unique minimum. In Fig. 4.4, the line B represents an absolute minimum, but an infinite number of lines misclassify only two samples as well.

(2) The cost function is not smooth. As a hyperplane is moved in a continuous manner, the number of points misclassified makes discrete jumps. Further, at points of **w** other than those where the cost function makes a discrete jump, the derivative of the cost function with respect to **w** is zero.

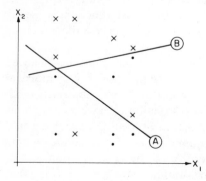

FIG. 4.4 Local minimums: line A misclassifies 3 samples and represents a local minimum; line B misclassifies 2 samples and represents an absolute minimum.

(3) Local minima are likely to exist. Figure 4.4 contains an example of a local minimum; line A cannot be moved continuously to line B without an increase in misclassification along the way.

(4) The cost function will not in general be convex.

Despite these drawbacks, it is still possible to use the number of misclassifications as a criterion. This choice corresponds to choosing the loss function

$$L[c(\mathbf{x}), i] = \begin{cases} 0 & \text{if } \mathbf{w}_i \cdot \mathbf{x} \geq \mathbf{w}_j \cdot \mathbf{x} \qquad \text{for all} \quad j \neq i, \\ 1 & \text{otherwise.} \end{cases} \tag{4.14}$$

Then Eq. (4.3) gives a risk proportional to the number of misclassifications, and Eq. (4.2) gives a risk proportional to the misclassifications weighted by the a priori probabilities. One can attempt to minimize the resulting $\tilde{R}$ with a search technique, keeping in mind the problems just discussed.

Let us examine a family of loss functions which yield a continuous and differentiable approximate risk and are thus easier to minimize. We note first that Eqs. (4.2) and (4.3) require the evaluation of the cost functions only at sample points. Loss function will thus be evaluated only at points whose classification are known; this fact will simplify our specification of the loss function.

Let us focus first on the two-class problem where we search for the hyperplane defined by $\mathbf{w}$, which separates the classes. The N-class problem will prove to be a simple if tedious extension of the approach to be developed. Equation (4.8) gives the shortest distance from a point to a hyperplane $\mathbf{w} \cdot \mathbf{x} = 0$. The distance from a hyperplane $\mathbf{w} \cdot \mathbf{x} = d$ to a point $\mathbf{y}$ is thus

$$|\mathbf{w} \cdot \mathbf{y} - d| / \|\boldsymbol{\omega}\|. \tag{4.15}$$

(The hyperplane in n-space, $\mathbf{w} \cdot \mathbf{x} = d$, is parallel to the hyperplane $\mathbf{w} \cdot \mathbf{x} = 0$ and a distance $d / \|\boldsymbol{\omega}\|$ away.) Note that this distance changes with scale changes of components of $\mathbf{x}$; (4.15) is a meaningful measure of distance only if a reasonable initial normalization of the pattern space has been employed. In any case, however, inclusion of the denominator makes the resulting loss function insensitive to multiplication of $\boldsymbol{\omega}$ by a constant. The inclusion of d in (4.15) deserves some discussion. The positive constant d specifies a dead zone $d / \|\boldsymbol{\omega}\|$ wide on either side of the hyperplane within which correctly classified sample points contribute to the cost function. In the case of separable classes, the algorithms which adjust the hyperplane so as to minimize cost will move the hyperplane so as to clear the dead zone of sample points if possible. This has the effect of putting the hyperplane in the "middle" of the empty space between the classes (provided d is correctly adjusted) and making a better choice among non-unique optimum hyperplanes.

Note that the effect of *d* can be diminished without moving the hyperplane by multiplying **w** by a constant. Thus sophisticated algorithms to minimize $R(\mathbf{w})$ will have provisions for adjusting the dead zone. If a fixed dead zone of distance d^* is specified *a priori*, then *d* can be set to $d^* \|\boldsymbol{\omega}\|$ as the algorithm proceeds. Alternatively (or supplementally), d^* can be adjusted on the basis of intermediate results of the algorithm. This is especially true in the separable case where it might be desired to specify the unique separating hyperplane with maximum dead zone.

We would consider the perfect separation in Fig. 4.5 an ideal situation, but suppose that perfect separation of classes were impossible. We are then faced with a situation such as that of Fig. 4.6—one or more sample points

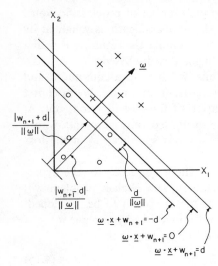

FIG. 4.5 Defining a dead zone. Underscored symbols are vectors. Samples: × class 1; ○ class 2.

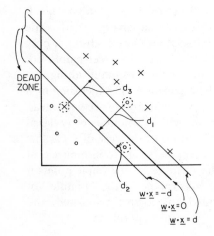

FIG. 4.6 Misclassified samples with a dead zone: × class 1; ○ class 2; ○ misclassified. Underscored symbols are vectors.

will be misclassified by any hyperplane. How do we decide in such a case when one hyperplane is better than another? More to the point, how do we define the loss associated with each sample point? It would be appropriate to define the loss as zero for samples on the correct side of the hyperplane and out of the "dead zone." Correspondingly, unsatisfactory points could constitute a loss equal to their distance from the appropriate hyperplane ($\mathbf{w} \cdot \mathbf{x} = d$ for samples in $\mathcal{Y}_1$ and $\mathbf{w} \cdot \mathbf{x} = -d$ for samples in $\mathcal{Y}_2$). Figure 4.6 contains three offending samples; the distances d_1, d_2, and d_3 indicated are the losses associated with each. Thus, we choose loss functions

$$L[c(\mathbf{x}), 1] = \begin{cases} 0, & \mathbf{w} \cdot \mathbf{x} \geq d, \\ \dfrac{d - \mathbf{w} \cdot \mathbf{x}}{\|\boldsymbol{\omega}\|} & \mathbf{w} \cdot \mathbf{x} < d, \end{cases} \tag{4.16a}$$

and

$$L[c(\mathbf{x}), 2] = \begin{cases} 0, & \mathbf{w} \cdot \mathbf{x} \leq -d, \\ \dfrac{\mathbf{w} \cdot \mathbf{x} + d}{\|\boldsymbol{\omega}\|}, & \mathbf{w} \cdot \mathbf{x} > -d. \end{cases} \tag{4.16b}$$

We can now minimize the cost function $\tilde{R}$ of Eq. (4.2) or (4.3). It is somewhat easier to do so by rewriting (4.3), when that expression is applicable, and (4.16) in terms of the set $\mathcal{Y}$:

$$\tilde{R} = \frac{1}{M} \sum_{j=1}^{M} f_i \left(\frac{d - \mathbf{w} \cdot \mathbf{y}_j}{\|\boldsymbol{\omega}\|} \right), \tag{4.17}$$

laigh minimum risk for greater d ✦

where

$$f_1(z) = \begin{cases} 0, & z \leq 0, \\ z, & z > 0, \end{cases} \tag{4.18}$$

and the subscript i in (4.17) indicates that other functions are acceptable. For notational simplicity, we shall consider Eq. (4.3) applicable and phrase our further discussion in terms of $\mathcal{Y}$. The reader should be able to translate any of the loss functions discussed into appropriate form for insertion into (4.2). Figure 4.7 illustrates the positions of the samples in augmented space. In terms of the *augmented* pattern space, $\mathbf{x} = (x_1, x_2, \ldots, x_n, 1)$, and the set $\mathcal{Y}$ of samples in $\mathcal{Y}_1$ and negatives of samples in $\mathcal{Y}_2$, the geometrical picture is considerably transformed. We are now seeking a hyperplane *through the origin* such that all the points in $\mathcal{Y}$ are on the positive side of that hyperplane. The reader is best advised to consider this notation (now conventional in the literature) as a convenient tool and translate his geometrical visualization into the unaugmented space with the original two classes. The author

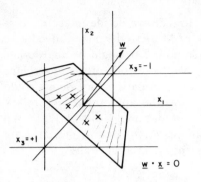

FIG. 4.7 Two-class separation in $(n+1)$-dimensional augmented pattern space. Underscored symbols are vectors.

will at times be guilty of phrasing his discussion in terms of the original problem while using notation referring to augmented space and the set $\mathcal{Y}$.

If we wished to consider the loss a *function* of the distance of a sample point from the hyperplane, e.g., the square of the distance, we could simply insert a function other than f_1 into Eq. (4.17), say,

$$f_2(z) = \begin{cases} 0, & z \le 0, \\ z^2, & z > 0, \end{cases} \tag{4.19}$$

or

$$f_3(z) = \begin{cases} 0, & z \le 0, \\ z^2, & 0 < z \le a, \\ 2az - a^2, & z > a, \end{cases} \tag{4.20}$$

where a is some positive constant. The advantage of f_2 and f_3 is that, unlike f_1, they have continuous derivatives.

4.5   MINIMIZING THE APPROXIMATE RISK

In most practical problems, the gradient technique or a variation thereof will prove the most efficient way to minimize $\tilde{R}(\mathbf{w})$. The general form is

$$\mathbf{w}^{(i+1)} = \mathbf{w}^{(i)} - \varepsilon_i \, \nabla \tilde{R}(\mathbf{w}^{(i)}), \qquad i = 0, 1, 2, \ldots. \tag{4.21}$$

Using (4.17) with f_1, we derive

$$\mathbf{w}^{(i+1)} = \mathbf{w}^{(i)} + \frac{\varepsilon_i}{M} \sum_{j \in J(\mathbf{w}^{(i)})} D(\mathbf{w}^{(i)}, \mathbf{y}_j), \tag{4.22a}$$

where

$$J(\mathbf{w}) = \{ j \mid \mathbf{w} \cdot \mathbf{y}_j < d, \quad \mathbf{y}_j \in \mathcal{Y} \} \tag{4.22b}$$

and

$$D(\mathbf{w}, \mathbf{y}) = \nabla\left(\frac{\mathbf{w} \cdot \mathbf{y} - d}{\|\omega\|}\right) = \frac{\mathbf{y}}{\|\omega\|} - \frac{(\mathbf{w} \cdot \mathbf{y} - d)\omega^*}{\|\omega\|^3}, \qquad (4.22c)$$

where ω^* is the $(n + 1)$-dimensional vector: $\omega^* = (\omega, 0)$. Similar equations can be obtained from f_2 and f_3.

In the preceding equations, all the samples are used in each iteration to obtain a new estimate of the weight vector from the old. This will be referred to as a *many-at-a-time* algorithm. This observation leads to an approximation of Eq. (4.22) by a one-at-a-time algorithm:

$$\mathbf{w}^{(i+1)} = \begin{cases} \mathbf{w}^{(i)} + \dfrac{\varepsilon_i}{M} D(\mathbf{w}^{(i)}, \mathbf{y}_j) & \text{if } \mathbf{w}^{(i)} \cdot \mathbf{y}_j < d, \\ \mathbf{w}^{(i)} & \text{if } \mathbf{w}^{(i)} \cdot \mathbf{y}_j \geq d, \end{cases} \qquad (4.23)$$

where the sample points of $\mathcal{Y}$ are arranged into some sequence $\mathbf{y}_1, \mathbf{y}_2, \ldots,$ and a single sample is used in each iteration. (The usual arrangement is to cycle through the sample points of $\mathcal{Y}$ repeatedly in a given order.) If ε_i in (4.23) is chosen sufficiently small relative to the ε_i in (4.22a), then the solution of (4.23) will tend to approach the solution of (4.22a) and to minimize $\tilde{R}$. It may, in fact, converge to the solution with fewer cycles through the sample points than the former algorithm. Of course, the algorithms corresponding to choices of f_2 or f_3 have matching one-at-a-time algorithms as well.

4.6   AN ALTERNATE COST FUNCTION

The cost functions of the previous two sections were stated in terms of the actual distance from the sample point to the hyperplane [Eq. (4.15)]. Since the quantity $(\mathbf{w} \cdot \mathbf{y} - d)$ is proportional to the distance, why not use that quantity in the loss functions? For example, why not use

$$\tilde{R}'(\mathbf{w}) = \frac{1}{M} \sum_{j=1}^{M} f(d - \mathbf{w} \cdot \mathbf{y}_j), \qquad (4.24)$$

with $f = f_1, f_2,$ or f_3? The resulting gradient would be much simpler, but a problem of interpretation exists. For a given $\mathbf{w}$, $\tilde{R}'(\mathbf{w})$ is proportional to the average distance (or squared distance, etc.) between the offending samples and the hyperplane, but the constant of proportionality is a function of $\mathbf{w}$. Hence, the average distance interpretation is not valid since $\tilde{R}'(\mathbf{w})$ is not comparable for different $\mathbf{w}$ by this interpretation; $\tilde{R}$ and $\tilde{R}'$ will *not* in general yield the same minimum. If we consider the discriminant function formulation, however, a natural interpretation arises.

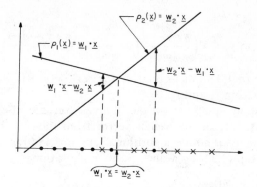

FIG. 4.8 Measuring misclassification error with discriminant functions. Underscored symbols are vectors.

Consider Fig. 4.8. We specify our problem in terms of finding discriminant functions as in Eq. (4.9). As mentioned earlier in the two-class case, the final decision boundary will be that for which

$$\rho_1(\mathbf{x}) = \rho_2(\mathbf{x}),$$

i.e.,

$$\mathbf{w}_1 \cdot \mathbf{x} - \mathbf{w}_2 \cdot \mathbf{x} = (\mathbf{w}_1 - \mathbf{w}_2) \cdot \mathbf{x} = 0.$$

Hence, in Eq. (4.10),

$$\mathbf{w} = \mathbf{w}_1 - \mathbf{w}_2.$$

Equation (4.24) can now be interpreted (with $d = 0$) as the average difference in the discriminant functions for misclassified samples. When $\tilde{R}' = 0$, all labeled samples are correctly classified. The constant d serves the same function as it did previously, tending to move the hyperplane away from points which are correctly classified but near the boundary. If we apply the gradient technique, we can interpret the resulting *algorithm* in a meaningful way as well. We obtain

$$\mathbf{w}^{(i+1)} = \mathbf{w}^{(i)} + \frac{\varepsilon_i}{M} \sum_{j \in J(\mathbf{w}^{(i)})} f'(d - \mathbf{w}^{(i)} \cdot \mathbf{y}_j)\mathbf{y}_j, \qquad (4.25)$$

where J is as in Eq. (4.22b), and f is either f_1, f_2, or f_3. We have, for $j \in J(\mathbf{w}^{(i)})$,

$$f_1'(d - \mathbf{w}^{(i)} \cdot \mathbf{y}_j) = 1$$

$$f_2'(d - \mathbf{w}^{(i)} \cdot \mathbf{y}_j) = 2(d - \mathbf{w}^{(i)} \cdot \mathbf{y}_j)$$

$$f_3'(d - \mathbf{w}^{(i)} \cdot \mathbf{y}_j) = \begin{cases} 2(d - \mathbf{w}^{(i)} \cdot \mathbf{y}_j) & \text{if } (d - \mathbf{w}^{(i)} \cdot \mathbf{y}_j) \le a, \\ 2a & \text{if } (d - \mathbf{w}^{(i)} \cdot \mathbf{y}_j) > a. \end{cases}$$

Many-at-a-time $\tilde{R}'$ Algorithm

Define

$$v(i) = \frac{1}{M} \sum_{j \in J(w^{(i)})} f'(d - w^{(i)} \cdot y_j) y_j. \qquad (4.26)$$

weighted average of vectors misclassified *(see below)* *※*

If $f = f_1$, $v(i)$ is proportional to (colinear with) the average of the sample vectors which do not satisfy $w^{(i)} \cdot y \ge d$. If $f = f_2$, $v(i)$ is proportional to a weighted average of the same sample vectors, with the weight of a sample point (or sample vector) proportional to the distance from that point to the hyperplane; thus, the worst offenders have the greatest influence on the sum. If $f = f_3$, the weighted average has a similar interpretation.

With this notation, Eq. (4.25) becomes

$$w^{(i+1)} = w^{(i)} + \varepsilon_i v(i). \qquad (4.27)$$

The discriminant function before the $(i + 1)$th iteration would have the value $w^{(i)} \cdot v^{(i)}$ for a sample point $v(i)$; afterward, it would have the value

$$w^{(i+1)} \cdot v(i) = [w^{(i)} + \varepsilon_i v(i)] \cdot v(i) = w^{(i)} \cdot v(i) + \varepsilon_i \|v(i)\|^2,$$

so that

$$w^{(i+1)} \cdot v(i) \ge w^{(i)} \cdot v(i).$$

We see that the new weight vector yields a higher value of discriminant function when evaluated at the average (or weighted average) of the sample points y_j such that $w^{(i)} \cdot y_j < d$. The change is in a direction which tends to reverse this latter inequality. Thus, we suspect that repeated application of Eq. (4.27) might yield a separating hyperplane if one exists or a decision surface if not. In fact, this is the case since the algorithm, if it converges, converges to the minimum of $\tilde{R}'$.

Another interpretation is provided by studying the effect of the iteration in weight space. The points $v(i)$ of sample space generate a hyperplane in weight space (see Fig. 4.9). All weight vectors w to the positive side the hyperplane $w \cdot v(i) = d$ will classify $v(i)$ satisfactorily. Since $v(i)$ is an average of sample points unsatisfactorily classified by $w^{(i)}$, the point $w^{(i)}$ in weight space will be on the wrong side of the hyperplane. As indicated in the figure, the algorithm represented by Eq. (4.27) moves the weight vector toward the hyperplane generated by v in a direction orthogonal to that hyperplane. If ε_i is large enough, $w^{(i+1)}$ will be on the positive side of the hyperplane. This latter objective is not necessarily advantageous: since the new weight vector can misclassify different sample points than the old, smaller corrections may be necessary for convergence. (This algorithm can converge to the minimum of $\tilde{R}'$, if the ε_i are sufficiently small.) However, if there exists a perfect separating hyperplane, there will always be a solution on the positive side of the hyperplane, so that larger corrections are merited. In general, however, one cannot know a priori if there is a separating hyperplane.

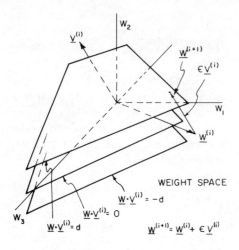

WEIGHT SPACE

$\underline{W} \cdot \underline{V}^{(i)} = -d$

$\underline{W} \cdot \underline{V}^{(i)} = 0$

$\underline{W} \cdot \underline{V}^{(i)} = d$

$\underline{W}^{(i+1)} = \underline{W}^{(i)} + \epsilon \underline{V}^{(i)}$

FIG. 4.9 A geometrical interpretation of the gradient technique. Underscored symbols are vectors.

This geometrical viewpoint provides a means for interpreting ε_i in the $\tilde{R}'$ algorithm. If ε_i is constant, we refer to (4.27) as the *fixed-increment* algorithm. If ε_i is the smallest integer which moves the weight vector to the other side of the hyperplane, that is,

$$\varepsilon_i = \left\{ \frac{|\mathbf{w}^{(i)} \cdot \mathbf{v}(i) - d|}{\|\mathbf{v}(i)\|^2} \right\}, \qquad (4.28)$$

where $\{x\} \equiv$ least integer greater than x, Eq. (4.27) is called *absolute error correction*. If we move a fraction λ of the distance to the hyperplane,

$$\varepsilon_i = \lambda \frac{|\mathbf{w}^{(i)} \cdot \mathbf{v}(i) - d|}{\|\mathbf{v}(i)\|^2}, \qquad (4.29)$$

we have *fractional correction*. (If $\lambda = 1$, we move to the hyperplane exactly; if $\lambda > 1$, we move to the other side.)

If there is a perfect separating hyperplane, fixed-increment and absolute error correction algorithms will find that solution in a finite number of steps, irrespective of the choice of initial weight vector or choice of fixed increment [36]. Fractional correction will also find the solution if $1 < \lambda < 2$. Since one seldom knows, however, that a perfect solution exists (even in the few practical cases where it does), engineering judgment must be imposed at some point in the iteration process if a solution has not been found and if ε_i is too large to allow convergence to the minimum of $\tilde{R}'$.

The many-at-a-time algorithm of Eqs. (4.26) and (4.27) can be transformed to a one-at-a-time algorithm:

$$\mathbf{w}^{(i+1)} = \begin{cases} \mathbf{w}^{(i)} + \varepsilon_i f'[d - \mathbf{w}^{(i)} \cdot \mathbf{y}(i)]\mathbf{y}(i) & \text{if} \quad \mathbf{w}^{(i)} \cdot \mathbf{y}(i) < d, \\ \mathbf{w}^{(i)} & \text{if} \quad \mathbf{w}^{(i)} \cdot \mathbf{y}(i) \geq d, \end{cases} \qquad (4.30)$$

where $\mathbf{y}(i) = \mathbf{y}_{i \bmod M}$ and we cycle through the samples repeatedly.† For the loss function f_1, we replace $\mathbf{v}(i)$ by $\mathbf{y}(i)$, approximating an average by one of the contributors to the average.

Both the geometrical and algebraic interpretations of the many-at-a-time algorithm apply to the one-at-a-time algorithm [36]. The same considerations on convergence hold as well. The one-at-a-time algorithm can provide accelerated convergence, particularly if a separating hyperplane exists.

Before proceeding to the N-class problem, let us consider a numerical example of how some of the aforementioned techniques are applied to a two-class two-dimensional problem. Let $\mathcal{Y}_1$ and $\mathcal{Y}_2$ be the sets of samples of class 1 and 2, respectively, while $\mathcal{Y}$ is the combined, augmented set of samples. All of the samples are listed in Table 4.1. The sample points of $\mathcal{Y}_1$ and $\mathcal{Y}_2$ are plotted in Fig. 4.10.

We apply the gradient approach to minimizing the approximate risk [Eq. (4.3)]. We chose f_1 [Eq. (4.18)], the alternate-distance, many at-a-time algorithm [Eq. (4.25)] with $d = 0$. We let ε_1 be adjustable so as to maintain a fixed step: $\varepsilon_i = 0.01/\|\mathbf{v}\|$. We chose, arbitrarily, the initial hyperplane to be that corresponding to the weight vector $\mathbf{w} = (-1, -2, 10)$. The initial hyperplane and those subsequently computed after 30, 50, 70, 90, and 114 iterations are shown in Fig. 4.10. The algorithm was halted at this point. If f_2 is

TABLE 4.1 Sample sets $\mathcal{Y}_1$, $\mathcal{Y}_2$, and $\mathcal{Y}$

$\mathcal{Y}_1$			$\mathcal{Y}_2$			$\mathcal{Y}$			
Sample no.	x_1	x_2	Sample no.	x_1	x_2	Sample no.	x_1	x_2	x_3
1	2	3	8	6	4	1	2	3	1
2	3	4	9	5	8	2	3	4	1
3	2	7	10	7	8	3	2	7	1
4	7	2	11	10	8	4	7	2	1
5	8	3	12	6	7	5	8	3	1
6	9	4	13	8	6	6	9	4	1
7	10	2	14	11	6	7	10	2	1
						8	-6	-4	-1
						9	-5	-8	-1
						10	-7	-8	-1
						11	-10	-8	-1
						12	-6	-7	-1
						13	-8	-6	-1
						14	-11	-6	-1

† The notation "mod M" means modulo M; i.e., when the count M is reached, we begin counting again at 1.

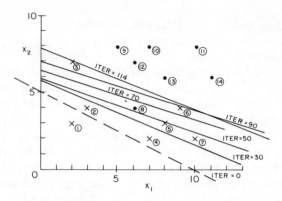

FIG. 4.10 The results of the algorithm of Eq. (4.25) at several iteration levels.

chosen [Eq. (4.19)], the final hyperplane is close to that for 90 iterations in Fig. 4.10, and it misclassifies 3 samples. This is due to the fact that the algorithm is minimizing a function of the distance of a misclassified sample to a hyperplane, not the number of misclassifications; since f_2 squares this distance, we intuitively expect that the algorithm will tend to prefer several small errors to one large one.

Table 4.2, which shows a portion of the iteration, is self-explanatory except that R, a measure of the total misclassified distance, is calculated by

$$R = \sum_{j=1}^{M} f_1\left(\frac{d - \mathbf{w} \cdot \mathbf{y}_j}{\|\boldsymbol{\omega}\|}\right)$$

rather than by (4.24), although (4.25) is minimized.

The choice of ε_i can produce dramatically different results. Using fractional correction [Eq. (4.29)] with $\lambda = 0.1$ and the same algorithm otherwise, the algorithm converges to essentially the same solution in only twelve iterations (Table 4.3). Unfortunately, no general rules are possible; a different sample distribution might produce an opposite result.

Although we have emphasized the gradient technique, $\tilde{R}'$ with f_1 can be attacked by linear programming as well (Section 4.8). All of the cost functions may be minimized by the reader's favorite search technique. It is clear that $\tilde{R}'$ yields much simpler algorithms than $\tilde{R}$.

The alternate cost function $\tilde{R}'$ has a hidden disadvantage which tends to reduce its computational advantages. $\tilde{R}'(\mathbf{w})$ is reduced in value by multiplying $\mathbf{w}$ by a fractional constant, which of course does not modify the separating hyperplane $\mathbf{w} \cdot \mathbf{x} = 0$. In minimizing $\tilde{R}'$, effort is hence wasted in reducing the magnitude of $\mathbf{w}$. This is not the case with the loss function R of Section 4.4; the loss function is in essence stated in terms of a weight vector of unit magnitude $\boldsymbol{\omega}/\|\boldsymbol{\omega}\|$. One may in many cases accomplish more

TABLE 4.2 Portion of iterative procedure $d = 0$

Iteration	w_1	w_2	w_3	R	Misclassified samples					
Initial	−1.000	−2.000	10.000	0.735	2	3	4	5	6	7
1	−0.991	−1.995	10.001	0.723	2	3	4	5	6	7
2	−0.983	−1.990	10.003	0.711	2	3	4	5	6	7
3	−0.974	−1.985	10.004	0.699	2	3	4	5	6	7
4	−0.965	−1.981	10.005	0.687	2	3	4	5	6	7
5	−0.957	−1.976	10.007	0.675	2	3	4	5	6	7
6	−0.948	−1.971	10.008	0.663	2	3	4	5	6	7
7	−0.940	−1.966	10.009	0.650	2	3	4	5	6	7
8	−0.931	−1.961	10.011	0.638	2	3	4	5	6	7
9	−0.922	−1.956	10.012	0.625	2	3	4	5	6	7
10	−0.914	−1.951	10.013	0.613	2	3	4	5	6	7
20	−0.829	−1.900	10.026	0.496	2	3	5	6	7	
21	−0.820	−1.895	10.028	0.485	2	3	5	6	7	
22	−0.812	−1.890	10.029	0.475	3	5	6	7		
23	−0.803	−1.885	10.030	0.465	3	5	6	7		
24	−0.795	−1.880	10.031	0.455	3	5	6	7		
25	−0.786	−1.875	10.033	0.445	3	5	6	7		
26	−0.777	−1.871	10.034	0.435	3	5	6	7		
27	−0.768	−1.866	10.035	0.425	3	5	6	7		
28	−0.760	−1.861	10.036	0.414	3	5	6	7		
29	−0.751	−1.856	10.037	0.404	3	5	6	7		
30	−0.742	−1.851	10.039	0.394	3	5	6	7		
45	−0.614	−1.776	10.057	0.242	3	5	6			
46	−0.606	−1.770	10.058	0.234	3	5	6			
47	−0.598	−1.764	10.059	0.226	3	5	6			
48	−0.590	−1.759	10.061	0.220	3	6				
49	−0.583	−1.752	10.062	0.215	3	6				
50	−0.576	−1.745	10.063	0.210	3	6				
70	−0.453	−1.589	10.087	0.143	3	6	8			
71	−0.447	−1.581	10.088	0.140	3	6	8			
72	−0.442	−1.573	10.089	0.137	3	6	8			
73	−0.436	−1.565	10.090	0.134	3	6	8			
89	−0.467	−1.454	10.099	0.117	3	8				
90	−0.475	−1.448	10.099	0.114	3	8				
91	−0.483	−1.442	10.099	0.113	3	6	8			
92	−0.478	−1.434	10.100	0.113	3	8				
113	−0.549	−1.294	10.108	0.086	3	6	8			
114	−0.543	−1.286	10.109	0.087	8					

TABLE 4.3 Results using fractional correction

Iteration	w_1	w_2	w_3	R	Misclassified samples					
Initial	−1.000	−2.000	10.000	0.735	2	3	4	5	6	7
1	−0.736	−1.851	10.041	0.388	3	5	6	7		
2	−0.624	−1.789	10.056	0.254	3	5	6			
3	−0.556	−1.739	10.067	0.200	3	6				
4	−0.510	−1.693	10.075	0.175	3	6	8			
5	−0.424	−1.572	10.092	0.133	3	6	8			
6	−0.363	−1.487	10.105	0.140	3	8				
7	−0.459	−1.415	10.105	0.116	3	8				
8	−0.536	−1.357	10.105	0.102	3	6	8			
9	−0.495	−1.299	10.113	0.100	8					
10	−0.517	−1.314	10.109	0.095	3	8				
11	−0.577	−1.269	10.109	0.089	6	8				
12	−0.461	−1.269	10.109	0.120	8					

per iteration of that algorithm, compensating for the computational penalty. If d in (4.24) is chosen to be a relatively large value, the tendency for $\|\mathbf{w}\|$ to shrink will be reduced; reducing $\|\mathbf{w}\|$ increases the width $(d/\|\boldsymbol{\omega}\|)$ of the dead zone and tends to increase $\tilde{R}'$.

4.7 THE N-CLASS PROBLEM

Most of the preceding discussion has been in terms of two-class recognition, where the emphasis is on the decision surface between the two classes. In the general N-class problem, we have N discriminant functions [Eq. (4.9)]. The weight vectors $\mathbf{w}_1, \mathbf{w}_2, \ldots, \mathbf{w}_N$ do *not* represent decision surfaces. If we examine only two of the classes, say classes i and j, the decision boundary is the surface where

$$\rho_i(\mathbf{x}) = \rho_j(\mathbf{x}),$$

that is, where

$$\mathbf{w}_i \cdot \mathbf{x} = \mathbf{w}_j \cdot \mathbf{x}. \tag{4.31}$$

The decision plane between the two classes is thus

$$(\mathbf{w}_i - \mathbf{w}_j) \cdot \mathbf{x} = 0. \tag{4.32}$$

How do we define the loss for an unsatisfactorily classified sample point? If a point $\mathbf{y}_m^{(i)}$ is satisfactorily classified, then

$$\mathbf{w}_i \cdot \mathbf{y}_m^{(i)} \geq \mathbf{w}_l \cdot \mathbf{y}_m^{(i)} + d \quad \text{for all} \quad l, \tag{4.33}$$

where we have again inserted a constant d to force points away from the boundary. (Of course, the algorithms may be employed with $d = 0$ if care is taken with the equality.) Inversely, a misclassified point will yield

$$\mathbf{w}_i \cdot \mathbf{y}_m^{(i)} < \mathbf{w}_j \cdot \mathbf{y}_m^{(i)} + d \qquad (4.34)$$

for at least one $j \neq i$.

If the point $\mathbf{y}_m^{(i)}$ is misclassified as being a member of class j, then the weight vector $\mathbf{w}_j$ must be the one that maximizes

$$z = (\mathbf{w}_j - \mathbf{w}_i) \cdot \mathbf{y}_m^{(i)}. \qquad (4.35)$$

One approach is to ignore temporarily the other weight vectors and to adjust $\mathbf{w}_i$ and $\mathbf{w}_j$ so as to tend to reduce z. More precisely, we can use the geometrical concepts developed earlier for the two-class problem and define the loss associated with the misclassified point $\mathbf{y}_m^{(i)}$ as the distance of $\mathbf{y}_m^{(i)}$ from the hyperplane $\mathbf{w} \cdot \mathbf{x} = 0$ which "separates" class i from class j, where $\mathbf{w} = \mathbf{w}_j - \mathbf{w}_i$, and $\mathbf{y}_m^{(i)}$ is on the wrong side (in this case the positive side) of $\mathbf{w}$. The technique described below is thus analogous to that of the two-class problem. We will therefore define

$$L[c(\mathbf{y}_m^{(i)}), i] = \begin{cases} 0 & \text{if } J(\mathbf{w}_1, \mathbf{w}_2, \ldots, \mathbf{w}_N; \mathbf{y}_m^{(i)}) \text{ is empty,} \\ f\left(\dfrac{(\mathbf{w}_j - \mathbf{w}_i) \cdot \mathbf{y}_m^{(i)} + d}{\|\boldsymbol{\omega}_j - \boldsymbol{\omega}_i\|} \right) & \text{otherwise,} \end{cases} \qquad (4.36)$$

where

$$J(\mathbf{w}_1, \ldots, \mathbf{w}_N; \mathbf{y}_m^{(i)}) = \{ p \mid \mathbf{w}_p \cdot \mathbf{y}_m^{(i)} > \mathbf{w}_i \cdot \mathbf{y}_m^{(i)} - d \}$$

and j is the integer contained in J that maximizes

$$[(\mathbf{w}_j - \mathbf{w}_i) \cdot \mathbf{y}_m^{(i)} + d]/\|\boldsymbol{\omega}_j - \boldsymbol{\omega}_i\|.$$

(The denominator has the same normalizing effect here as in the loss function.) Again, f may be f_1, f_2, f_3, or a similar function. Substitution of (4.36) into Eq. (4.2) or (4.3) gives a well-defined $\tilde{R}$ to be minimized. We write $\tilde{R}$ as

$$\tilde{R}(\mathbf{w}_1^{(k)}, \ldots, \mathbf{w}_N^{(k)}) = \sum_{l=1}^{N} \frac{p_l}{M_l} \sum_{m=1}^{M_l} u(\mathbf{y}_m^{(l)}) f\left(\frac{(\mathbf{w}_j^{(k)} - \mathbf{w}_l^{(k)}) \cdot \mathbf{y}_m^{(l)} + d}{\|\boldsymbol{\omega}_j^{(k)} - \boldsymbol{\omega}_l^{(k)}\|} \right),$$

where

$$u(\mathbf{y}_m^{(l)}) = \begin{cases} 0 & \text{if } \mathbf{w}_l^{(k)} \cdot \mathbf{y}_m^{(l)} > \mathbf{w}_j^{(k)} \cdot \mathbf{y}_m^{(l)} + d \quad \text{for all } j \neq l \\ 1 & \text{if } \mathbf{w}_j^{(k)} \cdot \mathbf{y}_m^{(l)} + d > \mathbf{w}_l^{(k)} \cdot \mathbf{y}_m^{(l)} \end{cases}$$

for the $j \in J(\mathbf{y}_m^{(l)})$ which maximizes

$$\frac{(\mathbf{w}_j^{(k)} - \mathbf{w}_l^{(k)}) \cdot \mathbf{y}_m^{(l)} + d}{\|\boldsymbol{\omega}_j^{(k)} - \boldsymbol{\omega}_l^{(k)}\|}.$$

If we apply the gradient technique, the gradient is with respect to *all* the parameters, to all $N(n + 1)$ components of $\mathbf{w}_1, \ldots, \mathbf{w}_N$. It will however, simplify the notation considerably if we define

$$\nabla_i = \left(\frac{\partial}{\partial w_{i1}}, \frac{\partial}{\partial w_{i2}}, \ldots, \frac{\partial}{\partial w_{i,\,n+1}}\right).$$

The gradient technique can then be rewritten

$$\mathbf{w}_i^{(k+1)} = \mathbf{w}_i^{(k)} - \varepsilon_k \nabla_i \tilde{R}(\mathbf{w}_1^{(k)}, \ldots, \mathbf{w}_N^{(k)}), \qquad \text{for} \quad i = 1, 2, \ldots, N. \quad (4.37)$$

We note that the weight vector $\mathbf{w}_i$ can appear in $\tilde{R}$ in two ways: (1) as the weight vector for the class containing $\mathbf{y}_m^{(l)}$, i.e., $i = l$; and (2) for $i \neq l$, $\mathbf{w}_i$ may appear as the vector $i = j$ that maximizes

$$\frac{((\mathbf{w}_j^{(k)} - \mathbf{w}_l^{(k)}) \cdot \mathbf{y}_m^{(l)} + d)}{\|\boldsymbol{\omega}_j^{(k)} - \boldsymbol{\omega}_l^{(k)}\|}.$$

We obtain

$$
\begin{aligned}
\nabla_i R = \ & \frac{p_i}{M_i} \sum_{m=1}^{M_i} u(\mathbf{y}_m^{(i)}) f'\!\left(\frac{(\mathbf{w}_j^{(k)} - \mathbf{w}_i^{(k)}) \cdot \mathbf{y}_m^{(i)} + d}{\|\boldsymbol{\omega}_j^{(k)} - \boldsymbol{\omega}_i^{(k)}\|}\right) \\
& \cdot D_1\!\left(\frac{(\boldsymbol{\omega}_j^{(k)} - \mathbf{w}_i^{(k)}) \cdot \mathbf{y}_m^{(i)} + d}{\|\boldsymbol{\omega}_j^{(k)} - \boldsymbol{\omega}_i^{(k)}\|}\right) \\
& + \sum_{l=1}^{N} \frac{p_l}{M_l} \sum_{m=1}^{M_l} u(\mathbf{y}_m^{(l)}) \gamma(\mathbf{y}_m^{(l)}, i) f'\!\left(\frac{(\mathbf{w}_j^{(k)} - \mathbf{w}_i^{(k)}) \cdot \mathbf{y}_m^{(l)} + d}{\|\boldsymbol{\omega}_j^{(k)} - \boldsymbol{\omega}_i^{(k)}\|}\right) \\
& \cdot D_2\!\left(\frac{(\mathbf{w}_j^{(k)} - \mathbf{w}_i^{(k)}) \cdot \mathbf{y}_m^{(l)} + d}{\|\boldsymbol{\omega}_j^{(k)} - \boldsymbol{\omega}_i^{(k)}\|}\right),
\end{aligned}
\qquad (4.38a)
$$

where $u(\mathbf{y}_m^{(l)})$ has been defined and we define $\gamma(\mathbf{y}_m^{(l)}, i)$ by

$$\gamma(\mathbf{y}_m^{(l)}, i) = \begin{cases} 1 & \text{if } j = i, \quad j \text{ defined by } J(\mathbf{y}_m^{(l)}), \\ 0 & \text{otherwise.} \end{cases}$$

D_1 is defined by

$$D_1\!\left(\frac{(\mathbf{w}_j^{(k)} - \mathbf{w}_i^{(k)}) \cdot \mathbf{y}_m^{(i)} + d}{\|\boldsymbol{\omega}_j^{(k)} - \boldsymbol{\omega}_i^{(k)}\|}\right) = \frac{\mathbf{y}_m^{(i)}}{\|\boldsymbol{\omega}_j^{(k)} - \boldsymbol{\omega}_i^{(k)}\|} + \frac{(\mathbf{w}_j^{(k)} - \mathbf{w}_i^{(k)}) \cdot \mathbf{y}_m^{(i)} + d}{\|\boldsymbol{\omega}_j^{(k)} - \boldsymbol{\omega}_i^{(k)}\|^3}$$
$$\cdot (\boldsymbol{\omega}_j^{(k)} - \boldsymbol{\omega}_i^{(k)})^* \qquad (4.38b)$$

where

$$(\boldsymbol{\omega}_j^{(k)} - \boldsymbol{\omega}_i^{(k)})^* = (\boldsymbol{\omega}_j^{(k)} - \boldsymbol{\omega}_i^{(k)}, 0).$$
$$\underset{(n+1)\text{th place}}{\uparrow}$$

For the case where $\gamma(\mathbf{y}_m^{(l)}, i) = 1$, we have $j = i$ and D_2 is defined by

$$D_2\left(\frac{(\mathbf{w}_i^{(k)} - \mathbf{w}_l^{(k)}) \cdot \mathbf{y}_m^{(l)} + d}{\|\boldsymbol{\omega}_i^{(k)} - \boldsymbol{\omega}_l^{(k)}\|}\right) = +\frac{\mathbf{y}_m^{(l)}}{\|\boldsymbol{\omega}_i - \boldsymbol{\omega}_l\|} - \frac{(\mathbf{w}_i^{(k)} - \mathbf{w}_l^{(k)}) \cdot \mathbf{y}_m^{(l)} + d}{\|\boldsymbol{\omega}_i^{(k)} - \boldsymbol{\omega}_l^{(k)}\|^3}$$

$$\cdot (\boldsymbol{\omega}_i^{(k)} - \boldsymbol{\omega}_l^{(k)})^* \qquad (4.38c)$$

This notational horror is the gradient technique in its pure form, the many-at-a-time form for $\tilde{R}$.

The one-at-a-time form requires that, for each sample vector $\mathbf{y}_m^{(i)}$, we update two weight vectors $\mathbf{w}_i$ and $\mathbf{w}_j$:

$$\mathbf{w}_i^{(k+1)} = \mathbf{w}_i^{(k)} - \varepsilon_i \nabla_i R$$

$$\mathbf{w}_j^{(k+1)} = \mathbf{w}_j^{(k)} - \varepsilon_j \nabla_j R$$

$$\nabla_i R = \frac{p_i}{M_i} u(\mathbf{y}_m^{(i)}) f'\left(\frac{(\mathbf{w}_j^{(k)} - \mathbf{w}_i^{(k)}) \cdot \mathbf{y}_m^{(i)} + d}{\|\boldsymbol{\omega}_j^{(k)} - \boldsymbol{\omega}_i^{(k)}\|}\right) D_1\left(\frac{(\mathbf{w}_j^{(k)} - \mathbf{w}_i^{(k)}) \cdot \mathbf{y}_m^{(i)} + d}{\|\boldsymbol{\omega}_j^{(k)} - \boldsymbol{\omega}_i^{(k)}\|}\right),$$

$$(4.39a)$$

where j, D_1, and $u(\mathbf{y}_m^{(i)})$ are as defined previously and

$$\nabla_j R = -\frac{p_i}{M_i} u(\mathbf{y}_m^{(i)}) f'\left(\frac{(\mathbf{w}_j^{(k)} - \mathbf{w}_i^{(i)}) \cdot \mathbf{y}_m^{(i)} + d}{\|\boldsymbol{\omega}_j^{(k)} - \boldsymbol{\omega}_i^{(k)}\|}\right) D_1\left(\frac{(\mathbf{w}_j^{(k)} - \mathbf{w}_i^{(k)}) \cdot \mathbf{y}_m^{(i)} + d}{\|\boldsymbol{\omega}_j^{(k)} - \boldsymbol{\omega}_i^{(k)}\|}\right).$$

$$(4.39b)$$

A further approximation which often accelerates convergence, and which may be used in either the one-at-a-time or many-at-a-time algorithm, is to use the weights for a given class as they are computed:

$$\mathbf{w}_i^{(k+1)} = \mathbf{w}_i^{(k)} - \varepsilon_k \nabla_i \tilde{R}[\mathbf{w}_1^{(k+1)}, \ldots, \mathbf{w}_{i-1}^{(k+1)}, \mathbf{w}_i^{(k)}, \ldots, \mathbf{w}_N^{(k)}], \qquad i = 1, 2, \ldots, N.$$

$$(4.40)$$

[Compare with (4.37).]

The alternate loss function discussed in the two-class case can also be extended to the N-class case:

$$L'[c(\mathbf{y}_m^{(i)}), i] = \begin{cases} 0 & \text{if } J(\mathbf{w}_1, \ldots, \mathbf{w}_N; \mathbf{y}_m^{(i)}) \text{ is empty,} \\ f[(\mathbf{w}_j - \mathbf{w}_i) \cdot \mathbf{y}_m^{(i)} + d] & \text{otherwise,} \end{cases} \qquad (4.41)$$

where J_i is as before and $j \in J$ now maximizes $(\mathbf{w}_j - \mathbf{w}_i) \cdot \mathbf{y}_m^{(i)} + d$. A similar geometrical interpretation of the resulting algorithm holds. The derivation of this case is much simpler and is suggested as an exercise for the reader.

4.8 SOLUTION BY LINEAR PROGRAMMING

The problem of finding a linear decision function can be stated as a linear programming problem with little modification; however, in the simplest form, a solution can only be obtained when perfect separation of the labeled samples is possible.

Smith [42] has suggested a formulation that yields a solution for the nonseparable case as well. It minimizes $\tilde{R}'$ of Eq. (4.24) with $f = f_1$. Suppose, for a sample $\mathbf{y}_i$ in $\mathcal{Y}$, we have

$$\mathbf{w} \cdot \mathbf{y}_i + h_i \geq d, \qquad h_i \geq 0. \qquad (4.42)$$

Then, if $h_i = 0$, $\mathbf{y}_i$ is on the correct side of the hyperplane and out of the dead zone. If $h_i > 0$ and is the minimum value such that (4.42) is satisfied, then $h_i = d - \mathbf{w} \cdot \mathbf{y}_i$, and h_i measures the misclassification error of $\mathbf{y}_i$ in the same sense as in Section 4.6. Hence, the linear programming formulation equivalent to minimizing $\tilde{R}'$ with $f = f_1$ is to find $\mathbf{w}$ such that

$$\mathbf{w} \cdot \mathbf{y}_i + h_i \geq d \qquad \text{for} \quad i = 1, 2, \ldots, M, \quad h_i \geq 0, \qquad (4.43a)$$

and such that

$$\sum_{i=1}^{M} h_i \qquad (4.43b)$$

is minimized. In this form, the amount of computation is largely determined by M, the number of samples. Smith published computational results which indicated that the gradient technique was better for most practical values of M. Grinold [14] noted that the dual problem, which is sensitive to n (the dimension of the samples) rather than M, could be solved by conventional linear programming packages which allow upper bounds on variables [22]; this provides a computational saving by a factor of the order of n/M, and should make linear programming competitive with search techniques.

Grinold posed another formulation suitable for the nonseparable case which minimizes the maximum error: maximize β such that

$$\mathbf{w} \cdot \mathbf{y}_i \geq \beta, \qquad i = 1, \geq 2, \ldots, M \qquad (4.44a)$$

and

$$\left(\frac{1}{M} \sum_{i=1}^{M} \mathbf{y}_i \right) \cdot \mathbf{w} = 1. \qquad (4.44b)$$

Equation (4.44b) is a normalization of $\mathbf{w}$ and does not affect the resulting solution. When a solution is obtained, $|\beta|$ is the maximum error. Again, the dual problem can be used to obtain a computationally superior solution.

linear hyperplane

4.9   EXTENSION TO GENERAL Φ FUNCTIONS

Suppose we wish to find the optimal discriminant functions of the form

$$\rho_i(\mathbf{x}) = \sum_{k=1}^{R} w_{ik}\, \varphi_k(\mathbf{x}) + w_{i,R+1}, \qquad i = 1, \ldots, N, \qquad (4.45)$$

where the φ_i are chosen functions. For example, a second-order polynomial in two variables is

$$\rho_i(\mathbf{x}) = w_{i1}x_2{}^2 + w_{i2}x_1 + w_{i3}x_2 + w_{i4}x_1{}^2 + w_{i5}x_1x_2 + w_{i6}. \qquad (4.46)$$

By comparison of (4.45) and (4.46), we obtain $\varphi_1(\mathbf{x}) = x_2{}^2$, $\varphi_2(\mathbf{x}) = x_1$, $\varphi_3(\mathbf{x}) = x_2$, $\varphi_4(\mathbf{x}) = x_1{}^2$, $\varphi_5(\mathbf{x}) = x_1 x_2$.

Such a problem can always be transformed into a linear problem of higher dimension by the mapping

$$x_k{}' = \varphi_k(\mathbf{x}), \qquad k = 1, 2, \ldots, R. \qquad (4.47)$$

The sample points may be mapped into this R-dimensional space and an optimum set of weights $\mathbf{w}_1, \mathbf{w}_2, \ldots, \mathbf{w}_N$, each $(R + 1)$-dimensional, derived by any of the preceding methods. The resulting discriminant functions $\rho_i(\mathbf{x}') = \mathbf{w}_i \cdot \mathbf{x}'$ are equivalent to (4.45) and are the optimum solutions sought.

Let us consider the one-dimensional, two-class example of Fig. 4.11.

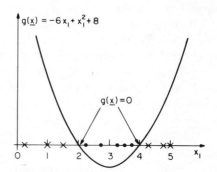

FIG. 4.11   A second-order discriminant function for a one-dimensional space. Underscored symbols are vectors.

Clearly, the two classes are not linearly separable. (A linear hyperplane in 1-space is, of course, a single point.) They *are* separable by the second-order polynomial shown. The function $g(\mathbf{x}) = -6x_1 + x_1{}^2 + 8$ is plotted; the boundary is given by the two points where $g(\mathbf{x}) = 0$. We can obtain this boundary by transforming the labeled samples into a two-dimensional space,

$$x_1{}' = \varphi_1(\mathbf{x}) = x_1, \qquad x_2{}' = \varphi_2(\mathbf{x}) = x_1{}^2,$$

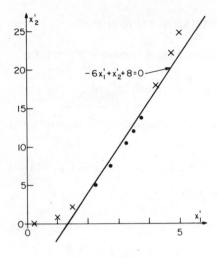

FIG. 4.12 The same discriminant transformed into a two-dimensional pattern space.

and finding a *linear hyperplane* $\mathbf{w} \cdot \mathbf{x}' = 0$ which separates the samples (Fig. 4.12). That hyperplane is given by the weight vector $\mathbf{w} = (-6, 1, 8)$; of course, the weight vector (without transformation) gives the coefficients of the second-order polynomial specified above. This method has the potential of allowing considerably more complex boundaries and of obtaining separating boundaries for multimodal regions using linear methods. It has the disadvantage of requiring an expansion of dimensionality in the most general case. This approach is further interpreted in Section 5.5.

It should be emphasized that Eq. (4.47) can be thought of as feature selection; after the transformation, we have samples in an R-dimensional space, and our problem is identical to the problem discussed throughout this chapter. In general, an rth-order polynomial in n variables will have $\binom{r+n}{r}$ coefficients,† leading to a high-dimensional space. (If $r = 5$ and $n = 20$, R is about 50,000.) We may use an approach such as feature ranking (Chapter IX) to select the terms used in (4.47) to reduce this problem, however.

4.10 THRESHOLD ELEMENTS IN THE REALIZATION OF LINEAR DISCRIMINANT FUNCTIONS

Threshold elements are a special-purpose realization of linear discriminant functions. They have received a great deal of attention in the pattern recognition literature because they are an efficient form of realizing linear discriminant functions and because the weights of the discriminant function correspond

---

† $\binom{m}{n}$ is the binomial coefficient and is equal to $m!/[n!(m-n)!]$.

directly to resistive elements which could be varied adaptively. Their popularity has decreased with the increasing availability of small general-purpose computers and the decreasing cost of integrated circuits. (Precision requirements often complicate their integration.)

4.10.1 Threshold Elements

There is an abundance of literature on threshold elements [2, 3, 6, 7, 8, 33, 35, 52, 53] most of which is oriented toward binary inputs (features) and the separable case. But threshold elements can be considered a physical realization of a linear decision boundary for the general case.

A threshold element is a device with a binary output f related to the input variables $x_1, x_2, \ldots, x_n$ by the equation

$$
f(x_1, x_2, \ldots, x_n) = \begin{cases} 1 & \text{if } \sum_{i=1}^{n} w_i x_i \geq -w_{n+1}, \\ 0 & \text{if } \sum_{i=1}^{n} w_i x_i < -w_{n+1}. \end{cases} \tag{4.48}
$$

The number $-w_{n+1}$ is called the threshold; $w_1, w_2, \ldots, w_n$ are real numbers called the weights of inputs $x_1, x_2, \ldots, x_n$, respectively. If the weights and threshold are fixed, $f(x_1, \ldots, x_n)$ is a well-defined and unique function, since every sample $\mathbf{x} = (x_1, x_2, \ldots, x_n)$ is mapped into either 0 or 1, which can correspond to the two classes to be identified in a two-class problem. The output of the element is clearly 0 if $\mathbf{w} \cdot \mathbf{x} < 0$, that is, if $\mathbf{x}$ is on the negative side of the hyperplane defined by $\mathbf{w} = (w_1, w_2, \ldots, w_{n+1})$ and is 1 if $\mathbf{x}$ is on the positive side of the hyperplane.

A threshold element is often denoted schematically as follows:

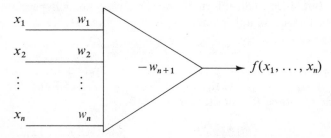

Threshold logic may be realized, for example, by several resistors feeding an active element such as a transistor, or by magnetic cores. Further, a threshold element is a simple model for a neuron, the assumed logic element of the brain, and thus of theoretical as well as practical importance.

4.10.2 Variable-Threshold Threshold Elements

A threshold element with a variable threshold and fixed weights is a *variable-threshold threshold element* [29, 30, 31]. The threshold can often be varied easily in a physical device, since it often corresponds simply to a voltage or a current level. In terms of linear discriminant functions, two hyperplanes with the same weights except for the constant term (the threshold) are parallel hyperplanes separated by a distance

$$\frac{|w'_{n+1} - w''_{n+1}|}{\|\omega\|}.$$

Varying the threshold thus corresponds to moving the hyperplane while maintaining its orientation; this can often be interpreted in a pattern classification problem as adjusting the a priori probabilities, modifying the expected relative frequency of occurrence of the two classes and favoring the most likely class. It also corresponds to a special piecewise-linear case discussed in Chapter VII, Section 7.6.

EXERCISES

4.1. What is wrong with the following argument: In terms of the augmented vectors $\mathbf{y} = (y_1, \ldots, y_n, 1)$ and $\mathbf{w} = (w_1, \ldots, w_n, w_{n+1})$, we can express the requirement that $\mathbf{y} \cdot \mathbf{w} = 0$ separate the sample points of two classes as the requirement that

$$\mathbf{y} \cdot \mathbf{w} > 0 \quad (see\ 4.13\ p.59)$$

for points $\mathbf{y}$ in class 1 and for the negative of points in class 2. That is, we must find a hyperplane such that the set of samples consisting of sample vectors from class 1 and negatives of sample vectors from class 2 lie to one side of it. But since that set is finite, we can always find a hyperplane farther out than the farthest sample point in a given direction. Hence, all sample sets are linearly separable.

4.2. A student is attempting to generate a separating linear hyperplane, $\sum_{i=1}^{3} w_i y_i + w_4$, in response to samples from two classes 1 and 2, as shown, using a one-at-a-time $\tilde{R}'$ algorithm with $d = 0$:

	y_1	y_2	y_3		w_1	w_2	w_3	w_4
				(initial)	1	1	1	1
sample (1)	0	1	0	class 2	1	−1	1	−1
sample (2)	1	0	0	class 1	2	−1	1	0
sample (3)	0	0	1	class 1		?		

(a)   Is he using fixed increment, absolute error correction, or fractional correction?   *P·68*
(b)   What is the missing weight vector?

4.3. Given the sample vectors

$$\mathbf{a} = (1, 1, -1, 0, 2) \qquad \mathbf{e} = (-1, 1, 1, 1, 0)$$
$$\mathbf{b} = (0, 0, 1, 2, 0) \qquad \mathbf{f} = (-1, -1, -1, 1, 0)$$
$$\mathbf{c} = (-1, -1, 1, 1, 0) \qquad \mathbf{g} = (-1, 1, 1, 2, 1)$$
$$\mathbf{d} = (4, 0, 1, 2, 1)$$

where

$$\{\mathbf{b}, \mathbf{d}, \mathbf{e}, \mathbf{f}\} \in \mathcal{Y}_1, \qquad \{\mathbf{a}, \mathbf{c}, \mathbf{g}\} \in \mathcal{Y}_2.$$

If they are presented in alphabetical order repeatedly, give the sequence of weight vectors and the solution generated using $w_0 = (1, 1, 1, -1, -1, 1)$ and
   (a)   fixed increment $\varepsilon_i = 1$,
   (b)   absolute correction, and
   (c)   fractional correction $\lambda = 2$,
for the one-at-a-time $\tilde{R}$ algorithm with $d = 0$ and $f = f_1$.

4.4. Express the problem of finding a set of 2nd-order polynomial discriminant functions for the following sample points in two dimensions as a problem of finding linear discriminant functions for a different set of points of higher dimensions:

$$\{(1, 1,), (0, -1), (4, 5)\} \in F_1, \qquad \text{see } (4.45)$$
$$\{(2, 2)(0, 2)(2, 3)\} \in F_2,$$
$$\{(-1, -1)(-2, 0)\} \in F_3.$$

List the set of points for the restated problem. *You need not solve.*

4.5. Given three pattern classes F_1, F_2, and F_3. Find linear discriminant functions for the sample points

$$\{(0, 1, -1, 2)\} \in F_1$$
$$\{(1, 1, 1, 1)(2, 1, 1, 1)\} \in F_2$$
$$\{(-1, 1, 0, -1)\} \in F_3$$

using the fixed increment algorithm with $\varepsilon_i = 1$ and applying the sample points in the order listed ($w_i^{(1)} = 0$) for the one-at-a-time $\tilde{R}'$ algorithm using $d = \frac{1}{2}$, f_1.

4.6. For the samples of Exercise 4.3, use the many-at-a-time $\tilde{R}'$ algorithm with $d = 0.1$, $\varepsilon_i = 1$, and the loss function with f_1, to do two iterations.

4.7. For the samples of Exercise 4.3, use the one-at-a-time $\tilde{R}'$ algorithm with $d = 0.1$, $\varepsilon_1 = 1$, and the loss function with f_2, to cycle through the seven samples twice.

4.8. Find the expressions corresponding to Eqs. (4.38) and (4.39) for the loss function of Eq. (4.41). *right!* $(195\,74\text{-}75)$

SELECTED BIBLIOGRAPHY

1. Amari, S., A Theory of Adaptive Pattern Classifiers, *IEEE Trans. Electron. Comput.* **16**, 299–307 (1967).
2. Breuer, M. A., Implementation of Threshold Nets by Integer Linear Programming, *IEEE Trans. Electron. Comput.* **14**, 950–952 (1965).
3. Cameron, S. H., The Generation of Minimal Threshold Nets by an Integer Program, *IEEE Trans. Electron. Comput.* **13**, 299–302 (1964).
4. Casey, R. G., An Experimental Comparison of Several Design Algorithms Used in Pattern Recognition, Watson Research Center, IBM Corp., Yorktown Heights, New York, Rept. RC 1500, 1965.
5. Chien, Y. T., and Fu, K. S., A Modified Recognition Machine Using Time-Varying Stopping Boundaries, *IEEE Trans. Information Theory* **12**, 206–214 (1966).
6. Chow, C. K., On the Characterization of Threshold Functions, *Switching Circuit Theory and Logical Design*, I.E.E.E. Conf. Rec. 34–38 (1961).
7. Chow, C. K., Statistical Independence and Threshold Functions, *IEEE Trans. Electron. Comput.* **14**, 66–68 (1965).
8. Coates, C. L., and Lewis, P. M., II, Linearly Separable Switching Functions, *J. Franklin Inst.*, **272**, 360–410 (1961).
9. Das, S. K., A Method of Decision Making in Pattern Recognition, *IEEE Trans. Comput.* **18**, 329–333 (1969).
10. Devyaterikov, I. P., Propoi, A. I., and Tsypkin, Ya. Z., Iterative Learning Algorithms for Pattern Recognition, *Automat. Remote Contr.* (1967).
11. Duda, R. O., and Singleton, R. C., Training a Threshold Logic Unit with Imperfectly Classified Patterns, presented at *Joint Western Comput. Conf., Los Angeles, California, August 1964*.
12. Fu, K. S., and Chen, C. H., A Sequential Decision Approach to Problems in Pattern Recognition and Learning, presented at *3rd Symp. Discrete Adaptive Processes, Chicago, October 1964*.
13. Gabelman, I. J., Properties and Transformations of Single Threshold Element Functions, *IEEE Trans. Electron. Comput.* **13**, 680–684 (1964).
14. Grinold, R. C., Comment on " Pattern Classification Design by Linear Programming," *IEEE Trans. Comput.* **18**, 378–379 (1969).
15. Grinold, R. C., A Note on Pattern Separation, *Oper. Res.* **18** (1970).
16. Hestenes, M. R., and Stiefel, E., Methods of Conjugate Gradients for Solving Linear Systems," *J. Res. Nat. Bur. Stand.* **49**, 409–436 (1952).
17. Highleyman, W. H., Linear Decision Functions, with Application to Pattern Recognition, *Proc. IRE* **50**, 1501–1514 (1962).
18. Highleyman, W. H., " Data for Character Recognition Studies," *IEEE Trans. Electron. Comput.* **12**, 135–136 (1963).

19. Ho, Y.-C., and Kashyap, R. L., An Algorithm for Linear Inequalities and Its Applications, *IEEE Trans. Electron. Comput.* **14** (1965).
20. Hoff, M. E., Jr., Learning Phenomena in Networks of Adaptive Switching Circuits, Stanford Electron. Labs., Stanford, California, Tech. Rept. 1554-1, 1962.
21. Ibaraki, T., and Muroga, S., Adaptive Linear Classifier by Linear Programming, *IEEE Trans. Sys. Sci. and Cybernetics*, **6**, 53–62 (1970).
22. IBM Publication H20-0476-1, Mathematical Programming System 360, Linear and Separable Programming—User's Manual.
23. Kailath, T., Adaptive Matched Filters, *in* "Mathematical Optimization Techniques" (R. Bellman, ed.), pp. 109–140, Univ. of California Press, Berkeley, 1963.
24. Kanal, L., Evaluation of a Class of Pattern-Recognition Networks, *in* "Biological Prototypes and Synthetic Systems, pp. 261–270, Plenum, New York, 1962.
25. Koford, J. S., Adaptive Pattern Dichotomization, Stanford Electron. Labs., Stanford, California, Rept. SEL-64-048 (TR No. 6201-1), 1964.
26. Koford, J. S., and Groner, G. F., The Use of an Adaptive Threshold Element to Design a Linear Optimal Pattern Classifier, *IEEE Trans. Information Theory* **12**, 42–50 (1966).
27. Mangasarian, O. L., Linear and Non-linear Separation of Patterns by Linear Programming, *Operations Research* **13**, 444–452 (1965).
28. Mays, C. H., Effect of Adaptation Parameters on Convergence Time and Tolerance for Adaptive Threshold Elements, *IEEE Trans. Electron. Comput.* **13**, 465–468 (1964).
29. Meisel, W. S., Variable-Threshold Threshold Elements, Univ. of Southern California, Los Angeles, Calif., Rept. USCEE 204, 1967.
30. Meisel, W. S., Variable-Threshold Threshold Elements, *IEEE Trans. Comput.* **17**, 656–667 (1968).
31. Meisel, W. S., Nets of Variable-Threshold Threshold Elements, *IEEE Trans. Comput.* **17**, 667–676 (1968).
32. Mengert, P. H., Solution of Linear Inequalities, NASA Electron. Res. Center, Cambridge, Massachusetts, 1969.
33. Minnick, R. C., Linear-Input Logic, *IRE Trans. Electron. Comput.* **10**, 6–16 (1961).
34. Motzkin, T. S., and Schoenberg, I. J., The Relaxation Method for Linear Inequalities, *Canad. J. Math.* **6**, 393–404 (1954).
35. Muroga, S., Toda, S., Theory of Majority Decision Elements, *J. Franklin Inst.* **271**, 376–418 (1961).
36. Nilsson, N. J., "Learning Machines," McGraw-Hill, New York, 1965.
37. Penrose, R. A., Generalized Inverse for Matrices, *Proc. Cambridge Phil. Soc.* **51**, 406–413 (1955).
38. Peterson, D. W., Discriminant Functions: Properties, Classes, and Computational Techniques, Stanford Electron. Labs., Stanford, California, Tech. Rept. 6761-2, 1965.
39. Ridgway, W. C., III, An Adaptive Logic System with Generalizing Properties, Stanford Electron. Labs., Stanford, California, Tech. Rept. 1556-1, 1962.
40. Rosen, C. A., and Hall, D. J., A Pattern Recognition Experiment with Near-Optimum Results, *IEEE Trans. Electron. Comput.* (*correspondence*) **15**, 666–667 (1966).
41. Rosen, J. B., Pattern Separation by Convex Programming, *J. Math. Anal. Appl.* **10**, 123–134 (1965).
42. Smith, F. W., Pattern Classifier Design by Linear Programming, *IEEE Trans. Comput.* **17**, 367–372 (1968).
43. Smith, F. W., Design of Multicategory Pattern Classifiers with Two-Category Classifier Design Procedures, *IEEE Trans. Comput.* **18**, 548–551 (1969).
44. Steinbuch, K., and Piske, V. A. W., Learning Matrices and Their Applications, *IEEE Trans. Electron. Comput.* **12** (1963).

45. Teng, T. L., and Li, C. C., On a Generalization of the Ho–Kashyap Algorithm to Multiclass Pattern Classification, *Proc. 3rd Ann. Conf. on Infor. Sci. and Systems, Princeton, 1969*, pp. 209–213.

46. Wee, W. G., and Fu, K. S., An Extension of the Generalized Inverse Algorithm to Multiclass Pattern Classification, *IEEE Trans. Syst. Sci. and Cybernetics* **4**, 192–194 (1968).

47. Widrow, B., Adaptive Sampled-Data Systems—A Statistical Theory of Adaptation, *1959 IRE WESCON Conv. Rec.*, Pt. 4, pp. 74–85, 1959.

48. Widrow, B., Generalization and Information Storage in Networks of Adaline "Neurons," *in* "Self-Organizing Systems—1962" (M. C. Yovits, G. T. Jacobi, and G. D. Goldstein, eds.), pp. 435–461, Spartan, Washington, D. C., 1962.

49. Widrow, B., and Hoff, M. E., Adaptive Switching Circuits, *1960 IRE WESCON Conv. Rec.*, Pt. 4, pp. 96–104, 1960.

50. Widrow, B., and Smith, F. W., Pattern-Recognizing Control Systems, *in* "Computer and Information Sciences," pp. 288–317, Spartan, Washington, D.C., 1964.

51. Widrow, B., Practical Applications for Adaptive Data-Processing System, presented at the *WESCON Conv., San Francisco*, Paper 11-4, *1963*.

52. Winder, R. O., Threshold Logic, Ph.D. dissertation, Princeton Univ., Princeton, New Jersey, 1962.

53. Winder, R. O., Threshold Logic in Artificial Intelligence, Sessions on Artifiicial Intelligence, *Proc. IEEE Winter General Meeting, January 1963*, pp. 107–128, 1963.

CHAPTER V

INDIRECT APPROXIMATION OF PROBABILITY DENSITIES

5.1 INTRODUCTION

In Chapter IV, we obtained decision rules by minimizing approximations to the expected loss. If we obtain approximations to the probability densities of each class, we can use the exact solution minimizing the risk with approximate densities. For example, we have noted in Chapter II that the optimum decision rule, given the loss function of Eq. (2.8), is

$$c(\mathbf{x}) = i \quad \text{if} \quad h_i \, p_i \, p_i(\mathbf{x}) \geq h_j \, p_j \, p_j(\mathbf{x}) \quad \text{for all} \quad j. \qquad (5.1)$$

Given approximations to $p_i(\mathbf{x})$ for all i, we have a fully defined decision rule; let us consider how to obtain such approximations using indirect methods. We will generally assume that Eq. (5.1) represents our decision rule, although extension to other rules is usually straightforward.

5.2 INTEGRAL-SQUARE APPROXIMATION

Let the unknown probability density of class i be $p_i(\mathbf{x})$, of interest in the region X of the vector space. Then we may seek parameters c_j such that

$$J(c_1^{(i)}, \ldots, c_R^{(i)}) = \int_X \left[p_i(\mathbf{x}) - \sum_{j=1}^{R} c_j^{(i)} \phi_j(\mathbf{x}) \right]^2 dX \qquad (5.2)$$

85

is minimized. We are given the samples $\{\mathbf{y}_1^{(i)}, \mathbf{y}_2^{(i)}, \ldots, \mathbf{y}_m^{(i)}\}$ of class i. For this criterion to be meaningful, the sample points should appear in a significant portion of the volume X; if not, $p_i(\mathbf{x})$ is zero over most of X.

The resulting discriminant functions

$$\rho_i(\mathbf{x}) = h_i \, p_i \sum_{j=1}^{R} c_j^{(i)} \phi_j(\mathbf{x}), \qquad i = 1, 2, \ldots, N \tag{5.3}$$

are well specified once the parameters $c_j^{(i)}$ are determined; for example, $p_i(\mathbf{x})$ will be a multivariate polynomial if the $\phi_j(\mathbf{x})$ are defined as in Section 4.9.

A necessary condition for the minimum of J [Eq. (5.2)] is that

$$\partial J / \partial c_k^{(i)} = 0, \qquad k = 1, 2, \ldots, R, \tag{5.4}$$

at the minimum. This yields, with some rearrangement, the linear equation

$$\sum_{j=1}^{R} c_j^{(i)} \int_X \phi_j(\mathbf{x}) \phi_k(\mathbf{x}) \, dX = \int_X \phi_k(\mathbf{x}) p_i(\mathbf{x}) \, dX, \qquad k = 1, 2, \ldots, R. \tag{5.5}$$

The integral on the right cannot be evaluated directly since $p_i(\mathbf{x})$ is unknown; but the expression on the right is the expectation of $\phi_k(\mathbf{x})$. An obvious approximation to Eq. (5.5) is then

$$\sum_{j=1}^{R} c_j^{(i)} \int_X \phi_j(\mathbf{x}) \phi_k(\mathbf{x}) \, dX = \frac{1}{M_i} \sum_{j=1}^{M_i} \phi_k(\mathbf{y}_j^{(i)}), \qquad k = 1, 2, \ldots, R, \tag{5.6}$$

the approximation of the expectation by the average.† Equation (5.6) may then be solved as any set of linear algebraic equations, or the $\{\phi_j\}$ may be chosen to be orthonormal. In this latter case, we obtain

$$c_k^{(i)} = \frac{1}{M_i} \sum_{j=1}^{M_i} \phi_k(\mathbf{y}_j^{(i)}), \qquad k = 1, 2, \ldots, R, \tag{5.7}$$

where

$$\int_X \phi_i(\mathbf{x}) \phi_j(\mathbf{x}) \, dx = \begin{cases} 1, & i = j, \\ 0, & i \neq j, \end{cases}$$

the definition of orthonormality.

The multivariate orthonormal functions may be obtained directly from a set of linearly independent functions by the Gram–Schmidt orthonormalization process [1], or by the extension of one-dimensional orthonormal functions

---

† If the distribution is sufficiently well-behaved, then

$$\frac{1}{M} \sum_{i=1}^{M} f(\mathbf{y}_i) \approx \int_X f(\mathbf{x}) p(\mathbf{x}) \, dX,$$

where $\mathbf{y}_1, \mathbf{y}_2, \ldots$ are samples of the density $p(\mathbf{x})$.

ch

(see Appendix A). A significant advantage of orthonormal functions, other than the elimination of the need for matrix inversion, is that the formulas for the coefficients are independent; hence, a higher order approximation may be obtained without recalculation of lower order coefficients.

Clearly, neither (5.6) nor (5.7) require storage of the sample points. The sum in either case may be accumulated as the sample points are presented, and the calculation performed when accumulation is complete. If new sample points are introduced sequentially and an adaptive modification of the discriminant is desired, the iterative formula

$$c_k^{(i)}(M + 1) = \frac{1}{M + 1} [Mc_k^{(i)}(M) + \phi_k(\mathbf{y}_{M+1})], \qquad c_k^{(i)}(0) = 0, \qquad (5.8)$$

exactly equivalent to (5.7), may be applied to obtain the exact solution for $M + 1$ sample points, given the solution for M sample points.

This latter formula provides an alternate interpretation for the approximation used in (5.6) and (5.7). For it will be noted that (5.8) may be written

$$c_k^{(i)}(M + 1) = c_k^{(i)}(M) + \frac{1}{M + 1} [\phi_k(\mathbf{y}_{M+1}) - c_k(M)], \qquad c_k(0) = 0. \quad (5.9)$$

This latter expression is in the form of a convergent stochastic approximation algorithm (see Chapter X), and in an appropriate sense, the integral of Eq. (5.2) converges to zero as M approaches infinity if the probability density can be represented exactly by the form chosen. The algorithm in (5.9) is a special case of an algorithm developed in the method of potential functions from a different viewpoint. (This point will be discussed further in Chapter VI.) The above discussion suggests that the particular choice of initial guess and weighting sequence represented by (5.9) are the "best" choice among stochastic approximation algorithms of this form, provided one accepts the premise that the best guess for the expectation is the average. The process in (5.9) converges to the solution of (5.6) at every step.

The method in (5.6) is clearly feasible for very complex systems, provided the ϕ_i are not too difficult to evaluate. For approximation by multivariate polynomials, the construction indicated in Appendix A is highly efficient.

If there are only two classes to be distinguished, or if we wish to obtain the pattern classes by successive dichotomies, we may approximate to

$$u(\mathbf{x}) = h_1 p_1 p_1(\mathbf{x}) - h_2 p_2 p_2(\mathbf{x}), \qquad (5.10)$$

the boundary rather than the discriminant function; that is, we minimize

$$J^*(c_1, \ldots, c_R) = \int_X \left[u(\mathbf{x}) - \sum_{i=1}^{R} c_i \phi_i(\mathbf{x}) \right]^2 dX. \qquad (5.11)$$

The appropriate decision rule is of course to decide class 1 if $\Sigma\, c_i \phi_i(\mathbf{x}) \geq 0$ and class 2 otherwise. The equivalents to Eqs. (5.6) and (5.7) are, respectively,

$$\sum_{j=1}^{R} c_j \int_X \phi_j(\mathbf{x})\phi_k(\mathbf{x})\, dX = \frac{h_1 p_1}{M_1} \sum_{j=1}^{M_1} \phi_k(\mathbf{y}_j^{(1)}) - \frac{h_2 p_2}{M_2} \sum_{j=1}^{M_2} \phi_k(\mathbf{y}_j^{(2)}),$$

$$k = 1, 2, \ldots, R, \quad (5.12)$$

and

$$c_k = \frac{h_1 p_1}{M_1} \sum_{j=1}^{M_1} \phi_k(\mathbf{y}_j^{(1)}) - \frac{h_2 p_2}{M_2} \sum_{j=1}^{M_2} \phi_k(\mathbf{y}_j^{(2)}), \qquad k = 1, 2, \ldots, R. \quad (5.13)$$

If p_1 and p_2 are estimated as

$$p_1 = \frac{M_1}{M_1 + M_2} \quad \text{and} \quad p_2 = \frac{M_2}{M_1 + M_2}, \quad (5.14)$$

and $h_1 = h_2 = 1$, (5.13) may be written simply as

$$c_k = \frac{1}{M_1 + M_2} \sum_{j=1}^{M_1+M_2} \mu(\mathbf{y}_j)\phi_k(\mathbf{y}_j), \quad (5.15a)$$

where

$$\mu(\mathbf{y}) = \begin{cases} 1 & \text{for} \quad \mathbf{y} \in \text{class 1} \\ -1 & \text{for} \quad \mathbf{y} \in \text{class 2.} \end{cases} \quad (5.15b)$$

The equations expressed in (5.12) and (5.13) yield exactly the same results as would the procedure of applying Eq. (5.6) or (5.7) separately to each class to find $p_1(\mathbf{x})$ and $p_2(\mathbf{x})$ and then substituting the results in (5.10). These results are equivalent to some of Sebestyen; his approach is somewhat different [8].

5.3 LEAST-MEAN-SQUARE APPROXIMATION

A major disadvantage of the above techniques is that a very high order of approximation may be necessary to get meaningful results if the sample points are confined to a relatively small volume of the region X. This situation is often the case in high-dimensional problems; e.g., a 20-cube with sides $\frac{1}{2}$ unit in length represents less than one-millionth of the volume of the unit 20-cube. The result is that a great deal of labor is expended in insuring that $p_i(\mathbf{x})$ approximates zero in regions of little interest. If we make the region X highly irregular in an attempt to fit the sample distribution, we are likely to find ourselves with a computationally infeasible problem in attempting to derive or evaluate orthonormal functions over that region.

This point should be emphasized. The curse of dimensionality (Section 1.5.1) leads to severe problems when integral-square minimization is utilized, significantly reducing its applicability in spaces of even moderate dimension for many applications. Figure 5.1 attempts to convey a situation which is likely to occur when the integration is over a rectangular parallelepiped enclosing all the samples. The probability density is near zero over most of the space; most of the integral-square error is measured over a region where samples will never occur, and a result such as illustrated might occur even with a high-order polynomial.

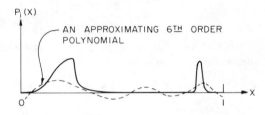

$P_i(X)$

AN APPROXIMATING 6TH ORDER POLYNOMIAL

FIG. 5.1 Integral-square approximation.

We could instead attempt to minimize

$$J_2 = \int_X \left[p_i(\mathbf{x}) - \sum_{j=1}^{R} c_j^{(i)} \phi_j(\mathbf{x}) \right]^2 P(\mathbf{x}) \, dX, \qquad (5.16)$$

where $P(\mathbf{x})$ is the probability density of appearance of sample points of any class, i.e.,

$$P(\mathbf{x}) = \sum_{l=1}^{N} p_l \, p_l(\mathbf{x}). \qquad (5.17)$$

Equation (5.16) is the mean-square error in the approximation. The emphasis is on minimizing the error where sample points occur. Direct application of the necessary condition for a minimum yields

$$\sum_{j=1}^{R} c_j^{(i)} \int_X \phi_j(\mathbf{x}) \phi_k(\mathbf{x}) P(\mathbf{x}) \, dX = \int_X \phi_k(\mathbf{x}) p_i(\mathbf{x}) P(\mathbf{x}) \, dX, \qquad k = 1, 2, \ldots, R.$$
$$(5.18)$$

Because of the product of unknown probabilities occurring on the right of (5.18), this does not reduce to an average as in the previous section. We can, however, reduce the problem somewhat by rewriting Eq. (5.16) as an average. Inserting (5.17) and interchanging summation and integration,

$$J_2 = \sum_{l=1}^{N} p_l \int_X \left[p_i(\mathbf{x}) - \sum_{j=1}^{R} c_j^{(i)} \phi_j(\mathbf{x}) \right]^2 p_l(\mathbf{x}) \, dX$$

$$= \sum_{l=1}^{N} p_l E_l \left\{ \left[p_i(\mathbf{x}) - \sum_{j=1}^{R} c_j^{(i)} \phi_j(\mathbf{x}) \right]^2 \right\}$$

$$\approx \sum_{l=1}^{N} \frac{p_l}{M_l} \sum_{k=1}^{M_l} \left[p_i(\mathbf{y}_k^{(l)}) - \sum_{j=1}^{R} c_j^{(i)} \phi_j(\mathbf{y}_k^{(l)}) \right]^2 \qquad (5.19)$$

It might appear at first glance that little has been accomplished, since $p_i(\mathbf{x})$ is unknown. We can proceed further for two reasons: (1) we need estimate $p_i(\mathbf{x})$ only at labeled samples, and (2) a rough estimate will be smoothed if the approximating function is continuous. If we denote the estimate of $p_i(\mathbf{y}_k^{(l)})$ by $\mu_i(\mathbf{y}_k^{(l)})$, we can minimize

$$J_2^* = \sum_{l=1}^{N} \frac{p_l}{M_l} \sum_{k=1}^{M_l} \left[\mu_i(\mathbf{y}_k^{(l)}) - \sum_{j=1}^{R} c_j^{(i)} \phi_j(\mathbf{y}_k^{(l)}) \right]^2 \tag{5.20}$$

if we can arrive at a reasonable estimate μ_i. (Note that J_2^*, the error averaged over the samples, is a reasonable criterion function independent of the derivation.) If we define

$$M = M_1 + M_2 + \cdots + M_N$$

and assume

$$p_i = M_i/M,$$

Eq. (5.20) becomes

$$J_2^* = \frac{1}{M} \sum_{k=1}^{M} \left[\mu_i(\mathbf{y}_k) - \sum_{j=1}^{R} c_j^{(i)} \phi_j(\mathbf{y}_k) \right]^2, \tag{5.21}$$

where the sum is over sample points of all classes. For notational simplicity, we shall refer hereafter to (5.21); modifications necessary for application to (5.20) should be obvious.

If μ_i is a known function, methods of varying usefulness are available for the resulting well-defined minimization problem. Solution of the linear system

$$A\mathbf{c}^{(i)} = \mathbf{b}^{(i)},$$

where

$$a_{mn} = \sum_{k=1}^{M} \phi_m(\mathbf{y}_k)\phi_n(\mathbf{y}_k) \quad \text{and} \quad b_j^{(i)} = \sum_{k=1}^{M} \phi_j(\mathbf{y}_k)\mu_i(\mathbf{y}_k), \tag{5.22}$$

with $A = [a_{mn}]$, $\mathbf{b}^{(i)} = (b_1^{(i)}, \ldots, b_R^{(i)})$, and $\mathbf{c}^{(i)} = (c_1^{(i)}, c_2^{(i)}, \ldots, c_R^{(i)})$, is sometimes feasible for medium values of R.† The problem is then to choose $\mu_i(\mathbf{x})$.

The simplest approach is to assign

$$\mu_i(\mathbf{x}) = \begin{cases} 1, & \mathbf{x} \text{ in class } i, \\ 0, & \text{if not.} \end{cases} \tag{5.23}$$

This should give a meaningful separation of classes. The disadvantage of this assignment is that for sample points not near the boundary of a class

---

† $R = 150$ is generally feasible for conventional matrix inversion routines of some quality.

the restriction to a constant value is unnecessarily severe, and may affect the quality of the approximation at the boundaries. Obviously, this estimate is unlikely to be accurate, and the "optimal" solution resulting from using it in Eq. (5.21) and minimizing may not provide a good approximation to the optimum boundary as defined by the true (but, alas, unknown) probability densities.

We can proceed adaptively, using the result of approximation to (5.23) to throw away samples far from the boundaries or to adjust the value of $\mu_i(\mathbf{x})$ at misclassified sample points, and then repeating the approximation. Concrete approaches are suggested in [3], but another approach suggested in that reference seems clearly superior. Potential function (Parzen estimator) techniques can approximate a probability density from samples of that density accurately by a simple formula:

$$\mu_i(\mathbf{x}) = \frac{1}{M_i} \sum_{l=1}^{M_i} \gamma(\mathbf{x}, \mathbf{y}_l^{(i)}), \qquad (5.24)$$

where γ is an appropriate "potential function." Chapter VI is devoted to potential function methods; we will assume for the present that we have defined $\mu_i(\mathbf{x})$ as in Eq. (5.24) and defer justification.

If Eq. (5.21) is minimized by solving the linear equation in (5.22), then μ_i need be calculated only once for each sample. It is of course efficient to calculate and store the MN numbers $\mu_i(\mathbf{y}_j)$ ($i = 1, 2, \ldots, N$; $j = 1, 2, \ldots, M$) once, if an adaptive optimization technique is used.

The reader may ask why one should expend such effort in minimizing (5.21) if (5.24) provides a good approximation to $p_i(\mathbf{x})$. The major point is that (5.21) can provide an *efficient* approximation [4]. (See Appendix B.) We wish the decision rule to be relatively simple and easy to calculate and Eq. (5.24) is not satisfactory in many applications. It, for example, requires storage of all the sample points in the form given. A less critical point is the fact that potential function methods can give probability densities with excessive variation; we have already noted the smoothing effect of the approximation procedure.

5.4 WEIGHTED MEAN-SQUARE APPROXIMATION

Equation (5.21) is probably closer to the problem we wish to solve than (5.2), but it might be argued that the discriminant function is most critical at the decision boundaries. Hence, one might minimize [3]

$$\int_X \left[\mu_i(\mathbf{x}) - \sum_{j=1}^{R} c_j^{(i)} \phi_j(\mathbf{x}) \right]^2 P(\mathbf{x}) g(\mathbf{x}) \, dX, \qquad (5.25)$$

where all is as before except $g(\mathbf{x})$ is a function reaching its maximum at the boundaries of the decision region. The concepts just discussed may be applied immediately. Let $\mu_i(\mathbf{x})$, $i = 1, 2, \ldots, N$, be the estimate of the probability density, and let

$$f(z) = \exp(-z^2/\sigma^2) \tag{5.26}$$

(or a similar function). Define

$$\max{}_1\{a_1, a_2, \ldots, a_m) = a_{i_1} \quad \text{and} \quad \max{}_2\{a_1, a_2, \ldots, a_m\} = a_{i_2}$$

if $a_{i_1} \geq a_{i_2} \geq \cdots \geq a_{i_m}$. Then, minimize

$$\frac{1}{M} \sum_{k=1}^{M} \left[\mu_i(\mathbf{y}_k) - \sum_{j=1}^{R} c_j^{(i)} \phi_j(\mathbf{y}_k) \right]^2 g(\mathbf{y}_k), \tag{5.27}$$

where

$$g(\mathbf{y}_k) = f[\max{}_1\{\mu_1(\mathbf{y}_k), \ldots, \mu_N(\mathbf{y}_k)\} - \max{}_2\{\mu_1(\mathbf{y}_k), \ldots, \mu_N(\mathbf{y}_k)\}].$$

Then g is large near boundaries. This is a well-defined minimization problem, which can still be solved by the solution of a linear system.

5.5 RELATION TO LINEAR DISCRIMINANT AND Φ-FUNCTION TECHNIQUES

Suppose that we had no particular interest in obtaining a characteristic discriminant function, an approximation to a probability density function. We could then simply find discriminant functions which minimized an estimate of the misclassification rate. In Fig. 5.2, two samples are misclassified by the existing discriminant functions; if the misclassification error is measured by the difference of the discriminant functions at those points, we can minimize the average misclassification error (or the average of some monotonic function f of the misclassification error):

$$R = \frac{p_1}{M_1} \sum_{i=1}^{M_1} f(\rho_2(\mathbf{y}_i^{(1)}) - \rho_1(\mathbf{y}_i^{(1)}) + d)$$

$$+ \frac{p_2}{M_2} \sum_{i=1}^{M_2} f(\rho_1(\mathbf{y}_i^{(2)}) - \rho_2(\mathbf{y}_i^{(2)}) + d), \tag{5.28}$$

where $d \geq 0$ and $f = f_1, f_2$, or f_3 of Eqs. (4.18), (4.19), and (4.20) or a similar function. If the argument of $f(z)$ is negative, there is no error, and $f(z)$ is zero. The constant d may be used to force the boundary away from samples which are almost misclassified. Suppose the discriminant functions are given

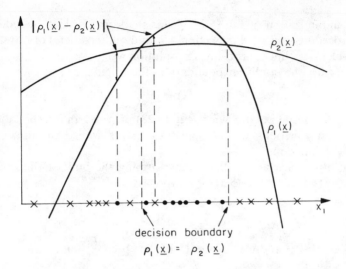

FIG. 5.2 Measuring misclassification error. Underscored letters indicate vectors.

by Eq. (5.3) with $h_i p_i = 1$, i.e., the constants are absorbed into $c_j^{(i)}$. Then

$$\rho_i(\mathbf{x}) = \mathbf{c}^{(i)} \cdot \boldsymbol{\phi}(\mathbf{x}), \tag{5.29}$$

where $\mathbf{c}^{(i)} = (c_1^{(i)}, \ldots, c_R^{(i)})$ and $\boldsymbol{\phi}(\mathbf{x}) = (\phi_1(\mathbf{x}), \ldots, \phi_R(\mathbf{x}))$. If we define the transformation

$$z_i = \phi_i(\mathbf{x}), \qquad i = 1, 2, \ldots, R, \tag{5.30a}$$

that is,

$$\mathbf{z} = \boldsymbol{\phi}(\mathbf{x}), \tag{5.30b}$$

then

$$\rho_i(\mathbf{x}) = \hat{\rho}_i(\mathbf{z}) = \mathbf{c}^{(i)} \cdot \mathbf{z}, \tag{5.31}$$

and the samples can be transformed into $\mathbf{z}$ space,

$$\mathbf{y}_i' = \boldsymbol{\phi}(\mathbf{y}_i). \tag{5.32}$$

If we define, as in Chapter IV, the set $\mathcal{Y}'$ of samples of class 1 and negatives of samples of class 2, and let $p_i = M_i/M$, Eq. (5.28) can be rewritten in terms of the samples in $\mathbf{z}$ space:

$$R = \frac{1}{M} \sum_{j=1}^{M} f[d - (\mathbf{c}^{(1)} - \mathbf{c}^{(2)}) \cdot \mathbf{y}_j']. \tag{5.33}$$

With $\mathbf{w} = \mathbf{c}^{(1)} - \mathbf{c}^{(2)}$, this is identically the minimization represented by Eq. (4.24). (The reader might note the similarity between Figs. 5.2 and 4.8.)

Hence the minimization of Eq. (5.28) yields the same decision boundary as does the procedure suggested in Section 4.9 (and outlined here) of transforming the problem to a linear problem. The solution weight vector $\mathbf{w}$ of the linear problem specifies the nonlinear boundary in the original space:

$$\mathbf{w} \cdot \boldsymbol{\phi}(\mathbf{x}) = 0. \tag{5.34}$$

From the opposite point of view, Eq. (5.28) provides an interpretation of the linear cost functions when applied to spaces whose coordinates are specified by ϕ functions.

We can also linearize the algorithms forming the bulk of this chapter. The equivalent of using Eq. (5.21) for two classes is

$$J = \frac{1}{M} \sum_{k=1}^{M} [d - \mathbf{w} \cdot \mathbf{y}_k']^2, \tag{5.35}$$

where $\mathbf{w} = \mathbf{c}^{(1)} - \mathbf{c}^{(2)}$ and $u(\mathbf{x})$ of Eq. (5.10) has been estimated as

$$u(\mathbf{y}) = \begin{cases} d, & \mathbf{y} \in \text{class } 1 \\ -d, & \mathbf{y} \in \text{class } 2. \end{cases} \tag{5.36}$$

Equation (5.35) corresponds to Eq. (4.24) with $f(z)$ given by

$$f_4(z) = z^2. \tag{5.37}$$

Least-square methods yield *two-sided* loss functions in this context; samples classified correctly still contribute to the cost. Equation (5.35) corresponds to what has, in the linear context, been called the LMS criterion [2]. Smith has published results suggesting that, at least for multivariate normal distributions, the LMS criterion appears more accurate than the one-sided criteria given by f_1, f_2, and f_3 of Eqs. (4.18), (4.19), and (4.20) [9].

5.6   EXTENSIONS

5.6.1   Updating the Discriminant Function

It appears at first that addition of new samples requires recalculation of the discriminant function from the start. However, one may simply note that the updated discriminant will be very close to the old discriminant; iterative techniques for solving linear equations [1] using the old discriminant function as the initial guess should converge quickly if at all.

5.6.2   Other Approximating Functions

There is no conceptual difficulty in substituting any parameterized function $g(\mathbf{x}; \mathbf{c})$ for $\sum c_i \phi_i(\mathbf{x})$ in the previous functions which were minimized. One cannot expect to find the optimum value of **c** by solving a linear equation in that case, but many other minimization techniques are available. If $g(\mathbf{x}; \mathbf{c})$ is an efficient approximation, one might get by with fewer parameters than in a general polynomial. Good general classes of parameterized functions for this use are (1) piecewise linear functions, and (2) composed functions (Meisel [4] and Appendix B).

Another generalization becomes apparent if we express Eq. (5.21) as

$$J_2^* = \frac{1}{M} \sum_{k=1}^{M} |\mu_i(\mathbf{y}_k) - g(\mathbf{y}_k; \mathbf{c})|;$$ (5.38)

parameters of a standard function

i.e., we may use the absolute value rather than the square. Again, this eliminates the possibility of solution by linear methods.

Can't take derivatives!

5.7 SUMMARY

The integral-square criterion (Section 5.2) is important from a theoretical standpoint and because of its extensive treatment in the pattern recognition literature; it has an elegantly simple solution. The mean-square criterion (Section 5.3) poses more computational difficulties, but is more valid in higher dimensions and more accurate where it counts for any dimensionality. The weighted mean-square error (Section 5.4) can reduce the required complexity of the discriminant by allowing larger approximation errors away from class boundaries.

The probability estimates required for the mean-square and weighted mean-square algorithms can be obtained by direct assignment (e.g., all equal 1), by adaptive modification, or by potential function (Parzen estimator) techniques; the last approach has a great advantage in accuracy.

Modified mean-square criteria which minimize the average error only at misclassified sample points lead directly to the algorithms of Chapter IV when linearized. The mean-square criteria can be linearized as well and yield two-sided loss functions which penalize correctly classified samples as well as incorrectly classified samples; these are most easily interpreted in the nonlinear form, although, of course, the algorithms are equivalent.

One need not limit consideration to polynomials for approximation; other forms may yield more efficient decision rules.

EXERCISES

5.1. Given $\mathcal{Y}_1 = \{(2, 0)(2, 2)(2, 4)(3, 3)\}$ and

$$\mathcal{Y}_2 = \{(0, 3)(-2, 2)(-1, -1)(1, -2)(3, -1)\},$$

find $\rho(\mathbf{x}) = c_1 x_1 + c_2 x_2 + c_3$ such that

$$\int_{-3}^{.5} \int_{-3}^{.5} [u(\mathbf{x}) - (c_1 x_1 + c_2 x_2 + c_3)]^2 \, dx_1 \, dx_2$$

is minimized, where $u(\mathbf{x})$ is given by Eq. (5.10) with $h_1 = h_2 = 1$. Use the method expressed in Eq. (5.15) with the orthonormal functions of Appendix A. Sketch the sample points and your solution.

5.2. Using the sample points of Exercise 5.1, find a mean-square approximation $c_1 x_1' + c_2 x_2' + c_3$ [minimizing Eq. (5.21)] to $p_1(\mathbf{x})$ and $p_2(\mathbf{x})$ by using Eq. (5.23) as the function to be approximated to. Sketch your result as before.

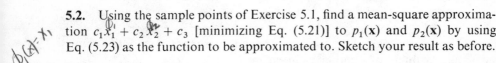

5.3. Describe an approach to the minimization of

$$\int_R \left| p_i(\mathbf{x}) - \sum_{j=1}^R c_j \phi_j(\mathbf{x}) \right| P(\mathbf{x}) \, dx$$

over $c_1, \ldots, c_R$. Write an iterative algorithm for finding a solution (based on the gradient technique).

5.4. Show that procedures (1) and (2) yield equivalent results given two sets of two-dimensional samples $\mathscr{Y}_1$ and $\mathscr{Y}_2$:

$$\mathscr{Y}_1 = \{\mathbf{y}_1^{(1)}, \mathbf{y}_2^{(1)}, \ldots, \mathbf{y}_{M_1}^{(1)}\}$$
$$\mathscr{Y}_2 = \{\mathbf{y}_1^{(2)}, \mathbf{y}_2^{(2)}, \ldots, \mathbf{y}_{M_2}^{(2)}\}:$$

(1) Find the second-order polynomial

$$q(\mathbf{x}) = c_1 + c_2 x_1 + c_3 x_2 + c_4 x_1^2 + c_5 x_1 x_2 + c_6 x_2^2$$

which minimizes

$$F(\mathbf{c}) = \sum_{k=1}^{M_1} [1 - q(\mathbf{y}_k^{(1)})]^2 + \sum_{k=1}^{M_2} [-1 - q(\mathbf{y}_k^{(2)})]^2;$$

classify $\mathbf{x}$ in class 1 if $q(\mathbf{x}) \geq 0$, in class 2 otherwise.

(2) Let $\phi_1 = 1$, $\phi_2 = x_1$, $\phi_3 = x_2$, $\phi_4 = x_1^2$, $\phi_5 = x_1 x_2$, $\phi_6 = x_2^2$. Transform the sets of two-dimensional samples $\mathscr{Y}_1$ and $\mathscr{Y}_2$ into two sets of six-dimensional samples Z_1 and Z_2 by the transformation

$$z_i = \phi_i(\mathbf{x}), \qquad i = 1, \ldots, 6;$$

(e.g., $\mathbf{z}_1^{(1)}$ in Z_1 has components $z_{11}^{(1)} = 1$, $z_{12}^{(1)} = y_{11}^{(1)}$, $z_{13}^{(1)} = y_{12}^{(1)}$, $z_{15}^{(1)} = y_{11}^{(1)} y_{12}^{(1)}$, etc.). From Z_1 and Z_2, form

$$Z = \{\mathbf{z}_1, \mathbf{z}_2, \ldots, \mathbf{z}_M\}, \qquad M = M_1 + M_2,$$

as the union of Z_1 and the negatives of samples of Z_2. Find the weight vector $\mathbf{c} = (c_1, c_2, \ldots, c_6)$ which minimizes

$$G(\mathbf{c}) = M^{-1} \sum_{k=1}^{M} (\mathbf{c} \cdot \mathbf{z}_k - 1)^2.$$

Classify $\mathbf{x}$ in class 1 if $\sum_{i=1}^{6} c_i \phi_i(\mathbf{x}) \geq 0$, in class 2 otherwise.

5.5. Apply the necessary condition for a minimum to Eq. (5.27) to find the appropriate modification of Eq. (5.22).

SELECTED BIBLIOGRAPHY†

1. Isaacson, E., and Keller, H. B., "Analysis of Numerical Methods," Wiley, New York, 1966.
2. Koford, J. S., and Groner, G. F., The Use of an Adaptive Threshold Element to Design a Linear Optimal Pattern Classifier, *IEEE Trans. Information Theory* **2**, 42–50 (1966).
3. Meisel, W. S., Least-Square Methods in Abstract Pattern Recognition, *Information Sciences* **1**, 43–54 (1968).
4. Meisel, W. S., The Efficient Representation of Functions for Pattern Classification and Feature Selection, *Proc. 1971 IEEE Sys. Sci. Cybernetics Conf.: Jt. Nat. Conf. Major Sys., Anaheim, California, October 1971.*
5. Patterson, J. D., and Womack, B. F., An Adaptive Pattern Classification System, *IEEE Trans. Sys. Sci. and Cybernetics* **2**, 62–67 (1966).
6. Patterson, J. D., Wagner, T. J., and Womack, B. F., A Mean-Square Performance Criterion for Adaptive Pattern Classification, *IEEE Trans. Automatic Control* **12**, 195–197 (1967).
7. Pitt, J. M., and Womack, B. F., Additional Features of an Adaptive, Multicategory Pattern Classification System, *IEEE Trans. Sys. Sci. and Cybernetics* **5**, 183–190 (1969).
8. Sebestyen, G. S., "Decision-Making Processes in Pattern Recognition," Macmillan, New York, 1962.
9. Smith, F. W., Design of Minimum-Error Optimal Classifiers for Patterns from Distributions with Gaussian Tails, *Proc. 2nd Int. Conf. Sys. Sci., Hawaii, January 1969*, pp. 38–41.

† See also bibliography for Chapters IV and VI.

DIRECT CONSTRUCTION OF PROBABILITY DENSITIES: POTENTIAL FUNCTIONS (PARZEN ESTIMATORS)

Way of estimating probability distributions from samples

Potential

6.1   INTRODUCTION

We have spent a great deal of space on indirect methods; we turn now to an important class of direct methods. As in any direct method, the validity of the result depends on the validity of the constructive algorithm; there is no criterion function to define an "optimal" solution. Potential function methods will be justified on first an intuitive and then a more formal basis.

The terminology "potential function" was introduced by Bashkirov *et al.* [6], although previous authors had employed the concept. The origin can perhaps be best traced to Parzen [15], whose suggestions in the one-dimensional case can be directly extended to the multivariate case [12, 13]. In fact, this approach is often called the "Parzen estimator" or "Parzen window" approach. Sebestyen employed a similar concept in his early paper on constructing probability densities from samples [17]. Aizerman *et al.* [1–5], Braverman [7], and Tsypkin [23] have studied extensively a particular class of potential function methods. Others have extended and elaborated upon the approach (see the bibliography).

Potential function methods proceed by constructing probability densities from samples. Given the conditional probability densities $p_i(\mathbf{x})$ for each class, an appropriate decision rule such as

(See p 40)

$$c(\mathbf{x}) = i \quad \text{if} \quad h_i p_i p_i(\mathbf{x}) \geq h_j p_j p_j(\mathbf{x}) \quad \text{for all} \quad j \tag{6.1}$$

can be invoked. Unless otherwise specified, we will be considering the labeled samples of only one class *i* at a time in order to estimate $p_i(\mathbf{x})$; we hence often omit the subscript indicating class membership for notational convenience. Further, since identical normalization constants for each class density cancel in comparisons such as (6.1), we often do not include such constants.

The estimated probability density $\hat{p}(\mathbf{x})$ is formed from the superposition of *potential functions* $\gamma(\mathbf{x}, \mathbf{y})$ over samples of $\hat{p}(\mathbf{x})$:

$$\hat{p}(\mathbf{x}) = \frac{1}{M} \sum_{j=1}^{M} \gamma(\mathbf{x}, \mathbf{y}_j). \quad \text{(6.2)}$$

The form of γ is typically as illustrated in Fig. 6.1 for a one-dimensional pattern space or Fig. 6.2 for a two-dimensional space, e.g.,

$$\gamma(\mathbf{x}, \mathbf{y}) = \frac{1}{(2\pi)^{n/2}\sigma^n} \exp\left(-\frac{\|\mathbf{x} - \mathbf{y}\|^2}{2\sigma^2}\right), \quad \text{(6.3)}$$

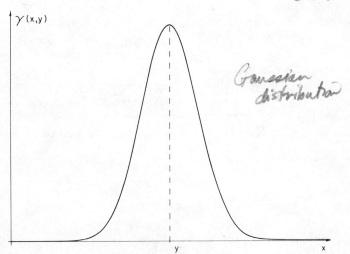

FIG. 6.1   A potential function (of one variable).

where $\|\mathbf{x}\|$ is a norm in *n*-dimensional pattern space. The potential function reflects the decreasing influence of a sample point **y** upon a point **x** as the distance $d(\mathbf{x}, \mathbf{y})$ between the points increases; the average of these "potentials" from samples of class *i* at a point **x** constitutes a measure of the degree of membership of point **x** in class *i*. To restate, $\gamma(\mathbf{x}, \mathbf{y})$ is a maximum when $\mathbf{x} = \mathbf{y}$ and becomes negligible when **x** and **y** are widely separated, varying continuously between.

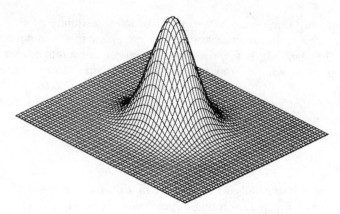

FIG. 6.2   A potential function (of two variables).

Equation (6.2) expresses the algorithm completely once γ is specified; $\hat{p}(\mathbf{x})$ may be evaluated directly for any value of $\mathbf{x}$. In the form specified, the sample points serve in effect as parameters of the distribution; Eq. (6.2) provides a decision rule which is inefficient in terms of computation and storage. We shall discuss in later sections the obtaining of efficient discriminants from potential function methods.

The choice of potential function is, of course, critical. Figure 6.3 is a plot of a possible $\hat{p}(\mathbf{x})$ when γ is overly peaked. It is clear that a sample lies beneath each peak. Figure 6.4 is the result of potential functions of intermediate width applied to the same samples; Fig. 6.5, the result of broad potential functions.

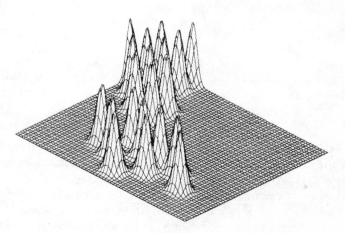

FIG. 6.3   A superposition of highly peaked potential functions.

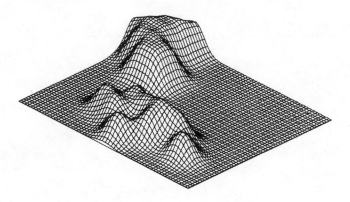

FIG. 6.4   A smoother superposition.

Either Fig. 6.4 or Fig. 6.5 could be considered an adequate representation. A later section discusses approaches to the choice of shape and size parameters determining the potential function, e.g., the constant σ in (6.3).

A computationally efficient potential function is

by hand

where

$$\gamma(\mathbf{x}, \mathbf{y}) = f\,[d(\mathbf{x}, \mathbf{y})],$$

$$d(\mathbf{x}, \mathbf{y}) = \sum_{i=1}^{n} |\,x_i - y_i\,| \qquad (6.4)$$

city block

and $f(d)$ is a piecewise linear function as in Fig. 6.6. The estimated probability

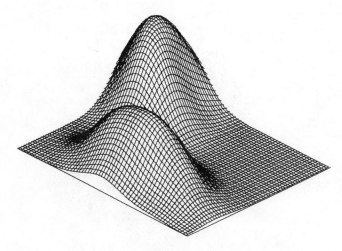

FIG. 6.5   An even smoother superposition.

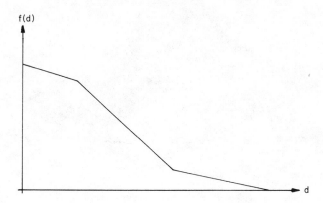

FIG. 6.6 Defining a piecewise linear potential function.

density $\hat{p}(\mathbf{x})$ corresponding to Fig. 6.4 but obtained using Eq. (6.4) is indicated in Fig. 6.7.

Note that, if

$$\int_X \gamma(\mathbf{x}, \mathbf{y}) \, dX = 1, \tag{6.5}$$

then

$$\int_X \hat{p}(\mathbf{x}) \, dX = \frac{1}{M} \sum_{i=1}^{M} \int_X \gamma(\mathbf{x}, \mathbf{y}) \, dX = \frac{1}{M} \sum_{i=1}^{M} 1 = 1;$$

p42

$p(\mathbf{x})$ will be normalized if γ is normalized. Equation (2.13) indicates the appropriate normalization for the most general form of Eq. (6.3).

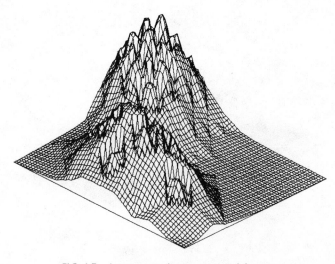

FIG. 6.7 A piecewise linear potential function.

6.2   AN ALTERNATE INTERPRETATION

Let us take the viewpoint proposed by Parzen [15]. Suppose we had one-dimensional samples, and we wished to estimate $p(x)$ at a particular point x. We could count the number of samples $N_h(x)$ in the interval $[x - h, x + h]$ and divide by the total number of samples M and the interval length $2h$ to obtain an estimate of the density at x:

$$\hat{p}(x) = N_h(x)/M(2h). \tag{6.6}$$

If we define

$$K(y) = \begin{cases} \frac{1}{2}, & |y| \le |1|, \\ 0, & |y| > |1|, \end{cases} \tag{6.7}$$

then we can write (6.6) as

$$\hat{p}(x) = \frac{1}{Mh} \sum_{j=1}^{M} K\left(\frac{x - y_j}{h}\right); \tag{6.8}$$

the jth term of the sum is zero if y_j falls outside $[x - h, x + h]$. Clearly, this corresponds to

$$\gamma(x, y) = \frac{1}{h} K\left(\frac{x - y}{h}\right), \tag{6.9}$$

which is sketched in Fig. 6.8. This leads immediately to the concept of generalizing K to forms such as we have suggested.

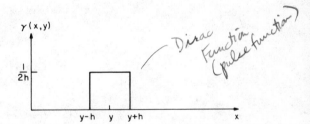

FIG. 6.8   A potential function equiv-alent to a modified histogram approach.

If we consider $\hat{p}(x)$ to be a function of the number of samples used in the estimate, $\hat{p}(x) \equiv \hat{p}(x; M)$, then Parzen shows that $\hat{p}$ is unbiased as $M \to \infty$ if $h \equiv h(M)$ and

$$\lim_{M \to \infty} h(M) = 0. \tag{6.10}$$

(The function K must satisfy certain conditions as well.) The potential function should become more peaked as the number of samples increases. This is a satisfying theoretical quality; but, since we are usually working with a small sample of fixed size, the problem encountered in practice is that of *deviation*   *total samples*

choosing a fixed h for a fixed M. (And, in higher dimensions, there are in general more shape and size parameters to specify.)

Permissible functions K include Eq. (6.7) and the following (one-dimensional case):

$$K(y) = (2\pi)^{-1/2} e^{-y^2/2}, \quad \text{z distribution} \tag{6.11a}$$

$$K(y) = [\pi(1 + y^2)]^{-1}, \quad \text{and} \tag{6.11b}$$

$$K(y) = \begin{cases} 1 - |y|, & |y| \le 1, \\ 0, & |y| > 1. \end{cases} \tag{6.11c}$$

6.3 GENERALITY OF POTENTIAL FUNCTION METHODS

The following theorem indicates the generality of potential function methods.

THEOREM [10] Let $Y = \{y_1, y_2, \ldots, y_M\}$ and $Z = \{z_1, z_2, \ldots, z_N\}$ be sets of samples of two classes such that no $y_i = z_k$. There exists a continuously differentiable potential function $\gamma(x, y)$ such that discriminant functions constructed according to Eq. (6.2) classify all points of Y and Z correctly using Eq. (6.1) with $p_1 = p_2$ and $h_1 = h_2$.

Proof Define

$$D = \underset{1 \le i \le M}{\text{Min}} \ \underset{1 \le j \le N}{\text{Min}} \ \|y_i - z_j\|, \quad \text{--- find smallest distance btw 2 points}$$

where $\|\cdot\|$ is again the usual Euclidean norm, and

$$\gamma(x, y) = \exp[-(1/\alpha)\|x - y\|^2], \tag{6.12}$$

where

$$\alpha < D^2/\ln[\text{Max}(N, M)]. \tag{6.13}$$

It will be shown that the potential function defined by Eqs. (6.12) and (6.13) satisfies the theorem.

Consider $y_k \in Y$. We have

$$\hat{p}_Z(y_k) = \frac{1}{N} \sum_{i=1}^{N} \exp[-(1/\alpha)\|y_k - z_i\|^2]$$

$$\le \underset{1 \le i \le N}{\text{Max}} \ \exp[-(1/\alpha)\|y_k - z_i\|^2] \quad \text{--- max when e is minimum.}$$

$$\le \exp[-(1/\alpha) \underset{1 \le i \le N}{\text{Min}} \|y_k - z_i\|^2] \le \exp(-D^2/\alpha)$$

$$< \exp(-\ln M) = 1/M = (1/M)\exp[-(1/\alpha)\|y_k - y_k\|^2]$$

$$< \frac{1}{M} \sum_{i=1}^{M} \exp[-(1/\alpha)\|y_k - y_i\|^2]$$

$$= \hat{p}_Y(y_k),$$

and $\mathbf{y}_k$ is classified correctly. With a change of notation, the above derivation shows that all points of Z are classified correctly as well. The potential functions and discriminant functions derived from them are continuously differentiable. The proof can clearly be extended to any number of classes or differing p_i and h_i.

The preceding theorem and its proof have some interesting implications. We have, since the proof is constructive, a pattern recognition algorithm which is "perfect" in terms of the commonly employed criteria of number of sample points misclassified (when applied to the design set). Performance on an independent test set undoubtedly would be better if a less irregular discriminant were generated. This theorem indicates, among other things, that it is not feasible to choose the shape parameters to optimize accuracy on the design set.

6.4 CHOOSING THE FORM OF POTENTIAL FUNCTION

Applying the intuitive interpretation given above, a reasonable set of criteria for a potential function $\gamma(\mathbf{x}, \mathbf{y})$ might be the following, phrased in intuitive terms:

(1) $\gamma(\mathbf{x}, \mathbf{y})$ should be maximum for $\mathbf{x} = \mathbf{y}$;

(2) $\gamma(\mathbf{x}, \mathbf{y})$ should be approximately zero for $\mathbf{x}$ distant from $\mathbf{y}$ and in the region of interest;

(3) $\gamma(\mathbf{x}, \mathbf{y})$ should be a smooth (continuous) function and tend to decrease in a monotonic fashion with the distance between $\mathbf{x}$ and $\mathbf{y}$; and

(4) if $\gamma(\mathbf{x}_1, \mathbf{y}_1) = \gamma(\mathbf{x}_2, \mathbf{y}_1)$, where $\mathbf{y}_1$ is a sample point, then the patterns represented by $\mathbf{x}_1$ and $\mathbf{x}_2$ should have approximately the same "degree of similarity" to $\mathbf{y}_1$.

The first criterion is fundamental and self-explanatory; however, as we shall see, allowing it to be only approximately satisfied can in some cases be useful.

The second criterion is important if the sample distribution is multimodal. In such a case, sample points from one cluster of a given class should not significantly affect the discriminant function in the vicinity of another cluster from the same class. For unimodal distributions, this requirement is unnecessary. Sebestyen treats in detail the "measure of similarity" $\|\mathbf{x} - \mathbf{y}\|^2$, where $\|\cdot\|$ represents the Euclidean norm [16]; note that this is equivalent to a potential function

$$\rho(\mathbf{x}, \mathbf{y}) = - \|\mathbf{x} - \mathbf{y}\|^2$$

which violates criterion (2).

If $\gamma(\mathbf{x}, \mathbf{y})$ is to be consistent with our intuitive concept of a potential, the third criterion requiring monotonicity is natural. It would be pedantic, however, to require monotonicity in the tail of the potential function where the potential is negligible.

The last criterion is more difficult to express in quantitative terms. It is closely related to proper normalization of the variables; the "shape" of the potential function should be such that a smooth probability density can be constructed. We shall discuss the choice of size and shape of the potential function in the next section.

There are two major classes of potential functions [8]. The potential functions we have described to this point are all potential functions of Type 1. Type 2 potential functions are of the following form:

$$\gamma(\mathbf{x}, \mathbf{y}) = \sum_{i=1}^{R} \lambda_i^2 \phi_i(\mathbf{x})\phi_i(\mathbf{y}), \tag{6.14}$$

where $\{\phi_i(\mathbf{x})\}$ is a complete set of multivariate orthonormal functions and the λ_i are constants. (We shall assume that $\lambda_i = 1$ for the sake of notational simplicity.) The justification for considering (6.14) to be a potential function is related to the fact that

$$\sum_{i=1}^{\infty} \phi_i(\mathbf{x})\phi_i(\mathbf{y}) = \delta(\mathbf{x} - \mathbf{y}), \tag{6.15}$$

where $\delta(\mathbf{x})$ is the Dirac δ function, if $\{\phi_i\}$ is a complete orthonormal set. The truncation in (6.14) could then be a good approximation to a potential function if it contained a sufficient number of terms.

Let us note, however, that the discriminant function resulting from (6.14) is

$$\hat{p}(\mathbf{x}) = \frac{1}{M} \sum_{i=1}^{M} \gamma(\mathbf{x}, \mathbf{y}_i) = \frac{1}{M} \sum_{i=1}^{M} \sum_{k=1}^{R} \phi_k(\mathbf{x})\phi_k(\mathbf{y}_i)$$

$$= \sum_{k=1}^{R} \phi_k(\mathbf{x})\left[\frac{1}{M} \sum_{i=1}^{M} \phi_k(\mathbf{y}_i)\right],$$

thus,

$$\hat{p}(\mathbf{x}) = \sum_{k=1}^{R} c_k \phi_k(\mathbf{x}), \tag{6.16}$$

where

$$c_k = \frac{1}{M} \sum_{i=1}^{M} \phi_k(\mathbf{y}_i). \tag{6.17}$$

But this is exactly the result we obtained in Section 5.2 in minimizing the integral-square error. Since this latter interpretation is valid irrespective of the number of terms, the author prefers to view this result from an integral-square point of view, and will not discuss the particular characteristics of Type 2 potential functions further.

6.5 CHOOSING SIZE AND SHAPE PARAMETERS

Let us phrase our discussion in terms of the potential function

$$\gamma(\mathbf{x}, \mathbf{y}) = \frac{1}{(2\pi)^{n/2}\sigma_1\sigma_2\cdots\sigma_n} \exp\left[-\frac{1}{2}\sum_{i=1}^{n} \frac{(x_i - y_i)^2}{\sigma_i^2}\right]. \tag{6.18}$$

How can we choose $\sigma_1, \sigma_2, \ldots, \sigma_n$?

If the features are normalized, e.g., by methods proposed in Section 1.5.1, then it is reasonable to set

$$\sigma_1 = \sigma_2 = \cdots = \sigma_n = \sigma. \tag{6.19}$$

We might also normalize the features by examining the marginal distributions of sample points, i.e., the samples projected on each axis. If the first component of the samples had a density as in Fig. 6.9, it would be reasonable to

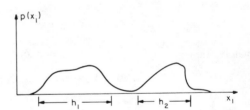

FIG. 6.9   A marginal distribution.

normalize that feature by dividing it by $(h_1 + h_2)/2$. Whatever the means we use to arrive at a reasonable normalization, let us assume we have only the size parameter σ to determine.

We shall adapt an approach proposed by Mucciardi and Gose in a somewhat different context [11]. Our objective is to choose σ so that the potential functions overlap significantly but not to an extreme degree. We may insure that, on the average, L sample points fall within a distance σ of each sample point. We can do so by calculating the average distance (in *normalized* space) of the Lth nearest sample; that is, if $D_L(\mathbf{y})$ is the distance of the Lth nearest sample from $\mathbf{y}$, we set

$$\sigma = \frac{1}{M}\sum_{i=1}^{M} D_L(\mathbf{y}_i). \tag{6.20}$$

Mucciardi and Gose suggest means for reducing the computation involved in (6.20).

The value of L depends in part on the sparseness of the samples, but one would expect an L of 10 to be the correct order of magnitude.

6.6 EFFICIENT DECISION RULES BASED ON POTENTIAL FUNCTION METHODS

6.6.1 Polynomial Potential Functions

If $\gamma(\mathbf{x}, \mathbf{y})$ is a polynomial of degree R in $x_1, x_2, \ldots, x_n$, then clearly $\hat{p}(\mathbf{x})$ as calculated in Eq. (6.2) is a multivariate polynomial of degree at most R. If we calculate the coefficients of that polynomial, we need not use the labeled samples as the parameters of our decision rule.

We will discuss the following potential functions which yield polynomial discriminant functions [10, 21]:

$$\text{A.} \qquad \gamma(\mathbf{x}, \mathbf{y}) = \frac{1}{(2\pi)^{n/2}\sigma^n} \exp\left(- \frac{\|\mathbf{x}\|^2 + \|\mathbf{y}\|^2}{2\sigma^2}\right) q\left[\frac{(\mathbf{x}, \mathbf{y})}{\sigma^2}\right] \qquad (6.21)$$

and

$$\text{B.} \qquad \gamma(\mathbf{x}, \mathbf{y}) = q(\|\mathbf{x} - \mathbf{y}\|^2), \qquad (6.22)$$

where $\|\mathbf{x}\|^2 = \sum_{i=1}^{n} x_i^2$, and $q(z)$ is a polynomial in z,

$$q(z) = \alpha_0 + \alpha_1 z + \alpha_2 z^2 + \cdots + \alpha_R z^R. \qquad (6.23)$$

TYPE A

Equation (6.21) gives a polynomial discriminant function; Eq. (6.21) is an approximation to Eq. (6.3) if $q(z)$ is an approximation to $\exp(z)$, and results in a discriminant function which is a polynomial multiplied by

$$\exp\left(- \frac{\|\mathbf{x}\|^2}{2\sigma^2}\right).$$

Using Eq. (6.21), we obtain a probability estimate†

$$\hat{p}(\mathbf{x}) = \frac{1}{(2\pi)^{n/2}\sigma^n} \exp\left(- \frac{\|\mathbf{x}\|^2}{2\sigma^2}\right) \sum_{K_R} a_{k_1 k_2 \cdots k_n} x_1^{k_1} x_2^{k_2} \cdots x_n^{k_n}. \qquad (6.24)$$

The result is a discriminant function which is a multivariate polynomial of degree R. If we had approximated the exponential function in (6.3) directly,

---

† See Eq. (6.33) for the definition of K_R.

as in (6.22), the order of the resulting polynomial would have been $2R$. (The square in the exponent would necessarily be retained if the result is to be a polynomial.) Since a polynomial of degree R in n variables has $\binom{R+n}{n}$ coefficients, this can result in a considerable saving. This windfall is not without a price, however, Let us examine the particular case proposed by Specht [21]:

$$q(z) = \sum_{k=0}^{R} \frac{z^k}{k!}, \qquad (6.25)$$

the Taylor series expansion of the exponential. For the sake of notational simplicity, let us drop the normalization factor and particularize to $\sigma = 0.5^{1/2}$. By the first criteria for a potential function, the function

$$\gamma(\mathbf{x}, \mathbf{y}) = \exp[-(\|\mathbf{x}\|^2 + \|\mathbf{y}\|^2)] \sum_{k=0}^{R} \frac{[2(\mathbf{x}, \mathbf{y})]^k}{k!}, \qquad (6.26)$$

referring to Eqs. (6.21) and (6.25), should have a maximum at $\mathbf{x} = \mathbf{y}$ for all $\mathbf{y}$. This is not the case, because

$$\frac{\partial \gamma}{\partial x_i} = \exp[-(\|\mathbf{x}\|^2 + \|\mathbf{y}\|^2)] \sum_{k=1}^{R} \frac{[2(\mathbf{x}, \mathbf{y})]^{k-1} 2 y_i}{(k-1)!}$$

$$- 2x_i \exp[-(\|\mathbf{x}\|^2 + \|\mathbf{y}\|^2)] \sum_{k=0}^{R} \frac{[2(\mathbf{x}, \mathbf{y})]^k}{k!} \qquad (6.27)$$

$$\frac{\partial \gamma}{\partial x_i} = 2 \exp[-(\|\mathbf{x}\|^2 + \|\mathbf{y}\|^2)] \left[(y_i - x_i) \sum_{k=0}^{R-1} \frac{[2(\mathbf{x}, \mathbf{y})]^k}{k!} - x_i \frac{[2(\mathbf{x}, \mathbf{y})]^R}{R!} \right].$$

A necessary condition for a maximum at $\mathbf{x} = \mathbf{y}$ is that the partials be zero at $\mathbf{x} = \mathbf{y}$; Eq. (6.27) indicates that this is the case if and only if $\mathbf{x} = \mathbf{y} = 0$. Except at the origin, the potential function so defined does not decline monotonically with distance from the sample point; it in fact peaks at a point other than the sample point. The fact that it only approximates this criterion is not necessarily damaging—the accuracy of the approximation is the essential question.

The distance from the desired location $\mathbf{y}$ of the maximum and the true location

$$\mathbf{x} = \mathbf{y} + \boldsymbol{\Delta}$$

of the maximum can be derived from Eq. (6.27). Let $x_i = y_i + \Delta_i$; $i = 1, 2,$ $\ldots, n$. The skew $\boldsymbol{\Delta} = (\Delta_1, \Delta_2, \ldots, \Delta_n)$ is a function of $\mathbf{y}$. Substituting for x_i in Eq. (6.27), we obtain

$$\Delta_i \sum_{k=0}^{R} \frac{2^k}{k!} \left[\sum_{i=1}^{n} (y_i + \Delta_i) y_i \right]^k + y_i \frac{2^R}{R!} \left[\sum_{i=1}^{n} (y_i + \Delta_i) y_i \right]^R = 0, \qquad i = 1, 2, \ldots, n. \qquad (6.28)$$

We may, for the sake of estimating the skew, consider $\mathbf{y} = (y_0, \ldots, y_0)$. The symmetry of the equations in (6.28) then allows us to set $\Delta_i = \Delta_0$ for $i = 1, 2, \ldots, n$ and obtain the single equation

$$\Delta_0 \sum_{k=0}^{R} \frac{2^k}{k!} [n(y_0 + \Delta_0)y_0]^k + y_0 \frac{2^R}{R!} [n(y_0 + \Delta_0)y_0]^R = 0. \qquad (6.29)$$

The magnitude of the skew at $\mathbf{y} = (y_0, \ldots, y_0)$ is then

$$\|\Delta\| = |\Delta_0|\sqrt{n}. \qquad (6.30)$$

Equation (6.29) can be solved for the exact value of Δ_0 for a given $\mathbf{y}$ (numerically, if necessary).

The above formulas are completely general if one interprets the variables as normalized in terms of standard deviations; that is,

$$\exp(-\|\mathbf{z} - \mathbf{w}\|^2/2\sigma^2)$$

can be represented as

$$\exp(-\|\mathbf{x} - \mathbf{y}\|^2)$$

if $\mathbf{x} = \mathbf{z}/\sigma\sqrt{2}$, $\mathbf{y} = \mathbf{w}/\sigma\sqrt{2}$. Thus, $y = (1/\sqrt{2}, 0, \ldots, 0)$ represents a point one standard deviation from the origin. A possible rule of thumb is that the skew should be considerably less than a standard deviation, i.e.,

$$\|\Delta\| \ll 1/\sqrt{2}. \qquad (6.31)$$

To get a quantitative feel for the actual skew we might encounter, we note from Eqs. (6.29) and (6.30) that

$$\|\Delta\| \approx \left| \frac{y_0\sqrt{n}}{(R+1)} \right|$$

if $|y_0| \gg 1$, $|\Delta_0| \ll 1$, and

$$(R - 1)! \ll (2ny_0^2)^R.$$

With $y_0 = 10$, $n = 16$, and $\|\Delta\| = 0.1$, Eq. (6.31) requires $R = 399$, a value much larger than required simply to approximate the exponential satisfactorily. On the other hand, the computational saving of the lower order polynomial is considerable if y_0 is small relative to a standard deviation; Specht [20] has reported on one such successful application of his algorithm. The skew is minimized if the origin is translated to minimize y_0.

The particular approximation chosen by Specht to $\exp[2(\mathbf{x}, \mathbf{y})]$ is an expansion about $(\mathbf{x}, \mathbf{y}) = 0$; consequently, the accuracy of the approximation suffers as $(\mathbf{x}, \mathbf{y})$ increases in magnitude. For a given sample point $\mathbf{y}_i$, $(\mathbf{x}, \mathbf{y}_i)$ is zero for $\mathbf{x}$ orthogonal to $\mathbf{y}_i$, and thus the approximation is sufficiently accurate in some hyperslice through the origin about a hyperplane orthogonal to $\mathbf{y}_i$ where $|(\mathbf{x}, \mathbf{y}_i)| \leq \varepsilon$; the probability estimate $\hat{p}(\mathbf{x}) = M^{-1} \sum_{i=1}^{M} \gamma(\mathbf{x}, \mathbf{y}_i)$ is sufficiently accurate only in the intersection of the hyperslices orthogonal to the sample points. With a reasonably high-order approximation, these hyperslices may, of course, be so large that their intersection covers the entire region of interest. One might ask, however, if the particular approximation chosen to $\exp[2(\mathbf{x}, \mathbf{y})]$ in the above algorithm is the best realization of a good idea. It is not a particularly difficult computational problem to find a poly-nomial approximation which, rather than predetermining the regions of poorest approximation, minimizes the error in the approximation in regions of interest for a particular problem. We can do so by seeking the polynomial $q(z) = \sum_{i=0}^{R} \alpha_i z^i$, which minimizes

$$F(\alpha) = \frac{1}{M^2} \sum_{j=1}^{M} \sum_{k=1}^{M} \exp\left(-\frac{\|\mathbf{y}_j\|^2 + \|\mathbf{y}_k\|^2}{2\sigma^2}\right)\left\{\exp\left[\frac{(\mathbf{y}_j, \mathbf{y}_k)}{\sigma^2}\right] - q\left[\frac{(\mathbf{y}_j, \mathbf{y}_k)}{\sigma^2}\right]\right\}^2$$

$$\approx E_{\mathbf{x}} E_{\mathbf{y}}\left\{\exp\left(-\frac{\|\mathbf{x} - \mathbf{y}\|^2}{2\sigma^2}\right) - \exp\left(-\frac{\|\mathbf{x}\|^2 + \|\mathbf{y}\|^2}{2\sigma^2}\right)q\left[\frac{(\mathbf{x}, \mathbf{y})}{\sigma^2}\right]\right\}^2, \quad (6.32)$$

where $E_{\mathbf{y}}$ denotes the expectation with respect to the distribution of $\mathbf{y}$. This measure is the mean squared error in the approximation. Taking partials with respect to the α_i and setting them equal to zero gives $R + 1$ linear equations in $R + 1$ unknowns. Using

$$\gamma(\mathbf{x}, \mathbf{y}) = \exp\left(-\frac{\|\mathbf{x}\|^2 + \|\mathbf{y}\|^2}{2\sigma^2}\right) q\left[\frac{(\mathbf{x}, \mathbf{y})}{\sigma^2}\right]$$

and generalizing Specht's derivation, we find the probability estimate

$$\hat{p}(\mathbf{x}) = \exp\left(-\frac{\|\mathbf{x}\|^2}{2\sigma^2}\right) \sum_{K_R} a_{k_1 k_2 \cdots k_m} x_1^{k_1} x_2^{k_2} \cdots x_n^{k_n},$$

where

$$K_R = \{(k_1, k_2, \ldots, k_k) \mid k_1 + k_2 + \cdots + k_n \leq R, \quad 0 \leq k_i \leq R\}$$

and

$$a_{k_1 k_2 \cdots k_n} = \frac{\alpha_h h! u(k_1, \ldots, k_n)}{\sigma^{2h} k_1! \cdots k_n!}, \quad (6.33)$$

with

$$h = k_1 + k_2 + \cdots + k_n$$

and

$$u(k_1, \ldots, k_n) = \frac{1}{M} \sum_{l=1}^{M} \exp\left(\frac{\|y_l\|^2}{2\sigma^2}\right) y_{l1}^{k_1} \cdots y_{ln}^{k_n}.$$

(The algorithm given by (6.26) corresponds to the choice $\alpha_h = 1/h!$, in which case Eq. (6.33) simplifies to Specht's result.)

For a given order of approximation R, the maximum skew at the sample points will generally be less using the approximation minimizing (6.32) than the Taylor series expansion. For type B polynomial potential functions, the skew may always be zero.

TYPE B

There will be no skew if the potential function is a scalar function with a maximum at zero for positive arguments and with an argument $\|\mathbf{x} - \mathbf{y}\|^2$. In particular, let

$$q(z) = \sum_{j=0}^{R} \alpha_j z^j \qquad (6.34)$$

a polynomial, be such a scalar function, approximately monotonically decreasing for positive arguments. Then $q(\|\mathbf{x} - \mathbf{y}\|^2)$ is a potential function of the type in Eq. (6.22). The polynomial $q(z)$ might be obtained, for example, by a one-dimensional least-squares approximation to $\exp(-az)$ on $[0, b]$, where b is the maximum distance in the region of interest. In any case, the resulting discriminant function is a multivariate polynomial of degree $2R$ in the n given variables:

$$\hat{p}(\mathbf{x}) = \sum_{K_R} a_{k_1 k_2 \cdots k_n} x_1^{k_1} x_2^{k_2} \cdots x_n^{k_n}, \qquad (6.35)$$

where

$$K_R = \{(k_1, k_2, \ldots, k_n) \mid k_1 + k_2 + \cdots + k_n \le 2R, \qquad 0 \le k_i \le 2R\}.$$

Let $\{\mathbf{y}_1, \mathbf{y}_2, \ldots, \mathbf{y}_M\}$ with $\mathbf{y}_i = (y_{i1}, y_{i2}, \ldots, y_{in})$ again be the set of samples of the class for which $\hat{p}(\mathbf{x})$ is being derived. We have

$$(\|\mathbf{x} - \mathbf{y}_i\|^2)^j = \left(\sum_{i=1}^{n} (x_i - y_{li})^2 \right)^j$$

$$= \sum_{\mathcal{N}_j} \frac{j!}{n_1! n_2! \cdots n_n!} (x_1 - y_{l1})^{2n_1} \cdots (x_n - y_{ln})^{2n_n}$$

$$= \sum_{\mathcal{N}_j} \frac{j!}{n_1! \cdots n_n!} \sum_{k_1=0}^{2n_1} \cdots \sum_{k_n=0}^{2n_n} \binom{2n_1}{k_1} \cdots \binom{2n_n}{k_n}$$

$$\cdot x_1^{k_1} \cdots x_n^{k_n} (-y_{l1})^{2n_1 - k_1} \cdots (-y_{ln})^{2n_n - k_n}, \qquad (6.36)$$

where

$$\mathcal{N}_j = \{(n_1, \ldots, n_n) \mid n_1 + n_2 + \cdots + n_n = j, \qquad 0 \le n_i \le j\}.$$

We have further that

$$q(\|\mathbf{x} - \mathbf{y}_l\|^2) = \sum_{j=1}^{R} \alpha_j (\|\mathbf{x} - \mathbf{y}_l\|^2)^j. \tag{6.37}$$

Inserting (6.36) into (6.37) and interchanging summations (noting that the inner summation is a function of j), we find

$$q(\|\mathbf{x} - \mathbf{y}_l\|^2) = \sum_{\mathcal{N}'_R} \frac{\alpha_h h!}{n_1! \cdots n_n!} \sum_{k_1=0}^{2n_1} \cdots \sum_{k_n=0}^{2n_n} \binom{2n_1}{k_1} \cdots \binom{2n_n}{k_n} x_1^{k_1} \cdots x_n^{k_n}$$

$$\cdot (-y_{l1})^{2n_1 - k_1} \cdots (-y_{ln})^{2n_n - k_n}, \tag{6.38}$$

where

$$\mathcal{N}'_R = \{(n_1, \ldots, n_n) \mid n_1 + \cdots + n_n \le R, \quad 0 \le n_i \le R\}$$

and

$$h = n_1 + n_2 + \cdots + n_n.$$

Define a function of $\mathbf{s} = (s_1, s_2, \ldots, s_n)$:

$$\mu(\mathbf{s}) = (-1)^{s_1 + \cdots + s_n} \frac{1}{M} \sum_{l=1}^{M} y_{l1}^{s_1} y_{l2}^{s_2} \cdots y_{ln}^{s_n}, \tag{6.39}$$

then

$$\hat{p}(\mathbf{x}) = \frac{1}{M} \sum_{l=1}^{M} q(\|\mathbf{x} - \mathbf{y}_l\|^2)$$

$$= \sum_{\mathcal{N}'_R} \frac{\alpha_h h!}{n_1! \cdots n_n!} \sum_{k_1=0}^{2n_1} \cdots \sum_{k_n=0}^{2n_n} \binom{2n_1}{k_1} \cdots \binom{2n_n}{k_n} \cdot x_1^{k_1} \cdots x_n^{k_n} \mu(2\mathbf{n} - \mathbf{k}), \tag{6.40}$$

where $2\mathbf{n} - \mathbf{k} = (2n_1 - k_1, \ldots, 2n_n - k_n)$. After a final interchange of summation and equating Eq. (6.40) to (6.35), we conclude that the following holds:

$$a_{k_1 k_2 \cdots k_n} = \sum_{N_k} \frac{\alpha_h h! \mu(2\mathbf{n} - \mathbf{k})}{n_1! n_2! \cdots n_n!} \binom{2n_1}{k_1} \cdots \binom{2n_n}{k_n}, \tag{6.41}$$

where

$$N_k = \{(n_1, n_2, \ldots, n_n) \mid n_1 + n_2 + \cdots + n_n \le R \quad \text{and} \quad k_i/2 \le n_i \le R, \\ 1 = 1, 2, \ldots, n\}.$$

The sums may be specified computationally:

$$\sum_{K_R} = \sum_{k_1=0}^{2R} \sum_{k_2=0}^{2R-k_1} \cdots \sum_{k_n=0}^{2R-k_1-\cdots-k_{n-1}},$$

$$\sum_{N_k} = \sum_{n_1=[k_1/2]}^{R} \sum_{n_2=[k_2/2]}^{R-n_1} \cdots \sum_{n_n=[k_n/2]}^{R-n_1-\cdots-n_{n-1}},$$

where $[x]$ is the least integer greater than or equal to x, and $\sum_a^b = 0$ if $b < a$.

To summarize briefly, the two types of polynomial potential functions have varying tradeoffs. Type A has fewer coefficients, but requires care in assuring that the effective potential function used is not overly skewed. Type B has no skew, but considerably more coefficients.

Equations (6.33) and (6.41) represent for type A and B, respectively, the closed form solutions for the coefficients of the polynomials. *Not all the terms need be used.* The coefficients can be calculated one at a time and the discriminant functions tested on a test set until a satisfactory level of accuracy is achieved; terms corresponding to coefficients of small magnitude may be discarded. Specht [20] found this approach highly effective.

6.6.2 Indirect Approximation

In Section 5.3, it was proposed that potential function methods be used to estimate $p_i(x)$ at the labeled samples and that a more efficiently calculated approximation be derived. If the approximation is a smooth function, this procedure may be relatively insensitive to variations in choice of shape and size parameters. In the two-class case, the decision boundary is

$$g(\mathbf{x}) = h_1 p_1 \hat{p}_1(\mathbf{x}) - h_2 p_2 \hat{p}_2(\mathbf{x}); \qquad (6.42)$$

we may approximate to the decision boundary rather than the probability densities. The approximation can be with respect to an integral-square, mean-square, or weighted mean-square criterion function, with the attendant tradeoffs of each (Chapter V). The approximation may be by polynomials or any efficient class of multivariate functions (see Appendix B). The optimization technique which determines the optimal parameters of the approximating function should be chosen for its efficiency given the first two choices.

The following chapter on piecewise linear discriminants contains a description of an algorithm which uses potential function estimates to find a piecewise linear decision boundary for N classes.

6.7 GENERALIZED POTENTIAL FUNCTIONS

If a potential function conforming to the criteria above constructs a satisfactory discriminant function when used in Eq. (6.1), then certain other potential functions, not necessarily conforming to those criteria, will be equally satisfactory. If a point $\mathbf{x}$ is such that

$$\rho_j(\mathbf{x}) > \rho_i(\mathbf{x}),$$

then

$$\text{(a)} \qquad \rho_j(\mathbf{x}) + g(\mathbf{x}) > \rho_i(\mathbf{x}) + g(\mathbf{x})$$

for any function $g(\mathbf{x})$, and

$$\text{(b)} \qquad f(\mathbf{x})\rho_j(\mathbf{x}) > f(\mathbf{x})\rho_i(x)$$

for $f(\mathbf{x}) > 0$.

Thus referring to Eq. (6.1), if $\gamma(\mathbf{x}, \mathbf{y})$ is a satisfactory potential function, so is

$$\text{(a)} \qquad \gamma(\mathbf{x}, \mathbf{y}) + g(\mathbf{x})$$

for any function $g(\mathbf{x})$, and so is

$$\text{(b)} \qquad f(\mathbf{x})\gamma(\mathbf{x}, \mathbf{y})$$

for $f(\mathbf{x}) > 0$.

For example, suppose

$$\gamma(\mathbf{x},\mathbf{y}) = \exp[-\|\mathbf{x} - \mathbf{y}\|^2] = \exp[-\|\mathbf{x}\|^2 - \|\mathbf{y}\|^2 + 2(\mathbf{x}, \mathbf{y})] \qquad (6.43)$$

where $\|\cdot\|$ is the Euclidean norm and $(\mathbf{x}, \mathbf{y})$ the inner product. Then

$$\gamma^*(\mathbf{x}, \mathbf{y}) = \exp(+\|\mathbf{x}\|^2)\,\gamma(\mathbf{x}, \mathbf{y}) = \exp[2(\mathbf{x}, \mathbf{y}) - \|\mathbf{y}\|^2] \qquad (6.44)$$

is a generalized potential function. Figure 6.10 is a plot of (6.44) for the one-dimensional case; one would hardly guess that this is a legitimate potential

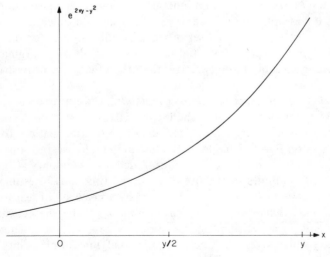

FIG. 6.10   A generalized potential function.

function by inspection. One might wish to use a generalized potential function if it were easier to compute or to approximate. This is exactly the case for type A polynomial potential functions; once they are computed, we need only compare the polynomial portions if the shape parameters are the same for all classes.

6.8   CONCLUSION

Potential function methods are a direct way of constructing general probability densities from a set of samples of a given class. The method of construction consists of a simple formula, requiring only the specification of the form of the potential function and of its associated size and shape parameters. The resulting probability densities provide discriminant functions which approach the theoretical optimal classification rate (Chapter II), but which, in the most direct form, are inefficient both in calculation and storage. Ways of overcoming these disadvantages include (1) using polynomial potential functions which yield polynomial discriminant functions directly, or (2) approximating the probability densities defined by potential functions with more efficient functional forms, such as ϕ-functions (Chapter V) or multivariate piecewise linear functions (Appendix B).

Because of the simplicity and generality of the potential function approach, it finds broad use as an aid to many aspects of the overall pattern recognition process:

(1) *Feasibility tests*   Potential function methods give an easy approximation to the Bayes-optimal set of samples; the result is a quick estimate of the best to be expected for a given set of features and samples for the problem at hand. For this purpose, potential function methods are marginally more costly, but considerably more effective, than the often used nearest-neighbor rule.

(2) *Criterion functions for indirect methods*   Class probability densities estimated by potential function methods can be used to estimate the optimality of decision boundaries for pattern classification or transformations for feature selection. Section 7.4 of Chapter VII illustrates their use in estimating the probability of error for a piecewise linear decision boundary. Chapter IX contains many examples of the use of potential functions in estimating the overlap of class probability densities defined by a given set of features.

(3) *Editing samples of overlapping distributions*   The theoretically optimum boundary in a decision theoretic sense (Chapter II) is not necessarily the boundary which gives 100 % accuracy in classifying sample points. Indeed, if the densities overlap, the optimal boundary should misclassify points from

a finite sample; the boundary is optimum relative to unlabeled samples as yet unavailable. Potential functions can be used to drop these "nuisance" samples in cases where this is appropriate (see Section 7.6).

EXERCISES

6.1. Show that

$$\gamma(x, y) = \begin{cases} x(x - 0.8xd + 1), & 0 \le d \le 1, \\ -0.2x^2(d - 2) + x, & 1 < d \le 2, \\ x, & d > 2, \end{cases}$$

(where

$$d \equiv d(x, y) = \left[\sum_{i=1}^{n} (x_i - y_i)^2 \right]^{1/2}$$

is the Euclidean distance), is a generalized potential function by finding a potential function (satisfying the criteria for a potential function) from which it may be derived.

6.2. Given the samples of classes 1 and 2: $\hat{p}(\underline{x}) = \frac{1}{M_i} \sum \sigma[d(x, r)]$

$\mathscr{Y}_1 = \{(2, 4)(2, 5)(3, 4)(3, 5)(-2, 0)(-3, 0)(-2, 1)(-3, 1)\}$, — *bimodal pyramids*

$\mathscr{Y}_2 = \{(1, 1)(1, 2)(1, 3)(0, 2)(-1, 1)(-1, 3)\}$. — *unimodal*

Using the potential function   *pyramid.* $\hat{p}_1(x) = \hat{p}_2(x)$
    boundary

$$\gamma[d(\mathbf{x}, \mathbf{y})] = \begin{cases} 1 - [d(\mathbf{x}, \mathbf{y})/3], & d(\mathbf{x}, \mathbf{y}) \le 3, \\ 0, & d(\mathbf{x}, \mathbf{y}) > 3, \end{cases} \text{ 3 pyramides}$$

with $d(\mathbf{x}, \mathbf{y}) = \sum_{i=1}^{2} |x_i - y_i|$, sketch the sample points and the boundary between classes which results from the potential function method.

6.3. Using the sample points from Exercise 6.2, and

$$q(z) = 1 - (z/7),$$

[see Eq. (6.22)] derive the coefficients of the polynomials

$$p_i(x_1, x_2) = a_{00}^{(i)} + a_{10}^{(i)} x_1 + a_{01}^{(i)} x_2 + a_{11}^{(i)} x_1 x_2 + a_{02}^{(i)} x_2^2 + a_{20}^{(i)} x_1^2, \qquad i = 1, 2$$

which result (a) by direct substitution, and (b) by Eq. (6.41). (c) Classify the points (0, 0) and (2, 2) using the above algorithm.

6.4. Let σ_{i1}^2 and σ_{i2}^2 be the variances of the first and second components, respectively, of class i. Let

$$p_i(\mathbf{x}) = \frac{1}{M_i} \sum_{j=1}^{M_i} \gamma_i(\mathbf{x}, \mathbf{y}),$$

where

$$\gamma_i(\mathbf{x}, \mathbf{y}) = f(d_i(\mathbf{x}, \mathbf{y})), \qquad f(d) = \begin{cases} 1 - (d/3), & d < 3, \\ 0, & d \geq 3, \end{cases}$$

and

$$d_i(\mathbf{x}, \mathbf{y}) = (|x_1 - y_1|/\sigma_{i1}) + (|x_2 - y_2|/\sigma_{i2}).$$

Apply this algorithm to the samples listed in Exercise 6.2. to determine the misclassification rate.

6.5. If a polynomial potential function is defined as

$$\gamma(\mathbf{x}, \mathbf{y}) = f(-d^2),$$

$$d^2(\mathbf{x}, \mathbf{y}) = \sum_{i=1}^{2} (x_i - y_i)^2,$$

with

$$f(z) = 1 + z + (z^2/2) + (z^3/3),$$

what is the coefficient of $x_1{}^4 x_2{}^2$ in the discriminant function? What is the coefficient of x_1?

SELECTED BIBLIOGRAPHY

1. Aizerman, M. A., Braverman, E. M., and Rozonoer, L. I., Theoretical Foundations of Potential Function Method in Pattern Recognition, *Avtomat. Telemekh.* **25**, 917–936 (1964).
2. Aizerman, M. A., Braverman, E. M., and Rozonoer, L. I., The Probability Problem of Pattern Recognition Learning and the Method of Potential Functions, *Avtomat. Telemekh.* **25**, 1307–1323 (1964).
3. Aizerman, M. A., Braverman, E. M., and Rozonoer, L. I., The Method of Potential Functions for the Problem of Restoring the Characteristics of a Function Converter from Randomly Observed Points, *Avtomat. Telemekh.* **25**, 1546–1556 (1964).
4. Aizerman, M. A., Braverman, E. M., and Rozonoer, L. I., The Robins–Monro Process and the Method of Potential Functions, *Avtomat. Telemekh.* **26**, 1951–1954 (1965).
5. Aizerman, M. A., Braverman, E. M., and Rozonoer, L. I., The Choice of Potential Function in Symmetric Spaces, *Avtomat. Telemekh.* **10**, 124–152 (1967).
6. Bashkirov, O. A., Braverman, E. M., and Muchnik, I. B., Potential Function Algorithms for Pattern Recognition Learning Machines, *Avtomat. Telemekh.* **25**, 692–695 (1964).
7. Braverman, E. M., On the Method of Potential Functions, *Avtomat. Telemekh.* **26**, 2130–2139 (1965).
8. Lemke, R. R., and Fu, K. S., Application of the Potential Function Method to Pattern Classification, *Proc. Nat. Electron. Conf.* **22**, 107–112 (1968).
9. Meisel, W. S., Mean-Square Methods in Abstract Pattern Recognition, *Information Sciences* **1**, 43–54 (1968).

10. Meisel, W. S., Potential Functions in Mathematical Pattern Recognition, *IEEE Trans. Comput.* **18**, 911–918 (1969).
11. Mucciardi, A. N., and Gose, E. L., An Algorithm for Automatic Clustering in *N*-Dimensional Spaces Using Hyperellipsoidal Cells, *Proc. IEEE Sys. Sci. Cybernetics Conf., Pittsburgh, Pennsylvania, October 1970*.
12. Murthy, V. K., Estimation of Probability Density, *Ann. Math. Statist.* **35**, 1027–1031 (1965).
13. Murthy, V. K., Nonparametric Estimation of Multivariate Densities with Applications, *in* "Multivariate Analysis" (P. R. Krishnaiah, ed.), pp. 43–58, Academic Press, New York, 1966.
14. Nadaraya, E., On Non-Parametric Estimates of Density Functions and Regression Curves, *Theory Probab. Its Appl.* **10**, 186–190 (1965).
15. Parzen, E., On Estimation of a Probability Density Function and Mode, *Ann. Math. Statist.* **33**, 1065–76 (1962).
16. Sebestyen, G. S., "Decision Making Processes in Pattern Recognition," Macmillan, New York, 1962.
17. Sebestyen, G. S., Pattern Recognition by an Adaptive Process of Sample Set Construction, *IEEE Trans. Information Theory*, **8**, S82–S91 (1962).
18. Sebestyen, G. S., and Edie, J., An Algorithm for Nonparametric Pattern Recognition, *IEEE Trans. Electron. Comput.* **15**, 908–915 (1966).
19. Specht, D. F., Generation of Polynomial Discriminant Functions for Pattern Recognition, Stanford Univ., Stanford, California, Stanford Rept. TR No. 6764–5, 1966.
20. Specht, D. F., Vectorcardiographic Diagnosis Using the Polynomial Discriminant Method of Pattern Recognition, *IEEE Trans. Bio-Med. Eng.* **14**, 90–95 (1967).
21. Specht, D. F., Generation of Polynomial Discriminant Functions for Pattern Recognition, *IEEE Trans. Electron. Comput.* **16**, 308–319 (1967).
22. Tsypkin, Ya. Z., Adaptation, Training, and Self-Organization in Automatic Systems, *Avtomat. Telemekh.* **27**, 16–51 (1966).
23. Tsypkin, Ya. Z., Use of the Stochastic Approximation Method in Estimating Unknown Distribution Densities from Observations, *Avtomat. Telemekh.* **27**, 94–96 (1966).
24. Van Ryzin, J., A Stochastic a Posteriori Updating Algorithm for Pattern Recognition, Dept. of Statistics, Stanford Univ., Stanford, California, Tech. Rept. 121, 1966.
25. Wolverton, C. T., and Wagner, T. J., Asymptotically Optimal Discriminant Functions for Pattern Classification, *IEEE Trans. Information Theory* **15**, 258–265 (1969).
26. Wolverton, C. T., and Wagner, T. J., Recursive Estimates of Probability Densities, *IEEE Trans. Sys. Sci. and Cybernetics* **5**, 246–247 (1969).
27. Zadeh, L. A., Fuzzy Sets, *Information and Control* **8**, 338–353 (1965).

CHAPTER VII

PIECEWISE LINEAR DISCRIMINANT FUNCTIONS

7.1 INTRODUCTION

A piecewise linear function is a function which is linear over subregions of the space. Figure 7.1a illustrates two piecewise linear discriminant functions of one variable. Each is linear for a given interval; the entire function specified in this way is, of course, very general and can, depending on the number of intervals, approximate rather arbitrary functions. A piecewise linear function of two variables is one which is linear over subregions of 2-space. In general, a piecewise linear discriminant function is specified by

$$\rho_i(\mathbf{x}) = \begin{cases} \boldsymbol{\omega}_{i1} \cdot \mathbf{x} + w_{i1, n+1}, & \mathbf{x} \in X_1(i), \\ \vdots & \\ \boldsymbol{\omega}_{iR} \cdot \mathbf{x} + w_{iR, n+1}, & \mathbf{x} \in X_R(i), \end{cases} \tag{7.1}$$

where $X_1, X_2, \ldots, X_R$ are disjoint subregions which cover the region of pattern space where samples occur.

Piecewise linear discriminant functions yield piecewise linear boundaries between classes. Possible boundaries are indicated in Fig. 7.1b. Alternatively, of course, one might aim to derive piecewise linear boundaries directly rather than through comparison of discriminant functions; both types of approaches are discussed in this chapter.

Piecewise linear discriminant functions and boundaries, because of their generality, are very powerful, although their generality is in some cases limited by the way in which those functions or boundaries are described.

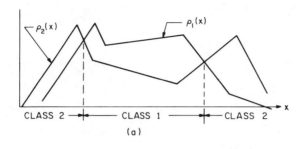

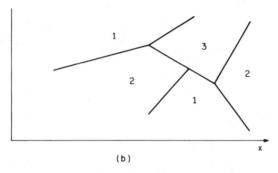

FIG. 7.1 Piecewise linear pattern classification: (a) discriminant functions; (b) boundaries.

7.2 IMPLICIT SUBCLASSES

One way of defining a piecewise linear discriminant function is to define it as a maximum of a set of linear discriminant functions:

$$\rho_i(\mathbf{x}) = \max_{1 \leq j \leq N_i} g_{ij}(\mathbf{x}) \qquad (7.2)$$

where

$$g_{ij}(\mathbf{x}) = \boldsymbol{\omega}_{ij} \cdot \mathbf{x} + w_{ij, n+1}.$$

This is equivalent to the representation in Eq. (7.1) if the regions are given by

$$X_k(i) = \{\mathbf{x} \mid \boldsymbol{\omega}_{ik} \cdot \mathbf{x} + w_{ik, n+1} \geq \boldsymbol{\omega}_{ij} \cdot \mathbf{x} + w_{ij, n+1} \quad \text{for all} \quad j \neq k\}. \qquad (7.3)$$

(This approach assures continuity of the discriminant functions.) Clearly, at any point in n-space, the functions $\rho_i(\mathbf{x})$ are determined by evaluating linear functions. The subregions are determined by comparison of the values of the same linear functions. This is not a completely general way of specifying piecewise linear functions since, with the preceding description, the value of the function corresponding to a given subregion must be larger than the

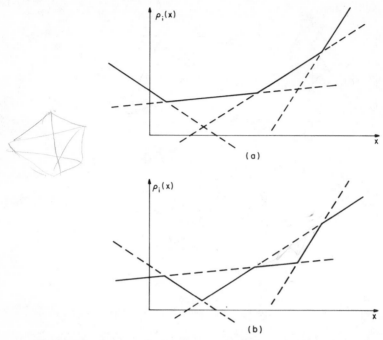

FIG. 7.2 Piecewise linear discriminant functions: (a) a concave function; (b) a non-concave function.

value of the other functions evaluated in that subregion; this is, of course, not a general requirement on piecewise linear functions. Figure 7.2a indicates a function constructed by this method. A little reflection will convince the reader that the concave nature of the function is a necessary result of this form of specification. The same hyperplanes could define the function of Fig. 7.2b if the form were not restricted to that of Eq. (7.2).

Let us consider a convenient interpretation of the approach of Eq. (7.2). Suppose that each class i were broken into N_i natural subclasses, that is, that the class i were formed of N_i distinct clusters. Then, supposing those subclasses were detected and denoted by $X_k(i)$, we could treat them as separate classes and derive a linear discriminant function, $\mathbf{w}_{ik} \cdot \mathbf{x}$, for each subclass. A given pattern could be classified in the kth subclass of the ith class if $\mathbf{w}_{ik} \cdot \mathbf{x}$ were greater than $\mathbf{w}_{jl} \cdot \mathbf{x}$ for all $j \neq k$ and all $l \neq k$. This is exactly the result achieved by Eq. (7.2); there the procedure just described is implemented as a two-stage process: (1) finding the dominant subclass for each original class, and (2) finding the dominant class overall by comparing dominant subclasses. This interpretation suggests that there should be a number of subsidiary functions for each class equal to the number of natural convex subclasses of that class, although exceptions exist [6].

p 30

To gain further insight to the approach described by Eq. (7.2), let us rewrite the result derived in Section 1.9.2 on prototype classification. There we noted that if $\mathbf{m}_i$ were a prototype of class i, then classifying a point $\mathbf{x}$ in the class to whose prototype it was nearest corresponded to choosing linear discriminant functions of the form

$$\rho_i(\mathbf{x}) = \mathbf{m}_i \cdot \mathbf{x} - \tfrac{1}{2}\|\mathbf{m}_i\|^2. \tag{7.4}$$

perpendicular bisectors

Assumes equal distributions

If $\mathbf{m}_{ij}$ is the prototype of subclass j of class i, then setting

$$g_{ij} = \mathbf{m}_{ij} \cdot \mathbf{x} - \tfrac{1}{2}\|\mathbf{m}_{ij}\|^2, \tag{7.5}$$

that is, setting

$$\omega_{ij} = \mathbf{m}_{ij} \tag{7.6a}$$

and

$$w_{ij,\,n+1} = -\tfrac{1}{2}\|\mathbf{m}_{ij}\|^2 \tag{7.6b}$$

yields a piecewise linear discriminant function corresponding to Eq. (7.2), based on defining the centers $\mathbf{m}_{ij}$ of subclasses.

Given a method of determining subclasses and their centers, a procedure for constructing the discriminant function is determined completely by Eqs. (7.6) and (7.2). Chapter VIII is devoted in large part to discussion of such cluster-seeking methods; hence, we will not discuss this approach further. It is worthwhile, however, to point out that the validity of the linear discriminant functions, assuming that the subclass centers were meaningfully defined, still depends on the Euclidean distance being appropriate and the space being meaningfully normalized; we discussed the difficulties of such an assumption in Chapter I. Once subclasses have been determined, *any* of the linear discriminant function techniques of chapter IV can be applied, treating each subclass as a separate class.

An error-correction method similar to those suggested earlier has been proposed for finding the weight vectors in Eq. (7.2) directly [6,14]. This procedure does not converge if the patterns are not separable by the piecewise linear discriminant function with the chosen number of subsidiary functions. No proof has ever been presented that it converges to a solution if one exists. However, it has the same intuitively appealing geometrical interpretation as proposed in Chapter IV. It proceeds as follows: The labeled samples are presented one at a time. If a sample is classified correctly by the current weights, no change in the weight vectors is made. If an error occurs, there is a correction in the weight vector which gave the highest value of all the subsidiary functions and in the weight vector which gave the largest value of subsidiary functions for the correct class. If these two weight vectors are $\mathbf{w}_{lm}$ and $\mathbf{w}_{ij}$, respectively, then the corrected weight vectors used in the $(k+1)$th iteration are

$$\mathbf{w}_{ij}^{(k+1)} = \mathbf{w}_{ij}^{(k)} + \varepsilon_k \mathbf{y}_k; \qquad \mathbf{w}_{lm}^{(k+1)} = \mathbf{w}_{lm}^{(k)} - \varepsilon_k \mathbf{y}_k, \tag{7.7}$$

where $\mathbf{w}_{ij} = (\boldsymbol{\omega}_{ij}, w_{ij,n+1})$ and $\mathbf{y}_k$ is augmented [the $(n+1)$th component is 1], and $\mathbf{y}_k$ is the kth labeled sample. The intuitive meaning is straightforward: The object is to increase the value of g_{ij} when evaluated at $\mathbf{y}_k$ while decreasing the value of g_{lm} when evaluated at $\mathbf{y}_k$.

The most extreme use of the subclass concept in constructing piecewise linear discriminant functions is to consider each sample point a subclass with its own linear discriminant function constructed using the prototype concept [Eqs. (7.5) and (7.6)], where each subclass consists of a single sample. This is in fact the nearest neighbor rule (Chapter I).

7.3 PERCEPTRONS AND LAYERED NETWORKS

Perceptron theory is oriented toward two category problems and conceptually toward threshold element realizations of the final decision rules. Historically, the orientation of the theory has been toward training of the threshold element networks as samples were presented [13, 14, 17].

The most common perceptron configuration is illustrated in Fig. 7.3, where the logical elements are threshold elements; the first layer of this two-layer network yields binary variables (two-valued variables, 0 or 1). The

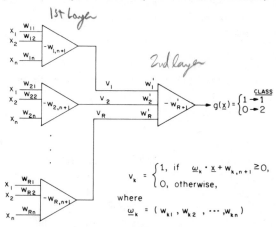

FIG. 7.3 A two-layer network of threshold elements. Underscored symbols are vectors.

second layer is a threshold element producing a binary variable using the binary variables of the first layer as inputs; the output value classifies an input vector $\mathbf{x}$ into one of two classes (e.g., $1 \to$ class 1; $0 \to$ class 2). Multiple layer networks, i.e., those for which we have inputs only from the previous layer, operate only with binary variables after the first layer (Fig. 7.4a).

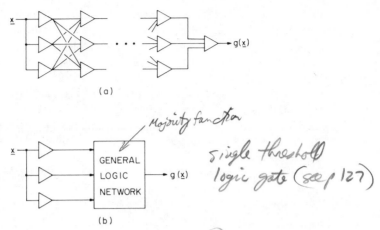

(a)

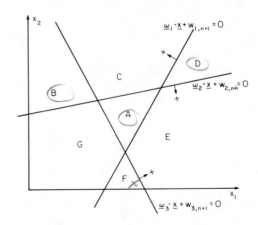

GENERAL

LOGIC → g(x)

NETWORK

Majority function

*single threshold
logic gate (see p 127)*

(b)

FIG. 7.4 Multilayer networks: (a) a general representation; (b) an equivalent representation. Underscored symbols are vectors.

This structure is equivalent to the first layer with all the following layers replaced by a switching network which operates on the binary variables of the first layer to produce an arbitrary switching function of those variables (since a network of threshold networks can realize any general switching function); see Fig. 7.4b.

Let us consider a geometrical interpretation of layered machines. Each of the first layer of threshold elements defines a hyperplane in pattern space; see Fig. 7.5, where the positive side of each of the hyperplanes has been indicated. The output of a given threshold element indicates on which side of the hyperplane the point **x** lies. Assume that the positive side of a hyperplane corresponds to an output of 1; and the negative side of a hyperplane

FIG. 7.5 Defining subregions with hyperplanes. Underscored symbols are vectors.

to an output of 0. The three hyperplanes in Fig. 7.5 would correspond to a perceptron with three threshold elements in the first layer. These particular hyperplanes divide the space into seven regions. These regions may be described by the output of the first layer; that is, region A is the region on the positive side of the first hyperplane, the positive side of the second hyperplane, and the positive side of the third hyperplane. This corresponds to the binary variables of the first layer being 1, 1, 1, respectively. Region E corresponds to 0, 1, 1. Region B corresponds to 1, 0, 0; in this last case, although the boundaries are determined entirely by the signs of the second and third hyperplanes, the first hyperplane must be positive for all points in B. Note that no region lies on the negative side of all three hyperplanes, so that the triplet 0, 0, 0 can never occur.

Since we allow only binary values as outputs of the first layer, the only information preserved after the first layer is the identity of the *subregion* in which the sample point occurs; no information on the location *within* the subregion is preserved. Suppose that the hyperplanes were chosen so carefully that no more than one class of sample points fell in each subregion. In particular, suppose that points falling in subregions A, B, and D were all members of class 1. Suppose that points falling in subregions C, G, and E were members of class 2, and finally, that no sample points fell in subregion F. Table 7.1 indicates desired values of the final output for given outputs of the first layer, where we have indicated a "don't care" situation by "d." This is a conventional formulation of a logic design problem [2]. It is a simple task to arrive at a logical expression relating the correct output to the outputs of the first layer:

$$g(\mathbf{v}) = v_2' \, v_3' + v_1' \, v_2' + v_1 \, v_2 \, v_3, \tag{7.8}$$

where the product corresponds to logical AND, the sum to logical OR, and the prime to logical NOT. Equation (7.8) can be implemented by many classes of logical networks. The case where the switching function in Fig.

TABLE 7.1

Region	v_1	v_2	v_3	$g(\mathbf{v})$
A	1	1	1	1
B	1	0	0	1
C	1	0	1	0
D	0	0	1	1
E	0	1	1	0
F	0	1	0	d
G	1	1	0	0
(no region)	0	0	0	d

7.4b is a *single* threshold logic gate has received a great deal of historical attention. [A *network* of threshold logic gates is complete in the sense that any logical functions may be realized by such a network; hence, a network of threshold elements is equivalent to any complete set of logic gates. The set of logical functions that can be implemented by a single threshold gate is more limited; for example, Eq. (7.8) represents a logical function that cannot be realized by a single threshold logic gate.]

One particular type of threshold logic gate is a majority element. A majority element is a logic gate in which the output is 1 if the majority of inputs are 1 and is 0 if the majority of inputs are 0; i.e., the output is the majority vote of the inputs. This specific element has been proposed as the switching function in Fig. 7.4b [14]. In this case, only the weights on the first stage, the inputs to the majority element, are modified; they are modified so as to tend to increase the number of correct classifications of labeled samples. The suggested procedure is an error-correction procedure similar to the procedures discussed in Chapter IV. If a threshold element is a contributor to an incorrect majority vote (i.e., votes with the majority), its weight vector is modified as in Eq. (7.7); the weight vector is incremented with opposite sign if it contributes to a *correct* decision. This procedure is based on intuitive, rather than theoretical, grounds.

It is clear that a powerful procedure would be one which resulted in a division of the space into cells (as in Fig. 7.5), where each cell contained samples of only one class or no samples at all. Then such a subregion could be assigned a corresponding class value or a " don't care," a logical equation such as Eq. (7.8) could be developed using classical switching theory algorithms, and every labeled sample would be classified correctly. One would not expect this ideal situation; a good set of hyperplanes would be one which misclassified the fewest number of samples, that is, one in which the class assignment of each subregion was least in question. One may use a structured random search to adjust the hyperplanes to minimize the misclassification rate. This measure has the disadvantage of discontinuity discussed in Chapter IV. The extension of the concepts of Chapter IV to obtain approximate measures of misclassification errors which are not discontinuous, e.g., the average distance of misclassified samples from the decision boundary, are much more difficult to formulate than in the single hyperplane case and have not been discussed in the literature. Using the distance of misclassified sample points to the nearest hyperplane, the most obvious approach, does not work well simply because moving a sample point to the other side of the hyperplane may not serve to classify it correctly. A better technique for defining decision boundaries will be described in Section 7.4; at this point we simply emphasize that, given such boundaries, the logical function for the switching function block in Fig. 7.4b can be easily determined.

One may either generalize or specialize the layered network of Fig. 7.4. The more general case of allowing any threshold element to be connected to any other threshold element has not resulted in many practical algorithms; such configurations are often studied by simulation as "neural nets." The special case of a layered network with no more than one threshold element per layer, generally referred to as a cascaded network, has received some attention [5]. Another special case of piecewise linear decision boundaries occurs in the N-class problem where linear decision boundaries are developed for each *pair* of classes, i.e., a decision boundary separating classes 1 and 2, classes 1 and 3, classes 2 and 3, and so on. In an N-class problem, $N - 1$ decision functions are evaluated for each class. A region is assigned to the class which receives the most "votes" [7, 18]. Figure 7.6 indicates the type

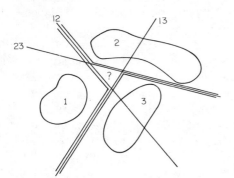

FIG. 7.6 A piecewise linear boundary obtained from pairwise linear boundaries.

of decision boundary which might result. As indicated, in some regions no decision will be reached. This is an attractive method from the point of view that it allows the relatively straightforward two-class linear discriminant techniques developed in Chapter IV to be used. Note that, if the classes used in this briefly described algorithm were in fact *subclasses* derived by a subset generation algorithm (Chapter VIII), this may be considered another method for deriving boundaries using the subclass concept. Sammon [18] suggests using the distance of an unlabeled sample from the hyperplane as a tie-breaking rule in questionable regions; he further points out that any two-class decision can itself be made by a piecewise linear discriminant.

7.4 INDIRECT APPROACHES TO DERIVING PIECEWISE LINEAR DISCRIMINANT FUNCTIONS

As in any indirect method, one must define a class of parameterized decision rules and a measure of quality. Suppose we consider the two-class case and define

$$q(\mathbf{y}) = h_1 p_1 p_1(\mathbf{y}) - h_2 p_2 p_2(\mathbf{y}), \tag{7.9}$$

where h_i is from the loss function of Eq. (2.3) and is usually 1. The probability densities can be estimated by potential function techniques (Chapter VI).

Let us further define

$$Q(X_i) = \sum_{\mathbf{y} \in X_i} q(\mathbf{y}); \qquad (7.10)$$

the notation indicates that the sum is taken over the samples which fall in subregion X_i. Then the decision rule may be

$$Q(X_i) \geq 0 \rightarrow \text{samples falling in } X_i \text{ assigned to class 1} \qquad (7.11\text{a})$$

$$Q(X_i) < 0 \rightarrow \text{samples falling in } X_i \text{ assigned to class 2.} \qquad (7.11\text{b})$$

The function $q(\mathbf{y})$ [Eq. (7.9)] is a measure of the degree of membership of a sample $\mathbf{y}$ in either class; i.e., the *sign* of $q(\mathbf{y})$ indicates the appropriate classification of $\mathbf{y}$, and the *magnitude* of $q(\mathbf{y})$ the confidence with which the assignment was made. Equation (7.10) is proportional to the average value of $q(\mathbf{y})$ for samples which fall in subregion X_i. The sign of this average provides a reasonable means for assigning a classification to subregion X_i; if $Q(X_i)$ is positive, the average of the quantities in Eq. (7.9) is positive and class 1 dominates the subregion, and vice versa. Figure 7.7 illustrates this point in the one-dimensional case. The weighted probability density for class 1 is more dominant, despite the fact that there are equal numbers of samples of each class; this dominance will be reflected in the sign of $Q(X_i)$.

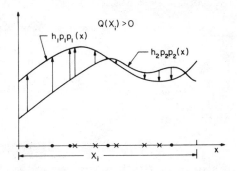

FIG. 7.7 Calculating the discriminatory quality of a subregion.

Two points should be emphasized: (1) the form of the probability densities is affected by samples outside of the subregion in question, and (2) the classification of the labeled samples is taken into account in generating the probability densities, but *not* in evaluating $Q(X_i)$, i.e., a sample may have a positive value of $q(\mathbf{y})$, but be in class 2.

Having defined a measure of the quality of a subregion, the measure of overall quality of a set of hyperplanes is the sum of the confidence by which each subregion is classified:

$$Q_T(\mathbf{w}_1, \mathbf{w}_2, \ldots, \mathbf{w}_R) = \sum_{i=1}^{R} |Q(X_i)|. \qquad (7.12)$$

(There is an implicit assumption that the number of labeled samples in each subregion is representative of the actual process; as defined, subregions are implicitly weighted by the number of samples they contain.)

The strong point of this approach is the suitability of the measure of quality; it is hardly exciting from a computational standpoint. A structured random search technique is perhaps the best approach to maximizing $Q_T(\mathbf{w}_1, \ldots, \mathbf{w}_R)$, which is a discontinuous function of $\mathbf{w}_1, \ldots, \mathbf{w}_R$. This computational procedure involves choosing an initial guess, perhaps by using one of the simpler techniques previously discussed. For each iteration of the algorithm, the sign of $\mathbf{w}_i \cdot \mathbf{y}_j$ is determined for all i and j, indicating which samples are in each subregion and which subregions are empty. Having thus sorted the samples, the calculation of Q_T is a straightforward process. It is important to note that $p_1(\mathbf{x})$ and $p_2(\mathbf{x})$ are evaluated only at the labeled samples $\mathbf{y}_i$ and need be evaluated and tabulated only *once*, prior to initiating the search procedure. Since $p_i(\mathbf{x})$ will be estimated in general by potential function methods,

$$p_i(\mathbf{x}) = \frac{1}{M_i} \sum_{j=1}^{M_i} \gamma(\mathbf{x}, \mathbf{y}_j^{(i)}),$$

there is a significant computational saving in tabulation.

This procedure is easily generalized to the N-class problem. Note that we can combine Eqs. (7.9) and (7.10) to obtain

$$Q(X_i) = h_1 p_1 \sum_{y \in X_i} p_1(\mathbf{y}) - h_2 p_2 \sum_{y \in X_i} p_2(\mathbf{y}). \tag{7.13}$$

Hence, given N classes, we define

$$Q'(X_i; j) = h_j p_j \sum_{y \in X_i} p_j(\mathbf{y}) \tag{7.14}$$

and we adopt the following decision rule:

X_i is labeled class k if $Q'(X_i; k) \geq Q'(X_i; j)$ for all j; (7.15)

that is, a subregion is assigned to the class for which the average weighted probability is the highest. The confidence may be defined analogously as

$$Q'(X_i) = \operatorname*{Min}_{j \neq k}\{Q'(X_i; k) - Q'(X_i; j)\}, \tag{7.16}$$

where k is fixed by $Q'(X_i; k) = \operatorname{Max}_l Q'(X_i; l)$. The confidence is thus the margin by which the assignment to class k is made. The object is then to maximize this measure of confidence:

$$Q_T' = \sum_{i=1}^{R} Q'(X_i). \tag{7.17}$$

7.5 PIECEWISE LINEAR DECISION BOUNDARIES BY LINEAR PROGRAMMING

Mangasarian has proposed a method for using linear programming to obtain piecewise linear decision boundaries for two-class problems [10]. The approach may be illustrated by reference to Fig. 7.8. Linear programming techniques are applied sequentially to the problem of dividing the pattern space into three regions by two parallel hyperplanes. One region, to the positive side of both hyperplanes, will contain only samples of class 1 (or no samples). The region to the negative side of both hyperplanes will contain only samples of class 2 (or no samples). The "confusion" region between the two hyperplanes will contain samples of both classes. The algorithm proceeds by applying the same procedure to samples which lie in the confusion region; this step yields a confusion region within the confusion region for which the process can be repeated, and so forth. In Fig. 7.8, the procedure terminates after only two iterations with no points in the confusion region. The boundary indicated by the heavy line in that figure is a piecewise linear decision boundary which separates the sample points with 100% accuracy. It is not necessary that this method continue until perfect classification results. One may simply terminate the algorithm after a predetermined number of iterations, leaving the confusion region which results as a residual error. The hyperplane for the last confusion region may be determined by any technique for the nonseparable case (see Chapter IV).

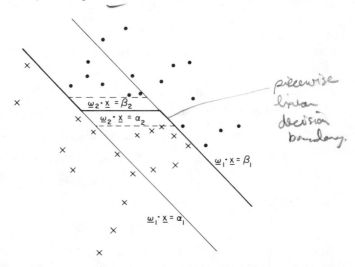

FIG. 7.8 Obtaining piecewise linear boundaries through linear programming. The underscored symbols are vectors.

Let us state the problem formally. We wish to find at each iteration hyperplanes $\boldsymbol{\omega} \cdot \mathbf{x} = \alpha$ and $\boldsymbol{\omega} \cdot \mathbf{x} = \beta$ such that the samples of class 1 are on the positive side of the first hyperplane, the samples of class 2 are on the negative side of the second hyperplane, and $\beta-\alpha$ is as small as possible (such that the confusion region is small). The problem is hence as follows:

$$\underset{\omega,\alpha,\beta}{\text{Min}}\{\beta-\alpha\} \qquad (7.18a)$$

subject to

$$\boldsymbol{\omega} \cdot \mathbf{y}_i^{(1)} \geq \alpha, \qquad i = 1, 2, \ldots, M_1; \qquad (7.18b)$$

$$\boldsymbol{\omega} \cdot \mathbf{y}_i^{(2)} \leq \beta, \qquad i = 1, 2, \ldots, M_2; \qquad (7.18c)$$

$$1 > \omega_k \geq -1, \qquad k = 1, 2, \ldots, n. \qquad (7.18d)$$

Equation (7.18d) is included as simply a normalization constraint; since this constraint does not prevent the ratio of coefficients of the linear hyperplane from taking any value, it does not reduce the generality of the problem. Unfortunately, this problem has a degenerate solution: $\boldsymbol{\omega} = 0$, $\alpha = \beta = 0$. Hence, we must add the constraint

$$\|\boldsymbol{\omega}\|^2 \geq \tfrac{1}{2}. \qquad (7.19)$$

This constraint does not restrict the generality of the result. It, however, introduces a difficulty; it is a quadratic rather than a linear constraint and cannot be solved by direct linear programming. One may, however, linearize this constraint by the following procedure. Suppose the solution is given by

$$\boldsymbol{\omega} = \mathbf{p} + \Delta\mathbf{p}, \qquad (7.20)$$

when $\mathbf{p}$ is near the solution (and hence $\|\Delta\mathbf{p}\|$ is small). Then we may obtain a linear approximation:

$$\|\boldsymbol{\omega}\|^2 = \boldsymbol{\omega} \cdot \boldsymbol{\omega} = (\mathbf{p} + \Delta\mathbf{p}) \cdot (\mathbf{p} + \Delta\mathbf{p}) = \mathbf{p} \cdot \mathbf{p} + 2\mathbf{p} \cdot \Delta\mathbf{p} + \|\Delta\mathbf{p}\|^2$$
$$\approx \mathbf{p} \cdot \mathbf{p} + 2\mathbf{p} \cdot \Delta\mathbf{p}. \qquad (7.21)$$

This equation may be rewritten to eliminate $\Delta\mathbf{p}$:

$$\|\boldsymbol{\omega}\|^2 \approx \mathbf{p} \cdot (\mathbf{p} + 2\,\Delta\mathbf{p}) = \mathbf{p} \cdot [2(\mathbf{p} + \Delta\mathbf{p}) - \mathbf{p}]$$
$$= \mathbf{p} \cdot (2\boldsymbol{\omega} - \mathbf{p}). \qquad (7.22)$$

Equation (7.19) is then approximated by

$$\mathbf{p} \cdot \boldsymbol{\omega} \geq \tfrac{1}{2}(\tfrac{1}{2} + \mathbf{p} \cdot \mathbf{p}). \qquad (7.23)$$

Given an initial guess $\mathbf{p}^{(0)}$ at the solution, Eqs. (7.18) and (7.23) can be solved by a linear program to obtain $\boldsymbol{\omega}$. Of course, the solution obtained is only an approximation to the solution with Eq. (7.19); the accuracy of that approximation is directly related to the accuracy of the choice of **p**. The algorithm converges to a solution of Eqs. (7.18) and (7.19) if Eq. (7.23) is used repeatedly, substituting the solution ω obtained in a given iteration for **p** in the next iteration.

To summarize, the problem of finding the parallel pair of hyperplanes may be solved by repeatedly solving (7.18) with (7.23), changing $\mathbf{p}^{(i)}$ at the ith iteration to be the solution $\omega^{(i-1)}$ of the previous iteration. The overall problem may be solved by repeatedly solving the parallel hyperplane problem until the misclassification error is accepted or the confusion region contains no samples. There is some chance of degeneracies arising in the numerical algorithms to prevent completion of the above process; Mangasarian has described techniques for overcoming such problems.

Hoffman and Moe have described a simpler algorithm with a similar objective [9]. They simply obtain the best linear separating hyperplane by any algorithm and then find the parallel hyperplanes to define the three regions as in Mangasarian's algorithm. They resolve the confusion region by applying a clustering technique (Chapter VIII) to the samples in the confusion region alone and a nearest-neighbor technique to the centers of the clusters. An advantage accrues if the confusion region contains many fewer sample points than the overall space.

7.6 LIMITING THE CLASS OF ACCEPTABLE BOUNDARIES (from p 117)

By limiting the class of piecewise linear boundaries we consider, we can reduce the computation involved in some algorithms and/or improve the efficiency of the resulting decision rule. Figure 7.9 indicates two approaches to reducing the number of parameters specifying the decision rule and the amount of computation (or hardware) required to use the decision rule.

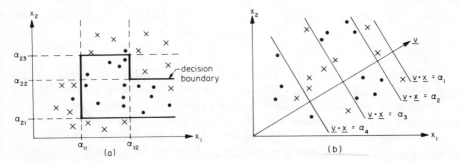

FIG. 7.9 Restricting the class of piecewise linear boundaries: (a) alignment with axes; (b) parallel hyperplanes. Underscored symbols are vectors.

In the first case (Fig. 7.9a), by using only hyperplanes orthogonal to the axes, only one rather than $n + 1$ parameters are necessary to specify each hyperplane. In the second case, by considering only parallel hyperplanes (Fig. 7.9b), we need $n + 1$ parameters to specify the first hyperplane, and only one parameter for each hyperplane thereafter.†

One way to utilize these restricted families of decision rules is to find the optimum parameters with respect to a cost function such as the one described in Section 7.4. The family of parallel hyperplanes is suited to using the average distance to misclassified points, in any of the various forms proposed in Chapter IV, as a criterion function; in this case, moving a misclassified point to the other side of the offending hyperplane will result in classifying it correctly (if there are no redundant hyperplanes).

Methods tailored to the first family of decision rules have been proposed. Henrichon and Fu [8] proposed an algorithm which develops hyperplanes orthogonal to the axes by considering projections of the samples on those axes; the approach has the advantage of being insensitive to scaling and the disadvantage of using only the projections of the samples. Meisel and Michalopoulos [11, 12] use the family of decision boundaries in Fig. 7.9a; they employ a two-stage process, a suboptimal procedure to obtain a *sufficient partition*, followed by a dynamic programming procedure to optimize the results of the first stage.

One efficient way to use the second family of decision boundaries (parallel hyperplanes) is, referring to Fig. 7.9b, to choose **v** by an algorithm which finds the direction **v** of maximum class separation (e.g., by discriminant analysis, Section 9.4), to plot the projections of the samples on **v** (i.e., $\mathbf{v} \cdot \mathbf{y}_1$, $\mathbf{v} \cdot \mathbf{y}_2, \ldots$), and to assign the values $\alpha_1, \alpha_2, \ldots, \alpha_R$ by inspection. Owen *et al.* [15] suggest (in a more general setting) optimal methods for assigning those values. Since they provide a programmable algorithm for choosing those values, one might modify **v** and readjust $\alpha_1, \ldots, \alpha_R$ until the misclassification rate (or the criterion function of Section 7.4) was minimized.

7.7   CONCLUSION

Piecewise linear decision boundaries and discriminant functions provide a powerful decision rule. In discussing them, we were often able to draw on concepts from previous chapters. Considering each class as composed of spacially contiguous subclasses, we used concepts from our discussion of linear discriminant functions. Two-class linear discriminants were used as well to generate piecewise linear boundaries for the N-class case.

---

† This second class of boundaries is considered piecewise linear because it can be shown to result from piecewise linear discriminant functions.

The perceptron approach led to a means of implementation of the decision rule and some possible algorithms. A proposed criterion function made indirect methods possible; it was computationally complex, but a reasonable measure of the quality of the decision boundary. Linear programming was proposed for a restricted class of boundaries; this computation is a substantial effort because a series of iterations are required to converge to the solution of each major iteration. Finally, low parameter families of piecewise linear boundaries were defined, and algorithms outlined for findings good members of those families. A piecewise linear discriminant also results when the cost functions of Chapter V are minimized with respect to the class of multivariate piecewise linear functions (Appendix B), as discussed in that chapter.

The subclass concept is very useful conceptually, and extends the material of Chapter IV to piecewise linear discriminants; however, finding subclasses, the subject of the next chapter, is difficult in itself. Error correction procedures will tend to give suboptimal results.

Layered networks illustrate an implementation of a decision rule with general piecewise linear boundaries that can be programmed or realized in hardware. Boundaries for the implementation can be chosen in most of the ways described in this chapter.

The indirect method proposed is computationally costly, but gives a near-to-optimum boundary for the given set of features. Less general boundaries are provided by linear programming.

By choosing a restricted, low-parameter form of piecewise linear boundary, computational cost is reduced. For linear segments aligned with the boundaries, efficient decision rules which closely approximate the statistically optimal boundary can be determined by a two-stage process; sufficient boundaries can be obtained by heuristic procedures and optimized by a dynamic programming algorithm.

EXERCISES

7.1. Suppose the *a priori* probabilities p_1 and p_2 were equal for two classes and the class-conditional probabilities were *Can get one line as mean $\rightarrow$ normalized*

$$p_1(\mathbf{x}) = K \sum_{j=1}^{3} \exp[-\tfrac{1}{2}\|\mathbf{x} - \mathbf{m}_{1j}\|^2], \qquad p_2(\mathbf{x}) = K \sum_{j=1}^{2} \exp[-\tfrac{1}{2}\|\mathbf{x} - \mathbf{m}_{2j}\|^2],$$

where K is the appropriate normalizing constant, $\mathbf{m}_{11} = (0, 0)$, $\mathbf{m}_{12} = (3, 0)$, $\mathbf{m}_{13} = (0, 3)$, $\mathbf{m}_{21} = (3, 3)$, $\mathbf{m}_{22} = (2, -2)$.

(a) Define piecewise linear discriminant functions which you would expect to classify samples of the above-defined classes quite accurately. Give your reasons.

(b) Sketch the decision boundaries in two-space, showing the $\mathbf{m}_{ij}$.

7.2. Given samples of three classes:

$$\mathcal{Y}_1 = \{(1, 1)\ (1, 2)\ (2, 1)\}$$
$$\mathcal{Y}_2 = \{(0, 0)\ (0, 1)\ (-1, 0)\}$$
$$\mathcal{Y}_3 = \{(-1, -1)\ (-2, -1)\ (-1, -2)\}.$$

(a) Define a decision function

$$v_{ij}(\mathbf{x}) = \begin{cases} i & \text{if} \quad \omega_{ij} \cdot \mathbf{x} + w_{ij,\,n+1} \geq 0, \\ j & \text{if} \quad \omega_{ij} \cdot \mathbf{x} + w_{ij,\,n+1} < 0, \end{cases}$$

for each pair of classes i, j by calculating the perpendicular bisector of the line segment between the mean of class i and the mean of class j.

(b) Let the decision function for the overall problem be

$$c(\mathbf{x}) = i$$

if the majority of the functions $v_{ij}(\mathbf{x})$ cast their vote for class i. Sketch the resulting decision boundaries and the classification of each subregion.

(c) Using the hyperplanes derived above, find an appropriate switching function for Fig. 7.4b. *majority function*

7.3. In two dimensions, the solution to the nonlinear programming problem represented by Eqs. (7.18) and (7.19) can often be found by inspection. Given the sample points

$$\mathcal{Y}_1 = \{(2, 2)\ (4, 4)\ (6, 0)\},$$
$$\mathcal{Y}_2 = \{(2, 1)\ (4, 2)(0, 6)\},$$

what are the decision boundaries resulting from Mangasarian's algorithm?

SELECTED BIBLIOGRAPHY

1. Akers, S. B., Techniques of Adaptive Decision-Making, General Electric Electron. Lab., Syracuse, New York, Tech. Inform. Series Rept. R64 ELS-12, 1965.
2. Bartee, T. C., Lebow, I. L., and Reed, I. S., "Theory and Design of Digital Machines," McGraw-Hill, New York, 1962.
3. Beakley, G. W., and Tuteur, F. B., Comments on "A Nonparametric Partitioning Procedure for Pattern Classification," *IEEE Trans. Comput.* **19**, 362–363 (1970).
4. Blokh, A. Sh., On Linear Perceptrons, *Automat. Remote Contr.* **25**, 1191–1193 (1964).
5. Cadzow, J. A., Synthesis of Nonlinear Decision Boundaries by Cascaded Threshold Gates, *IEEE Transactions Comput.* **17**, 1165–1172 (1968).
6. Duda, R. O., and Fossum, H., Pattern Classification by Iteratively Determined Linear and Piecewise Linear Discriminant Functions, *IEEE Trans. Electron. Comput.* **15**, 220–232 (1966).
7. Fukunaga, H., and Olsen, D. R., Piecewise Linear Discriminant Functions and Classification Errors for Multiclass Problems, *IEEE Trans. Information Theory,* **16**, 99–100 (1970).

8. Henrichon, E. G., Jr., and Fu, K. S., A Nonparametric Partitioning Procedure for Pattern Classification, *IEEE Trans. Comput.* **18**, 614-624 (1969).
9. Hoffman, R. L., and Moe, M. L., Sequential Algorithm for the Design of Piecewise Linear Classifiers, *IEEE Trans. Sys. Sciences and Cybernetics*, **5**, 166–168 (1969).
10. Mangasarian, O. L., Multisurface Method of Pattern Separation, *IEEE Trans. Information Theory* **14**, 801-807 (1968).
11. Meisel, W. S., and Michalopoulos, D. A., A Partitioning Algorithm with Application in Pattern Classification, Piecewise-Constant Approximation, and the Optimization of Decision Trees, to be published.
12. Michalopoulos, D. A., "An Optimum Partitioning Algorithm for Pattern Recognition and Piecewise-Constant Approximation with Application to Self-Programming Computers," Ph.D. Thesis, Univ. of Southern California, Los Angeles, California, October, 1971.
13. Minsky, M., and Papert, S., "Perceptrons: An Introduction to Computational Geometry," MIT Press, Cambridge, Massachusetts, 1969.
14. Nilsson, N. J., "Learning Machines," McGraw-Hill, New York, 1965.
15. Owen, J., Brick, D. B., and E. Henrichon, E., A Nonparametric Approach to Pattern Recognition, *Pattern Recognition* **2**, 227–234 (1970).
16. Peterson, D. W., and Mattson, R. L., A Method for Finding Linear Discriminant Functions for a Class of Performance Criteria, *IEEE Trans. Information Theory*, **12**, 380–387 (1966).
17. Rosenblatt, F., "Principles of Neurodynamics," Spartan, Washington, D.C., 1962.
18. Sammon, J. W., Jr., An Optimal Discriminant Plane, *IEEE Trans. Comput.* 826–829, **19** (1970).
19. Smith, F. W., A Trainable Nonlinear Function Generator, *IEEE Trans. Automatic Control*, **11**, 212–218 (1966).

CHAPTER VIII

CLUSTER ANALYSIS
AND UNSUPERVISED LEARNING

8.1   INTRODUCTION

A set of sample points of reasonable complexity is usually formed of discernible subsets. These may be of the nature of convex clusters as in Fig. 8.1a or of sheets (near lower-dimensional surfaces) as in Fig. 8.1b. Describing and locating these clusters provides a description of the data structure which is of use in itself and which simplifies or solves the pattern classification problem. We shall study in this chapter methods for describing and locating such subsets, a process which we shall refer to as *cluster analysis.* Other terminology used for the same or related concepts includes "cluster seeking," "subset generation," "unsupervised learning," "unsupervised estimation," "learning without a teacher," "decision-directed learning," "learning with a probabilistic teacher," and "decomposition of probability density functions."

The difference between pattern classification and cluster analysis is the fact that in cluster analysis the samples are *unlabeled.* We may interpret this state of affairs in two fundamental ways:

(1) The samples correspond to samples of *one* class and the clusters to *subclasses* of that class, just as lower case "a" and upper case "A" are subclasses of the class consisting of the first letter of the alphabet. We can use this information in structuring a decision function for pattern recognition.

(2) The samples have no assigned class membership. The intent of cluster analysis might be to find "natural" clusters corresponding to "natural"

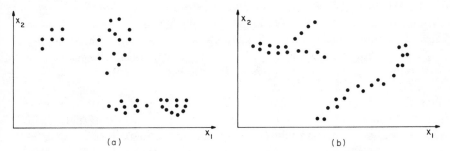

FIG. 8.1   Types of clusters: (a) convex clusters; (b) clusters in sheets.

classes in the data, to break up all the samples in a pattern classification problem into smaller groups so that a simpler pattern classification problem can be solved on each subregion, to reconstruct a probability density from the samples, to get the most out of a small set of labeled samples by extrapolating class membership to unlabeled samples, or simply to understand better the system from which the data arises.

The problem may be stated somewhat more formally. Given samples $\mathbf{y}_1, \mathbf{y}_2, \ldots, \mathbf{y}_M$ in a pattern space X, we seek subregions $X_1, X_2, \ldots, X_R$ such that every $\mathbf{x}$ in X falls in one of the subregions and no $\mathbf{x}$ in X falls in two subregions:

$$X_1 \cup X_2 \cup \cdots \cup X_R = X, \tag{8.1a}$$

and

$$X_i \cap X_j = \varnothing \quad \text{for} \quad i \neq j. \tag{8.1b}$$

Each subregion hopefully contains the multidimensional analog of what we would intuitively call a "cluster" in two-dimensional space. (This concept will be formulated statistically in Section 8.3.)

The formulation of Eqs. (8.1) assumes that we wish to partition the pattern space so that we can categorize samples not used in generating the clusters. In some applications, only the given samples are of interest, and it is sufficient to define sample subsets corresponding to clusters. In other applications, one might want to allow cluster subregions to overlap; some organisms, for example, can be considered both plants and animals.

Cluster analysis algorithms can be characterized as direct or indirect, depending, respectively, upon the lack of or use of a criterion function defining the quality of the clustering. Another major difference between cluster analysis algorithms is whether the number of clusters R is specified or must be determined.

In this chapter, we shall first discuss means of defining subregions. Discussion of a statistical formulation will follow. Several sections are devoted to direct cluster analysis methods whose validity is based upon the logic of the construction employed. A class of criterion functions suggested for indirect methods provides a further choice of algorithms which are generally more computationally costly and often require an initial approximation to the cluster subregions by direct methods. The concepts of unsupervised learning and decision-directed learning are outlined. Final sections discuss the use of cluster analysis in data analysis and in pattern classification.

8.2   DESCRIBING THE SUBREGIONS

Let us first discuss how one might describe subregions corresponding to clusters before we discuss algorithms for finding specific parameters in those descriptions.

8.2.1   Piecewise Linear Clusters

Suppose that we have a set of R hyperplanes in n-space:

$$\mathbf{w}_1 \cdot \mathbf{x} = 0, \ldots, \mathbf{w}_R \cdot \mathbf{x} = 0. \tag{8.2}$$

As in Fig. 7.5, the cells defined by the intersecting hyperplanes form subregions which might correspond to clusters. We have discussed in Section 7.3 the technique of tagging each subregion with the appropriate signs of all the hyperplanes.

The extension from hyperplanes to general Φ-function boundaries may be made as in Chapter IV.

dead zone p64   Cat-2

8.2.2   Center-Distance Descriptions

A cluster may be defined by defining a set of centers $\mathbf{m}_1, \mathbf{m}_2, \ldots, \mathbf{m}_R$ and a measure of proximity $d_i(\mathbf{x}, \mathbf{m}_i)$. A cluster is then the set of points which are nearer (as defined by the given measure of proximity) to the particular cluster center, that is

$$X_i = \{\mathbf{x} \mid d_i(\mathbf{x}, \mathbf{m}_i) \leq d_j(\mathbf{x}, \mathbf{m}_j) \text{ for all } j \neq i\}. \tag{8.3}$$

The proximity measures may be distance measures or more complex calculations of the dissimilarity between two vectors [5]; the particular measure used may differ with each center to which it is applied, as indicated by the subscript in Eq. (8.3). One distance in which we shall be interested is the weighted Euclidean distance

$$d_i^2(\mathbf{x}, \mathbf{m}_i) = \sum_{j=1}^{n} \left(\frac{x_j - m_{ij}}{\sigma_{ij}} \right)^2. \tag{8.4}$$

In this latter case, the clusters are described by a set of R means and a set of R variance vectors,

$$\mathbf{m}_i = (m_{i1}, m_{i2}, \ldots, m_{in}) \tag{8.5a}$$

and

$$\boldsymbol{\sigma}_i = (\sigma_{i1}, \ldots, \sigma_{in}), \tag{8.5b}$$

$2n$ parameters for each cluster. The boundaries of clusters defined in this way are piecewise quadratic. Although the boundary between regions described in this manner is a function of the distribution of centers and can be quite complex, it is interesting to note the natural cluster shape implied by such a distance measure by asking what the locus of points equidistant from the cluster center might look like. With the distance measure of Eq. (8.4), the locus of equidistant points (obtained by setting d_i equal to a constant) is an ellipsoid aligned with the axes (see Fig. 8.2).

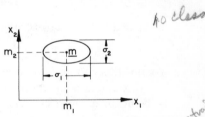

FIG. 8.2   Locus of $d(\mathbf{x}, \mathbf{m}) = \frac{1}{2}$. Underscored symbols are vectors.

8.2.3   Proximal Surfaces

If the sample points lie in sheets, that is, near lower-dimensional surfaces, they may be described by those surfaces along with a means of measuring the distance to those surfaces. If the surface is defined by $f(\mathbf{x}) = 0$, the deviation of $f(\mathbf{x})$ from 0, appropriately normalized, may be used as a measure of the distance of a point from the surface. Depending upon the form of $f(\mathbf{x})$, the appropriate normalization may or may not be obvious. In the case of linear hyperplanes it is, of course, the magnitude of the weight vector $\boldsymbol{\omega}$ (see Chapter IV).

8.2.4   Definition by Sample Subsets

The finite subset of sample points constituting a cluster or sheet define the cluster in themselves. This may be a sufficient definition for the cluster, particularly if data analysis is the end aim (see Section 8.10).

If data analysis is not the end aim, however, a means of defining a cluster membership of a new sample point, given a finite subset of samples, is necessary. One means of doing so is to define a measure of distance to the subset. A new point is assigned to a cluster if it is nearest to the samples of that cluster in terms of the distance measure. A method applicable to sheets as well as clusters is to use the average distance to the sample points in the cluster, or, more generally, the localized distance to the cluster, that is, the average distance to the *closer* points. (Localized distances are discussed further in Section 9.4.)

8.2.5 Definition by Discriminant Functions

Since each cluster can be considered a subclass, it is natural to propose the use of a discriminant function as well as a boundary oriented approach, as we did in the pattern classification case. All the considerations of Section 1.5.2 apply if one substitutes "clusters" for "classes." Hence, an alternative statement of the problem is to use the unlabeled samples to generate *cluster discriminants*

$$\rho^{(i)}(\mathbf{x}), \qquad i = 1, 2, \ldots, K, \tag{8.6a}$$

such that the cluster decision rule is

$$c'(\mathbf{x}) = i \qquad \text{if} \quad \rho^{(i)}(\mathbf{x}) \geq \rho^{(j)}(\mathbf{x}) \qquad \text{for all} \quad i \neq j. \tag{8.6b}$$

Again, this can be viewed as simply a convenient way to define clusters, or the discriminant functions may be proportional to the likelihood of a point $\mathbf{x}$ being in a given cluster. In Section 8.3, we shall discuss a probabilistic formulation of the clustering problem in which the discriminants are probability densities.

Center-distance descriptions of clusters can be interpreted as discriminant functions

$$\rho^{(i)}(\mathbf{x}) = -d_i^{2}(\mathbf{x}, \mathbf{m}_i); \tag{8.7}$$

see Eq. (8.3).

8.2.6 Hierarchical Procedures

The analogy to pattern classification suggests hierarchical procedures, equivalent to successive dichotomies (Section 1.5.2). Subsets can be defined by breaking the space into two subregions, breaking each subregion into two further subregions, and so on. The same considerations apply here as in Section 1.5.2. Most of the proposed methods of describing subregions can be used to describe the dichotomy at each level.

8.3   CLUSTER ANALYSIS AS DECOMPOSITION OF PROBABILITY DENSITIES

A complex probability distribution could conceivably be represented as a sum or superposition of simpler probability densities, a *mixture*:

$$p(\mathbf{x}) = \sum_{i=1}^{R} p^{(i)} p^{(i)}(\mathbf{x}). \qquad (8.8)$$

If $p^{(i)}(\mathbf{x})$ is a probability density for all i and the following conditions hold,

$$\sum_{i=1}^{R} p^{(i)} = 1, \qquad (8.9a)$$

$$p^{(i)} \geq 0, \qquad \text{all } i, \qquad (8.9b)$$

then $p(\mathbf{x})$ as defined by Eq. (8.8) is a legitimate probability density; that is, it is appropriately normalized. If we interpret $p^{(i)}(\mathbf{x})$ as describing the probability of $\mathbf{x}$ falling in the subset X_i, and define $p^{(i)}$, a constant, as the *a priori* probability of $\mathbf{x}$ falling in subset X_i, then Eq. (8.8) can be interpreted as the probability density of the unlabeled samples expressed in terms of the statistics of the natural clusters of those samples. In most cases, each cluster will correspond to a *mode* (local maximum) of the probability density $p(\mathbf{x})$. Further, if

$$p^{(j)}(\mathbf{x}) p^{(i)}(\mathbf{x}) \approx 0 \qquad \text{for all } \mathbf{x} \qquad \text{and for } j \neq i, \qquad (8.10)$$

that is, if the cluster probability densities have little overlap, then Eq. (8.8) is approximately represented as

$$p(\mathbf{x}) \approx p^{(i)} p^{(i)}(\mathbf{x}) \qquad \text{if } \mathbf{x} \in X_i, \qquad (8.11a)$$

where

$$X_i = \{\mathbf{x} \mid p^{(i)} p^{(i)}(\mathbf{x}) \geq p^{(j)} p^{(j)}(\mathbf{x}) \text{ for all } j\}. \qquad (8.11b)$$

In this latter case, if the subregions are defined in any of the ways described in Section 8.2, we may choose an appropriate probability density for the samples of that subregion.

Alternatively, we may view the problem of cluster analysis as the problem of finding component probability densities in Eq. (8.8). If this latter viewpoint is adopted, one may simply parametrize the $p^{(i)}(\mathbf{x})$ and attempt to find those parameters satisfying some criterion function. This statistical formulation is usually utilized under the heading of unsupervised learning or unsupervised estimation, which we shall discuss further in Section 8.8. However, it provides a useful statistical interpretation of almost all cluster-seeking algorithms, and hence the concept of cluster-seeking as the location of modes (local maximums) of a probability density is an important unifying concept.

The concept is similar to those in potential function methods. The points of highest local concentration of samples are modal points $\mathbf{m}_1, \mathbf{m}_2, \ldots \mathbf{m}_R$; we may reconstruct the probability density corresponding to those modal points as

(see (6.2) p 99)

$$p(\mathbf{x}) \approx \hat{p}(\mathbf{x}) = \frac{1}{N} \sum_{i=1}^{R} n_i \gamma(\mathbf{x}, \mathbf{m}_i), \tag{8.12}$$

where γ is a normalized potential function (see Chapter VI), n_i is the number of samples in cluster i (corresponding to mode i), and N is the total number of samples used to estimate $p(\mathbf{x})$. Clearly, this corresponds to Eq. (8.8) with

$$p^{(i)} = n_i/N. \tag{8.13}$$

The statistical formulation leads directly to a means for using cluster-seeking algorithms as pattern classification algorithms. If we use Eq. (8.8) to estimate $p_j(\mathbf{x})$ for a given class by applying clustering algorithms to samples of that class alone, and do so for each class, we may simply use those estimated probability densities to determine class membership. Clustering for pattern classification is discussed further in Section 8.11.

8.4   MODE SEEKING ON PROBABILITY ESTIMATES

Given a probability density $p(\mathbf{x})$ describing a distribution of sample points, one would expect that the locations of local maximums, or modes, of that probability density would define meaningful cluster centers. Given such centers, they might be used in a center-distance definition of clusters or in estimating the parameters of a mixture distribution.

Potential function methods provide a means of constructing a smooth probability density function from sample points. Clearly, to estimate mode locations, we want the function to be very smooth so that a local maximum does indeed represent a meaningful cluster. Hence, for the purpose of mode seeking, the potential functions used to form the probability density should be perhaps less peaked than one might otherwise use.

Having created an estimate of the probability density, the problem of finding local maximums is, of course, not particular to pattern recognition. A wide variety of literature on optimum-seeking methods has been published. The important point in this regard is that the optimums that we seek need not be at all accurate and, hence, a rather simple optimum-seeking technique is justified. One might use random search to find local maximums, followed by local gradient searches to find better estimates of those local maximums.

Butler proposed this direct approach to mode estimation with a particular potential function; he suggests a means for rapid estimation of the modes [12].

It is difficult to describe the clusters appropriately when the cluster centers are determined in this manner. There does not appear to be any natural measure of proximity for this method.

8.5 ITERATIVE ADJUSTMENT OF CLUSTERS

There is a family of iterative processes which assumes (1) that the number of clusters can be estimated, and (2) that adequate initial guesses of the cluster centers can be made. Other methods, such as those discussed in Sections 8.4 and 8.6, for example, can be used to find these initial estimates. Suppose initial estimates of the cluster centers are $\mathbf{m}_1^{(0)}$, $\mathbf{m}_2^{(0)}$, ..., $\mathbf{m}_R^{(0)}$, and a distance measure $d(\mathbf{x}, \mathbf{y})$ is defined. The iterative procedure is then as follows [7, 11, 13, 16, 29] (the *center adjustment* algorithm):

(1) Assign every sample $\mathbf{y}$ to the cluster whose center is closest, using the current estimate of the centers $\mathbf{m}_i^{(k)}$:

$$\mathbf{y} \quad \text{in} \quad C_i^{(k)}(\text{the } i\text{th cluster}) \qquad \text{if} \quad d(\mathbf{y}, \mathbf{m}_i^{(k)}) \leqslant d(\mathbf{y}, \mathbf{m}_j^{(k)}) \quad \text{for all} \quad j. \tag{8.14}$$

(For the first iteration, $k = 0$.)

(2) Calculate new centers for each cluster as the point which is of minimum average distance to points in that cluster:

$$\mathbf{m}_i^{(k+1)} \quad \text{minimizes} \quad Q_i(\mathbf{m}) = \sum_{\mathbf{y} \in C_i^{(k)}} d(\mathbf{y}, \mathbf{m}). \tag{8.15}$$

If $d(\mathbf{x}, \mathbf{y})$ is the "city-block" distance [Eq. (1.5)], then this step is accomplished by simply calculating the mean of the samples currently in the cluster, that is,†

$$\mathbf{m}_i^{(k+1)} = \frac{1}{|C_i^{(k)}|} \sum_{\mathbf{y} \in C_i^{(k)}} \mathbf{y}. \tag{8.16}$$

If the average squared distance is used in (8.15), the same result holds for the familiar Euclidean distance.

(3) The entire sequence is repeated using the latest value of the centers. The procedure terminates when no samples change classification in step (1).

The procedure will converge, but of course the result to which it converges is highly dependent upon the number and location of the initial centers. Methods for splitting old clusters or adding new clusters as the algorithm

---

† If S is a set, $|S|$ is the number of elements in the set.

proceeds have been proposed, but the approach is most effective as a means of "adjusting" clusters estimated by other algorithms suggested in this chapter.

The procedure can be strengthened by generalizing it to a distance measure depending on the cluster, as in Eq. (8.3). In particular, let the distance measure be defined by Eq. (8.4). Then the procedure discussed above may modify the variances as well as the means. This is accomplished by placing a subscript i on the distance measure in Eq. (8.14) and appending to (8.16) the equation for modifying the variance:

$$\sigma_{ij}^{(k+1)} = \left[\frac{1}{|C_i^{(k)}|} \sum_{y \in C^{(k)}_i} \left(y_j - m_{ij}^{(k+1)} \right)^2 \right]^{1/2} \qquad j = 1, 2, \ldots, n. \quad (8.17)$$

This expression is, of course, exactly the standard deviation of the samples which fall in the cluster. The distance measure then reflects the ellipsoidal shape of each cluster (see Fig. 8.2). We will refer to this as the *center-variance adjustment algorithm,* as opposed to the center adjustment algorithm. Equation (8.15) does not directly apply, and this approach, while intuitively appealing, does not have as obvious convergence qualities as the center adjustment algorithm. The adaptive sample set method described in Section 8.6 provides initial estimates of means and variances for the center-variance adjustment algorithm.

Both algorithms can be viewed as approximate algorithms for minimizing the average distance of samples to the center of the cluster in which they fall:

$$Q = \sum_{j=1}^{R} \sum_{y \in Cj} d_j(\mathbf{y}, \mathbf{m}_j). \quad (8.18)$$

(In the center adjustment algorithm, the distance function does not vary with the cluster.) The results of minimizing Q for the constant-distance-function case are dependent on the normalization of the space. Friedman and Rubin [19] suggested a family of criteria which are invariant to nonsingular linear transformations. Fukunaga and Koontz [20] showed that the constant-distance-function criterion of the form (8.18) could be made invariant by applying a data-dependent linear transformation to the samples before clustering. The general form of Eq. (8.18) and the center-variance adjustment algorithm could be considered equivalent to application of the constant-distance or center-adjustment approach to a *nonlinearly* transformed space.

— log or x^2 for example

8.6 ADAPTIVE SAMPLE SET CONSTRUCTION

Sebestyen proposed a clustering algorithm [49], which he later refined in conjunction with Edie [50]; in both cases, the algorithm was discussed as part of a procedure for constructing probability densities from samples. (Bonner

proposed a somewhat simpler algorithm with similar characteristics [9,10].)
Features of this efficient algorithm include the following:

(1) samples are taken sequentially and need not be stored;
(2) the order in which samples are taken affects the clusters arrived at;
(3) a center-distance representation of the clusters results, using the
distance of Eq. (8.4); the algorithm automatically derives the σ_i;
(4) a " guard zone " is used to postpone classification of doubtful samples
and to minimize the effect of the initial parameters of the algorithm and of
the sequence of the samples on the final result; and
(5) the number of clusters need not be prespecified.

The basic idea of the algorithm is to take the sample points serially, in
some arbitrary order, and build up clusters. The samples that have contributed
to a given cluster determine the centers of the clusters, and the relative
weights on the axes are determined by approximations to the variances of the
contributing samples. Because the process takes the samples in sequence, a
sample that was placed in a given cluster and hence contributed to its formation may fall in another cluster at the end of the process.

If t represents the number of samples in a cluster, and another sample
$y(t + 1)$ falls in the cluster, the mean and variance are adjusted as follows:

$$m(t + 1) = \frac{1}{t + 1}[tm(t) + y(t + 1)], \qquad (8.19a)$$

$$\sigma_i^2(t + 1) = \frac{1}{t + 1}\{t\sigma_i^2(t) + [y_i(t + 1) - m_i(t + 1)]^2\} \qquad \text{for} \quad i = 1, 2, \ldots, n,$$

$$(8.19b)$$

where $m(t)$ and $\sigma(t)$ are the mean and approximate standard deviation of
the cluster after t samples have been inserted. (Lower bounds should be
placed on the variances to keep cells from becoming too small.) At any
given stage in the sequence of samples, the distances $d_i(\mathbf{x}, \mathbf{m}_i)$, as specified
by Eq. (8.4), are well-defined. Three regions are defined during cluster
creation:

(1) the interior of the cluster cell

$$d_i^2(\mathbf{x}, \mathbf{m}_i) \leq \theta\tau; \qquad (8.20a)$$

(2) a guard zone

$$\theta\tau < d_i^2(\mathbf{x}, \mathbf{m}_i) \leq \tau; \qquad (8.20b)$$

(3) the exterior of the cell

$$d_i^2(\mathbf{x}, \mathbf{m}_i) > \tau. \qquad (8.20c)$$

(See Fig. 8.3.) If a new sample falls interior to an established cluster, it is used to modify the cluster description by Eqs. (8.19). If a new sample falls outside all present clusters, it forms the center of a new cluster with prespecified initial variances. If a sample falls in the guard zone, it is set aside. After the queue of samples which fell in guard zones reaches a certain length, those samples are forced into the nearest cluster. Sebestyen and Edie suggest specific formulas for bounding the number of samples allowed in the guard zone and for choosing parameters of the algorithm.

Mucciardi and Gose [32] suggest an approach to specifying the parameters τ and θ. They recommend that, after the samples are normalized by the initial variances (determined from examination of the marginal distributions), the value τ be set to the average squared distance between all samples and their L_1th nearest sample and $\theta\tau$ be the set to the average squared distance between all samples and their L_2th nearest sample, where $L_2 < L_1$, and, for example, $L_1 = 4$ and $L_2 = 2$. Experimental evidence and a geometrical argument suggest that, after the samples are normalized, the average squared distance to the Lth nearest sample is proportional to the number of dimensions included in the calculation; this approximation can save a great deal of computation.

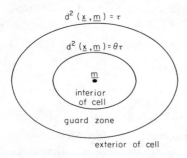

$d^2(\underline{x}, \underline{m}) = \tau$

$d^2(\underline{x}, \underline{m}) = \theta\tau$

$\underline{m}$

interior of cell

guard zone

exterior of cell

FIG. 8.3 Defining three regions of the evolving cluster. Underscored symbols are vectors.

8.7 GRAPH-THEORETIC METHODS

8.7.1 Simultaneous Use of Samples

A disadvantage of a method such as adaptive sample set construction is that the results are dependent upon the ordering of the samples. One could argue that, by considering all the samples simultaneously, one might determine the clusters more accurately. The graph-theoretic approaches discussed in this section do so at a substantial cost in rapid-access storage and a possible increase in computation time. They are, however, capable of detecting sheets as well as convex clusters.

Basically, all such methods depend upon an analysis of the intersample distances

$$d_{ij} = d(\mathbf{y}_i, \mathbf{y}_j), \qquad i = 1, 2, \ldots, M; \quad j = 1, 2, \ldots, M. \qquad (8.21)$$

It is often convenient to speak of an $M \times M$ interpoint-distance matrix A with elements d_{ij}. There are $M(M-1)/2$ nonredundant intersample distances for M samples. Computational feasibility for most algorithms requires storage of all nonredundant values of d_{ij} for at least some part of the procedure. This can be a severe restriction; one thousand samples generate about a half-million interpoint distances. Several of the algorithms discussed in this section accept this as a limitation on the number of samples that can be clustered; others reduce the severity of this constraint by various ploys.

Another means of extending the of applicability graph-theoretic methods is to apply them to the cluster centers resulting from an algorithm such as adaptive sample set construction when the initial cell sizes are chosen small to create many clusters. Graph-theoretic methods can indicate which clusters should be grouped together.

8.7.2 The Similarity Matrix

Suppose we chose a threshold θ and constructed a *similarity matrix* S from the intersample distances such that each element s_{ij} were as follows:

$$s_{ij} = \begin{cases} 1, & d_{ij} \leq \theta, \\ 0, & d_{ij} > \theta. \end{cases} \qquad (8.22)$$

The quantities s_{ij} are binary and hence require only one bit of storage rather than the word of storage required by d_{ij}. The similarity matrix tells whether a pair of samples are closer than a distance θ and no more; the choice of θ is critical. A set of eight two-dimensional samples are plotted in Fig. 8.4. We can indicate the effect of the thresholding by connecting pairs of points for which $d_{ij} \leq \theta$; the result is indicated in Fig. 8.5 for three values of θ. If θ is

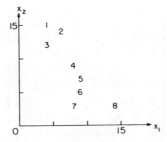

FIG. 8.4 Eight two-dimensional samples.

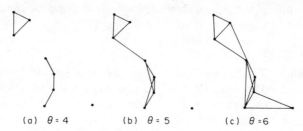

(a) $\theta = 4$ (b) $\theta = 5$ (c) $\theta = 6$

FIG. 8.5 Graphs generated by thresholding Fig. 8.4.

chosen correctly, a cluster is defined by disjoint connected subgraphs of the graph so defined [1]. In Fig. 8.5, three clusters result for $\theta = 4$, two for $\theta = 5$, and one for $\theta = 6$.

One might choose θ on the basis of sample statistics, e.g., as some function of average distance μ to the nearest point and the standard deviation σ of this distance. Zahn [59] suggests that a small value of σ relative to μ increases the likelihood of this approach succeeding. On the other hand, a large value of σ suggests that no single value of θ is appropriate for the entire space.

Algorithms are available for finding connected subgraphs of a larger graph [4,53]. One simple algorithm follows:

(1)   Choose the row of the similarity matrix with the greatest number of 1's, say row i. (An arbitrary decision can be made in the event of a tie.)

(2)   Form a cluster consisting of all the samples corresponding to 1's in row i. Add a sample to that cluster if there is a 1 in the column corresponding to that sample in a row corresponding to a sample already chosen for that cluster.

(3)   Remove columns and rows corresponding to samples placed in a completed cluster, and repeat the procedure for the reduced matrix.

(4)   Continue until the similarity matrix is exhausted.

Let us demonstrate this procedure. The following similarity matrix corresponds to Fig. 8.5a:

$$S = \begin{bmatrix} 1 & 1 & 1 & 0 & 0 & 0 & 0 & 0 \\ 1 & 1 & 1 & 0 & 0 & 0 & 0 & 0 \\ 1 & 1 & 1 & 0 & 0 & 0 & 0 & 0 \\ 0 & 0 & 0 & 1 & 1 & 0 & 0 & 0 \\ 0 & 0 & 0 & 1 & 1 & 1 & 0 & 0 \\ 0 & 0 & 0 & 0 & 1 & 1 & 1 & 0 \\ 0 & 0 & 0 & 0 & 0 & 1 & 1 & 0 \\ 0 & 0 & 0 & 0 & 0 & 0 & 0 & 1 \end{bmatrix}.$$

If we choose row 1 as the initial row, we note the 1's in columns 2 and 3. Since there are no additional samples with 1's in rows 2 and 3, the first cluster is $\{y_1, y_2, y_3\}$. The following submatrix results from removing rows and columns 1, 2, and 3:

$$S' = \begin{array}{c} 4 \\ 5 \\ 6 \\ 7 \\ 8 \end{array} \begin{bmatrix} 1 & 1 & 0 & 0 & 0 \\ 1 & 1 & 1 & 0 & 0 \\ 0 & 1 & 1 & 1 & 0 \\ 0 & 0 & 1 & 1 & 0 \\ 0 & 0 & 0 & 0 & 1 \end{bmatrix}.$$

We may choose row 5 or 6 (retaining the same numbering system) to initiate the next step. If we choose 5, samples 4, 5, and 6 are drawn into the cluster. Since row 6 has a 1 in column 7, y_7 is added to the cluster, resulting in the cluster $\{y_4, y_5, y_6, y_7\}$ and leaving $\{y_8\}$ for the final cluster.

The final clusters are described by their members, as discussed in Section 8.2.4. A new sample may be placed in a cluster by comparing the average localized distance to samples in each cluster.† A more efficient cluster description can be obtained by labeling the samples with their cluster membership and solving the resulting pattern classification problem to determine cluster boundaries. Since the graph-theoretical approach can define sheets as clusters, simple center-distance definitions may fail; the mean of samples in a sheet may not lie anywhere near the sheet.

8.7.3 Minimal Spanning Trees

The problem of choosing θ can be avoided by dealing directly with the interpoint-distance matrix, the elements of which are defined by Eq. (8.21). One such approach is through the use of minimal spanning trees from graph theory. The initial graph is defined by the interpoint distances. It has M nodes, each corresponding to a sample. All pairs of nodes are connected, and each such edge of the graph is weighted by the corresponding intersample distance.

Let us define a minimal spanning tree of an edge-weighted linear graph. A *tree* is a connected graph with no closed circuits. A *spanning tree* of a connected graph G is a tree in G which contains every node of G. The *weight* of a tree is the sum of the weights of its edges. A *minimal spanning tree* is the spanning tree of minimal weight. Returning to Fig. 8.4, we find its minimal spanning tree to be that diagrammed in Fig. 8.6, where the weights of each edge of the minimal tree are indicated. Zahn [59] discusses the use of minimal

† Localized distances are discussed in Section 9.4.

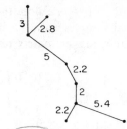

FIG. 8.6   A minimal spanning tree for Fig. 8.4.

spanning trees in clustering and references algorithms for finding the minimal spanning tree.

By definition, the minimal spanning tree connects all nodes and does not define clusters without further processing. It provides a reduced graph which one can argue on both theoretical and intuitive grounds contains all the essential information necessary for clustering. Many intuitive algorithms are possible. For example, an edge with a large weight relative to the other branches from its nodes is a candidate to be broken to form a cluster. In Fig. 8.6, the edges with weights 5 and 5.4 might be broken to form three clusters. This approach allows, in effect, varying θ in the similarity matrix approach as a function of the local character of the sample distribution. Zahn [59] discusses such intuitive decomposition of the minimal spanning tree.

8.8   INDIRECT METHODS IN CLUSTERING

Most of the methods discussed to this point have been direct methods which depended upon the validity of the constructive algorithm employed. The emphasis on direct methods is due to their computational efficiency relative to indirect methods, where a criterion function is defined and minimized. Indirect methods are generally more efficient in pattern classification than cluster analysis because there are generally more clusters than pattern classes and because the number of clusters is usually unknown.

Indirect methods can easily be posed. Section 8.2 lists parameterized descriptions of subregions,

$$X_i \equiv X_i(\alpha), \qquad i = 1, 2, \ldots, R. \tag{8.23}$$

Section 8.5 mentioned several criterion functions, Eq. (8.18) being the prime example. If the subregions are defined by Eqs. (8.3)–(8.5), then Q of Eq. (8.18) could be minimized directly with respect to $\mathbf{m}_1, \mathbf{m}_2, \ldots, \mathbf{m}_R$ and $\sigma_1, \sigma_2, \ldots, \sigma_R$

(2*Rn* parameters) if *R* is known. Equation (8.18) is not suitable for minimization with respect to *R*, the number of clusters, since *Q* will be minimized if there is one sample per cluster—an intuitively nonoptimal optimum.

Section 8.3 provides us with the concepts for a very general criterion function. If the probability density of the samples is adequately represented by Eq. (8.8), each component $p^{(i)}(\mathbf{x})$ will correspond to a natural cluster to the degree that Eq. (8.10) is satisfied. A measure of the overlap of the component densities is

$$I(\boldsymbol{\alpha}; R) = E_{\mathbf{x}}\left\{\sum_{i=1}^{R} \sum_{\substack{j=1 \\ j \neq 1}}^{R} p^{(i)}p^{(j)}p^{(i)}(\mathbf{x})p^{(j)}(\mathbf{x})\right\}, \tag{8.24a}$$

$$\sum_{i=1}^{R} p^{(i)} = 1, \tag{8.24b}$$

where $p^{(i)}(\mathbf{x})$ is the probability density of samples falling in $X_i(\boldsymbol{\alpha})$ and the expectation $E_{\mathbf{x}}$ is with respect to $p(\mathbf{x})$ of Eq. (8.8). The component densities can be estimated by potential function methods:

$$p^{(i)}(\mathbf{x}) = \frac{1}{M^{(i)}} \sum_{\mathbf{y} \in X_i(\boldsymbol{\alpha})} \gamma(\mathbf{x}, \mathbf{y}), \tag{8.25}$$

where $M^{(i)}$ is the number of samples $\mathbf{y}$ which fall in $X_i(\boldsymbol{\alpha})$. The expectation can be approximated with an average over all *M* samples to obtain an equally valid criterion function for minimization:

$$I'(\boldsymbol{\alpha}; R) = \frac{1}{M} \sum_{k=1}^{M} \left\{\sum_{i=1}^{R} \sum_{\substack{j=1, \\ j \neq i}}^{R} p^{(i)}p^{(j)}p^{(i)}(\mathbf{y}_k)p^{(j)}(\mathbf{y}_k)\right\}. \tag{8.26}$$

The value of I' will be zero if the component densities do not overlap at all and large if all densities are coincident. One can minimize I' with respect to the parameters $\boldsymbol{\alpha}$ defining the subregions and with respect to *R* because of the normalizing effect of (8.24b); this latter constraint is automatically satisfied by setting

$$p^{(i)} = M^{(i)}/M. \tag{8.27}$$

Equation (8.26) can be further simplified by noting that

$$p^2(\mathbf{x}) = \left(\sum_{i=1}^{R} p^{(i)}p^{(i)}(\mathbf{x})\right)\left(\sum_{j=1}^{R} p^{(j)}p^{(j)}(\mathbf{x})\right)$$

$$= \sum_{i=1}^{R} \sum_{j=1}^{R} p^{(i)}p^{(j)}p^{(i)}(\mathbf{x})p^{(j)}(\mathbf{x})$$

$$= \sum_{i=1}^{R} \sum_{\substack{j=1 \\ j \neq i}}^{R} p^{(i)}p^{(j)}p^{(i)}(\mathbf{x})p^{(j)}(\mathbf{x}) + \sum_{i=1}^{R} [p^{(i)}p^{(i)}(\mathbf{x})]^2.$$

Hence, Eq. (8.26) can be rewritten as

total variance   *item variance*

$$I'(\boldsymbol{\alpha}; R) = C - \sum_{i=1}^{R} C_i(\boldsymbol{\alpha}), \quad = correlation \tag{8.28a}$$

where

$$C = \frac{1}{M} \sum_{k=1}^{M} p^2(\mathbf{y}_k) \tag{8.28b}$$

and

$$C_i(\boldsymbol{\alpha}) = \frac{1}{M} \sum_{k=1}^{M} [p^{(i)} p^{(i)}(\mathbf{y}_k)]^2. \tag{8.28c}$$

points — *actual variance for y_i*   *diagonal*   *if correlation is zero then*

If the component densities are estimated by (8.25) and $p^{(i)}$ by (8.27), then (8.28c) becomes

$$C_i(\boldsymbol{\alpha}) = \frac{1}{M} \sum_{k=1}^{M} \left\{ \frac{1}{M} \sum_{\mathbf{y}' \in X_i(\boldsymbol{\alpha})} \gamma(\mathbf{y}_k, \mathbf{y}') \right\}^2. \tag{8.29}$$

Note that C of Eq. (8.28b) is represented as independent of $\boldsymbol{\alpha}$ by the argument that the overall probability density of a set of samples is independent of the way in which they are partitioned. Since the equivalence of (8.26) and (8.28) assumed a particular partition-dependent representation of $p(\mathbf{x})$, however, this is only approximately true, and C should remain a part of the criterion function. Equation (8.28) can be minimized by a random search method such as described in Chapter III.

Watanabe [54] has proposed a general indirect formulation of clustering algorithms into which many algorithms, including that proposed in (8.28) by the author, fall. If K is the cost of a partition of a set $\mathcal{O}$ into clusters $\mathcal{O}_1, \mathcal{O}_2, \ldots, \mathcal{O}_R$, then

$$K = C(\mathcal{O}) - \sum_{i=1}^{R} C(\mathcal{O}_i), \tag{8.30}$$

where $C(\mathcal{O}_i)$ is the *cohesion* of $\mathcal{O}_i$. Note that this corresponds directly to (8.28) with the cohesion defined by (8.28c). An alternate form can be stated in terms of the anticohesion $A(\mathcal{O}_i)$ measuring the lack of cohesion of $\mathcal{O}_i$:

$$K = \sum_{i=1}^{R} A(\mathcal{O}_i) - A(\mathcal{O}). \tag{8.31}$$

Watanabe's formulation generalizes the clustering problem toward the more general problem in artificial intelligence, where the similarity of samples can be defined in a much more complex manner than we have here.

8.9 UNSUPERVISED AND DECISION-DIRECTED LEARNING

8.9.1 Pattern Classification with Unlabeled Samples

We have repeatedly alluded to the relation between pattern classification and cluster analysis. The clusters can be considered "natural" pattern classes in themselves or subclasses of larger pattern classes. Considering clusters as subclasses of larger known pattern classes, one may use cluster analysis as part of a conventional pattern classification algorithm, as discussed further in Section 8.10. On the other hand, one may consider that the unlabeled samples form natural but unknown pattern classes, and that the process of cluster analysis is the detection and recognition of those classes. Particularly when the samples are processed sequentially rather than simultaneously, this process is tagged as *unsupervised learning* or *learning without a teacher*. All of the algorithms we have discussed in this Chapter are generally applicable to this problem, although the viewpoint of what is occurring is often somewhat different.

One example of unlabeled samples might occur in code breaking. Suppose a code is employed in which letters of the alphabet are replaced in a systematic manner with more than a single symbol; for example, the letter "*a*" may occur as a "*b*," a " +," and a " !." When presented to us to decode, none of these symbols is labeled as to its correct designation. We may, given text expressed in this code, be able to select pertinent features: for example, the frequency with which the symbol appears at the end of a word, the frequency with which the symbol appears at the beginning of a word, the maximum number of times the symbol appears following another symbol, the number of times the symbol appears alone, etc. Hence, each character gives rise to a sample point. We do not know the classification of these sample points, but it is reasonable to assume that each cluster will tend to correspond to a single character of the alphabet. We may, at least as an initial approach, replace all symbols in a given cluster by a single character, and attempt to decode the text thus obtained. This is an example of a situation where we are searching for known pattern classes, but with unlabeled samples. Another class of applications occurs when the classes to be recognized are unknown, but it is important to detect the existence of class differences and to characterize those differences. One could not know what classes of objects an unmanned explorer of the moon or a planet would encounter or what samples of rock or animal and plant life, if any, should be collected. The unmanned device could, however, be designed to collect differing samples; it could use clustering algorithms to search out items which form a new cluster relative to prior observations in an appropriately defined pattern space.

Similarly, an ICBM warhead may be surrounded by a cloud of various types of decoys. A clustering algorithm in a feature space defining the characteristics of the objects observed could conceivably detect a cluster with a single member (the warhead), even if the exact characteristics of the decoys were unknown.

A somewhat different point of view is to consider that we have a limited number of labeled samples and that we wish to design a system which will modify the decision rule as it is used to classify samples. If the unlabeled samples are converted into labeled samples by assuming the classification assigned by the current decision rule is correct, and pattern classification algorithms utilized to modify the decision rule, the procedure is designated *decision-directed learning.*

8.9.2   Unsupervised Learning

As we have noted, most algorithms in this chapter are directly applicable to the unsupervised learning problem, since it is to some extent an interpretation of cluster analysis rather than a different problem. In much of the recent literature, the statistical formulation of Section 8.3 has been adopted as the formal description of the problem; procedures derived are means of finding the parameters of a mixed distribution. Much excellent work along these lines is available [3, 14, 16, 18, 23, 24, 25, 28, 30, 34, 36, 37, 38, 39, 40, 45, 51, 52, 56, 57, 58]. Space and time constraints prevent the inclusion in this volume of the statistical preliminaries necessary to discuss and relate this work; the author must reluctantly refer the reader to the bibliography.

8.9.3   Decision-Directed Learning

Some decision-directed schemes are straightforward modifications of pattern classification algorithms. Supposing we have a reasonable estimate of the decision boundary (perhaps from a small labeled sample set), the algorithms to be discussed may work.

Given the initial decision boundary, samples may be classified by that decision boundary, the resulting labeled samples used to obtain a new decision boundary, and the procedure repeated until no samples change classification [33]. Alternatively or concurrently, one may allow only samples sufficiently far from the boundary to be labeled and hence to modify the decision rule [25]. Other more formally based procedures have been proposed (e.g., [22, 35, 41]).

Agrawala [2] has proposed a variation of the basic decision-directed scheme with some theoretical advantages. The label placed on a given sample is generated randomly from a problem-defined probability density. This procedure is *learning with a probabilistic teacher.*

8.10 CLUSTERING AS DATA ANALYSIS

The number of clusters in a set of data and their location give a great deal of information about the structure of that data. Having obtained clusters of sample points, one can obtain statistics for each cluster and derive an understanding of the qualitative aspects of the system represented by the data. The noted differences between the clusters can be related to the locations of the subsets. Hence, one can view cluster analysis as generalized correlation analysis in certain applications. Further, clustering indicates anomalous points, points which are widely separated from other sample points, and which may be a result of error in measurement or in data preparation.

Cluster analysis has found wide application in the social and behavioral sciences. A typical application was reported by Ringwald *et al.* [42], where cluster analysis was used to define typical types of students. A group of students was clustered on the basis of information gathered, and the typical member of each cluster described.

In *numerical taxonomy*, the natural classification of biological species on the basis of descriptive measurements may be attempted by cluster analysis. Usually a hierarchical decision rule is sought.

8.11 CLUSTER ANALYSIS AND PATTERN CLASSIFICATION

Cluster analysis may form a part of a pattern classification algorithm. The intention may be simply to divide up the space into natural subregions such that a classification algorithm can be applied separately to those subregions; in this case, the clustering algorithm is applied to all samples irrespective of class. For example, the shape of the clusters in the adaptive sample set algorithm may be used as the local shape of the potential function in the potential function method; that is, the variances obtained in that method may be used to determine the shape of the potential function in the given subregion.

On the other hand, a clustering algorithm may be applied separately to samples of each class. For example, if probability densities for each class are derived separately and described by Eq. (8.8) or (8.11), we have estimates of the probability densities $p_i(\mathbf{x})$ of each class and can compare them as usual.

EXERCISES

8.1. Given the samples (1, 5)(2, 5)(3, 4)(6, 4)(7, 4)(8, 5), define the two appropriate subsets by all six methods suggested in Section 8.2 (by inspection). Sketch the resulting subregions. In which subset would each method place (4.5, 4)?

8.2. Assuming that the clusters of Exercise 8.1 were *locally* bivariate normal of the form

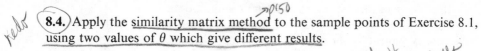

$$p^{(i)}(\mathbf{x}) = K \exp\left[-\left(\frac{x_1^2}{\sigma_1^2} + \frac{x_2^2}{\sigma_2^2}\right)\right],$$

specify $p(\mathbf{x})$ in Eq. (8.8) from the data available.

8.3. Choose reasonable constants in the Sebestyen–Edie algorithm for application to the samples of Exercise 8.1, and apply the algorithm. Show each step. Explain your choices of constants.

8.4. Apply the similarity matrix method to the sample points of Exercise 8.1, using two values of θ which give different results.

8.5. Describe an application where overlapping clusters are acceptable, that is, where a point may be in more than one cluster. Suggest a modification of the discriminant function approach which would define such clusters; in particular, show how the center-distance description might be modified.

8.6. Given unlabeled samples: (1, 3)(1, 4)(2, 4)(3, 3)(4, 0)(4, 1)(4, 2)(4, 3)(4, 4) (5, 0)(5, 1)(5, 2)(6, 0)(6, 1)(6, 2):

   (a)   Use the algorithm specified by Eqs. (8.14) and (8.16) to find clusters for $R = 2$, $\mathbf{m}_1^{(0)} = (3, 3)$, and $\mathbf{m}_2^{(0)} = (6, 1)$.

   (b)   Repeat (a) for $R = 3$, $\mathbf{m}_1^{(0)}$ and $\mathbf{m}_2^{(0)}$ as above, and $\mathbf{m}_3^{(0)} = (1, 4)$.

   (c)   Cluster the samples using the same algorithm with the modification of Eq. (8.17) with $R = 2$, $\mathbf{m}_1^{(0)} = (2.5, 3.5)$, $\mathbf{m}_2^{(0)} = (6, 1)$, and $\sigma_1^{(0)} = \sigma_2^{(0)} = (1, 1)$.

SELECTED BIBLIOGRAPHY

1. Abraham, C., Evaluation of Clusters on the Basis of Random Graph Theory, IBM Research Memo., IBM Corp., Yorktown Heights, New York, November 1962.
2. Agrawala, A. K., Learning with a Probabilistic Teacher, *IEEE Trans. Information Theory* **16**, 373–379 (1970).
3. Alens, N., and Cover, T. M., Compound Bayes Learning without a Teacher, *Proc. Conf. Inform. Sci. Sys., Princeton, March, 1967*, p. 109.
4. Baker, J. J., A Note on Multiplying Boolean Matrices, *Comm. ACM* **5**, (1962).
5. Ball, G. H., Data Analysis in the Social Sciences: What About the Details? *Proc. Fall Joint Comput. Conf., December 1965*, pp. 553–559.
6. Ball, G. H., Classification Analysis, Stanford Research Institute, Menlo Park, California, Tech. note, Contract NONR-4918(00), November 1970.
7. Ball, G. H., and Hall, D. J., ISODATA. An Iterative Method of Multivariate Data Analysis and Pattern Classification, *Proc. IEEE Int. Commun. Conf., June 1966*, pp. 116–117.

8. Blaydon, C., and Ho, Y.-C., On the Abstraction Problem in Pattern Classification, *Proc. Nat. Electron. Conf. 1966*, **22**, 857–862 (1966).

9. Bonner, R. E., A "Logical Pattern" Recognition Program, *IBM J. Res. Develop.* **6**, 353–359 (1962).

10. Bonner, R. E., On Some Clustering Techniques, *IBM J. Res. Develop.* **8**, 22–32 (1964).

11. Braverman, E. M., The Method of Potential Functions in the Problem of Training Machines to Recognize Patterns without a Trainer, *Automat. Remote Cont.* **27**, 1748–1771 (1966).

12. Butler, G. A. A Vector Field Approach to Cluster Analysis, *Pattern Recognition*, **1**, 291–299 (1969).

13. Casey, R. G., and Nagy, G., An Autonomous Reading Machine, *IEEE Trans. Comput.* **17**, 492–503, (1968).

14. Cooper, D. B., and Cooper, P. W., Nonsupervised Adaptive Signal Detection and Pattern Recognition, *Information and Control*, **7**, 416–444 (1964).

15. Cooper, P. W., Hyperplanes, Hyperspheres, and Hyperquadrics as Decision Boundaries, in Computer and Information Sciences (J. T. Tou, ed.), pp. 111–139, Spartan, Washington, D.C., 1964.

16. Dorofeyuk, A. A., Teaching Algorithm for a Pattern Recognition Machine without a Teacher, Based on the Method of Potential Functions, *Automat. Remote Contr.* **27**, 1728–1737 (1966).

17. Firschein, O., and Fischler, M., Automatic Subclass Determination for Pattern-Recognition Applications, *IEEE Trans. Electron. Comput.* **12** 137–141 (1963).

18. Fralick, S. C., Learning to Recognize Patterns without a Teacher, *IEEE Trans. Information Theory* **13**, 57–64 (1967).

19. Friedman, H. P., and Rubin, J., On Some Invariant Criteria for Grouping Data, *J. Amer. Statist. Assoc.* **62**, 1159–1178 (1967).

20. Fukunaga, K., and Koontz, W. L. G., A Criterion and an Algorithm for Grouping Data, *IEEE Trans. Comput.* **19**, 917–923 (1970).

21. Gitman, I., and Levine, M. D., An Algorithm for Detecting Unimodal Fuzzy Sets and Its Application as a Clustering Technique, *IEEE Trans. Comput.* **19**, 583–593 (1970).

22. Gregg, W. D., and Hancock, J. C., An Optimum Decision-Directed Scheme for Gaussian Mixtures, *IEEE Trans. Information Theory* **14**, 451–561 (1968).

23. Hancock, J. C., and Patrick, E. A., Iterative Computation of a posteriori Probability for M-ary Nonsupervised Adaptation, *IEEE Trans. Information Theory* **12**, 483–484 (1966).

24. Hilborn, C. G., Jr., and Lainiotis, D. G., Optimal Adaptive Pattern Recognition, *Proc. Conf. Inform. Sci. Sys., Princeton, March 1967*, pp. 259–263.

25. Ide, E. R., and Tunis, C. J., An Experimental Investigation of an Unsupervised Adaptive Algorithm, IBM Sys. Develop. Div., Endicott, New York, Rept. TR-01-967, 1966.

26. Kaminuma, T., Takekawa, T., and Watanabe, S., Reduction of Clustering Problems to Pattern Recognition, *Pattern Recognition* **1**, 196–205 (1969).

27. Kashyap, R. L., and Blaydon, C. C., Recovery of Functions from Noisy Measurements Taken at Randomly Selected Points and Its Application to Pattern Classification, *Proc. IEEE* **54**, 1127–1129 (1966).

28. Lainiotis, D., A Nonlinear Adaptive Estimation Algorithm, *IEEE Trans. Automatic Control* **13**, 197 (1966).

29. MacQueen, J., Some Methods for Classification and Analysis of Multivariate Observations, *Proc. 5th Symp. Statist. Probab., Berkeley, 1967*, pp. 281–297, Univ. of California Press, Berkeley, California, 1967.

30. Mahalanabis, A. K., and Das, P. An Example of Nonsupervised Adaptive Pattern Classification, *IEEE Trans. Automatic Control* **13**, 107–108 (1968).
31. Mattson, R. L., and Dammann, R. L., A Technique for Determining and Coding Subclasses in Pattern Recognition Problems, *IBM J. Res. Develop.* **9**, 294–302 (1965).
32. Mucciardi, A. N., and Gose, E. L., An Algorithm for Automatic Clustering in *N*-Dimensional Spaces Using Hyperellipsoidal Cells, *Proc. IEEE Sys. Sci. Cybernetics Conf., Pittsburgh, October 1970.*
33. Nagy, G., and Shelton, G. L., Jr., Self-Corrective Character Recognition System, *IEEE Trans. Information Theory* **12**, 215–222 (1966).
34. Patrick, E. A., On a Class of Unsupervised Estimation Problems, *IEEE Trans. Information Theory*, **14**, 407–415 (1968).
35. Patrick, E. A., and Costello, J. P., Asymptotic Probability of Error Using Two Decision-Directed Estimators for Two Unknown Mean Vectors, *IEEE Trans. Information Theory*, **14**, 160–162 (1968).
36. Patrick, E. A., and Costello, J. P., Bayes Related Solutions to Unsupervised Estimation, *Proc. Nat. Electron. Conf., 1969.*
37. Patrick, E. A., and Costello, J. P., On Unsupervised Estimation Algorithms, *IEEE Trans. Information Theory*, **16**, 556–570 (1970).
38. Patrick, E. A., and Fischer, F. P., II, Cluster Mapping with Experimental Computer Graphics, *IEEE Trans. Comput.*, **18**, 987–991 (1969).
39. Patrick, E. A., and Hancock, J. C., Nonsupervised Sequential Classification and Recognition of Patterns, *IEEE Trans. Information Theory*, **12**, 362–372 (1966).
40. Patrick, E. A., and Liporace, L., Unsupervised Estimation of Parametric Mixtures, Purdue Univ. Lafayette, Indiana, Rept. TR-EE-70-31, 1970.
41. Patrick, E. A., Costello, J. P., and Monds, F. C., Decision-Directed Estimation of a Two-Class Decision Boundary, *IEEE Trans. Comput.* **19**, 197–205 (1970).
42. Ringwald, B. E., Mann, R. D., Rosenwein, R., and McKeachie, W. J., Conflict and Style in the College Classroom—An Intimate Study, *Psychology Today*, **4**, 45–47 (1971).
43. Rosenblatt, F., "Principles of Neurodynamics; Perceptrons and the Theory of Brain Mechanism," Spartan, Washington, D.C., 1962.
44. Rosenfeld, A., Huang, H. K., and Schneider, B. V., An Application of Cluster Detection to Text and Picture Processing, *IEEE Trans. Information Theory*, **15**, 672–681 (1969).
45. Sammon, J. W., Jr., Adaptive Decomposition of Superpositions of Probability Density Functions, Rome Air Development Center, Rome, New York, Tech. Rept. No. RADC-TR-66-540, 1966.
46. Sammon, J. W., Jr., An Adaptive Technique for Multiple Signal Detection and Identification, *in* "Pattern Recognition" (L. Kanal, ed.), pp. 409–439, Thompson, Washington, D.C., 1968.
47. Sammon, J. W., Jr., On-Line Pattern Analysis and Recognition System, Rome Air Development Center, Rome, New York, Tech. Rept. No. RADC-TR-68-263, 1968.
48. Scudder, H. J., III, Probability of Error of Some Adaptive Pattern Recognition Machines, *IEEE Trans. Information Theory*, **11**, 363–371 (1965).
49. Sebestyen, G. S. Pattern Recognition by an Adaptive Process of Samples Set Construction, *IEEE Trans. Information Theory*, **8**, S82–S91 (1962).
50. Sebestyen, G. S., and Edie, J., An Algorithm for Nonparametric Pattern Recognition, *IEEE Trans. Electron. Comput.* **15**, 908–915 (1966).
51. Spragins, J., Learning without a Teacher, *IEEE Trans. Information Theory*, **12**, 223–229 (1966).
52. Swerling, P., Classes for Signal Processing Procedures Suggested by Exact Minimum Mean Square Error Procedures, *SIAM J. Appl. Math.* **14**, 1199–1224 (1966).

53. Warshall, S., A Theorem on Boolean Matrices, *J. ACM*, **9**, 11–13 (1962).
54. Watanabe, S., A Unified View of Clustering Algorithms, *Proc. Intnat. Fed. Info. Proc. Soc., Czechoslovakia, 1971.*
55. Wilks, S. S., Multidimensional Statistical Scatter, *in* Contributions to Probability and Statistics (I. Oskin, S. Ghurye, W. Hoeffding, W. Madow, and H. Mann, eds.), Standford Univ. Press, Stanford, California, 1960.
56. Yakowitz, S. J., Unsupervised Learning and the Identification of Finite Mixtures, *IEEE Trans. Information Theory*, **16**, 330–338 (1970).
57. Yakowitz, S. J., and J. Spragins, On the Identifiability of Finite Mixtures, *Ann. Math. Statist.* **39**, (1968).
58. Young, T. Y., and Coraluppi, G., Stochastic Estimation of a Mixture of Normal Density Functions Using an Information Criterion, *IEEE Trans. Information Theory* **6**, 258–264 (1970).
59. Zahn, C. T. Graph-Theoretical Methods for Detecting and Describing Gestalt Clusters, *IEEE Trans. Comput.* **20**, 68–86 (1971).

CHAPTER IX

FEATURE SELECTION

9.1 INTRODUCTION

9.1.1 The General Problem

Feature extraction always amounts to finding a transformation from one space to another. One might seek a direct transformation from measure space to pattern space; alternatively, the feature extraction process may be considered as a set of transformations applied in series, in parallel, or both. The ultimate objective is to obtain a pattern space consistent with the four criteria discussed in Section 1.6: (1) low dimensionality, (2) retention of sufficient information, (3) enhancement of distance in pattern space as a measure of the similarity of physical patterns, and (4) comparability of features among samples.

It is somewhat artificial to consider feature selection as an independent step; it is intimately related to the overall pattern recognition process. The division between pattern classification and feature selection is usually advisable, however, because (1) the computational feasibility of many pattern classification algorithms is restricted to relatively low dimension, (2) practical sample sizes restrict the dimensionality of the space for which the concepts upon which those algorithms are based are valid, and (3) the multistage process often results in a more efficient decision rule.

Feature selection algorithms can be valuable in themselves in data analysis. They can be used to find the intrinsic dimensionality of data in a much more

general sense than can factor analysis or discriminant analysis [7, 27, 38, 67].
Feature selection techniques may be used to find a two- or three-dimensional
representation of high-dimensional data which retains the essential structure
of the original data, but allows direct visual examination [64]. One can use
feature ranking techniques to compare the effectiveness of different system
measurements. In data analysis, features determined as most powerful in
separating classes give qualitative information on the underlying causes of
class differences.

The nature of the application may suggest a natural set of features, as is
often the case in some image recognition problems [44, 61]. This chapter is
concerned, however, with applications in which we wish to determine " good "
features from a set of samples alone. Further, the approach is generally nonparametric: it is not assumed that the samples arise from a probability
density of simple form.

While the preprocessing and feature selection process may consist of
several stages, we will formulate the problem as if there were one stage, and
leave it to the reader to devise sequences of procedures when it appears of
advantage. At every stage of the process, the samples are specified in a given
space, and we wish to find a transformed space where the samples have a
satisfactory distribution; we will denote the given space as Z-space, with
components $\mathbf{z} = (z_1, \ldots, z_m)$ [or occasionally $\mathbf{f} = (f_1, \ldots, f_m)$]. We wish to
find a transformation $\mathbf{F}$ which maps Z into a pattern space X with components
$\mathbf{x} = (x_1, \ldots, x_n)$, that is,

$$\mathbf{x} = \mathbf{F}(\mathbf{z}), \tag{9.1}$$

or

$$x_i = F_i(z_1, \ldots, z_m), \qquad i = 1, 2, \ldots, n.$$

The objective of this transformation is usually to lower dimensionality, to
obtain a simpler sample distribution, or to normalize. Dividing each component in Z-space by the range of that component in a set of samples, as
suggested in Section 1.5.1, is an example of a normalizing transformation.

This chapter begins with a discussion of direct versus indirect methods in
feature selection. Some discussion of direct methods follows, but the bulk of
methods discussed will be indirect methods. As usual, indirect methods involve
a choice of (a) a definition of the cost of a set of features, (b) a parameterized
set of transformations, and (c) an optimization technique. The chapter is
organized into a discussion, first, of classes of parameterized transformations
and, second, of alternative measures of separability.

Parameterized transformations discussed will include general linear
transformations and, in particular, orthonormal transformations: general
nonlinear transformations and, in particular, piecewise linear transformations.

The similarity between an orthonormal transformation and the expansion of a function (or image) in orthonormal functions is discussed in a later section.

Different measures of separability to be discussed include measures based on interset distances, where the concept of a localized distance is introduced. Measures of separability based upon estimating the overlap of the class probability densities are discussed, and similarity to the concept of localized distances is indicated. Other more specialized measures of optimality are discussed, including criteria which measure the preservation of structure by the transformation and the fidelity in representation of a set of samples. It is indicated how measures of separability for pattern classification may be used to give a criteria for feature selection which measures the optimality of features for the class of decision rules *to be used*, rather than optimality *independent* of the class of decision rules used.

Direct methods of constructing orthonormal functions are discussed. The optimum Karhunen–Loève expansion is discussed along with a suboptimal but more efficient approach. Feature ranking, the ordering of a set of features by their utility in separating pattern classes (or preserving structure) is discussed. Finally, the cost of the features are incorporated as a tradeoff against the quality of the features using a dynamic programming algorithm.

9.1.2 Direct versus Indirect Methods

As in pattern classification algorithms, there are direct (constructive) methods and indirect (optimization) methods. An indirect feature selection strategy is defined by choosing: (1) a class of parameterized transformations; (2) a criterion function, a measure of the quality of the distribution of transformed sample points; and (3) an optimization procedure to find the optimum transformation with respect to the measure of quality [49]. The class of transformations is specified parametrically:

$$\mathscr{F} = \{\mathbf{F}(\mathbf{z}; \boldsymbol{\alpha}) \,|\, \boldsymbol{\alpha} = (\alpha_1, \alpha_2, \ldots, \alpha_R) \in \mathscr{A}\}, \qquad (9.2)$$

where $\mathscr{A}$ is some allowable region for the parameters. For example, a member of the class of linear transformations is given by

$$x_1 = F_1(\mathbf{z}; \mathbf{w}_1) = w_{11}z_1 + w_{12}z_2 + \cdots + w_{1m}z_m$$
$$\vdots$$
$$x_n = F_n(\mathbf{z}; \mathbf{w}_n) = w_{n1}z_1 + w_{n2}z_2 + \cdots + w_{nm}z_m$$

or, in matrix notation,

$$\mathbf{x} = \mathbf{F}(\mathbf{z}; \mathbf{W}) = \mathbf{Wz},$$

where $\mathbf{W}$ is an $n \times m$ matrix with elements w_{ij}.

The measure of quality Q is an estimate of the probability of misclassification and/or the separability of the pattern classes. Because the sample points in Z-space are given, the distribution of sample points in X-space is determined solely by the transformation $\mathbf{F}(\mathbf{x}; \alpha)$ and hence by α; thus, Q is to be optimized with respect to α:

$$Q \equiv Q(\alpha). \tag{9.3}$$

Constraints are often involved in defining either $\mathscr{F}$ or Q; these constraints may often be implemented by optimization with respect to another function $G(\alpha)$ incorporating those constraints. For example, suppose the constraint were of the form $g(\alpha) = 0$ and Q was to be minimized; one could then minimize

$$G(\alpha) = Q(\alpha) + \lambda[g(\alpha)]^2, \qquad \lambda > 0. \tag{9.4}$$

(This approach has the advantage of allowing a loosening or tightening of the constraint by variation of the value of λ.) The optimum solution is specified completely by choosing $\mathscr{F}$ and Q. A wide range of optimization techniques provide a wide choice of possible algorithms; but the solution is indirectly determined as soon as $\mathscr{F}$ and Q are specified.

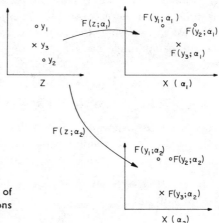

FIG. 9.1 Comparing the separability of samples transformed by two transformations determined by different parameters.

Figure 9.1 is an attempt to represent graphically the indirect process. Here we have chosen a hypothetical set of parameterized transformations; the results of applying the two particular members of this class of transformations determined by parameters α_1 and α_2 to the labeled samples are illustrated. A measure of quality Q can be defined which measures the "quality" of the resulting distribution:

$$Q(\alpha) = Q[\mathbf{F}(\mathbf{y}_1; \alpha), \mathbf{F}(\mathbf{y}_2; \alpha), \mathbf{F}(\mathbf{y}_3; \alpha)].$$

If Q measures the cohesion of the classes, then one would expect $Q(\alpha_2)$ to be greater than $Q(\alpha_1)$, i.e., $F(z; \alpha_2)$ to be a better transformation than $F(z; \alpha_1)$. The optimum solution is obtained by finding the value of α which gives the best distribution of transformed samples in X as measured by Q.

We have stated the indirect formulation in terms of a single criterion function. There may in fact be several conflicting criteria by which one can judge a set of features. Techniques are available which give a spectrum of "non-inferior" solutions for multiple criteria [5]; they give results such as in Section 9.8.3, where the cost of features, as well as the separability of samples, is taken into account.

Direct methods do not have the satisfying quality, as do indirect methods, of defining an "optimal" solution. They construct a (hopefully) satisfactory solution.

Since there are literally hundreds of possible triplets of $\mathscr{F}$, Q, and optimization technique, the procedure followed in this chapter will be to first discuss and compare families of parameterized transformations and then to discuss and compare measures of quality. Occasionally, we will discuss a particular triplet when it has aspects of particular interest. Special attention is devoted to the particular characteristics of the processing of a measurement space obtained by sampling a continuous time function. Feature ranking algorithms based upon developed measures of quality will be presented. Finally, we will consider the choice of an optimum subset of features when the cost of calculating, measuring, or implementing each feature is taken into account.

9.2 DIRECT METHODS

A *principle of decomposition* forms a conceptual basis for direct feature selection methods. It is simply a recognition of the paradox inherent in attempting to isolate pattern classification and feature selection:

The selection of a set of features which efficiently describe a system in terms of a pattern to be recognized in those features is itself pattern recognition. Each feature describes some aspect of the pattern and amounts to a decomposition of the quality to be recognized in the overall problem into a set of more easily recognized qualities.

Once stated, this principle is almost self-evident; however, it provides a framework for the integration of many techniques. In essence, it states that a given problem can be decomposed into a set of simpler problems, and, in fact, that each of these problems may in turn be decomposed.

An important conclusion of this principle is that pattern classification algorithms may be used for feature selection by using them appropriately to "recognize" an aspect of the overall pattern recognition problem. We hence may *construct* a feature directly. The constructed features must generate a scalar output which is a measure of some characteristic of the system. This objective may be accomplished through two approaches: (1) generation of a single discriminant function which measures the given quality continuously or (2) by defining subclasses in the subproblem such that the class labels measure monotonically the characteristic in question. In the first case, the feature is a discriminant function measuring the degree of the quality represented in the measurements:

$$x_i = \rho(\mathbf{z}). \tag{9.5}$$

[Of course, $\rho(\mathbf{z})$ may in general depend only on some subset of the components of Z-space.] In the second case,

$$x_i = k \qquad \text{if} \quad \mathbf{z} \in \mathcal{U}_k, \tag{9.6}$$

where $\mathcal{U}_1, \mathcal{U}_2, \ldots, \mathcal{U}_N$ are appropriately chosen subclasses.

When the form of Eq. (9.5) is used to obtain an equation for a feature, it is important to use suitable techniques in generating the discriminant function. The method used must be one which extracts a characteristic discriminant function for the feature in question; that is, the value of the discriminant evaluated at a point in pattern space must be an indication of the degree of membership in the class of patterns having the particular feature in question. One must be able to generate this discriminant from the single class; this is much like reconstructing a probability density function from samples of a random process. Error-correction methods, which depend on *differences* between classes, do not necessarily yield characteristic discriminant functions for each class, nor in many cases are samples of the inverse class available. Potential function methods, for example, generate characteristic discriminant functions (see Chapter VI).

A hypothetical example will serve to illustrate this approach. Let us assume that we wish to distinguish between the characters O, D, and H. The degree of curvature or straightness seems to be a characteristic of importance in distinguishing members of these sets (Fig. 9.2a). We might recognize these

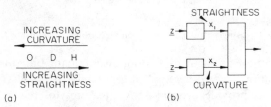

(a)   (b)

FIG. 9.2 The principle of decomposition: (a) distinguishing O, D, and H; (b) the decomposed formulation. Underscored symbols are vectors.

characters by decomposing the problem to one of recognizing the degree of straightness and one of recognizing the degree of curvature, followed by one of recognizing the given characters using the features which estimate the curvature and straightness. Figure 9.2b indicates diagramatically the decomposed problem. It is presumably a simpler problem to measure the degree of straightness or curvature of a character than to recognize the character. If ten features were used to measure curvature and ten others to measure straightness, the decomposition yields two ten-dimensional problems followed by one two-dimensional pattern classification problem rather than the single twenty-dimensional problem obtained by using all twenty features concurrently.

Often, analytic or heuristic techniques can be used to construct a feature. For example, aspects of radar " cross section " can be computed analytically from a target model and might provide features for target discrimination.

The above examples illustrate the implications of the principle of decomposition when the constructed features have clear interpretations. The principle applies as well to situations where the constructed features have no obvious interpretation. The following generalization will also provide a theoretical interpretation of the principle of decomposition.

Referring to Fig. 9.3, we note that one may in general decompose any

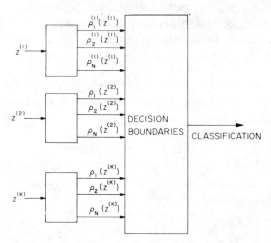

FIG. 9.3 Using pattern classification algorithms to generate features.

pattern recognition problem by finding discriminant functions for N classes using classification algorithms applied separately to K subsets of a given set of features. This provides a total of NK features for the final classification algorithm. That is, one might, for example, solve three ten-dimensional two-class problems and one six-dimensional two-class problem instead of a thirty-dimensional two-class problem. The motivation for doing so might be that computational considerations and sample size restrict the classification algorithms to ten dimensions.

The justification for decomposition resides in the fact that, barring willful sabotage, the classification error for the overall system should be the same as or less than that of any of the K component problems. Hence, the best obtainable results for a given number of features will be improved by composition with other subproblems. For example, consider any subproblem with feature vector $\mathbf{z}^{(i)}$ and resulting discriminant functions $\rho_1(\mathbf{z}^{(i)})$, $\rho_2(\mathbf{z}^{(i)})$, ..., $\rho_N(\mathbf{z}^{(i)})$. Choosing decision boundaries as usual [by classifying $\mathbf{z}^{(i)}$ in class k if $\rho_k(\mathbf{z}^{(i)}) > \rho_j(\mathbf{z}^{(i)})$ for all $j \neq i$] gives a certain rate of misclassification of the sample points. If this subproblem is part of the decomposition of Fig. 9.3, then the pattern space on which the final decision rule is based will contain $\rho_1(\mathbf{z}^{(i)})$, ..., $\rho_N(\mathbf{z}^{(i)})$ as components; a pattern classification algorithm which tended to minimize classification error should do no worse than the decision boundary defined by the above discriminants alone—since that boundary is itself available.

Indeed, much more information than the boundary is available from the subproblem. Conceptualizing the discriminant functions as estimate of probability densities, it is clear that the values of the discriminant function contain a great deal more information than simply which is larger. Perceptrons and layered machines (Section 7.3) are a special case of the principle of decomposition where only the *classification* produced by the subproblem is utilized in succeeding stages.

9.3 INDIRECT METHODS: PARAMETERIZED TRANSFORMATIONS

9.3.1 Linear Transformations: Normalization

Section 1.5.1 contained a brief discussion of normalization of a given pattern space. It was suggested that each component of the pattern space be divided by the standard deviation of that component of the samples. Such a transformation does not reduce dimensionality of the space; hence, in this case, $m = n$. The corresponding transformation can be represented as

$$x_i = b_i z_i, \qquad i = 1, \ldots, n,$$

or, in matrix notation,†

$$\mathbf{x} = \mathbf{Bz},$$

† We will consider *column* vectors $\mathbf{x}$ and $\mathbf{z}$ in matrix equations for most of this chapter.

where **B** is a diagonal matrix:

$$\mathbf{B} = \begin{bmatrix} b_1 & & & \\ & b_2 & & 0 \\ & & \ddots & \\ 0 & & & b_n \end{bmatrix}.$$

(9.7)

In the example cited, the particular criterion $G(b_1, \ldots, b_n)$ minimized by that result is given in Exercise 1.1; we were able to get a closed form result to the minimization problem. The constraint used in this case to prevent the space from shrinking was to require

$$\prod_{i=1}^{n} b_i = 1.$$

(9.8)

More generally, we can obtain the optimum normalization with regard to other criteria proposed in later sections.

9.3.2 Linear Transformations; Selecting n out of m Features

Suppose by some procedure (to be discussed) that we have selected the "best" n features out of m, $n < m$. Suppose the given features are z_1 through z_m and the chosen set of features are z_{i_1} through z_{i_n}; hence,

$$x_k = z_{i_k}, \qquad k = 1, \ldots, n,$$

(9.9a)

or in matrix notation,

$$\mathbf{x} = \mathbf{Tz},$$

$$\mathbf{T} = \begin{bmatrix} \boldsymbol{\beta}_1 \\ \vdots \\ \boldsymbol{\beta}_n \end{bmatrix},$$

(9.9b)

$$\boldsymbol{\beta}_k = (0, \ldots, 0, 1, 0, \ldots, 0).$$
$$\uparrow$$
$$\text{position } i_k$$

The parameters of this transformation are, of course, the set of integers $\{i_1, i_2, \ldots, i_n\}$.

9.3.3 Linear Transforms: Orthonormality

Let us consider a more general linear transform:

$$\mathbf{x} = \mathbf{Tz}$$

(9.10)

$$\mathbf{T} = \begin{bmatrix} \mathbf{w}_1 \\ \vdots \\ \mathbf{w}_n \end{bmatrix},$$

(9.11)

where the row vectors satisfy

$$\mathbf{w}_i \cdot \mathbf{w}_j = 0, \qquad i \neq j, \tag{9.12}$$

if **T** is *orthogonal*, and satisfy in addition

$$\|\mathbf{w}_i\|^2 = 1, \qquad i = 1, \ldots, n, \tag{9.13}$$

if **T** is *orthonormal*. *(if not normalized, projection is not equal to $z \cdot \mathbf{w}$)*
Referring to Eqs. (9.10) and (9.11), we see that

$$x_i = \mathbf{w}_i \cdot \mathbf{z}, \qquad i = 1, \ldots, n, \tag{9.14}$$

that is, that the *i*th component of a vector $\mathbf{x} \in X$ corresponding to $\mathbf{z} \in Z$ is obtained by projecting **z** on the vector $\mathbf{w}_i \in Z$. If $\mathbf{w}_1, \ldots, \mathbf{w}_n$ are orthonormal, we can interpret them as basis vectors defining a subspace in Z, that is, as defining orthogonal axes of that *n*-dimensional subspace. An orthogonal transformation equally well defines the axes but the row vectors are not of unit length and hence can arbitrarily determine the length of the resulting vector **x**. As we shall see in Section 9.8, Eq. (9.14) defines the vector **x** which approximates the vector **z** in the subspace of lower dimensionality with the least-mean-square error. One could choose an orthonormal transformation rather than an arbitrary matrix in a minimization procedure to prevent shrinking of the space and to insure that the transformation in actuality does result in an *n*-dimensional space. Many measures of separability could easily result in the set of row vectors of a general matrix being linearly dependent—hence, redundant. The extreme case would be if two row vectors were equal. Requiring orthonormality or orthogonality prevents the row vectors from becoming linearly dependent.

How might we insure orthonormality? Suppose $Q(\mathbf{w}_1, \ldots, \mathbf{w}_n)$ is our measure of separability of the sample points in X-space for the transform **T**. If we form *criterion function*

$$\begin{aligned}
G(\mathbf{w}_1, \ldots, \mathbf{w}_n) = Q(\mathbf{w}_1, \ldots, \mathbf{w}_n) &+ \lambda[(\mathbf{w}_1 \cdot \mathbf{w}_2)^2 + (\mathbf{w}_1 \cdot \mathbf{w}_3)^2 + \cdots \\
&+ (\mathbf{w}_1 \cdot \mathbf{w}_n)^2 + (\mathbf{w}_2 \cdot \mathbf{w}_3)^2 + \cdots + (\mathbf{w}_n \cdot \mathbf{w}_{n+1})^2 \\
&+ (\|\mathbf{w}_1\|^2 - 1)^2 + \cdots + (\|\mathbf{w}_n\|^2 - 1)^2],
\end{aligned} \tag{9.15}$$

the expression in brackets will be zero if and only if **T** is orthonormal. Hence, G will tend to be minimized by the orthonormal transformation minimizing Q. The positive constant λ is a scale factor which balances the error in the orthonormality with the deviation from the minimum of Q. If λ is large, the minimization procedure will keep the transformation orthonormal with a high degree of accuracy at the expense of minimizing the separability measure Q. If λ is small, the emphasis will be the opposite. Since in most minimization procedures of high dimensionality one might stop relatively far from the absolute minimum, the matrix which results may not be exactly orthonormal.

orthogonal

there exist, however, procedures, one of which is discussed in Section 9.8.3, by which one can generate, from a set of <u>linearly independent vectors</u>, a set of orthonormal vectors which represent exactly the same subspace. Such a method could be applied to a solution obtained by minimizing an expression such as Eq. (9.15). *See 9.18 too*

Adding the constraint to the criterion function, as in Eq. (9.15), complicates the optimization procedure and creates the problem of choosing and/or adjusting λ. Patrick and Fischer [56] suggest an alternate procedure where the <u>gradient of Q is projected onto a hyperplane which locally satisfies orthonormality.</u> This problem accounts for the popularity of criterion functions which lead to w_1, w_2, ..., w_n being eigenvectors of some matrix; distinct eigenvectors are automatically orthogonal.

If we desire to normalize the space resulting from an orthonormal transformation, we may do so after we derive the solution to the minimization problem in Eq. (9.15). If we do so, the final transformation, referring to Eq. (9.7), is given by

$$\mathbf{x} = \mathbf{B}(\mathbf{Tz}) = (\mathbf{BT})\mathbf{z} = \begin{bmatrix} b_1\mathbf{w}_1 \\ \vdots \\ b_n\mathbf{w}_n \end{bmatrix} \mathbf{z}. \tag{9.16}$$

Thus, normalization following an orthonormal transformation amounts to modifying the lengths of the orthonormal vectors. The equivalent operation can be performed in a single step by finding an optimum orthogonal transformation rather than an orthonormal transformation. To prevent the space from collapsing, a constraint such as Eq. (9.8) must be applied, which in this case translates to

$$\prod_{i=1}^{n} \|\mathbf{w}_i\|^2 = 1. \tag{9.17}$$

unit hypercube

The equivalent of Eq. (9.15) is then

$$G = Q + \lambda[(\mathbf{w}_1 \cdot \mathbf{w}_2)^2 + (\mathbf{w}_1 \cdot \mathbf{w}_3)^2 + \cdots$$

$$+ (\mathbf{w}_{n-1} \cdot \mathbf{w}_n)^2 + (\prod_{i=1}^{n} \|\mathbf{w}_i\|^2 - 1)^2]. \tag{9.18}$$

This is no more complex than Eq. (9.15) and does double duty if eventual normalization is required.

9.3.4 General Nonlinear Transforms

A parameterized nonlinear transform amounts to n parameterized nonlinear functions,

$$x_i = F_i(\mathbf{z}; \boldsymbol{\alpha}_i), \qquad i = 1, \dots, n, \tag{9.19}$$

where

$$\boldsymbol{\alpha}_i = (\alpha_{i1}, \alpha_{i2}, \dots, \alpha_{iN_i}).$$

Perhaps the most obvious class of such functions are multivariate polynomials of a given order or ratios of such polynomials. For example, a general second-order polynomial (without the constant term) can be expressed as†

$$F_i(\mathbf{z}) = \mathbf{z}' \mathbf{A}_i \mathbf{z} + \mathbf{b}_i \cdot \mathbf{z}, \tag{9.20}$$

where $\mathbf{A}_i$ is a symmetric $m \times m$ matrix. The matrix has $m(m + 1)/2$ nonredundant terms, so the number of parameters required to specify a general second-order polynomial for all n features is

$$n[m(m + 1)/2 + m]. \tag{9.21}$$

If $n = 10$ and $m = 20$, there are 2300 parameters to be determined; optimizing a complex nonlinear function with respect to such a large number of parameters verges on infeasibility. We must apparently limit the generality of our choice of $\mathbf{F}$.

We might limit ourselves in an arbitrary manner. For example, the matrices $\mathbf{A}_i$ in (9.20) might be constrained to be diagonal, i.e., all cross-product terms dropped. This gives $2mn$ parameters—400 for $m = 20$, $n = 10$.

One might be less arbitrary by optimizing the measure of quality over a large set of parameters, but employing a modified random search which searched only those vectors $\boldsymbol{\alpha}$ with at least K components zero. This makes the search more efficient and imposes a limit on the resulting number of terms in the polynomial.

A similar objective is achieved by minimizing

$$F(\boldsymbol{\alpha}) = Q(\boldsymbol{\alpha}) - \lambda \sum_{i=1}^{R} f(\alpha_i) \tag{9.22}$$

with

$$f(\alpha_i) = \exp(-\alpha_i{}^2/2\sigma^2). \tag{9.23}$$

The effect is that, if a coefficient approaches zero, there will be a strong tendency to approach it more closely. This algorithm provides a continuous function amenable to a gradient technique.

Another means to the same end ensures that a coefficient remains zero once it approaches it. If $\boldsymbol{\alpha}^{(k)}$ is the kth estimate of the optimum $\boldsymbol{\alpha}$ in a search technique, one simply sets

$$\alpha_j^{(k)} = 0, \qquad k > l,$$

whenever

$$|\alpha_j^{(l)}| \leq K.$$

Thus, as the search proceeds, the number of parameters being searched decreases. On the other hand, unlike the previous algorithm, there is no

---

† Here $\mathbf{z}'$ denotes the transpose of $\mathbf{z}$; $\mathbf{z}'\mathbf{A}\mathbf{z} = \mathbf{z} \cdot \mathbf{A}\mathbf{z}$.

mechanism tending to cause coefficients to become small and the solution can become trapped in the quadrant of the initial guess.

A point which mitigates the difficulty of the minimization process is that a suboptimal solution is often completely satisfactory.

9.3.5 Piecewise Linear Transformations

Piecewise linear transformations have been proposed for feature selection [51].† A piecewise linear transformation is linear over subregions of Z-space with

$$\mathbf{x} = \mathbf{F}(\mathbf{z}) = \begin{cases} \mathbf{T}_1 \mathbf{z} + \mathbf{a}_1, & \mathbf{z} \in Z_1, \\ \vdots \\ \mathbf{T}_R \mathbf{z} + \mathbf{a}_R, & \mathbf{z} \in Z_R, \end{cases} \tag{9.24}$$

where $Z_1, \ldots, Z_R$ are disjoint subregions of Z-space, the union of which covers the region of Z-space where samples may occur, $\mathbf{T}_1, \ldots, \mathbf{T}_R$ are $n \times m$ matrices, and $\mathbf{a}_1, \ldots, \mathbf{a}_R$ are constant vectors.‡ Figure 9.4 illustrates a piece-

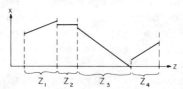

FIG. 9.4 A piecewise linear function.

wise linear transformation for $m = n = 1$. A piecewise linear transformation can approximate any feasible nonlinear transform if enough subregions are used; such transforms are hence very general.

The number of parameters in (9.24) is $nR(m + 1)$; for $n = 10$, $m = 20$, and 10 subregions, there are 2100 parameters. We can reduce the number of parameters by choosing

$$\mathbf{T}_l = \begin{bmatrix} \mathbf{v}_1^{(l)} \\ \vdots \\ \mathbf{v}_n^{(l)} \end{bmatrix} \qquad l = 1, \ldots, R, \tag{9.25}$$

$$\mathbf{v}_i^{(l)} = (v_{i1}^{(l)}, \ldots, v_{im}^{(l)}),$$

and

$$v_{ik}^{(l)} = 0 \qquad \text{for all} \quad i \quad \text{and for} \quad k \in \mathcal{K}_l,$$

---

† E. A. Patrick also suggested the approach in the "Author's Reply" to Meisel [50].

‡ Constant terms, previously omitted, are included here for reasons that the example following will indicate; in Eq. (9.10) or (9.20), they would simply correspond to a translation of *all* sample points.

where $\mathcal{K}_l$ is a subset of $\{1, 2, \ldots, m\}$. For example, let $n = 3$, $m = 5$, and $R = 2$; then if $\mathcal{K}_1 = \{1, 3\}$ and $\mathcal{K}_2 = \{2, 5\}$, the matrices are of the form

$$\mathbf{T}_1 = \begin{bmatrix} 0 & v_{12} & 0 & v_{14} & v_{15} \\ 0 & v_{22} & 0 & v_{24} & v_{25} \\ 0 & v_{32} & 0 & v_{34} & v_{35} \end{bmatrix}, \qquad \mathbf{T}_2 = \begin{bmatrix} v_{11} & 0 & v_{13} & v_{14} & 0 \\ v_{21} & 0 & v_{23} & v_{24} & 0 \\ v_{31} & 0 & v_{33} & v_{34} & 0 \end{bmatrix}. \quad (9.26)$$

[One possible restriction on Eq. (9.25) is that a given integer k cannot be in all $\mathcal{K}_i$; if so, z_k would never be used.] The number of parameters can be as few as nm—the same as a single linear transform. The form of the row vectors is such that, in each subregion, only the projection of the sample points in a lower-dimensional subspace is used. In the preceding example z_1 and z_3 are not used in subregion Z_1, and z_2 and z_5 are not used in subregion Z_2.

An example should indicate the power of this class of piecewise linear transforms. Suppose Z-space is two-dimensional and samples of two classes are distributed as in Fig. 9.5a. We wish to transform into a one-dimensional

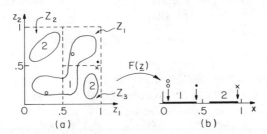

FIG. 9.5 The effect of a piecewise linear transformation. Underscored symbol is a vector.

pattern space. As indicated in Fig. 9.5a, we choose (by inspection) the subregions

$$\begin{aligned} Z_1 &= \{\mathbf{z} \,|\, \tfrac{1}{2} \le z_1 \le 1, \quad \tfrac{1}{2} \le z_2 \le 1\} \\ Z_2 &= \{\mathbf{z} \,|\, 0 \le z_1 < \tfrac{1}{2}\} \\ Z_3 &= \{\mathbf{z} \,|\, \tfrac{1}{2} \le z_1 \le 1, \quad 0 \le z_2 < \tfrac{1}{2}\}. \end{aligned} \quad (9.27)$$

The reader may verify that the transformation given by

$$x = \begin{cases} z_1 - \tfrac{1}{2}, & \mathbf{z} \in Z_1 \\ z_2, & \mathbf{z} \in Z_2 \\ 2z_1 - 1, & \mathbf{z} \in Z_3 \end{cases} \quad (9.28)$$

maps all the points of class 1 into the interval $[0, \tfrac{1}{2}]$ and of class 2 into $[\tfrac{1}{2}, 1]$, as indicated in Fig. 9.5b, making them easily separable in X. Here $\mathcal{K}_1 = \{2\}$, $\mathcal{K}_2 = \{1\}$, and $\mathcal{K}_3 = \{2\}$. Only the projections on the z_1 axis of points in Z_1, on the z_2 axis of points in Z_2, and on the z_3 axis of points in Z_3 are transformed into X. Our success is due to the fact that the classes are separable in these projections. Note that:

(1) the transformation is not one-to-one; both open circles in the figure are mapped into the same point; and

(2) the transformation is discontinuous; the small dot and cross, close in Z, are widely separated in X.

The first characteristic is advantageous; it allows the modality of a distribution to be reduced. A complex distribution can be considerably simplified.

The second characteristic, discontinuity, can be advantageous in reducing dimensionality, e.g., unfolding a sphere or a "doughnut" onto a plane (Section 9.6). Discontinuous transforms, however, make the careful choice of boundaries between regions $Z_1, Z_2, \ldots, Z_R$ critical and allow the transformation on each subregion to be largely independent of samples in the other subregions, in some cases not utilizing all the information available. The problem becomes more difficult analytically when we require that the piecewise linear transforms be continuous, i.e., that

$$\mathbf{T}_i \mathbf{z} + \mathbf{a}_i = \mathbf{T}_j \mathbf{z} + \mathbf{a}_j \tag{9.29}$$

for all points $\mathbf{z}$ on the boundary between Z_i and Z_j, but computational requirements may be reduced because the number of free parameters in the specification of Eq. (9.24) are reduced. Appendix B discusses the use of continuous piecewise linear transformations.

The transformation in Eq. (9.25) is powerful, yet efficient, if the subregions and zero columns are appropriately chosen. Let us discuss algorithms for choosing both.

A Direct Algorithm

One class of algorithms is described by the following procedures:

A. Choose the subregions by a cluster analysis technique which partitions the measurement space such that each partition contains a natural "cluster" of sample points. Such methods define the regions $Z_1, \ldots, Z_R$ such that the boundaries tend to occur in areas of the space which are sparse in samples, as in Fig. 9.6.

B. For each subregion, find a subset of features (usually different in each subregion) such that the samples from that subregion can be adequately separated by class when projected onto the subspace so defined. (In Fig. 9.5, the samples in each subregion are completely separable when projected onto the appropriate axis.) This may be accomplished by ranking the coordinates $z_1, z_2, \ldots, z_m$ using the samples in a given subregion and one of the feature

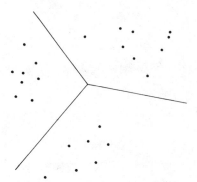

FIG. 9.6   Using clusters to define subregions.

ranking algorithms to be proposed in Section 9.9. For each subregion, the columns in the matrix of Eq. (9.25) which correspond to the coordinates ranked lowest are set to zero.

C.   The nonzero parameters are chosen by an appropriate search technique to optimize the chosen measure of quality.

None of these steps, except perhaps the last, is difficult computationally; the last is of course simplified by the smaller number of nonzero parameters and the possible acceptability of a local optimum. It is worth emphasizing the fact that the number of parameters can be as few as the number required for a single linear transformation.

An Indirect Algorithm

Alternatively, the subregions $Z_1, Z_2, \ldots, Z_R$ can be parametrized and the optimum transformation found with respect to these parameters as well, eliminating steps A and B, but increasing the number of parameters. The most obvious way of describing the subregions is by linear hyperplanes with undetermined coefficients; restricting those hyperplanes to be perpendicular to the axes reduces the number of parameters to one per hyperplane. Any of the methods of describing subregions suggested in Section 8.2 however, could be employed.

An example will serve to illustrate the indirect approach. Suppose we have samples of two classes in a two-dimensional Z-space, as illustrated in Fig. 9.7. We will allow two regions, Z_1 and Z_2, separated by a hyperplane (a line, in this case):

$$z_1 + w_1 z_2 + w_2 = 0. \tag{9.30}$$

The transformation sought is of the form

$$
\begin{aligned}
x &= F(\mathbf{z}; w_1, w_2; a_1, a_2, a_3; b_1, b_2, b_3) \\
&= \begin{cases} a_1 z_1 + a_2 z_2 + a_3 & \text{if} \quad z_1 + w_1 z_2 \geq 0 \\ b_1 z_1 + b_2 z_2 + b_3 & \text{if not,} \end{cases}
\end{aligned} \tag{9.31}
$$

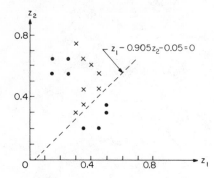

FIG. 9.7 Two subregions defined by a single hyperplane.

which will transform the two-dimensional space into a one-dimensional space. We choose to minimize the measure of quality given in Section 9.4, the sum of intraset distances divided by the interset distance. Using an adaptive random search technique, locally optimum values of the parameters can be determined in 20 iterations: $w_1 = -0.905$, $w_2 = -0.05$, $a_1 = 8.13$, $a_2 = 7.43$, $a_3 = 1.601$, $b_1 = -0.613$, $b_2 = -0.0207$, $b_3 = 1.197$. The hyperplane defining the subregions is plotted in Fig. 9.7; the one-dimensional samples obtained from transforming the samples in Fig. 9.7 are illustrated in Fig. 9.8. The two

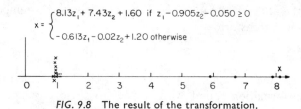

$$x = \begin{cases} 8.13z_1 + 7.43z_2 + 1.60 & \text{if } z_1 - 0.905z_2 - 0.050 \geq 0 \\ -0.613z_1 - 0.02z_2 + 1.20 & \text{otherwise} \end{cases}$$

FIG. 9.8 The result of the transformation.

classes are transformed into linearly separable distributions.

OTHER EFFICIENT NONLINEAR TRANSFORMATIONS

An efficient parametrized transformation is one which is specified by a low number of parameters relative to its generality. Piecewise linear multivariate functions in general, and the proposed subclass of piecewise linear functions in particular, are an important class. If continuous, they form a subclass of the general class of multivariate splines. The algorithms suggested for piecewise linear transformations are applicable directly to piecewise rth-order multivariate polynomials if the transformation suggested in Section 4.10 is performed first; the problem is then piecewise linear.

Another more difficult class of efficient transformations is the class of composed functions: $F(\mathbf{x}) = G[H(\mathbf{x})]$. A low-parameter transformation of the form $F(\mathbf{x}; \boldsymbol{\alpha}) = \alpha_1[x_1 + \alpha_2(x_2 + \alpha_3 x_3)^4]^5$ would certainly be preferable to a general twentieth-order polynomial in three variables (with 1771 coefficients) if the former were sufficiently accurate.

Parametrized composed functions and continuous piecewise linear functions are discussed in Appendix B.

9.4 MEASURES OF QUALITY: INTERSET AND INTRASET DISTANCES

Given two pattern classes, we would like to maximize the distance between transformed samples of different classes (the *interset distance*) while minimizing the internal scatter of each transformed class (the *intraset distance*) (see Fig. 9.9). The distance between two sets is, of course, an ill-defined concept.

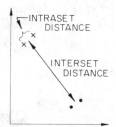

FIG. 9.9 Intraset versus interset distances.

One measure of the distance between two sets is the distance between their means; this is reasonable only for unimodal distributions. A measure which is less oriented toward unimodal distributions is the average squared distance between points of separate classes. A measure of the internal scatter of the samples is the average squared distance between points in each cluster summed over the clusters. Define the interset distance

$$S = \frac{1}{M_1 M_2} \sum_{q=1}^{M_1} \sum_{p=1}^{M_2} d^2[\mathbf{F}(\mathbf{y}_q^{(1)}), \mathbf{F}(\mathbf{y}_p^{(2)})], \qquad (9.32)$$

and the intraset distance

$$R_i = \frac{2}{M_i(M_i - 1)} \sum_{j=1}^{M_i} \sum_{k>j}^{M_i} d^2[\mathbf{F}(\mathbf{y}_j^{(i)}), \mathbf{F}(\mathbf{y}_k^{(i)})] \qquad (9.33)$$

for class i, with $d(\mathbf{x}, \mathbf{y})$ a distance measure. Then we can minimize

$$Q(\boldsymbol{\alpha}) = (R_1 + R_2)/S, \qquad (9.34)$$

or, similarly, maximize S subject to $S + R_1 + R_2 = $ constant.

With conventional distance measures, Eq. (9.34) is to some extent oriented toward the formation of each class into unimodal distributions, i.e., those where the samples of each class form a single cluster. If a class is multimodal or consists of a sheet of sample points, minimizing Eq. (9.34) does not necessarily achieve the objective of separating the classes. In Fig. 1.7, the average distance between all pairs of samples in the same class does not indicate the cohesiveness of the sheet or clusters constituting that class; pairs of points in different clusters of the same class or at different ends of a long sheet dominate the average squared intersample distance. Similarly, the interclass distance is distorted; the distances between the most separated clusters of different classes dominate rather than the distances between adjacent clusters of different classes. Minimizing (9.34) with respect to a limited class of transformations might *degrade* the separability of certain distributions.

We can generalize by defining a *localized distance*:

$$d^*(\mathbf{x}, \mathbf{y}) = \begin{cases} d(\mathbf{x}, \mathbf{y}) & \text{for} \quad d(\mathbf{x}, \mathbf{y}) \le D \\ D & \text{for} \quad d(\mathbf{x}, \mathbf{y}) > D \end{cases} \qquad (9.35)$$

(see Fig. 9.10a). The effect of using this distance in Eqs. (9.32) and (9.33) is

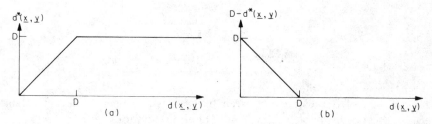

FIG. 9.10 Localized distance: (a) a localized distance; (b) another representation. Underscored symbols are vectors.

to consider only interset and intraset distances which are less than D. Bringing points of the same class closer together will not change Q so defined as long as those points are more than a distance D apart; separating points of different classes more than D has no effect on Q. Another way of noting this effect is to think of maximizing $D - d^*(\mathbf{x}, \mathbf{y})$ rather than minimizing $d^*(\mathbf{x}, \mathbf{y})$, and vice versa. Figure 9.10b indicates that, in this case, samples more than D apart contribute nothing to the sum.

Other choices of d^* can be made, e.g.,

$$d^*(\mathbf{x}, \mathbf{y}) = 1 - \exp\left[-\frac{1}{2D^2} d^2(\mathbf{x}, \mathbf{y})\right], \qquad (9.36)$$

a continuously differentiable function of $d(\mathbf{x}, \mathbf{y})$, illustrated in Fig. 9.11. (In this case, it is convenient to replace $d^2(\mathbf{x}, \mathbf{y})$ in Q with $d^*(\mathbf{x}, \mathbf{y})$, i.e., (to drop

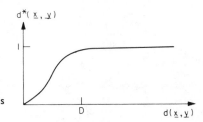

FIG. 9.11   A localized distance with a continuous derivative. Underscored symbols are vectors.

the square.) The next section will lead more formally to the concept of a localized distance.

If D in (9.35) or (9.36) is fixed, that fact may favor an expansion or shrinking of the space; to reduce this problem, D may be made proportional to the sum of component variances throughout the optimization (at a computational cost). We can also directly define

$$d^2(\mathbf{x}, \mathbf{y}) = \sum_{i=1}^{n} \left(\frac{x_i - y_i}{\sigma_i} \right)^2 \tag{9.37}$$

and derive σ_i from the distribution of transformed samples (so that it becomes a function of the parameters of the transformation).

A specialized solution is available to the problem of finding the linear transformation maximizing S subject to $S + R_1 + R_2 = \text{constant}$ [65] [see Eqs. (9.32) and (9.33)]. We pose the problem in terms of a linear transform of the form

$$\mathbf{x} = \mathbf{Wz}, \qquad \mathbf{W} = \begin{bmatrix} \mathbf{w}_1 \\ \vdots \\ \mathbf{w}_n \end{bmatrix}.$$

Then we wish to maximize

$$S = \frac{1}{M_1 M_2} \sum_{q=1}^{M_1} \sum_{p=1}^{M_2} \| \mathbf{W}\mathbf{y}_q^{(1)} - \mathbf{W}\mathbf{y}_p^{(2)} \|^2 \tag{9.38a}$$

such that

$$F = \frac{2}{M(M-1)} \sum_{q=1}^{M} \sum_{p=1}^{M} \| \mathbf{W}\mathbf{y}_q - \mathbf{W}\mathbf{y}_p \|^2 - K = 0, \tag{9.38b}$$

where the last sum is over the samples of both classes. More explicitly,

$$S = \frac{1}{M_1 M_2} \sum_{q=1}^{M_1} \sum_{p=1}^{M_2} \sum_{i=1}^{n} \left[\sum_{j=1}^{m} w_{ij}(y_{qj}^{(1)} - y_{pj}^{(2)}) \right]^2$$

$$F = \frac{2}{M(M-1)} \sum_{q=1}^{M} \sum_{p=1}^{M} \sum_{i=1}^{n} \left[\sum_{j=1}^{m} w_{ij}(y_{qj} - y_{pj}) \right]^2 - K = 0,$$

or

$$S = \sum_{i=1}^{n} \sum_{j=1}^{m} \sum_{k=1}^{m} w_{ij} w_{ik} b_{jk}, \tag{9.39a}$$

where

$$b_{jk} = \frac{1}{M_1 M_2} \sum_{q=1}^{M_1} \sum_{p=1}^{M_2} (y_{qj}^{(1)} - y_{pj}^{(2)})(y_{qk}^{(1)} - y_{pk}^{(2)})$$

and

$$F = \sum_{i=1}^{n} \sum_{j=1}^{m} \sum_{k=1}^{m} w_{ij} w_{ik} c_{jk} - K = 0 \tag{9.39b}$$

where

$$c_{jk} = \frac{2}{M(M-1)} \sum_{q=1}^{M} \sum_{p=1}^{M} (y_{qj} - y_{pj})(y_{qk} - y_{pk}).$$

We can solve this problem using the method of Lagrange multipliers; that is, we maximize

$$G = S - \lambda F$$

and find the value of λ satisfying the constraint (9.39b). Setting

$$\partial G / \partial w_{ij} = 0,$$

we get

$$\sum_{k=1}^{m} w_{ik}(b_{jk} - \lambda c_{jk}) = 0, \qquad i, j = 1, \ldots, n. \tag{9.40}$$

Defining matrices

$$\mathbf{B} = (b_{jk}), \qquad \mathbf{C} = (c_{jk}),$$

Eq. (9.40) may be expressed as

$$\mathbf{w}_1(\mathbf{B} - \lambda \mathbf{C}) = 0, \tag{9.41}$$
$$\vdots$$
$$\mathbf{w}_n(\mathbf{B} - \lambda \mathbf{C}) = 0.$$

Since $\mathbf{C}$ is positive definite, $\mathbf{C}^{-1}$ exists, so we may write (9.41) as

$$\mathbf{w}_i(\mathbf{BC}^{-1} - \lambda \mathbf{I}) = 0, \qquad i = 1, \ldots, n, \tag{9.42}$$

i.e.,

$$\mathbf{w}_i \mathbf{BC}^{-1} = \lambda \mathbf{w}_i; \qquad i = 1, \ldots, n.$$

Hence, the λ are the eigenvalues of $\mathbf{BC}^{-1}$ and the $\mathbf{w}_i$ are the eigenvectors. It can be shown that for the optimal $\mathbf{w}_i$ and λ_i

$$Q_{\text{opt}} = \sum_{i=1}^{m} \lambda_i \mathbf{w}_i \mathbf{C} \mathbf{w}_i', \qquad (9.43)$$

which is maximum if all λ_i equal the maximum eigenvalue and all $\mathbf{w}_i$ equal the corresponding eigenvector, a transformation into a one-dimensional space. This optimum one-dimensional line can define a discriminant function itself; this approach has been called *discriminant analysis*. An *n*-dimensional space can be formed from the *n* (orthogonal) eigenvectors corresponding to the largest *n* eigenvalues. (It should be noted that determining the eigenvectors and eigenvalues of a large matrix is a difficult computation.)

We have discussed in detail a special solution. The value of Q can certainly be minimized by search methods with respect to any parameterized transformation, including linear transformations; the space must be prevented from collapsing by imposing constraints such as orthogonality or by using a form of criterion function such as (9.34) which is invariant to pure shrinkage of the space.

A very similar measure of quality can be minimized to give the *Fisher discriminant* [21]. This particular measure was the distance of samples of a given class to their mean as an intraset distance, and the distance between the means of two classes as interset distance. The optimum is always a transformation to a one-dimensional space; hence, the Fisher discriminant defines a direction of maximum separation and can be used as a pattern classification algorithm. See reference [18] of Chapter VII for a summary of the equations and an extension to the *N*-class problem.

9.5   MEASURES OF QUALITY UTILIZING PROBABILITY ESTIMATES

9.5.1   Some Measures of Separability

Several measures of separability are stated in terms of the *a priori* class probabilities p_i and the conditional probability densities $p_i(\mathbf{x})$ of the *transformed* samples; we shall list them prior to discussing their meaning. One such is the divergence [36, 40, 41]:

$$\text{max:} \quad Q_1 = \int_X [p_1 p_1(\mathbf{x}) - p_2 p_2(\mathbf{x})] \log\left[\frac{p_1 p_1(\mathbf{x})}{p_2 p_2(\mathbf{x})}\right] dX, \qquad (9.44)$$

where $\mathbf{x} = \mathbf{F}(\mathbf{z}; \boldsymbol{\alpha})$. Another is the Bhattacharyya distance [8, 36]:

$$\text{min:} \quad Q_2 = -\log \int_X [p_1(\mathbf{x}) p_2(\mathbf{x})]^{1/2} dX. \qquad (9.45)$$

Tou and Heydorn [71, 72] suggest similar measures. Butler [11] proposes a measure of mutual information oriented toward feature ranking. Another measure has been proposed by Patrick and Fischer [56]:

$$\text{max:} \quad Q_3^2 = \int [p_1 p_1(\mathbf{x}) - p_2 p_2(\mathbf{x})]^2 \, dX. \tag{9.46}$$

Meisel [50] proposed a modification of (9.46) which can be advantageous in higher dimensions:

$$\text{max:} \quad Q_4^2 = \frac{p_1}{M_1} \sum_{k=1}^{M_1} \{p_1 p_1[\mathbf{F}(\mathbf{y}_k^{(1)})] - p_2 p_2[\mathbf{F}(\mathbf{y}_k^{(1)})]\}^2$$
$$+ \frac{p_2}{M_2} \sum_{k=1}^{M_2} \{p_1 p_1[\mathbf{F}(\mathbf{y}_k^{(2)})] - p_2 p_2[\mathbf{F}(\mathbf{y}_k^{(2)})]\}^2. \tag{9.47}$$

This last expression is an estimate of the expectation with respect to $\mathbf{x}$ of $[p_1 p_1(\mathbf{x}) - p_2 p_2(\mathbf{x})]^2$. The relation between Q_3 and Q_4 is similar to that between the integral-square and mean-square criteria discussed in Chapter V. The measure Q_3 may calculate the error over a large portion of the space where the probability densities are almost zero; Q_4 measures the same error only at the sample points.

More direct, but discontinuous, is an estimate of the misclassification rate of the Bayes optimal decision rule:

$$\text{min:} \quad Q_5 = \frac{p_1}{M_1} \sum_{i=1}^{M_1} \mu\{p_2 p_2[\mathbf{F}(\mathbf{y}_i^{(1)})] - p_1 p_1[\mathbf{F}(\mathbf{y}_i^{(1)})]\}$$
$$+ \frac{p_2}{M_2} \sum_{i=1}^{M_2} \mu\{p_1 p_1[\mathbf{F}(\mathbf{y}_i^{(2)})] - p_2 p_2[\mathbf{F}(\mathbf{y}_i^{(2)})]\}, \tag{9.48}$$

where

$$\mu(x) = \begin{cases} 1, & x \geq 0, \\ 0, & x < 0. \end{cases}$$

Three measures which are stated directly in terms of the *N*-class case are

$$\text{max:} \quad Q_6 = \int_X \max_{1 \leq j \leq N} \{p_j p_j(\mathbf{x})\} \, dX, \tag{9.49}$$

$$\text{min:} \quad Q_7 = \int_X p^2(\mathbf{x}) \, dX - \int_X \left[\sum_{i=1}^{N} [p_i p_i(\mathbf{x})]^2 \right] dX, \tag{9.50}$$

and

$$\text{min:} \quad Q_8 = \frac{1}{M} \sum_{j=1}^{M} \left[p^2(\mathbf{F}(\mathbf{y}_j)) - \sum_{i=1}^{N} [p_i p_i(\mathbf{F}(\mathbf{y}_j))]^2 \right], \tag{9.51}$$

where

$$p(\mathbf{x}) = \sum_{i=1}^{N} p_i p_i(\mathbf{x}). \tag{9.52}$$

(Q_7 and Q_8 are related in the same manner as Q_3 and Q_4; Q_8 is usually preferable for a higher dimensional X-space.)

Measures stated for the two-class case can be converted to the N-class case by optimizing the sum of all pairwise measures of quality or by maximizing the minimum of pairwise measures of quality.

All of the criterion functions listed measure explicitly or implicitly the overlap of the class-conditional probability densities of the *transformed* samples. Figure 9.12 illustrates two possible one-dimensional distributions

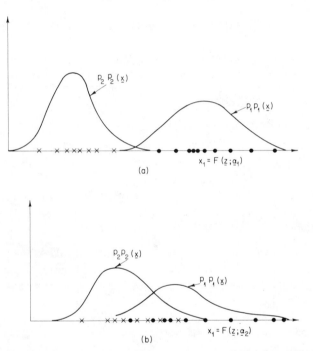

FIG. 9.12 Measuring overlap of the class probability densities: (a) small overlap, easy separability; (b) large overlap, poor separability. Underscored symbols are vectors.

of samples resulting from two transformations applied to the same distribution in Z-space. The transformation which results in the least overlap of probability densities will yield the space with the least expected classification error with respect to the Bayes optimal decision rule. All of the measures are optimized when there is no overlap and take their worst value when the class densities are identical (maximum overlap). For example, if the class densities do not overlap, then $p_i(\mathbf{x})p_j(\mathbf{x}) = 0$ for $i \neq j$ and

$$\max_{1 < j < N} \{p_j p_j(\mathbf{x})\} = \sum_{j=1}^{N} p_j p_j(\mathbf{x}).$$ (9.53)

Then

$$Q_6 = \sum_{i=1}^{N} p_j \int_X p_j(\mathbf{x}) \, dX = \sum_{i=1}^{N} p_j = 1. \tag{9.54}$$

If $p_j(\mathbf{x}) = p_i(\mathbf{x})$ for all i, j, then

$$\max_{i \leq j \leq N} \{p_j p_j(\mathbf{x})\} = p_j(\mathbf{x}) \max_{i \leq j \leq N} \{p_j\} \tag{9.55}$$

and

$$Q_6 = \int_X p_j(\mathbf{x}) \, dx \cdot \max_{i \leq j \leq N} \{p_j\} = \max_{i \leq j \leq N} \{p_j\}. \tag{9.56}$$

These are upper and lower bounds on Q_6; the nearer Q_6 to 1, the better. The measures Q_7 and Q_8 are easily interpreted by noting that

$$p^2(\mathbf{x}) - \sum_{i=1}^{N} [p_i p_i(\mathbf{x})]^2 = \sum_{i=1}^{N} \sum_{\substack{j=1 \\ i \neq j}}^{N} p_i p_j p_i(\mathbf{x}) p_j(\mathbf{x}), \tag{9.57}$$

correlation

which clearly measures the overlap when integrated. (This is analogous to the criterion proposed by the author for clustering in Chapter VIII.) The optimum values of Q_7 and Q_8 are zero.

Given that the above measures (and others!) all aim at measuring the overlap of class densities, there are still characteristics we can use in choosing between them:

(1) *Theoretical differences:* There are theoretical differences between some of the measures, relating them to one another and to the actual probability of error defined by the densities. Most such results are based upon the assumption that the class densities are Gaussian; in such cases, measures such as the divergence and Bhattacharyya distance [Eqs. (9.44) and (9.45)] can be expressed efficiently in terms of the means and covariance matrices of the Gaussian distributions.

(2) *Effect of the "curse of dimensionality":* In higher dimensions, criterion functions which measure overlap where the samples occur avoid the hidden difficulties of minimizing over large regions of the space where the probability densities are very small. The equations for Q_4, Q_5, and Q_8 are expressed directly in this form; Q_1 can be approximated as a summation over the samples by expressing the expectation as an average over those samples.

(3) *Computational considerations:* If the densities are not of a known or sufficiently simple form, the integration required in some measures may have to be computed numerically—usually an infeasible procedure in spaces of more than a few dimensions. This problem can be overcome in several ways: (a) by avoiding it, as do Q_4, Q_5, and Q_8, and potentially Q_1; (b) by

using a potential function estimate of the densities and converting the integral of a sum to the sum of integrals of easily integrable potential functions, as we will illustrate; and (c) by being clever about the numerical integration procedure (e.g., see Butler [11]). Once the problem of feasibility is solved, measures can be compared directly in terms of operation count. If the general N-class case must be considered, Q_6, Q_7, and Q_8 start out with a considerable advantage over two-class measures which must be summed over all pairs of classes.

In the "worst case," where the densities are nonzero in a small portion of the space X, where the number of classes is fairly large, and where the class probabilities are not Gaussian, the reader will probably find Q_8 [Eq. (9.51)] as good a measure as any. Equation (9.48), Q_5, has the significant advantage that its value is the probability of misclassification and hence has a direct interpretation; its disadvantage is discontinuity.

9.5.2 Estimating the Probability Density

All of these measures depend on an estimate of the probability densities. This can always be accomplished nonparametrically by potential function methods (Chapter VI);

$$p_i(\mathbf{x}) = \frac{1}{M_i} \sum_{j=1}^{M_i} \gamma[\mathbf{x}, \mathbf{F}(\mathbf{y}_j^{(i)})].\tag{9.58}$$

This estimate inserted in any of the measures discussed in the previous subsection provides a measure of the quality of the distribution of labeled samples in the transformed space. The result is, however, dependent upon the quality of the estimate of Eq. (9.58). The potential functions must be of appropriate shape and size if $p_i(\mathbf{x})$ is to be accurately reconstructed; Chapter VI contained a proof of the fact that one can always make the potential functions $\gamma(\mathbf{x}, \mathbf{y})$ sufficiently peaked to assure arbitrarily small overlap for *any* sample distribution. In pattern classification, the problem is solved by a thoughtful one-time choice of shape and size parameters; in feature selection, the transformed samples move with varying parameters α in the transformation $F(\mathbf{z}; \alpha)$, and we must insure that the size and shape parameters will be appropriate for any allowable variation. For example, if the potential function were fixed, multiplying $F(\mathbf{z}; \alpha)$ by a large constant would effectively shrink the potential function and improve any measure of overlap. We can attack this problem by (1) imposing constraints on the transformation which prevent shrinkage, or (2) by structuring the size and shape parameters so that they vary with the transformation and remain appropriate.

The first approach has the disadvantage of not allowing shrinkage of the axes relative to one another when that is a meaningful aspect of the feature selection. A constraint applicable to general nonlinear transformations is

$$\sigma_i^2(X) = 1; \qquad i = 1, \ldots, n, \tag{9.59}$$

where $\sigma_i^2(X)$ is the variance of the ith component of the transformed samples, independent of class; this constraint yields a "squared-up" set of samples in X-space. A familiar constraint for linear transformations is orthonormality (Section 9.3.3); this will prevent shrinkage.

9.5.3 A Particular Case and Its Relation to Localized Distance

Patrick and Fischer [56] show a revealing relationship between their measure [Eq. (9.46)] and localized distance. If the $p_i(\mathbf{x})$ are estimated in Q_3, using the potential function method, we have

$$Q_3^2 = \int_X \left\{ \frac{p_1}{M_1} \sum_{j=1}^{M_1} \gamma[\mathbf{x}, \mathbf{F}(\mathbf{y}_i^{(1)})] - \frac{p_2}{M_2} \sum_{j=1}^{M_2} \gamma[\mathbf{x}, \mathbf{F}(\mathbf{y}_i^{(2)})] \right\}^2 dX. \tag{9.60}$$

Expanding the integrand,

$$Q_3^2 = \int_X \sum_{r=1}^{2} \sum_{s=1}^{2} \sum_{j=1}^{M_1} \sum_{k=1}^{M_2} \xi_{rs} (p_r p_s / M_r M_s) \gamma[\mathbf{x}, F(\mathbf{y}_j^{(r)})]\gamma[\mathbf{x}, F(\mathbf{y}_k^{(s)})] dX, \tag{9.61}$$

where

$$\xi_{rs} = \begin{cases} 1, & r = s, \\ -1, & r \neq s. \end{cases}$$

We can then write (9.61) in the form

$$Q_3^2 = \frac{p_1^2}{M_1^2} \sum_{j=1}^{M_1} \sum_{k=1}^{M_1} C_{jk}^{1,1} + \frac{p_2^2}{M_2^2} \sum_{j=1}^{M_2} \sum_{k=1}^{M_2} C_{jk}^{2,2} \tag{9.62}$$

$$- \frac{2p_1 p_2}{M_1 M_2} \sum_{j=1}^{M_1} \sum_{k=1}^{M_2} C_{jk}^{1,2},$$

where

$$C_{jk}^{rs} = \int_X \gamma[\mathbf{x}, F(\mathbf{y}_j^{(r)})] \cdot \gamma[\mathbf{x}, F(\mathbf{y}_k^{(s)})] dX. \tag{9.63}$$

If C_{jk}^{rs} could be interpreted as an inverse distance between $\mathbf{y}_j^{(r)}$ and $\mathbf{y}_k^{(s)}$ [i.e., if C_{jk}^{rs} got larger as $d(\mathbf{y}_j^{(r)}, \mathbf{y}_k^{(s)})$ got smaller], then Eq. (9.62) could be interpreted as minimizing intraset distances while maximizing interset distance.

Referring to the one-dimensional case illustrated in Fig. 9.13, we see

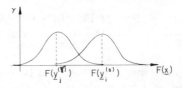

FIG. 9.13 Equivalence to localized distance. Underscored symbols are vectors.

(9.63) can indeed be interpreted as an inverse distance. The integral of the product of the potential functions does measure inversely a non-Euclidean distance between $F(\mathbf{y}_j^{(r)})$ and $F(\mathbf{y}_i^{(s)})$. If those points are far apart, C_{ij}^{rs} is very small, since the product of the two functions is almost zero everywhere; if the two points coincide, C_{ij}^{rs} is maximum. This function is a *localized* distance measure, since it changes very little after the points have moved sufficiently far apart.

Particularizing, let

$$\gamma(\mathbf{x}, \mathbf{y}) = \left(\frac{1}{\sqrt{2\pi}\sigma}\right)^n \exp\left(-\frac{1}{2\sigma^2}\|\mathbf{x} - \mathbf{y}\|^2\right). \qquad (9.64)$$

Then (see [56]),

$$C_{jk}^{rs} = \frac{p_r p_s}{M_r M_s}\left(\frac{1}{\sqrt{2\pi}\sigma}\right)^n \exp\left(-\frac{1}{4\sigma^2}\|F(\mathbf{y}_j^{(r)}) - F(\mathbf{y}_k^{(s)})\|^2\right). \qquad (9.65)$$

It is clear that this is very close to the localized distance of Eq. (9.37) and Fig. (9.11).

The criterion of Eq. (9.47) can also be written as Eq. (9.62) with [50]

$$C_{jk}^{rs} = \frac{p_1}{M_1}\sum_{l=1}^{M_1}\gamma[F(\mathbf{y}_l^{(1)}), F(\mathbf{y}_j^{(r)})]\gamma[F(\mathbf{y}_l^{(1)}), F(\mathbf{y}_k^{(s)})]$$

$$+ \frac{p_2}{M_2}\sum_{l=1}^{M_2}\gamma[F(\mathbf{y}_l^{(2)}), F(\mathbf{y}_j^{(r)})]\gamma[F(\mathbf{y}_l^{(2)}), F(\mathbf{y}_k^{(s)})]. \qquad (9.66)$$

Let us consider computational tradeoffs among the many alternate forms of similar criterion functions. If $\gamma(\mathbf{x}, \mathbf{y})$ is chosen as in (9.64), calculating Q_3 in the form (9.62) requires

$$M_1{}^2 + M_2{}^2 + M_1 M_2 = (M_1 + M_2)^2 - M_1 M_2 \qquad (9.67)$$

calculations of the exponential, and the form (9.66) requires $2(M_1 + M_2)$ times that amount in calculations of $\gamma(\mathbf{x}, \mathbf{y})$. But if Q_4 is calculated using the form (9.47) directly, only $(M_1 + M_2)^2$ calculations of γ are necessary, $M_1 M_2$ more than calculations of the exponential; since γ can be considerably more efficiently defined in the latter case (the tails need not be accurate), one pays little, if any, price for the advantages of mean-square error.

9.6 MEASURES OF QUALITY: THE PRESERVATION
OF STRUCTURE

The measures that have been discussed to this point have been aimed at finding a transformation which tended to minimize the classification error; we used class separation as the pertinent objective. This resulted in preserving only information relevant to separating the classes.

Another approach is to attempt to preserve as much structural information as possible while transforming to a lower-dimensional space. For example, if a set of 100-dimensional samples all lay on a two-dimensional hyperplane in 100-space, they could be represented exactly in a two-dimensional space; that is, all distances between sample points would remain unchanged. One might hence like to transform into lower-dimensional spaces so that inter-sample distances are preserved (or are proportional).

Let $y_1, \ldots, y_M$ be a set of samples in Z-space. Then

$$Q_9 = \frac{2}{M(M-1)} \sum_{i<j} \{d_n[F(y_i), F(y_j)] - d_m(y_i, y_j)\}^2, \tag{9.68}$$

where d_n and d_m are distance measures defined in n- and m-space, respectively, measures the mean-square error in corresponding distances [38, 64].

Often to "unfold" a set of sample points lying on a curved surface as in the projection of a globe onto a map, the larger distances in either the given space or transformed space must be ignored. A modification which accomplishes this objective by placing a greater weight on the smallest distances is

$$Q_9' = \frac{2}{M(M-1)} \sum_{i<j} [d_n(i, j) - d_m(i, j)]^2 f[d_n(i, j)], \tag{9.69}$$

where we have adopted an obvious shorthand, and

$$f(d) = \exp\left(-\frac{1}{2\sigma^2} d^2\right) \tag{9.70}$$

or a similar monotonically decreasing function for positive arguments.†

Another function which has been proposed as a measure of the preservation of local distances is [67]

$$Q_{10} = \frac{\sum_{i \neq j} [d_m^2(i, j)/d_n^4(i, j)]}{[\sum_{i \neq j} [1/d_n^2(i, j)]]^2}. \tag{9.71}$$

† We may substitute $f(d_m)$ for $f(d_n)$ with little conceptual change.

The denominator is a normalizing factor necessary to make Q_{10} invariant with shrinkage of X. The numerator can be written as

$$\sum_{i \neq j} \left(\frac{d_m(i,j)}{d_n(i,j)} \right)^2 \frac{1}{d_n{}^2(i,j)}.$$

Terms of the sum corresponding to large distances in X-space have little effect on the sum due to the weighting factor $1/d_n{}^2$. Since the overall expression is invariant to shrinkage of X-space, the optimum is achieved when all the small distances in X-space are proportional to all the small distances in Z-space.

This procedure, also referred to as *nonlinear mapping* and *multidimensional scaling*, has been investigated by several researchers [7, 12, 38, 64, 66, 67]. It provides an extremely powerful means of viewing the relationship among high-dimensional samples in a two-dimensional space. For this purpose, no transformation $\mathbf{F}(\mathbf{z}; \boldsymbol{\alpha})$ need be explicitly defined; the components of the samples in X-space may be adjusted to minimize a measure of preservation of structure, and the result will be a distribution of samples in the lower-dimensional space which exhibit the same local distance relationships as the original samples (if the minimum value of Q is small). This latter procedure does *not* yield any obvious means to transform a new sample into X-space and hence is not easily adapted to pattern classification. It further requires that Q be minimized with respect to nM parameters (n the dimension of X-space and M the number of samples), which can limit the number of samples to which this algorithm is applied. If Q is minimized with respect to a parameterized transformation (e.g., piecewise linear), a well-defined transformation results and the number of parameters is not directly related to the number of samples. On the other hand, if we wish simply to extract the structure of the data, we may use cluster analysis to reduce the number of samples to a set of "typical" cluster centers to extend the conventional procedure.

9.7   INDIRECT METHODS: OTHER MEASURES OF QUALITY

9.7.1   Class-Independent Criteria

Preservation-of-structure criterion functions are stated without reference to class. There are other measures of quality which emphasize fidelity in the representation of the samples rather than class separation. Expansion of samples in orthonormal functions is a typical approach which minimizes the integral-square or mean-square error in the approximation; we shall discuss this approach further in Section 9.8. That section will describe the equivalence of such expansions to the determination of best-fitting linear subspaces. This approach is particularly suitable as a preprocessing step when the samples are originally of very high dimension. The user must take care, however, that he does not destroy the information distinguishing the classes by losing critical details of the original samples which may not substantially contribute to the integral-square error.

9.7.2   Tailoring the Measure to the Decision Rule

We have isolated feature selection from pattern classification by defining measures of quality which yielded pattern spaces in which good decision rules could be defined. Once we restrict our consideration to a particular form of decision rule, this procedure may be suboptimal. The transformation which minimizes the overlap of class densities may not be the transformation which minimizes the misclassification by a linear hyperplane.

If potential function methods or methods which give similarly complex boundaries are used in the pattern classification stage following feature selection, most proposed measures of quality are directly related to the performance of the decision rule $c(\mathbf{x})$. However, a large family of algorithms can be specified by defining

$$Q_{11}(\alpha) = p_2 \int_{X_1(\alpha)} p_2(\mathbf{x}) \, dX + p_1 \int_{X_2(\alpha)} p_1(\mathbf{x}) \, dX, \qquad (9.72)$$

where

$$X_i(\alpha) = \{\mathbf{x} \,|\, \mathbf{x} \text{ is classified in class } i \text{ by } c(\mathbf{x}) \text{ with } \mathbf{x} = \mathbf{F}(\mathbf{z}; \alpha)\}.$$

The quantity Q_{11} measures the probability of error due to the decision rule to be used. This procedure can be difficult; it in essence involves applying a chosen pattern classification algorithm repeatedly for different values of α until the best value of α is chosen. The decision rule is determined at the same time as the features. If the pattern classification algorithm is indirect, i.e., $c(\mathbf{x}) \equiv c(\mathbf{x}; \beta)$, then $Q_{11}(\alpha) \equiv Q_{11}(\alpha; \beta)$, and we minimize Q_{11} with respect to the parameters of the parameterized decision rule and the parameterized transformation. The computational difficulties of this approach are obvious; it is best suited to linear discriminant function decision rules.

The value of Q_{11} may be difficult to evaluate; alternate criterion functions include (1) the misclassification rate due to the decision rule, and (2) approximations to the misclassification rate such as the average distance to misclassified samples (Chapter IV).

9.8.   CUSTOM ORTHONORMAL TRANSFORMATIONS

9.8.1   Orthonormal Transformations and Expansion in Orthonormal Functions

Many physical patterns can be thought of as functions of one or two variables. As in Fig. 9.14a, an electrocardiogram can be regarded as a function of time. As in Fig. 9.14b, a visual pattern may be regarded as a

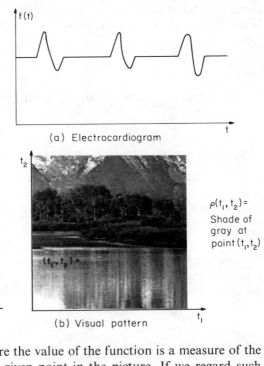

(a) Electrocardiogram

$\rho(t_1, t_2) =$
Shade of
gray at
point (t_1, t_2)

FIG. 9.14   Physical patterns as one-
or two-dimensional functions.

(b) Visual pattern

function of two variables, where the value of the function is a measure of the gray scale (the darkness) at a given point in the picture. If we regard such patterns as giving rise to continuous functions, hence infinite-dimensional measure spaces, we may consider the expansion of these given functions into a sum of simpler functions and use the coefficients of the truncated expansion as the features. We would expect such features to have the characteristics mentioned in Section 9.1, for a small change in the coefficients should result in a small change in the function represented by the expansion.

Because the processing of these patterns will in most likelihood be done digitally, it is often useful to view the infinite-dimensional patterns as high-dimensional vectors resulting from sampling the infinite-dimensional functions; thus, in the case of the elctrocardiogram, we may represent it by a series of values measured at small increments in time. In the case of a visual image we may view it as a set of values measured at discrete grid points in the visual field. In either case, the pattern is represented by a high-dimensional vector representing the values of the function listed in some prespecified order. Thus, corresponding to a function $f(t)$ is a vector with components $f_1, \ldots, f_m$:

$$f(t) \Leftrightarrow (f_1, \ldots, f_m) = \mathbf{f}. \tag{9.73}$$

We will use this notation to represent interchangeably a function or a vector; hence, in what follows, one may replace the vectors with functions where the inner product $(\mathbf{f}_1, \mathbf{f}_2)$ of two vectors for functions corresponds to an integration for functions,†

$$(\mathbf{f}_1, \mathbf{f}_2) \Leftrightarrow \int_{\mathcal{R}} f_1(t) f_2(t) \, dt, \tag{9.74}$$

and the norm of a vector is correspondingly

$$\|\mathbf{f}\|^2 = (\mathbf{f}, \mathbf{f}) \Leftrightarrow \int_{\mathcal{R}} f^2(t) \, dt. \tag{9.75}$$

Our objective is then to express a given vector, i.e., pattern, as an expansion of a finite number of vectors $\boldsymbol{\phi}_1, \ldots, \boldsymbol{\phi}_n$:

$$\mathbf{f} \approx \sum_{i=1}^{n} a_i \boldsymbol{\phi}_i,$$

$$\boldsymbol{\phi}_i = (\phi_{i1}, \ldots, \phi_{im}). \tag{9.76}$$

Suppose we choose to approximate $\mathbf{f}$ so as to minimize the average squared error in the approximation. That is, given the set of orthonormal vectors and the function $\mathbf{f}$, what are the a_i such that

$$\left\| \mathbf{f} - \sum_{i=1}^{n} a_i \boldsymbol{\phi}_i \right\|^2 \tag{9.77}$$

is minimized, or, more explicitly, such that

$$\sum_{k=1}^{m} \left(f_k - \sum_{i=1}^{n} a_i \phi_{ik} \right)^2 \tag{9.78}$$

is minimized?

If we take the partial derivatives of this function with respect to the coefficients a_l and set those partial derivatives equal to zero, we obtain a linear equation in the coefficients:

$$\sum_{i=1}^{n} a_i (\boldsymbol{\phi}_i, \boldsymbol{\phi}_l) = (\mathbf{f}, \boldsymbol{\phi}_l), \qquad l = 1, \ldots, n. \tag{9.79}$$

---

† The inner $(\mathbf{f}_1, \mathbf{f}_2)$ product and dot product $\mathbf{f}_1 \cdot \mathbf{f}_2$ are identical for vectors.

This is a set of n equations in n unknowns, and can be solved directly by any numerical means for solving a set of linear equations. Since, however, this is not one of the most efficient procedures computationally, we would like, if possible, to avoid repeating such procedures every time we wished to transform a sample into the pattern space. If the ϕ_i were such that

$$(\phi_i, \phi_l) = \begin{cases} 0, & i \neq l, \\ 1, & i = l, \end{cases} \tag{9.80}$$

that is, if the ϕ_i were orthonormal, then Eq. (9.79) reduces to

$$a_l = (f, \phi_l), \qquad l = 1, \ldots, n, \tag{9.81}$$

ch.

an obvious improvement. Thus, in almost every practical case where we care to use such an expansion, it will pay to use orthonormal (or orthogonal) functions.

Since we are choosing $x_i = a_i$, Eq. (9.81) implies that

$X = Tz$

$$\mathbf{x} = \mathbf{Tf}, \tag{9.82}$$

$$\mathbf{T} = \begin{bmatrix} \phi_1 \\ \vdots \\ \phi_n \end{bmatrix} \tag{9.83}$$

see p. 170

with $\{\phi_i\}$ orthonormal row vectors. This corresponds exactly to an orthonormal transformation where $\mathbf{f}$ defines what we usually call z-space (Section 9.3.3). Thus, expanding a discretized function $\mathbf{f}$ in discretized orthonormal functions ϕ_i corresponds to finding an orthonormal transformation of the m-dimensional samples $\mathbf{f}$ into an n-dimensional space. Clearly, the previous work in this chapter is directly applicable to this problem.

Most readers will be familiar with the expansion of a function in a Fourier series, at least a one-dimensional Fourier expansion. This is but one sort of an orthonormal expansion; there are many fast computational procedures for a wide class of orthonormal transformations [3]. Another straightforward expansion is expansion in a multivariate polynomial.

Of course, choosing such expansions without specific regard for the problem at hand may result in an approximation to the functions which is inefficient in the sense that it does not approximate the function as closely as possible for the number of terms used. On the other hand, using standard orthonormal functions avoids the need for deriving specialized functions. One might, however, be willing to derive orthonormal functions of a more general type if there was reason to believe that such effort would improve the approximation for a given number of terms. The number of terms is of critical importance since the number of terms is equal to the number of coefficients and hence to the number of features in the pattern space. The next subsection will discuss the derivation of orthogonal functions specific to the problem at hand and, in a specified sense, optimal for the problem at hand.

9.8.2 Karhunen–Loève Expansion and Factor Analysis

If we had a representative set of samples of the functions to be approximated to, how might we choose a set of orthonormal functions that on the average approximated those sample functions better than any other set of functions? Suppose those functions are represented as vectors as before:

$$
\begin{aligned}
\mathbf{f}_1 &= (f_{11}, f_{12}, \ldots, f_{1m}), \\
\mathbf{f}_2 &= (f_{21}, \ldots, f_{2m}), \\
&\ \vdots \\
\mathbf{f}_M &= (f_{M1}, \ldots, f_{Mm}).
\end{aligned}
\tag{9.84}
$$

The problem is then to find similarly represented orthonormal functions:

$$
\begin{aligned}
\boldsymbol{\phi}_1 &= (\phi_{11}, \ldots, \phi_{1m}), \\
&\ \vdots \\
\boldsymbol{\phi}_n &= (\phi_{n1}, \ldots, \phi_{nm}),
\end{aligned}
\tag{9.85}
$$

such that

$$
\begin{aligned}
Q_{12}(\boldsymbol{\phi}_1, \cdots, \boldsymbol{\phi}_n) &= \frac{1}{M} \sum_{i=1}^{M} \left\| \mathbf{f}_i - \sum_{j=1}^{n} a_j^{(i)} \boldsymbol{\phi}_j \right\|^2 \\
&= \frac{1}{M} \sum_{i=1}^{M} \sum_{t=1}^{m} \left(f_{it} - \sum_{j=1}^{n} a_j^{(i)} \phi_{jt} \right)^2
\end{aligned}
\tag{9.86}
$$

with

$$
a_j^{(i)} = (\mathbf{f}_i, \boldsymbol{\phi}_j)
\tag{9.87}
$$

is minimized. We wish to minimize the mean-square error in the approximation, hence finding the set of functions which yield the least error averaged over all the sample points.

The solution to this problem is the generalized Karhunen–Loève expansion [16]. One method of solution is as follows; let

$$
k_{rs} = \frac{1}{M} \sum_{i=1}^{M} f_{ir} f_{is}, \qquad \mathbf{K} = [k_{rs}].
\tag{9.88}
$$

$Av = \lambda v$

$\sqrt{} \ |A - \lambda I| v = 0$

closed samples

Then **K** is an $m \times m$ covariance matrix. Solve the eigenvalue problem

$$\mathbf{K}\boldsymbol{\phi}_k = \sigma_k^2 \boldsymbol{\phi}_k, \qquad k = 1, 2, \ldots, m, \qquad (9.89)$$

perhaps by a numerical method. The normalized eigenvectors of the co-variance matrix form a set of orthonormal vectors. Choose the eigenvectors corresponding to the n largest eigenvalues to construct the transformation **T** [Eq. (9.82)].

This approach requires a difficult computation of the eigenvalues and eigenvectors of a large matrix.

Equation (9.82) indicated the equivalence of orthonormal transformations and expansion in orthonormal vectors. Hence, (9.86) can be interpreted as measuring the mean-square distance between samples in m-dimensional Z-space and their projection on the n-dimensional X-space. Minimizing Q_{12} gives the subspace of dimension n which best fits (in a least-mean-square sense) the sample points and thus which loses the least information in the projection (see Fig. 9.15). This interpretation indicates the equivalence of the

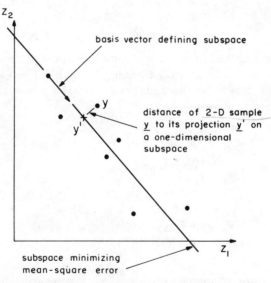

FIG. 9.15 Factor analysis. Underscored symbols are vectors.

Karhunen–Loève expansion to *factor analysis* [73] (sometimes *principal components analysis*).

Fukunaga and Koontz [26] suggest a suboptimal means for employing the Karhunen–Loève expansion to choose a transformation which emphasizes class differences rather than fidelity of representation.

9.8.3 A Simpler Custom Expansion

A suboptimal set of orthonormal functions may be obtained from a set of samples in a much simpler fashion than through the use of an optimality criterion employing all the samples. The procedure employs the Gram–Schmidt orthonormalization process, which constructs a set of orthonormal functions (vectors) from an equal number of linearly independent functions (vectors).

THE GRAM–SCHMIDT ORTHONORMALIZATION PROCESS

Given a set of linearly independent vectors $\mathbf{f}_1, \mathbf{f}_2, \ldots, \mathbf{f}_m$, we wish to construct a set of orthonormal vectors $\boldsymbol{\phi}_1, \boldsymbol{\phi}_2, \ldots, \boldsymbol{\phi}_r$ which span the same space. Suppose we hypothesize that the orthonormal functions can be constructed by a procedure of the following form:

$$\begin{aligned}
\boldsymbol{\phi}_1 &= d_1[\mathbf{f}_1], \\
\boldsymbol{\phi}_2 &= d_2[\mathbf{f}_2 - c_{12}\boldsymbol{\phi}_1], \\
&\vdots \\
\boldsymbol{\phi}_r &= d_r[\mathbf{f}_r - c_{1r}\boldsymbol{\phi}_1 \cdots - c_{r-1,r}\boldsymbol{\phi}_{r-1}],
\end{aligned} \tag{9.90}$$

where each orthonormal function is obtained from the previous orthonormal function and one new function. Requiring that $(\boldsymbol{\phi}_i, \boldsymbol{\phi}_j) = 0$ for $i \neq j$ results in $c_{jk} = (\boldsymbol{\phi}_j, \mathbf{f}_k)$. Imposing the additional normality condition $(\boldsymbol{\phi}_j, \boldsymbol{\phi}_j) = 1$ yields the following algorithm:

$$\begin{aligned}
\boldsymbol{\Psi}_1 &= \mathbf{f}_1 \\
\boldsymbol{\phi}_1 &= (\boldsymbol{\Psi}_1, \boldsymbol{\Psi}_1)^{-1/2}(\boldsymbol{\Psi}_1) \\
c_{12} &= (\boldsymbol{\phi}_1, \mathbf{f}_2) \\
\boldsymbol{\Psi}_2 &= \mathbf{f}_2 - c_{12}\boldsymbol{\phi}_1 \\
&\vdots \\
c_{jk} &= (\boldsymbol{\phi}_j, \mathbf{f}_k), \quad j = 1, \ldots, k-1 \\
\boldsymbol{\Psi}_k &= \mathbf{f}_k - c_{1k}\boldsymbol{\phi}_1 - \cdots - c_{k-1,k}\boldsymbol{\phi}_{k-1} \\
\boldsymbol{\phi}_k &= (\boldsymbol{\Psi}_k, \boldsymbol{\Psi}_k)^{-1/2}\boldsymbol{\Psi}_k \\
&\vdots
\end{aligned} \tag{9.91}$$

(If we only require orthogonal functions, we can remove the normalization constraint.)

GENERATION FROM TYPICAL SAMPLES

Suppose that we wish a space of dimension n. Then we choose n typical samples representative of all classes; preferably, these samples should be as dissimilar as possible, i.e., typical of different classes or types of samples.

Given such samples, we may apply the Gram–Schmidt orthonormalization process to them directly, deriving *n* orthonormal functions into which all samples can be expanded. In terms of the original pattern space the transformation to the new pattern space is

$$x_i \equiv a_i = (\mathbf{f}, \boldsymbol{\phi}_i), \quad i = 1, 2, \ldots, n. \tag{9.92}$$

The equivalent linear transformation is given by (9.82) and (9.83).

This is clearly more oriented to the specific problem than would be a general expansion. The suboptimality of the expansion is a result of the fact that while all of the samples used to generate the orthonormal vectors can be represented *exactly* by an *n*-term expansion in the derived functions, we have only considered *n* samples. The hypothesis is then that this is optimal in the sense that if the generating samples were truly typical, we would expect other samples to be represented closely by expansion in these functions. We note, that in any case, as is true for all orthonormal functions, Eq. (9.92) gives the best expansion of **f** in the least-mean-square sense for the given set of orthonormal functions.

In terms of our alternative interpretation, the subspace generated by this method is suboptimal in the sense that the samples used to generate the orthonormal functions lie exactly in the subspace; thus, this procedure is optimal in the sense that it minimizes exactly (over the set of orthonormal vectors)

$$Q = \sum_{i=1}^{n} \left\| \mathbf{y}_{k_i} - \sum_{j=1}^{n} (\mathbf{y}_{k_i}, \boldsymbol{\phi}_j)\boldsymbol{\phi}_j \right\|^2, \tag{9.93}$$

where $\mathbf{y}_{k_i}$, $i = 1, \ldots, n$ is the set of typical samples. The minimum value of Q is, of course, zero and is achieved by this procedure.

9.9 CHOOSING *n* OF *m* FEATURES

9.9.1 Feature Ranking

Given an arbitrary *m*-dimensional *Z*-space, the problem is to rank the features in that *Z*-space by some criterion related to their usefulness in recognizing the pattern, hence, to obtain an ordering of the given features $z_1, z_2, \ldots, z_m$:

$$i_1, i_2, \ldots, i_m; \quad i_k \in \{1, 2, \ldots, m\}. \tag{9.94}$$

Then, the first *n* features ordered in this manner are chosen for the pattern space or perhaps for further consideration. The transformation from *Z* into *X* is then given by Eq. (9.9). The transformation is completely determined by the ordering in Eq. (9.94) and the value of *n*.

Feature ranking provides one means for choosing from an oversized set of proposed measurements. It is most useful in situations where the features are chosen by knowledge of the system, that is, intuitively, and we wish to find some objective way of ranking a large set of candidate features. Feature ranking is also useful in sequential pattern recognition, where features are computed sequentially and a decision may be made before all the features of a given sample are computed; a ranking then gives the order in which to calculate features. This will be further discussed in Chapter X. It should be noted that this problem is somewhat different from the less general problem of picking the best subset of n members from an m member set; in the latter case, there is no need to rank the features in the chosen subset. This latter problem is discussed in the next subsection, although of course the feature ranking method is a possible approach.

We are given a set of samples in Z-space of each class j:

$$\mathbf{y}_i^{(j)} = (y_{i1}^{(j)}, \ldots, y_{im}^{(j)}), \qquad i = 1, \ldots, M_j, \quad j = 1, \ldots, N. \tag{9.95}$$

Let us discuss measures of quality of a feature which can be calculated using only the component of these samples corresponding to that feature.

LIMITATIONS OF PROJECTIONS ONTO ONE DIMENSION

Clearly, if we look at the component of the samples corresponding to the feature whose quality is to be measured, that is, if we project the sample points onto the corresponding axis and consider only that projection in estimating the feature, we are losing a great deal of information. For example, in Fig. 9.16, the projections upon the z_1 axis in all cases are exactly the same

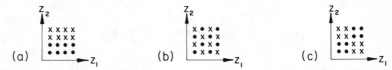

FIG. 9.16　Three two-dimensional sample distributions.

and the three situations are indistinguishable considering only z_1. Yet, they are clearly distinctly different situations. In the first, the sample points are easily separable, in the second, they are not. On the other hand, almost any method of ranking would rank feature z_2 above feature z_1 in case (a)—certainly the correct ranking.

A major difficulty of considering one-dimensional projections is illustrated, however, by case (c), where the points are clearly separable but can only be separated by using both features concurrently. Here again, however, the features would receive an equal ranking and neither would be dropped unless the other were dropped. A third feature of less importance could easily be ranked higher, since the projections on either axis give no hint of the separability of the samples, and are, in fact, identical to the projections in (b).

POSSIBLE RANKING FORMULAS

The following formulas allow ranking the features by numerical ordering of the values assigned by those formulas:

$$r_{i_1} \geq r_{i_2} \geq \cdots \geq r_{i_m}$$

implies the ordering

$$i_1, i_2, \ldots, i_m.$$

Any of the measures of quality to be proposed for multidimensional sample distributions can be transformed into a ranking formula for feature z_i by applying it directly to the one-dimensional distribution obtained by projecting the sample points on the ith axis (taking the ith component of all samples); i.e., a measure Q defined for a general n-dimensional distribution can be evaluated for a one-dimensional distribution as well, and thus r_i can be set equal to Q evaluated using the projection of samples on the ith axis. Another possible one-dimensional ranking formula with many advantages is

$$r_i = \text{SCORE}_i,$$

with SCORE_i evaluated as described by Henrichon and Fu [32].

We can get away from the limitations of one-dimensional projections by utilizing one of the measures of separability Q defined in earlier sections. A measure of separability can measure the quality of a set of labeled samples expressed in terms of any subset of features; we can denote this dependence of Q on the features chosen by

$$Q \equiv Q(i_1, i_2, \ldots, i_m),$$

i.e., $Q(i_1, \ldots, i_m)$ is the measure calculated for samples whose components are $x_{i_1}, x_{i_2}, \ldots, x_{i_m}$.

Suppose a larger value of Q corresponds to better separability. Then, given n features to rank, one might define the ranking formula

$$r_k = -Q(1, 2, \ldots, k - 1, k + 1, \ldots, n), \qquad k = 1, 2, \ldots, n. \quad (9.96)$$

The larger r_k, the better the feature x_k relative to the set of n features; for, $r_i > r_j$ implies that the samples are more separable with feature x_j deleted, and, hence, trading x_i for x_j improves separability. Unlike ranking based on one-dimensional projections, this approach will signal the importance of a feature which is useless alone but valuable in combination with another feature; when either is dropped, the quality will degrade significantly.

On the other hand, this approach fails when two or more features are strong, but measure very similar aspects of the pattern; dropping any of them at one time would result in very little degradation in quality because of the presence of the others. But, since all would receive a low ranking, all might be dropped from the ultimate set of features. Very similar features should not be ranked in this manner. We can avoid this problem by a generalization; we define a Kth-*order ranking formula*

$$r_{i_1 i_2 \cdots i_K} = -Q(\mathbf{i}),$$

where $\mathbf{i}$ is a vector of all integers between 1 and n except $i_1, i_2, \ldots, i_K$. Then, $r_{i_1 i_2 \cdots i_K} > r_{j_1 j_2 \cdots j_K}$ implies that the *set* of features $\{x_{i_1}, x_{i_2}, \ldots, x_{i_K}\}$ is better than the *set* of features $\{x_{j_1}, x_{j_2}, \ldots, x_{j_K}\}$. If r_i and r_j are relatively small, but r_{ij} is relatively large, the features x_i and x_j are highly correlated in a generalized sense, and both should not be retained, but one of them should since $\{x_i, x_j\}$ is a highly ranked pair. If $r_i, r_j, r_k, r_{ij}, r_{jk}$, and r_{ik} are relatively small, but r_{ijk} is large relative to other third-order rankings, then the three features are highly correlated (again in a generalized sense), but one should be retained. The argument can be extended to any order, but becomes unwieldy computationally if all orders are taken into account. Generally, the analyst must restrict his consideration to low-order interactions.

An alternate approach to choosing the best of a set of n features is the following procedure:

(1) Rank the n features by (9.96). Discard the worst single feature.
(2) Rank the remaining features by (9.96) with n replaced by $(n-1)$. Discard the worst single feature.
(3) Continue until a sufficiently small number of features remains.

This procedure will not remove a group of features useful together by the nature of the measure, and should drop all but one of a group of redundant (highly correlated) features. One advantage of this procedure relative to the method suggested previously is that no interpretation of the results is necessary to arrive at the final set of n features; but, on the other hand, no insight into the dependencies among features is obtained.

To reduce m features to n features, the latter procedure requires $(m-n)$ $(m+n-1)/2$ calculations of $Q(\mathbf{i})$; the former procedure requires $m(m+1)/2$ calculations to obtain both first- and second-order rankings. For $m = 30$, $n = 10$, the former quantity is 390; the latter quantity is 465, although one may, of course, limit the pairs of features ranked to reduce this number.

If the features are obtained by the Karhunen–Loève expansion or discriminant analysis, the ordering of the eigenvalues gives a natural feature ordering [17].

9.9.2 Best *n* of *m*

Feature ranking provides a means of choosing the best *n* of *m* features, but does not take into account the final number of features *n* which will be adopted. Hence, to pick the best *n* features out of *m*, one should in theory compare all possible combinations of *n* features; Q could be evaluated for all subsets, and the best chosen. The drawback to this procedure is, of course, that there are $\binom{m}{n}$ possible subsets, e.g.,

$$\binom{20}{10} = 184{,}756.$$

Mucciardi and Gose [53] provide experimental comparisons of several suboptimal methods.

9.9.3 Incorporating the Cost of Features

We have ignored any consideration other than the usefulness of a feature in ranking. If there are significant differences in the cost of calculating or collecting features, cost could be taken into account [55]. One way this modified problem can be formulated is to choose decision variables m_i $(i = 1, \ldots, m)$ such that the overall cost is less than some maximum cost C_{max}, where

$$m_i = \begin{cases} 1 & \text{if variable} \quad z_i \quad \text{is chosen,} \\ 0 & \text{if not.} \end{cases} \tag{9.97}$$

We solve the problem of maximizing

$$\sum_{i=1}^{m} m_i r_i \tag{9.98a}$$

subject to

$$\sum_{i=1}^{m} m_i c_i \leq C_{max}, \tag{9.98b}$$

where r_i is a ranking formula as above and c_i is the cost of using feature z_i.

We can solve this program using dynamic programming with invariant imbedding. Define

$$f(v, r) = \max_{m_1, \ldots, m_r} \sum_{i=1}^{r} m_i r_i \tag{9.99a}$$

subject to

$$\sum_{i=1}^{r} m_i c_i \leq v. \tag{9.99b}$$

We can easily calculate (or tabulate)

$$f(v, 1) = \max_{m_1} m_1 r_1 \qquad (9.100a)$$

subject to

$$m_1 c_1 \leq v \qquad (9.100b)$$

as a function v. Having done so, other members of the family of problems in (9.99) can be obtained iteratively:

$$f(v, r) = \max_{m_r, \ldots, m_1} \left[m_r r_r + \sum_{i=1}^{r-1} m_i r_i \right]$$

$$= \max_{m_r} \left[m_r r_r + \max_{m_{r-1}, \ldots, m_1} \sum_{i=1}^{r-1} m_i r_i \right],$$

where $\max_{m_r}$ is subject to $m_r c_r \leq v$ and $\max_{m_{r-1}, \ldots, m_1}$ is subject to

$$\sum_{i=1}^{r-1} m_i c_i \leq v - m_r c_r.$$

Hence,

$$f(v, r) = \max_{m_r \in \{0, 1\}} [m_r r_r + f(v - m_r c_r, r - 1)] \qquad (9.101a)$$

subject to

$$m_r c_r \leq v. \qquad (9.101b)$$

We can iterate to the solution $f(C_{max}, m)$ desired using (9.100) and (9.101). See Nelson and Levy [55] for an example of the calculation procedure.

Let us examine the type of result provided by this approach. If the costs and ranking values for 10 features are as in Table 9.1, the results will be as in Table 9.2.† The results for a range of maximum cost are automatically

TABLE 9.1

Features (i)	Costs (c_i)	Rank (n)
1	1	0.0001074
2	2	0.0000013
3	3	0.0007472
4	4	0.0003326
5	5	0.0311158
6	6	0.0780098
7	7	0.7156781
8	8	0.0314356
9	9	0.3823075
10	10	0.0004071

† The author is indebted to W. W. Yuan for this example.

TABLE 9.2

Max cost (C_{max})	Total return [$f(C_{max}, 10)$]	Features chosen	Max cost (C_{max})	Total return [$f(C_{max}, 10)$]	Features chosen
0	0.0	0	16	1.0979852	7, 9
1	0.0001074	1	17	1.0980920	1, 7, 9
2	0.0001074	1	18	1.0980920	1, 7, 9
3	0.0007472	3	19	1.0987319	3, 7, 9
4	0.0008546	1, 3	20	1.0988397	1, 3, 7, 9
5	0.0311157	5	21	1.1291008	5, 7, 9
6	0.0780098	6	22	1.1759948	6, 7, 9
7	0.7156780	7	23	1.1761026	1, 6, 7, 9
8	0.7157854	1, 7	24	1.1761026	1, 6, 7, 9
9	0.7157854	1, 7	25	1.1767425	3, 6, 7, 9
10	0.7164252	3, 7	26	1.1768493	1, 3, 6, 7, 9
11	0.7165326	1, 3, 7	27	1.2071104	5, 6, 7, 9
12	0.7467938	5, 7	28	1.2072181	1, 5, 6, 7, 9
13	0.7936879	6, 7	29	1.2072181	1, 5, 6, 7, 9
14	0.7937952	1, 6, 7	30	1.2078580	3, 5, 6, 7, 9
15	0.7937952	1, 6, 7			

provided by the algorithm. It is clear that setting the maximum cost at 20 yields very little over a maximum cost of 16, but going from 15 to 16 yields a significant improvement in the total return.

9.10 CONCLUSION

There are few direct methods in feature selection that are not application-specific. This does not negate the importance of features constructed utilizing problem knowledge, but limits the discussion that can be attempted in this text. A context for conceptualizing direct feature selection methods was presented as a "principle of decomposition," which stated that feature selection tended to reduce the overall pattern recognition problem to a series of simpler pattern recognition problems. Direct methods may stand alone, or may precede the more abstract feature selection or feature ranking algorithms of the remainder of the chapter.

A very large number of indirect feature selection algorithms can be constructed by varying one's choice of cost function, of parameterized transformation, and of optimization technique. The variety of options open to the designer is further increased by some of the specialized techniques such as custom orthonormal transformations which can be used alone or as preprocessing techniques prior to some of the more complex feature selection methods. The variety poses few fundamental choices, however; measures of quality which measure the overlap of probability densities can often be expressed as measures of interset versus intraset distances using localized distances. Caution is required in the use of measures which are conceptually based upon unimodal pattern classes, such as those which do not use localized distances. Computational considerations make linear transforms attractive as a class of parameterized transformations. Nonlinear transforms require arbitrary choices of nonlinear terms or the use of an efficiently defined class of functions, e.g., piecewise linear functions. Feature ranking, essentially a linear transform, utilizes the measures of quality to rank a proposed set of features.

There are difficulties in practice which have not been fully treated here. Often certain "measurements" are simply nominal values and are difficult to use directly in a feature selection algorithm. For example, in classifying personnel, marital status may be represented by the values 1, 2, 3, 4, 5 for married, single, widowed, separated, and divorced, respectively, a completely arbitrary assignment which inserts an assumption ordering the categories. Such problems may be approached by an appropriate application of concepts similar to structure-preserving transformations ("multidimensional scaling") [7, 14a, 27, 28a, 38, 39a, 45a, 45b, 51b, 64, 66, 67, 70].

We have discussed in this chapter, as noted, the more abstract approaches to feature selection; a great deal can be done in more specific problem areas. Some of this, particularly in waveform or image processing, comes under the category of heuristic or linguistic feature extraction. A discussion of this approach is contained in Section 10.4 of Chapter X. The problem of choosing features sequentially, i.e., being able to reach a decision before all the features are calculated, is often called sequential feature selection and is discussed in Section 10.3.

EXERCISES

9.1. Given

$$\mathbf{f}_1 = (1, 1, 1, 2), \qquad \mathbf{f}_2 = (0, 1, 0, 1), \qquad \text{and} \qquad \mathbf{f}_3 = (-1, 1, 1, -1).$$

(a) Use the Gram–Schmidt orthonormalization process to obtain three orthonormal "functions" from the above linearly independent "functions." Plot them.

(b) What is the least-mean-square error in expanding $\mathbf{f}_4 = (1, 1, 1, 0)$ in the functions derived?

— *Can plot in 3 dimensions* $a_j = f \cdot \phi_j$ — *projection*

9.2. Suppose we wished to apply the principle of decomposition in a manner similar to the character identification example in the text. We design four

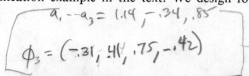
$a_1 - a_3 = 1.14, -.34, .85$
$\phi_3 = (-.31, .41, .75, -.42)$

curvature *straightness*

features z_1, z_2, z_3, z_4 such that the first two are measures that we feel can discriminate curvature in the physical pattern and the last two are measures of straightness. We calculate features z_1, z_2 for 9 samples of curved characters and obtain

$z_1 + z_2$

$$(3, 3.5, -, -) \quad (4.5, 2, -, -,) \quad (5, 3, -, -)$$
$$(4, 3, -, -,) \quad (4.5, 3.5, -, -) \quad (5, 4, -, -)$$
$$(4, 4, -, -,) \quad (4.5, 5, -, -) \quad (6, 3.5, -, -).$$

From samples of straight characters, we obtain

$z_3 + z_4$

$$(-, -, 2, 1.5) \quad (-, -, 4, 1) \quad (-, -, 5, 3)$$
$$(-, -, 3, 1) \quad (-, -, 4, 3) \quad (-, -, 5.5, 4)$$
$$(-, -, 3, 2) \quad (-, -, 4.5, 2) \quad (-, -, 5.5, 5).$$
$$(-, -, 3.5, 1.5) \quad (-, -, 4.5, 4)$$

(a) Use these samples to construct 2 features measuring curvature and straightness, respectively.

(b) Using these features, transform the following two sample sets into a two-dimensional pattern space and plot them. Indicate a linear separating surface if possible:

$$\mathcal{Y}_1 = \{(3, 2, 3, 2)(7, 5, 5, 4)(2, 3, 4, 2)(4, 1, 6, 5)\} \quad \text{— straight}$$
$$\mathcal{Y}_2 = \{(5, 3, 2, 4)(4, 3, 5, 1)(5, 5, 7, 2)(4, 4, 1, 1)\}. \quad \text{— curved}$$

9.3. Given samples in Z-space:

p.179

$$\mathcal{Y}_1 = \{(1, 1, 1)(0, 1, 1)(2, 2, -2)(2, 0, 1)(1, -2, -1)\}$$
$$\mathcal{Y}_2 = \{(2, -5, -2)(1, -4, 1)(-1, -5, 0)(2, -1, 2)\}.$$

(a) Find the *orthonormal* transformation into a two-dimensional X-space which minimizes Q in (9.34), using Euclidean distance in that equation.

(b) Find the optimum *orthogonal* transformation with respect to (9.34).

(c) Plot both results.

9.4. Given samples of 2 classes: 3 regions

$$\mathcal{Y}_1 = \{(6, 0, 8, 0, -3) \quad (7, -1, 12, 8, 1) \quad (10, 4, 6, 2, -1)$$
$$(-1, 6, 14, 4, -4) \quad (2, 7, 10, 10, -2) \quad (2, 0, -1, 0, 1)$$
$$(4, 7, 2.5, 7, 2)(2.5, 2, 2.5, 10, 2) \quad (1, 5, 1, 5, 2)\}$$
$$\mathcal{Y}_2 = \{(4, 3, 4, 4, 3)(-1, 1, 15, 10, -2) \quad (8, 9, 8, 0, -2)$$
$$(1, 8, 2.5, 5, -1)(6, 9, 10, 3, -3)\}. \quad p.174$$

Find a piecewise linear transformation of the form of Eq. (9.25) into a two-dimensional X-space such that the classes are linearly separable. Use three subregions, i.e., $R = 3$ in Eq. (9.24).

— Use direct algorithm

9.5. Using the samples in Exercise 9.4, rank the five features
 (a) using the Fisher criterion [21],

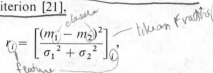

$$r_i = \left[\frac{(m_1 - m_2)^2}{\sigma_1^2 + \sigma_2^2} \right]_i ,$$

where the means and variances are of the ith components of the samples of the indicated class, and
 (b) using Eq. (9.34) with the localized distance [Eq. (9.35)], where the equation is applied in turn to the one-dimensional projections of sample points.

9.6. Given the sample points $(0, 0, 0)$, $(2, 0, 2)$, $(1, 0, 1)$, and $(1, 1, 2)$, find a set of corresponding two-dimensional samples such that all (Euclidean) distances are retained exactly. Find a continuous transformation which produces the derived mapping.

SELECTED BIBLIOGRAPHY

1. Alexandridis, N. A., and Klinger, A., Walsh Orthogonal Functions in Geometrical Feature Extractions, *Proc. Symp. Appl. of Walsh Functions, April 1971.*
1a. Ahlgren, R. C., Ryan, H. F., and Swonger, C. W., A Character Recognition Application of an Iterative Procedure for Feature Selection, *IEEE Trans. Comput.* **20**, 1067–1074 (1971).
1b. Alt, F. L., Digital Pattern Recognition by Moments, *in* "Optical Character Recognition," pp. 153–180, Spartan, Washington, D.C., 1962.
2. Andrews, H. C., Multidimensional Rotations in Feature Selection, *IEEE Trans. Comput.* **20**, 1045–1050 (1971).
3. Andrews, H. C., and Caspari, K. L., A Generalized Technique for Spectral Analysis, *IEEE Trans. Comput.* **19**, 16–25 (1970).
4. Bakis, R., Herbst, N., and Nagy, G., An Experimental Study of Machine Recognition of Handprinted Numerals, *IEEE Trans. Sys. Science and Cybernetics* **3**, 119–132 (1968).
4a. Bastien, P. L., and Dunn, L. A., Global Transformations in Pattern Recognition of Bubble Chamber Photographs, *IEEE Trans. Comput.* **20**, 995–1001 (1971).
4b. Beck, F., The Special Features of POLLY: How They Are Used for Automatic Scanning, *IEEE Trans. Comput.* **20**, 1002–1006 (1971).
5. Beeson, R. M., and Meisel, W. S., Optimization of Complex Systems with Respect to Multiple Criteria, *Proc. IEEE Systems, Man, and Cybernetics Conf.: Joint Nat. Conf. on Major Systems, Anaheim, Calif., October 1971.*
6. Bellman, R. E., "Dynamic Programming," Princeton Univ. Press, Princeton, New Jersey, 1957.
7. Bennett, R. S., The Intrinsic Dimensionality of Signal Collections, *IEEE Trans. Information Theory* **15**, 517–525 (1969).
8. Bhattacharyya, A., On a Measure of Divergence between Two Statistical Populations Defined by Their Probability Distributions, *Bull. Calcutta Math. Soc.* **35**, 99–109 (1943).

9. Bledsoe, W. W., and Browning, I., Pattern Recognition and Reading by Machines, *Proc. Eastern Joint Comput. Conf., Boston, December* 1959, pp. 225–233.

10. Block, H. D., Nilsson, N. J., and Duda, R. O., Determination and Detection of Features in Patterns, *in* Computer and Information Sciences (J. Tou and R. H. Wilcox, eds.), pp. 75–110, Spartan, Washington, D.C., 1964.

11. Butler, G. A., Evaluating Feature Spaces for the Two-Class Problem, *Proc. Systems Science and Cybernetics Conf., Joint Nat. Conf. on Major Systems, Anaheim, California, October 1971.*

12. Calvert, T. W., Nonorthogonal Projections for Feature Extraction in Pattern Recognition, *IEEE Trans. Comput.* **19**, 447–452 (1970).

13. Calvert, T. W., and Young, T. Y., Randomly Generated Nonlinear Transformations for Pattern Recognition, *IEEE Trans. Sys. Science and Cybernetics* **5**, 266–278 (1969).

14. Caprihan, A., and Figueiredo, R. J. P., On the Extraction of Pattern Features from Continuous Measurements, *IEEE Trans. Syst. Science and Cybernetics* **6**, 110–115 (1970).

14a. Carroll, J. D., and Chang, J-J., Analysis of Individual Differences in Multi-Dimensional Scaling via an *N*-way Generalization of "Eckart–Young" Decomposition, *Psychometrika* **3**, 283–319 (1970).

15. Chen, C. H., Theoretical Comparison of a Class of Feature Selection Criteria in Pattern Recognition, *Proc. IEEE Symp. on Feature Extraction and Selection, Argonne, Illinois, October 1970.*

16. Chien, Y. T., and Fu, K. S., On the Generalized Karhunen–Loève Expansion, *IEEE Trans. Information Theory* **13**, 518–520 (1967).

17. Chien, Y. T., and Fu, K. S., Selection and Ordering of Feature Observations in a Pattern Recognition System, *Information and Control* **12**, 395–414 (1968).

18. Clark, M. T., Optimization of the Representation of Sampled Data Signals on Orthonormal Bases, *IEEE Proc. 7th Symp. on Adaptive Processes, UCLA, December 1968.*

19. Collins, D. C., Meisel, W. S., and Shaw, D. E., Distortion-Invariant Structural Analysis of Waveforms, Technology Service Corp., Santa Monica, California, Rept. No. 027, December 1970.

19a. Collins, D. C., and Meisel, W. S., Structural Analysis of Biological Waveforms, *Proc. Ann. Conf. Eng. Medicine Biology, Las Vegas, Nevada, October 1791.*

19b. Das, S. K., Feature Selection with a Linear Dependence Measure, *IEEE Trans. Comput.* **20**, 1106–1109 (1971).

20. de Figueiredo, R. J. P., and Netravali, A. N., Direct Optimization in Subspaces of Splines with Application to Feature Selection, *Symp. on Feature Extraction and Selection, Argonne, Illinois, October 1970.*

20a. Deuser, L. M., A Hybrid Multispectral Feature Selection Criterion, *IEEE Trans. Comput.* **20**, 1116–1117 (1971).

21. Fisher, R. A., The Statistical Utilization of Multiple Measurements, *Ann. Eugen.* **8**, 376–386 (1938).

22. Fisher, R. A., The Use of Multiple Measurements in Taxionomic Problems, *in* "Contributions to Mathematical Statistics," pp. 32.179–32.188, Wiley, New York, 1950.

23. Flanagan, J. L., "Speech Analysis, Synthesis and Perception," Springer-Verlag, Berlin and New York, 1965.

24. Fu, K. S., "Sequential Methods in Pattern Recognition and Machine Learning," Academic Press, New York, 1969.

25. Fu, K. S., Min, P. J., and Li, T. J., Feature Selection in Pattern Recognition, *IEEE Trans. Sys. Science and Cybernetics.* **6**, 33–39 (1970).

26. Fukunaga, K., and Koontz, W. L. G., Application of the Karhunen–Loève Expansion to Feature Selection and Ordering, *IEEE Trans. Comput.* **19**, 311–318 (1970).

27. Fukunaga, K., and Olsen, D. R., An Algorithm for Finding the Intrinsic Dimensionality of Data, *Proc. IEEE Sys. Sci. and Cybernetics Conf. Pittsburgh, October 1970.*

27a. Geselowitz, D. B., Use of the Multipole Expansion to Extract Significant Features of the Surface Electrocardiogram, *IEEE Trans. Comput.* **20**, 1086–1088 (1971).

28. Gose, E. E., Improving the Population of Elements in a Pattern Recognition Network, *IEEE Int. Symp. on Information Theory, San Remo, Italy, September 1967.*

28a. Guttman, L., A General Nonmetric Technique for Finding the Smallest Coordinate Space for a Configuration of Points, *Psychometrika* **33**, (1968).

28b. Hall, E. L., *et al.*, A Survey of Preprocessing and Feature Extraction Techniques for Radiographic Images, *IEEE Trans. Comput.* **20**, 1032–1044 (1971).

29. Hart, P. E., A Brief Survey of Preprocessing for Pattern Recognition, Rome Air Development Center, Rome, New York. Tech. Rept. No. RADC-TR-66-819, January 1967.

30. Henderson, T. L., and Lainiotis, D. G., Comments on Linear Feature Extraction, *IEEE Trans. Information Theory* **15**, 728–730 (1969).

31. Henderson, T. L., and Lainiotis, D. G. Application of State Variable Techniques to Optimal Feature Extraction–Multichannel Analog Data, *IEEE Trans. Information Theory* **16**, 396–406 (1970).

32. Henrichon, E. G., Jr., and Fu, K. S., A Nonparametric Partitioning Procedure for Pattern Classification, *IEEE Trans. Comput.* **18**, 614–624 (1969).

32a. Heydorn, R. P., Redundancy in Feature Extraction, *IEEE Trans. Comput.* **20**, 1051–1053 (1971).

32b. Hoffman, R. L., and Fukunaga, K., Pattern Recognition Signal Processing for Mechanical Diagnostics Signature Analysis, *IEEE Trans. Comput.* **20**, 1095–1099 (1971).

33. Hu, M. K., Visual Pattern Recognition by Moment Invariants, *IRE Trans. Information Theory* **8**, 179–187 (1962).

34. Huggins, W. H., Representation and Analysis of Signals: I—The Use of Orthogonalized Exponentials, Johns Hopkins Univ., Baltimore, Maryland, Rept. AFCR-TR-57-357, September 1957.

35. Kadota, T. T., and Shepp, L. A., On the Best Set of Linear Observables for Discriminating Two Gaussian Signals, *IEEE Trans. Information Theory* **13**, 278–284 (1967).

36. Kailath, T., The Divergence and Bhattacharyya Distance Measure in Signal Selection, *IEEE Trans. Commun. Technol.* **15**, 52–60 (1967).

37. Kamentsky, L. A., and Liu, C. N., Computer Automated Design of Multifont Print Recognition Logic, *IBM J. Res. Develop.* **7**, 2–13 (1962).

37a. Kelly, K. K., Calvert, T. W., Longini, R. L., and Brown, J. P., Feature Enhancement of Vectorcardiograms by Linear Normalization, *IEEE Trans. Comput.* **20**, 1109–1110 (1971).

37b. Klinger, A., Pattern Width at a Given Angle, *Comm. ACM* **14**, 15–20 (1971).

37c. Klinger, A., Kochman, A., and Alexandridis, N., Computer Analysis of Chromosome Patterns: Feature Encoding for Flexible Decision Making, *IEEE Trans. Comput.* (Special Issue on Feature Extraction and Selection in Pattern Recognition) **20**, 1014–1022 (1971).

37d. Kozlay, D., Feature Extraction in an Optical Character Recognition Machine, *IEEE Trans. Comput.* **20**, 1063–1066 (1971).

38. Kruskal, J. B., Multidimensional Scaling by Optimizing Goodness of Fit to a Nonmetric Hypothesis, *Psychometrika* **29**, 1–27 (1964).

39. Kruskal, J. B., Nonmetric Multidimensional Scaling: A Numerical Method, *Psychometrika* **29**, 115–129 (1964).

39a. Kruskal, J. B., and Carroll, J. D., Geometrical Models and Badness-of-Fit Functions, *in* "Multivariate Analysis—II," (P. R. Krishnaiah, ed.), Academic Press, New York, 1969.

40. Kullback, S., "Information Theory and Statistics," pp. 197–200, Wiley, New York, 1959.

41. Lainiotis, D. G., Optimal Feature Extraction in Pattern Recognition, *Proc. 1967 Int. Symp. on Information Theory.*

42. Lainiotis, D. G., A Class of Upper Bounds on Probability of Error for Multihypothesis Pattern Recognition, *IEEE Trans. Information Theory* **15**, 730–731 (1969).

43. Lainiotis, D. G., Sequential Structure and Parameter-Adaptive Pattern Recognition— Part I: Supervised Learning, *IEEE Trans. Information Theory* **16**, 548–556 (1970).

44. Levine, M. D., Feature Extraction: A Survey, *Proc. IEEE*, **57**, 1391–1407 (1969).

45. Lewis, P. M., The Characteristic Selection Problem in Recognition Systems, *IEEE Trans. Information Theory* **8**, (1962).

45a. Lingoes, J. C., Recent Computational Advances in Nonmetric Methodology for the Behavioral Sciences, *Proc. Int. Symp. Mathematical and Computational Methods in Social Sciences*, pp. 1–38. International Computation Centre, Rome, Italy, 1966.

45b. Lingoes, J. C., The Multivariate Analysis of Qualitative Data, *Multivariate Behavioral Research*, **3**, 61–94 (1968).

46. Liu, C. N., A Programmed Algorithm for Designing Multifont Character Recognition Logics, *IEEE Trans. Electron. Comput.* **13**, 586–593 (1964).

46a. Makhoul, J., Speaker Adaptation in a Limited Speech Recognition System, *IEEE Trans. Comput.* **20**, 1057–1062 (1971)

47. Marill, T., and Green, D. M., On the Effectiveness of Receptors in Recognition Systems, *IEEE Trans. Information Theory* **9**, 11–27 (1963).

48. Meisel, W. S., Potential Functions in Pattern Classification Algorithms, *Proc. Symp. on Adaptive Processes, Pennsylvania State University, November 1969.*

49. Meisel, W. S., Dimensionality Reduction in Pattern Recognition, Pattern Recognition Workshop, *Sys. Sci. and Cybernetics Conf. Pittsburgh, October 1970.*

50. Meisel, W. S., On Nonparametric Feature Selection, *IEEE Trans. Information Theory* **17**, 105–106 (1971).

51. Meisel, W. S., The Efficient Representation of Functions for Pattern Classification and Feature Selection, *Proc. IEEE Systems, Man, and Cybernetics Conf.: Joint Nat. Conf. on Major Systems, Anaheim, Calif., October 1971.*

51a. Meisel, W. S., and Michalopoulos, D. A., A Partitioning Algorithm with Application in Pattern Classification, Piecewise-Constant Approximation, and the Optimization of Decision Trees, to be published.

51b. Meisel, W. S., Computer-Based Analysis of Medical Data, Pattern Recognition Workshop, *Joint Nat. Conf. on Major Systems, Anaheim, Calif., October 1971*; Abstract to be published in *IEEE Trans. Systems, Man, and Cybernetics.*

52. Min, P. J., A Non-Parametric Method of Feature Selection, *IEEE Proc. 7th Symp. on Adaptive Processes, UCLA, December 1968.*

52a. Mohn, W. S., Jr., Two Statistical Feature Evaluation Techniques Applied to Speaker Identification, *IEEE Trans. Comput.* **20**, 979–987 (1971).

53. Mucciardi, A. N., and Gose, E. E., A Comparison of Seven Techniques for Choosing Subsets of Pattern Recognition Properties, *IEEE Trans. Comput.* **20**, 1023–1031 (1971).

54. Munson, J. H., Duda, R. O., and Hart, P. E., Experiments with Highleyman's Data, Stanford Research Institute, Menlo Park, California, Research Rept., October 1967.

55. Nelson, G. D., and Levy, D. M., A Dynamic Programming Approach to the Selection of Pattern Features, *IEEE Trans. Sys. Science and Cybernetics* **4**, 145–151 (1968).

56. Patrick, E. A., and Fischer, F. P., II, Nonparametric Feature Selection, *IEEE Trans. Information Theory* **15**, 577–584 (1969).

57. Patrick, E. A., Fischer, F. P., II, and Shen, L. Y. L., Computer Analysis and Classification of Waveforms and Pictures: Part I—Waveforms, Purdue University, Lafayette, Indiana, RADC-TR-69-279, September 1969.

58. Pavlidis, T., Linguistic Analysis of Waveforms, *in* "Computer and Information Sciences III: Software Engineering, Vol. 2" (J. Tou, ed.), Academic Press, New York, 1971.

58a. Pols, L. C. W., Real-Time Recognition of Spoken Words, *IEEE Trans. Comput.* **20**, 972–978 (1971).

58b. Preston, K., Jr., Feature Extraction by Golay Hexagonal Pattern Transforms, *IEEE Trans. Comput.* **20**, 1007–1013 (1971).

59. Raviv, J., and Streeter, D. N., Linear Methods for Biological Data Processing, IBM Corp., Yorktown Heights, New York, Research Rept. RC-1577, December 1965.

60. Ray, W. D., and Driver, R. M., Further Decomposition of the Karhunen–Loève Series Representation of a Stationary Random Process, *IEEE Trans. Information Theory* **16**, 663–668 (1970).

61. Rosenfeld, A., "Picture Processing by Computer," Academic Press, New York, 1969.

62. Ryan, H. F., The Information Content Measure as a Performance Criterion for Feature Selection, *IEEE Proc. 7th Symp. on Adaptive Processes, UCLA, December 1968.*

63. Sammon, J. W., Jr., On-Line Pattern Analysis and Recognition System, Rome Air Development Center, Rome, New York, Tech. Rept. No. RADC-TR-68-263, August 1968.

64. Sammon, J. W., Jr., A Nonlinear Mapping for Data Structure Analysis, *IEEE Trans. Comput.* **18**, 401–409 (1969).

65. Sebestyen, G., "Decision-Making Processes in Pattern Recognition," Macmillan, New York, 1962.

66. Shepard, R. N., The Analysis of Proximities: Multidimensional Scaling with an Unknown Distance Function, *Psychometrika* **27**, 125–139, 219–246 (1962).

67. Shepard, R. N., and Carroll, J. D., Parametric Representation of Data Structures, *in* "Multivariate Analysis" (P. R. Krishnaiah, ed.), Academic Press, New York, 1966.

68. Shoenfelt, J. E., Tappert, C. C., and Goetze, A. J., Techniques for Efficient Encoding of Features in Pattern Recognition, *IEEE Trans. Comput.* **20**, 1104–1105 (1971).

68a. Smith, F. W., and Wright, M. H., Automatic Ship Photo Interpretation by the Method of Moments, *IEEE Trans. Comput.* **20**, 1089–1094 (1971).

69. Tappert, C. C., *et al.*, The Use of Dynamic Segments in the Automatic Recognition of Continuous Speech, Rome Air Development Center (prepared by IBM), RADC-TR-70-26, 1970.

70. Torgerson, W. S., "Theory and Methods of Scaling," Chap. 11. Wiley, New York, 1958.

71. Tou, J. T., Feature Extraction in Pattern Recognition, *Pattern Recognition* **1**, 3–11 (1968).

72. Tou, J. T., and Heydorn, R. P., Some Approaches to Optimum Feature Extraction, *in* "Computer and Information Sciences—II" (J. T. Tou, ed.), pp. 57–89, Academic Press, New York, 1967.

72a. Young, T. Y., The Reliability of Linear Feature Extractors, *IEEE Trans. Comput.* **20**, 967–971 (1971).

73. Watanabe, S., Karhunen–Loève Expansion and Factor Analysis—Theoretical Remarks and Applications, *Proc. Conf. Infor. Theory, 4th, Prague, Czechoslovakia, 1965.*

74. Watanabe, S., Lambert, P. F., Kulikowski, C. A., Buxton, J. L., and Walker, R., Evaluation and Selection of Variables in Pattern Recognition, *in* "Computer and Information Sciences—II" (J. T. Tou, ed.), pp. 91–122, Academic Press, New York, 1967.
75. White, H. S., Finding Events in a Sea of Bubbles, *IEEE Trans. Comput.* **20**, 988–994 (1971).
76. Whitney, A. W., A Direct Method of Nonparametric Measurement Selection, *IEEE Trans. Comput.* **20**, 1100–1103 (1971).

CHAPTER X

SPECIAL TOPICS

10.1   INTRODUCTION

There are many aspects of pattern recognition that are beyond the scope of this book. There is such a great deal of work making substantial contributions to particular areas such as image processing, character recognition, and speech processing that the author must be content with listing a few references at the end of this chapter. On the other hand, there are some areas which we can touch upon constructively because they spring naturally from material covered previously. The remainder of this chapter is devoted to a few such topics.

10.2   BINARY VARIABLES

If the features were restricted to binary values, say 0 and 1, one could develop particularized algorithms. Such problems can arise, for example, if an image is quantized by a bank of photocells, each of which indicate only the presence of light intensity below or above a fixed threshold. Clearly, none of our previous work involves any restrictions against variables taking only two values, but we are presently interested in methods which take advantage of this information.

Pure histogram approaches become more feasible, and assumptions such as independence of features or Markovian dependence of the variables are easier to justify.

↳ Previous trial predicts next trial

If samples composed of binary features are linearly separable, the problem becomes a conventional problem in designing a threshold logic element which gives an output of 1 for samples of one class and of 0 for samples of the other class. References [2, 3, 6–8, 30, 31, 33, 35, 52, 53] of Chapter IV discuss this problem.

Binary variables are often an inefficient means of creating a pattern space, and can be approached in some cases by creating from them features with more information. A common approach, for example, is to create new features which are weighted linear sums of the binary variables.

10.3 SEQUENTIAL FEATURE SELECTION

In Section 9.9.3 we introduced the concept of a nonuniform cost of features. If the cost of computing or collecting features is extreme, one might wish to compute only as many features as necessary to make a decision with some level of confidence, that is, to use the features *sequentially*. One might imagine, for example, that the application was one of diagnosing an illness and that each feature required a difficult (and perhaps dangerous) test on the patient. K. S. Fu [B4] introduced this problem in a pattern recognition context.

We can extend the concepts of Chapter II to this problem by defining a likelihood ratio λ_n which is a function of the number of features utilized:

$$\lambda_n = \frac{p_1(x_1, x_2, \ldots, x_n)}{p_2(x_1, x_2, \ldots, x_n)}. \tag{10.1}$$

Wald [B6] suggested a sequential probability ratio test (SPRT): Continue taking new features until (a) $\lambda_n \geq A$, or (b) $\lambda_n \leq B$. In the first case, decide class 1. In the second case, decide class 2. For example, suppose $A = 1.2$ and $B = 1/1.2 = 0.833$; then, no decision will be made until one conditional probability exceeds the other by 20%.

The SPRT may not provide a solution in a finite number of features, so the modified SPRT (MSPRT) of Chien and Fu [B3] might be used; define $g_1(n)$ and $g_2(n)$ as monotonically nonincreasing and nondecreasing functions of n, respectively. Then:

Continue taking new features until $\lambda_n > e^{g_1(n)}$ or $\lambda_n < e^{g_2(n)}$.

In the first case, decide class 1; in the second case, decide class 2. If

$$g_1(n) = a'\left(1 - \frac{n}{R}\right)^{r_1}, \qquad g_2(n) = -b'\left(1 - \frac{n}{R}\right)^{r_2}, \tag{10.2}$$

$$0 \leq r_1, r_2 \leq 1, \quad a' > 0, \quad b' > 0,$$

then $g_1(R) = g_2(R) = 0$, and a decision *must* be made with R features unless the probabilities are identical.

The sequential problem can be treated as R different problems, where R is the maximum number of features, and an expression for λ_n for $n = 1, 2, \ldots, R$ can be derived, for example, with potential function estimates of the probabilities.

A remaining problem is the order of choice of the features. One logical approach is to use a ranking formula to determine the relative efficacy of the features (Section 9.9) and to choose the features in order of rank (or in the order of the product of their rank and their cost of utilization). This approach yields a fixed order of feature utilization and requires that only R decision rules be estimated from labeled samples or otherwise.

One might attempt, instead, to determine which of the features should optimally be chosen given the values of the features already chosen. This is a considerably more difficult problem. A dynamic programming solution may be formulated [B4], but suboptimal solutions appear to be required for computational feasibility.

10.4 STRUCTURAL, LINGUISTIC, AND HEURISTIC ANALYSIS OF PATTERNS

It is impossible here to go into the varieties of approaches which fall under the above and similar labels or into the structure of formal language theory, so this section must be limited to some general concepts. Structural, linguistic, and heuristic methods attempt to utilize more *a priori* knowledge about the problem than the approaches proposed to this point, and have largely been limited to visual patterns or to waveforms where humans have a rather detailed understanding of the types of patterns to expect. When the application is suitable, they can reduce or eliminate the need for labeled samples. The applications are usually those in which the human could do the job readily by inspection of the waveform or image, but the task is to be performed automatically.

Without attempting to do full justice to the subject, let us consider a simple example of linguistic constructions. The "elements" of the language are

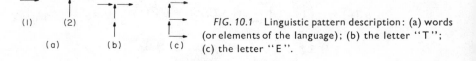

FIG. 10.1 Linguistic pattern description: (a) words (or elements of the language); (b) the letter "T"; (c) the letter "E".

illustrated in Fig. 10.1a; there are only two elements. There are several operators:

$$\rightarrow\!\leftarrow \quad \text{head to head,}$$
$$\rightarrow\!\rightarrow \quad \text{head to tail,}$$
$$\leftarrow\!\leftarrow \quad \text{tail to head, and}$$
$$\leftarrow\!\rightarrow \quad \text{tail to tail.}$$

Then, if the "head" is denoted by the arrow of the element and the head or tail under consideration is that of the last element added,

$$(1)\!\rightarrow\!\rightarrow\!(1)\!\leftarrow\!\leftarrow\!(2)\!\leftarrow\!\leftarrow\!(2)$$

is a "sentence" describing Fig. 10.1b, the letter "*T*"; and

$$(1)\!\leftarrow\!\leftarrow\!(2)\!\leftrightarrow\!(1)\!\leftarrow\!\leftarrow\!(2)\!\leftrightarrow\!(1)$$

represents Fig. 10.1c, the letter "E." As a recognition problem, the elements and their relationship would have to be extracted from the representation of the pattern in measurement space, and that "sentence" analyzed. A FORTRAN compiler is a pattern recognizer in the same sense; it "recognizes" whether a given program is a legitimate member of the FORTRAN language or is not.

There are clearly two stages in linguistic analysis: (1) the extraction of the sentence from measurement space; and (2) the interpretation of that sentence. Most work to date has emphasized the latter aspect.

The extraction of the characterization of the pattern is analogous to feature selection; the interpretation of the representation is analogous to pattern classification. The effect of the linguistic approach in practice seems to be to place the burden of the procedure on the selection of features which allow a manageable linguistic solution. If the overall procedure is considered, the distinction between the linguistic and statistical approaches becomes fuzzy. Watanabe [C25] presents a strong argument for the similarity of the two approaches and describes some of the pitfalls and limitations of the linguistic approach.

Structural, linguistic, or heuristic approaches allow the utilization of knowledge of the particular application in question to minimize sample requirements and improve accuracy. Since humans are notoriously inept at describing their innate pattern recognition algorithms, such procedures must be undertaken with care. The heuristic approach is to define features with clear interpretations and, rather than using labeled samples to derive decision boundaries, to *describe* from knowledge of the problem the exact equations and logic of the decision rule. Those equations and logic might be in the form of a formal language or might be anything the designer can program.

Consider, for example, the approach to waveform analysis proposed by Pavlidis [C21]. He was concerned with the representation of waveforms in such a manner as to facilitate their processing by linguistic or heuristic approaches and in such a manner as to preserve the *details* of structure so important in applications such as electrocardiogram analysis. He described algorithms for approximating the waveform with a piecewise linear function such that the maximum difference between the representation and the actual waveform was less than a prespecified bound. Figure 10.2 illustrates a wave-

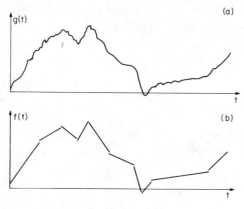

FIG. 10.2 Waveform representation: (a) the original waveform; (b) a reduced representation.

form and its representation. The representation preserves detailed structure which might be lost in a least-squares approximation such as the expansions in orthonormal functions described in Chapter IX. Using such a representation, it is easier to design explicit algorithms for extracting features which can be described in a fuzzy manner: "the presence of a small notch in a large peak," "a rapid but brief drop to negative values," etc.

Collins and co-workers [C6, C6a] have described a means for using such a representation to obtain features which give a continuous value measuring the *degree* to which such fuzzy characteristics exist; their formulation, *distortion-invariant feature extraction,* is such that the description of the characteristic of interest may be changed by varying *parameters* of the algorithm rather than the algorithm itself. Such continuous features allow the exploitation of the full power of conventional pattern classification algorithms when samples are available. Meisel and Collins generalized this concept to *structural languages* [C15a]. Patrick *et al.* [C20] describe a means of extracting continuous features from waveforms using *intervalized basis functions*.

An oversimplification may be useful in illustrating the effect of the heuristic rather than statistical approach. Suppose x_1 and x_2 were two features measuring the degree to which two different characteristics were present in a waveform or picture. In the heuristic approach, the designer might, through his interpretation of the features, choose two constants, α_1

and α_2, such that $x_i \geq \alpha_i$ implied characteristic i was present and $x_i < \alpha_i$ implied it was not. The decision rule employed might be as follows: If characteristic 1 *and* characteristic 2 are present or if neither characteristic 1 or 2 are present, then the sample is in class 1; if characteristic 1 but not 2 or characteristic 2 but not 1 are present, the sample is in class 2. This decision rule results in the boundaries of Fig. 10.3a.

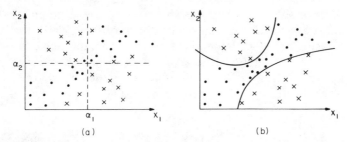

(a) (b)

FIG. 10.3 Heuristic versus statistical approaches: (a) heuristic boundaries; (b) boundaries derived by pattern classification algorithms.

In that figure, we have included samples of the two classes; if conventional pattern classification algorithms are applied, the boundaries of Fig. 10.3b might be obtained. These boundaries do not admit of an easy word statement of the logic employed, but they represent more closely the actual physical patterns. Hence, given the same features and a sufficient set of labeled samples, the statistical approach is perhaps preferable. The obvious advantage of heuristic or linguistic methods is that they often require *no samples*.

10.5 ASYMPTOTIC CONVERGENCE AND STOCHASTIC APPROXIMATION

Many important theoretical results can be obtained for algorithms by studying their behavior as the number of samples M approaches infinity, their *asymptotic convergence* to optimal or suboptimal solutions. For example, Parzen [E9] showed the conditions under which potential function estimators converged to the actual probability densities; Cover and Hart [E4] showed that nearest-neighbor methods converged asymptotically to a value of risk which could be related to the risk of the optimal decision rule. This text has largely omitted discussion of these results for two related reasons: it is difficult to (1) orient this text toward applied rather than theoretical results, and (2) obtain enough samples to approach the asymptotic case in high-dimensional spaces.

Stochastic approximation is a technique which has achieved some popularity because of its ability to converge asymptotically to the optimum of appropriate cost functions in the presence of statistical noise. The algorithms obtained by this approach do not generally differ in form from algorithms obtained by considering the minimization of loss functions without consideration of asymptotic properties; the usual impact of such considerations is to impose limitations upon the parameters of the algorithm. We noted in Section 3.2, for example, that one choice of ε_i in the gradient technique corresponded to a stochastic approximation algorithm. We further noted in Section 5.2, that an algorithm derived by approximating the expectation by an average over the samples could be put in the form of a stochastic approximation algorithm. Stochastic approximation has hence proved a powerful technique for theoretical interpretation and justification of many algorithms.

10.6 NONSTATIONARY PATTERN RECOGNITION

Suppose the probability densities describing the class distributions were nonstationary, i.e., time-varying:

$$p_i(\mathbf{x}) \equiv p_i(\mathbf{x}; t), \tag{10.3a}$$

$$p_i \equiv p_i(t). \tag{10.3b}$$

There are two major types of nonstationarities which allow pattern recognition to proceed [D2]:

(1) The variation with time is of the form

$$p_i(\mathbf{x}; t) \equiv p_i[\mathbf{x}; f_1(t), \dots, f_K(t)], \tag{10.4a}$$

$$p_i(t) = p_i[g_1(t), \dots, g_L(t)], \tag{10.4b}$$

where $g_i(t)$ and $f_i(t)$ can be measured or estimated; and

(2) The variation with time is sufficiently slow, relative to the rate at which samples are taken, to allow labeled samples to be used for classification.

The first case becomes a stationary problem if the *a priori* probabilities p_i are stationary and $f_1(t), f_2(t), \dots, f_K(t)$ can be treated as features. Then

$$p_i(\mathbf{x}; t) \equiv p_i(\hat{\mathbf{x}}), \tag{10.5}$$

where $\hat{\mathbf{x}} = (x_1, x_2, \dots, x_n, f_1, \dots, f_K)$, and the problem is conventional. If the dependence is periodic, one can design special algorithms to extract this dependence; for example, we could add a feature $x_{n+1} = \sin \omega t$, and minimize one of the measures of quality suggested in Chapter IX with respect to ω. The amount of improvement in the measure of quality indicates the degree of periodic dependence and the minimizing value of ω the optimum periodicity. It is worth noting that, if the time dependence is of the form (10.4) and if $f_1, f_2, \ldots, f_K$ cannot be measured or estimated, then the presence of these unknown quantities simply adds statistical uncertainty; classical techniques may still be successful. Figure 10.4 indicates the improvement in separability

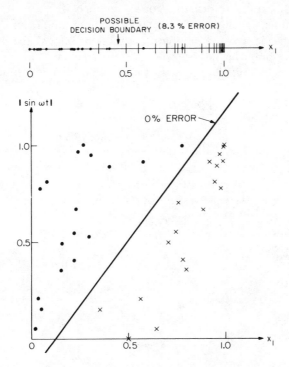

FIG. 10.4 Using periodicity as a feature.

of a set of artificial samples using $|\sin \omega t|$ as a feature, but a respectable result could be obtained, as indicated, using only the single feature x_1 [D2].

In the second case, slow-varying dependence, the major impact is that the optimum decision boundary varies slowly and the latest samples are the most valid. If the samples are ordered as they occur, then they might be assigned weights such that

$$0 < \alpha_1 < \alpha_2 < \cdots < \alpha_M, \tag{10.6}$$

e.g.,

$$\alpha_i = a^i, \qquad a > 1, \tag{10.7}$$

if M is the index of the last labeled sample. Then, most of the algorithms proposed can be modified such that the latest samples affect the decision boundary the most. Potential function methods become

$$\hat{p}(\mathbf{x}) = \frac{1}{M} \sum_{i=1}^{M} \alpha_i \gamma(\mathbf{x}, \mathbf{y}_i),$$ (10.8)

a simple modification. (Normalization is retained if $\sum \alpha_i = 1$.) We can use the one-at-a-time algorithms of Chapter IV without modification if we do not cycle through the labeled samples; in these methods, the hyperplane is adjusted using only the last sample. Alternatively, we can modify indirect methods by including the weight factor in the cost function, e.g.,

$$\tilde{R} = \frac{1}{M} \sum_{i=1}^{M} \alpha_i f(d - \mathbf{w} \cdot \mathbf{y}_i).$$ (10.9)

In summary, the tools developed throughout this text can be used directly or modified for the nonstationary case.

EXERCISES

10.1. *Sequential feature selection.* Given

$$p_1(\mathbf{x}) = K \exp\left[-\frac{\pi}{10} \|\mathbf{x}\|^2\right], \qquad p_2(\mathbf{x}) = K \exp\left[-\frac{\pi}{10} \|\mathbf{x} - (2, 2, \ldots, 2)\|^2\right]$$

for $\mathbf{x}$ of any dimension; further given sequential features of a vector $\mathbf{x}$ to be classified:

$$x_1 = 1$$
$$x_2 = 2$$
$$\vdots$$
$$x_i = i$$
$$\vdots$$

(a)   Using Wald's SPRT, what values of stopping boundaries A and B will cause a decision to be made on x_3? On x_4? What is the decision?

(b)   Plot the likelihood ratio λ_i as a function of i for $1 \le i \le 10$.

10.2. *Sequential feature selection.* Using the modified SPRT with

$$g_1(n) = \left(1 - \frac{n}{5}\right)^{.5}, \qquad g_2(n) = -\left(1 - \frac{n}{5}\right)^{.5}$$

on pattern classes represented by multivariate normal distributions (with unknown means and variances), an experimenter notes the following behavior:

$x_1 = 1, x_2 = 1:$ decision made for class 2
$x_1 = 0, x_2 = +1, x_3 = 0:$ decision made for class 1
$x_1 = 0, x_2 = 0, x_3 = 1, x_4 = 0, x_5 = 0:$ decision made for class 1

Find two normal distributions $p_1(x_1, \ldots, x_n)$, $p_2(x_1, x_2, \ldots, x_n)$, $n = 1, \ldots, 5$, for which the above behavior could hold.

10.3. *Nonstationary pattern recognition.* Suppose $h_1 = h_2$, $p_1 = p_2$, and

$$p_i(\mathbf{x}; t) = K \exp[-\tfrac{1}{2}\|\mathbf{x} - \mathbf{m}_i(t)\|^2],$$

with

$$\mathbf{m}_1(t) = (1, 1)t + (1, 1) \quad \text{and} \quad \mathbf{m}_2(t) = (-1, -1)t + (-1, -1).$$

Find the optimum decision boundary and show that it does not vary with time.

SELECTED BIBLIOGRAPHY

A. *Binary Features*

A1. Abend, K., Harley, T. J., and Kanal, L. N., Classification of Binary Random Patterns, *IEEE Trans. Information Theory* **11**, 538–544 (1965).

A2. Bledsoe, W. W., Further Results on the n-tuple Pattern Recognition Method, *IRE Trans. Electron. Comput.* **10**, 96 (1961).

A3. Bledsoe, W. W., and Browning, I., Pattern Recognition and Reading by Machine, *1959 Proc. Eastern Joint Computer. Conf.*, Sandia Corp., Alburquerque, New Mexico, Reprint SCR-132, March 1960.

A4. Chow, C. K., A Class of Nonlinear Recognition Procedures, *IEEE Trans. Sys. Science and Cybernetics* **2**, 101–109 (1966).

A5. Chow, C. K., and Liu, C. N., An Approach to Structure Adaptation in Pattern Recognition, *IEEE Trans. Sys. Science and Cybernetics* **2**, 73–80. (1966).

A6. Chow, C. K., and Liu, C. N., Approximating Discrete Probability Distributions with Dependence Trees, *IEEE Trans. Information Theory* **14**, 462–567 (1968).

A7. Highleyman, W. H., Further Comments on the n-tuple Pattern Recognition Method, *IRE Trans. Electron. Comput.* **10**, 97 (1961).

A8. Lewis, P. M., Approximating Probability Distributions to Reduce Storage Requirement, *Information and Control* **2**, 214–225 (1959).

A9. Roy, R. J., and Sherman, J., Two Viewpoints of k-tuple Pattern Recognition, *IEEE Trans. Sys. Science and Cybernetics* **3**, 117–120 (1967).

A10. Sklansky, J., Threshold Training of Two-Mode Signal Detection, *IEEE Trans. Information Theory* **11**, 353–362 (1965).

A11. Toussaint, G. T., Note on Optimal Selection of Independent Binary-Valued Features for Pattern Recognition, *IEEE Trans. Information Theory* **17**, 618 (1971).

A12. Winder, R. O., Threshold Logic in Artificial Intelligence, *Proc. IEEE Winter Gen. Meet., Sessions on Artificial Intelligence, January 1963*, pp. 107–128.

B.   *Sequential Feature Selection*

B1.   Chien, Y. T., and Fu, K. S., Sequential Decisions, Pattern Recognition and Machine Learning, Purdue University, Lafayette, Indiana, TR-EE65-6, April 1965.
B2.   Chien, Y. T. and Fu, K. S., On the Finite Stopping Rules and Nonparametric Techniques in a Feature Ordered Sequential Recognition System, Purdue University, Lafayette, Indiana, Rept. TR-3366-16, October 1966.
B3.   Chien, Y. T., and Fu, K. S., Sequential Recognition Using a Nonparametric Ranking Procedure, *IEEE Trans. Information Theory* **13**, 484–492 (1967).
B4.   Fu, K. S., "Sequential Methods in Pattern Recognition and Machine Learning," Academic Press, New York, 1969.
B5.   Fu, K. S., Min, P. J., and Li, T. J., Feature Selection in Pattern Recognition, *IEEE Trans. Sys. Science and Cybernetics* **6**, 33–39 (1970).
B6.   Wald, A., "Sequential Analysis," Wiley, New York, 1967.

C.   *Linguistic and Structural Approaches*

C1.   Anderson, R. H., Syntax-Directed Recognition of Hand-Printed Two-Dimensional Mathematics, *in* "Symposium on Interactive Systems for Experimental Applied Mathematics" (M. Klerer and J. Reinfelds, eds.), pp. 436–459, Academic Press, New York, 1968.
C2.   Chomsky, N., "Syntactical Structures," Mouton, The Hague, 1957.
C3.   Chomsky, N., Linguistic Theory, *in* "Northeast Conference on The Teaching of Foreign Languages; Working Committee Report," (R. C. Mead, ed.), p. 43, 1966.
C4.   Clowes, M. B., Perception, Picture Processing and Computers, *in* Machine Intelligence (N. Collins and D. Mitchie, eds.), pp. 81–197, Oliver and Boyd, Edinburgh, 1967.
C5.   Clowes, M. B., Transformational Grammars and the Organization of Pictures, *in* Automatic Interpretation and Classification of Images (A. Grasselli, ed.), Academic Press, New York, 1969.
C6.   Collins, D. C., Meisel, W. S., and Shaw, D. E., Distortion-Invariant Structural Analysis of Waveforms, Technology Service Corp., Santa Monica, California, Rept. No. 027, December 1970.
C6a.   Collins, D. C., and Meisel, W. S., Structural Analysis of Biological Waveforms, *Proc. Ann. Conf. Engr. Medicine Biology, Las Vegas, Nevada, November 1971.*
C7.   Evans, T. G., Descriptive Pattern-Analysis Techniques: Potentialities and Problems, *in* "Methodologies of Pattern Recognition," (S. Watanabe, ed.), p. 147, Academic Press, New York, 1969.
C8.   Feder, J., The Linguistic Approach to Pattern Analysis—A Literature Survey, Department of Electrical Engineering, New York University, New York, Tech. Rept. 400-133, February 1966.
C9.   Feder, J., Languages, Automata, and Classes of Chain-Encoded Patterns, New York University, New York, Tech. Rept. 400-165 (AD668081), August 1967.
C10.   Feder, J., Linguistic Specification and Analysis of Classes of Line Patterns, Department of Electrical Engineering, New York University, New York, Tech. Rept. 403-2, April 1969.
C11.   Grenander, U., Foundations of Pattern Analysis, *Quart. Appl. Math.* **27**, 1–55 (1969).
C12.   Ledley, R. S., and Ruddle, F. H., Chromosome Analysis by Computer, *Scientific American*, 40–46 (April 1966).
C13.   Ledley, R., and Wilson, J., Concept Analysis by Syntax Processing, *Proc. Amer. Documentation Inst.* **1**, (October 1964).

C14. Ledley, R. S., Rotolo, L. S., Golab, T. J., Jacobsen, J. D., Ginsberg, M. D., and Wilson, J. B., FIDAC: Film Input to Digital Automatic Computer and Associated Syntax-Directed Pattern Recognition Programming System, *in* "Optical and Electro-Optical Information Processing" J. T. Tippett, (D. A. Berkowtiz, L. C. Clapp, C. J. Koester, and A. Vanderburgh, Jr., eds.), pp. 591–713, MIT Press, Cambridge, Massachusetts, 1965.

C15. Lipkin, L. E., Watt, W. C., and Kirsch, R. A., The Analysis, Synthesis, and Description of Biological Images, *Ann. N. Y. Acad. Sci.* **128**, 984–1012 (1966).

C15a. Meisel, W. S., and Collins, D. C., Biomedical Signal Analysis Using Interactive Graphics, *San Diego Biomedical Symp., San Diego, California, February 1972*.

C16. Miller, W. F., and Shaw, A. C., Linguistic Methods in Picture Processing—A Survey, *Proc. Fall Joint Comput. Conf. 1968*, pp. 279–290, Spartan, Washington, D. C.

C17. Miller, W. F., and Shaw, A. C., A Picture Calculus, *in* "Emerging Concepts in Computer Graphics," pp. 101–121, Benjamin, New York, 1968.

C18. Narasimhan, R., Labeling Schemata and Syntactic Descriptions of Pictures, *Information and Control* **7**, 151 (1964).

C19. Nir, M., Recognition of General Line Patterns with Application to Bubble Chamber Photographs and Handprinted Characters, Ph.D. Thesis, Department of Electric Engineering, University of Pennsylvania, 1967.

C20. Patrick, E. A., Fischer, F. P., II, and Shen, L. Y. L., Computer Analysis and Classification of Waveforms and Pictures: Part I—Waveforms, Purdue University, Lafayette, Indiana, RADC-TR-69-279, September 1969.

C21. Pavlidis, T., Linguistic Analysis of Waveforms, "Software Egineering Vol. 2," (J. Tou, ed.), Academic Press, New York, 1971.

C22. Rosenfeld, A., *et al.*, Sequential Operations in Digital Picture Processing, *J. Assoc. Comput. Mach.* **13**, 471 (1966).

C23. Shaw, A. C., The Formal Description and Parsing of Pictures, Ph.D. Thesis, Computer Science Department, Stanford University (1968). Also available from Stanford Linear Accelerator Center, Stanford, California, SLAC Rept. No. 84, 1968.

C24. Swain, P. H., and Fu, K. S., Nonparametric and Linguistic Approaches to Pattern Recognition, Purdue University, Lafayette, Indiana, Lars Information Note 051970, TR-EE 70-20, June 1970.

C25. Watanabe, S., Ungrammatical Grammar in Pattern Recognition, *Pattern Recognition* (to appear).

D. *Nonstationary Pattern Recognition*

D1. Amari, S., A Theory of Adaptive Pattern Classifiers, *IEEE Trans. Electron. Comput.* **16**, 299–307 (1967).

D2. Meisel, W. S., and Yuan, W. W., Nonstationary Pattern Recognition (to be published).

D3. Nilsson, N. J., "Learning Machines," McGraw-Hill, New York, 1965.

E. *Asymptotic Convergence and Stochastic Approximation*

E1. Aizerman, M. A., Braverman, E. M., and Rozonoer, L. I., Method of Potential Functions in the Problem of Restoration of Functional Converter Characteristic by Means of Points Observed Randomly, *Automat. Remote Control* **25**, (December 1964).

E2. Blum, J., Multidimensional Stochastic Approximation Methods, *Ann. Math. Statist.* **25**, 373–407 (1954).

E3. Cover, T. M., Rates of Convergence for Nearest Neighbor Classification, *Proc. 1st Ann. Hawaii Conf. on Sys. Theory, January 1968.*

E4. Cover, T. M., and Hart, P. E., Nearest Neighbor Pattern Classification, *IEEE Trans. Information Theory* **13**, 21–26 (1967).

E5. Dvoretzky, A., On Stochastic Approximation, *Proc. 1960 Berkeley Symp. Math. Stat. and Prob., Vol.* 1, pp. 39–55.

E6. Kashyap, R. L., and Blaydon, C. C., Recovery of Functions from Noisy Measurements Taken at Randomly Selected Points and Its Application to Pattern Classification, *Proc. IEEE* **54**, 1127–1129 (1966).

E7. Kashyap, R. L., and Blaydon, C. C., Estimation of Probability Density and Distribution Functions, *IEEE Trans. Information Theory* **14**, 549–556 (1968).

E8. Nikolic, Z. J., and Fu, K. S., A Mathematical Model of Learning in an Unknown Random Environment, *1966 Proc. Nat. Electron. Conf., Vol.* 22, pp. 607–612.

E9. Parzen, E., On Estimation of Probability Density Function and Mode, *Ann. Math. Statist.* **33**, 1065–1076 (1962).

E10. Peterson, D. W., Some Convergence Properties of a Nearest Neighbor Decision Rule, *IEEE Trans. Information Theory* **16**, 26–31 (1970).

E11. Robbins, H., and Monro, S., A Stochastic Approximation Method, *Ann. Math. Statist.* **22**, (1951).

E12. Tsypkin, Ya. Z., Application of Stochastic Approximation Method to the Estimation of the Unknown Distribution by Observation, *Automat. Remote Control* **26**, (March 1966).

E13. Wagner, T. J., The Rate of Convergence of an Algorithm for Recovering Functions from Noisy Measurements Taken at Randomly Selected Points, *IEEE Trans. Sys. Science and Cybernetics* **4**, 151–154 (1968).

E14. Wolverton, C. T., and Wagner, T. J., Asymptotically Optimal Discriminant Functions for Pattern Recognition, Laboratories for Electronics and Related Science Research, University of Texas, Austin, Tech. Rept. No. 45, February, 1968.

F. *Other*

F1. Andrews, H. C., "Computer Techniques in Image Processing," Academic Press, New York, 1970.

F2. Andrews, H. C., and Pratt, W. K., Transform Image Coding, *Symp. on Comput. Processing in Communications*, Polytechnic Institute of Brooklyn, New York, April 1969.

F2a. Arcelli, C., and Levialdi, S., Picture Processing and Overlapping Blobs, *IEEE Trans. Comput.* **20**, 1111–1115 (1971).

F3. Arcese, A., Mengert, P. H., and Trombini, E. W., Image Detection Through Bipolar Correlation, *IEEE Trans. Information Theory* **16**, 534–540 (1970).

F4. Bellman, R., Dynamic Programming, Pattern Recognition, and Location of Faults in Complex Systems, *J. Appl. Probability* **3**, 268–271 (1966).

F5. Chow, C. K., On Optimum Recognition Error and Reject Tradeoff, *IEEE Trans. Information Theory* **16**, 41–47 (1970).

F6. Dreyfus, H. L., Alchemy and Artificial Intelligence, Rand Report P-3244, Rand Corp., Santa Monica, California, December 1965.

F7. Drucker, H., Computer Optimization of Recognition Networks, *IEEE Trans. Comput.* **18**, 918–923 (1969).

F8. Eden, M., Handwriting and Pattern Recognition, *IRE Trans. Information Theory* **8**, 160 (1962)

F9. Grasselli, A. (ed.), "Automatic Interpretation and Classification of Images," Academic Press, New York, 1969.

F10. Harley, T. J., Jr., Kanal, L. N., and Randall, N. C., System Considerations for Automatic Imagery Screenin, *in* "Pictorial Pattern Recognition," (G. C. Cheng *et al.*, eds.), Thompson, Washington, D.C., 1968.

F11. Holt, A. W., Comparative Religion in Character Recognition Machines, *Computer Group News* **2**, 3–11 (1968).

F12. Highleyman, W. H., Data for Character Recognition Studies, *IEEE Trans. Electron. Comput.* **12**, 135–136 (1963).

F13. Kanal, L. N., (ed.), "Pattern Recognition," Thompson, Washington, D.C., 1968.

F14. Ledley, R. S., Rotolo, L. S., Golab, T. J., Jacobsen, J. D., Ginsberg, M. D., and Wilson, J. B., FIDAC: Film Input to Digital Automatic Computer and Associated Syntax-Directed Pattern Recognition Programming System, *in* "Optical and Electro-Optical Information Processing" (J. T. Tippet, D. A. Berkowitz, L. C. Clapp, C. J. Koester, and A. Vanderburgh, Jr., eds.), pp. 591–613, MIT Press, Cambridge, Massachusetts, 1965.

F15. Lipkin, B. S., and Rosenfeld, A., "Picture Processing and Psychopictorics," Academic Press, New York, 1970.

F16. Minsky, M., Steps Toward Artificial Intelligence, *Proc. IRE* **49**, 8 (1961).

F17. *Pattern Recognition*, Special Issue on Image Enhancement **2** (2) (1970).

F18. Pratt, W. K., Kane, J., and Andrews, H. C., Hadamard Transform Image Coding, *Proc. IEEE* **57**, 58–67 (1969).

F19. Richardson, J. M., Theory of Property Filtering in Pattern Recognition, Hughes Aircraft Research Labs., Malibu, California, Tech. Rept. No. RADC-TR-66-531, September 1966.

F20. Rosenfeld, A., "Picture Processing by Computer," Academic Press, New York, 1969.

F21. Sammon, J. W., Jr., Interactive Pattern Analysis and Classification, *IEEE Trans. Comput.* **7**, 594–616 (1970).

F22. Watanabe, S., Mathematical Explication of Classification of Objects, *in* "Information and Prediction in Science," (S. Dockx and P. Bernays, eds.), p. 39, Academic Press, New York, 1965.

F23. Watanabe, S., "Knowing and Guessing," Wiley, New York, 1969.

F24. Watanabe, S., Pattern Recognition as an Inductive Process, *in* "Methodologies of Pattern Recognition" (S. Watanabe, ed.), p. 521, Academic Press, New York, 1969.

F25. Watanabe, S., Modified Concepts of Logic, Probability and Information Based on Generalized Continuous Characteristic Function, *Information and Control* **15**, 1 (1969).

F26. Zadeh, L. A., Fuzzy Sets, *Information and Control* **8**, 368–353 (1965).

A SET OF
ORTHONORMAL POLYNOMIALS

The polynomials in one dimension defined by

$$Q_m(x) = \sum_{k=0}^{m} (-1)^k \binom{m}{k} \binom{m+k}{k} x^k, \qquad m = 1, 2, 3, \ldots, \qquad Q_0(x) = 1,$$

have the property that

$Q_1(x) = 1 - 2x$

$$\int_0^1 Q_n(x) Q_m(x)\, dx = \begin{cases} 0, & n \neq m, \\ \dfrac{1}{2n+1}, & n = m. \end{cases}$$

Hence, the polynomials

$$P_n(x) = (2n + 1)^{1/2}\, Q_n(x), \qquad n = 0, 1, 2, \ldots$$

are orthonormal in [0, 1]. A set of multivariate orthonormal polynomials of degree R in n variables is then

$$\{\phi_{m_1 m_2 \cdots m_n}(\mathbf{x}) \,|\, 0 \leq m_1 + m_2 + \cdots + m_n \leq R, 0 \leq m_i \leq R\},$$

where

$$\phi_{m_1 m_2 \cdots m_n}(\mathbf{x}) = P_{m_1}(x_1) P_{m_2}(x_2) \cdots P_{m_n}(x_n). \tag{A.1}$$

The reader may verify that these functions are indeed orthonormal and that

$$\sum_{\mathcal{M}} a_{m_1 m_2 \cdots m_n} \phi_{m_1 \cdots m_n}(\mathbf{x}),$$

where $\mathcal{M} = \{(m_1, m_2, \ldots, m_n) | 0 \leq m_1 + m_2 + \cdots + m_n \leq R, \ 0 \leq m_i \leq R\}$ represents a general multivariate polynomial of degree R.

Note that the multiplication in (A.1) represents an efficient way of computing the orthonormal functions and of storing the algorithm for doing so.

If the sample points y occur in the region $a_1 \leq y_1 \leq b_1$, $a_2 \leq y_2 \leq b_2, \ldots,$ $a_n \leq y_n \leq b_n$, they may be transformed into the unit cube by the substitution

$$x_i = \frac{(y_i - a_i)}{(b_i - a_i)}, \qquad i = 1, 2, \ldots, n.$$

EFFICIENT REPRESENTATION
AND APPROXIMATION
OF MULTIVARIATE FUNCTIONS

B.1 INTRODUCTION

Functions of multiple variables present problems in numerical analysis which can seldom be efficiently solved by the direct extension of univariate methods. A relatively unexplored area of extreme importance is that of the efficient representation and approximation of multivariate functions. In some cases, a mapping can be represented *exactly* by a more efficiently computed functional form than that in which it was given. In other cases, the objective is an efficiently represented *approximation*. Further, the function may be fully specified, specified only at sample points, or only implicitly specified as the minimum of a criterion function.

The concept of an efficient representation of a function must remain somewhat vague at this point. We shall simply note that there are two aspects of an efficient representation; among the class of functional representations which approximate a given mapping with a given degree of accuracy, an efficient approximation is among those which (a) are specified by a small number of parameters and (b) can be computed most efficiently. Two classes of efficiently defined functions are (1) piecewise linear form functions and (2) composed functions.

An *explicit* approximation problem is a conventional problem: minimize

$$\|F - f\| \quad \text{over} \quad f \in \mathscr{F}, \quad \mathscr{F} \quad \text{a family of functions,} \quad \text{(B.1)}$$

where $\mathbf{x} = (x_1, x_2, \ldots, x_n)$ and $F(\mathbf{x})$ is a given function. Another form of the problem occurs when only sampled values of F are given:

$$F(\mathbf{y}_1), F(\mathbf{y}_2), \ldots, F(\mathbf{y}_M); \tag{B.2}$$

the problem is then to find $f \in \mathscr{F}$ such that

$$f(\mathbf{y}_i) \approx F(\mathbf{y}_i), \qquad i = 1, 2, \ldots, M, \tag{B.3}$$

or, more formally, such that

$$\|\mathbf{F} - \mathbf{f}\|, \tag{B.4}$$

where $\mathbf{f} = [f(\mathbf{y}_1), \ldots, f(\mathbf{y}_M)]$ and $\mathbf{F} = [F(\mathbf{y}_1), \ldots, F(\mathbf{y}_M)]$, is minimized. Both forms are explicit approximation problems.

A problem which is not generally considered part of classical approximation theory, but which has much in common with the problem just postulated, is the approximation of implicitly defined functions. In particular, we will be concerned with finding efficient approximations of a function implicitly defined as a minimum of a *criterion function* $Q(f)$ for $f \in \mathscr{F}^*$, a given family of functions. If $\mathscr{F} \subset \mathscr{F}^*$, where $\mathscr{F}$ is the family of efficient approximations, then the criterion function is an excellent measure of the error in approximating the minimizing function, since the criterion function measures, by definition, the characteristics of the function of interest; the problem then becomes to find the minimum of

$$Q(f), \qquad f \in \mathscr{F}. \tag{B.5}$$

(Here again f may be either a vector or a function depending on whether $Q(f)$ is defined at sample points as in Eqs. (B.2) and (B.3) or is a measure which utilizes the full function f.) Most of the work described in the remainder of this discussion can be applied to the approximation of explicitly or implicitly defined functions; the work, in fact, indicates the relationship of the two problems and emphasizes their similarities rather than their differences.

It is worth emphasizing that we wish to be able to handle the problem posed in Eqs. (B.2)–(B.4) in its full generality. While for univariate functions, this problem is seldom considered of a significantly different nature than the problem posed in (B.1), it imposes considerable difficulties in a multivariate problem. Many multivariate methods which are extensions of univariate methods require griding of the space and hence the values of F at grid points in space. This information is available if the function F is given, but is not available if the problem is specified in the alternate form.

When the problem is phrased in either form, and a family of parameterized functions $\mathscr{F}$ is chosen, i.e.,

$$\mathscr{F} = \{f \mid f(\mathbf{x}) \quad \text{is defined for} \quad \mathbf{x} \in X,$$
$$f = f(\mathbf{x}; \boldsymbol{\alpha}) \quad \text{for some} \quad \boldsymbol{\alpha} \in \mathscr{A}\}, \tag{B.6}$$

then

$$Q(f) = Q[f(\mathbf{x}; \boldsymbol{\alpha})] \equiv Q(\boldsymbol{\alpha}). \tag{B.7}$$

The approximation problem then becomes one of finding the optimum value of the finite-dimensional vector $\boldsymbol{\alpha}$. The theory of the optimization of multivariate functions with respect to a finite set of parameters is relatively well developed, and hence a solution of a problem so formulated is feasible in many cases. The major characteristic determining computational feasibility, given a fixed criterion function Q, is the dimension of $\boldsymbol{\alpha}$. The key problem attacked here is the specification of *efficient* families of parametrized functions for approximation. Without attempting a formal definition, let us simply note that an efficient family of functions is one in which the number of parameters utilized in specifying a member of that family is low relative to the generality of the class of functions. Admittedly, this is a very vague statement of the problem, but the intention of this work can be made more clear by noting the major families of functions proposed for study:

(1) *Piecewise linear form functions*, i.e.,

$$f(\mathbf{x}; \boldsymbol{\alpha}_1, \ldots, \boldsymbol{\alpha}_R) = \begin{cases} \boldsymbol{\alpha}_1 \cdot \boldsymbol{\phi}(\mathbf{x}) & \text{for } \mathbf{x} \in X_1, \\ \boldsymbol{\alpha}_2 \cdot \boldsymbol{\phi}(\mathbf{x}) & \text{for } \mathbf{x} \in X_2, \\ \quad\vdots \\ \boldsymbol{\alpha}_R \cdot \boldsymbol{\phi}(\mathbf{x}) & \text{for } \mathbf{x} \in X_R, \end{cases} \tag{B.8a}$$

where

$$\boldsymbol{\phi}(\mathbf{x}) = [\phi_1(\mathbf{x}), \phi_2(\mathbf{x}), \ldots, \phi_R(\mathbf{x})], \tag{B.8b}$$

$$\boldsymbol{\alpha}_i = (\alpha_{i1}, \alpha_{i2}, \ldots, \alpha_{im}), \tag{B.8c}$$

$$X_1 \cup X_2 \cup \cdots \cup X_R = X, \tag{B.8d}$$

$$X_i \cap X_j = \phi, \tag{B.8e}$$

i.e., $X_1, X_2, \ldots, X_R$ partition the space of definition X. The expression $\boldsymbol{\alpha} \cdot \boldsymbol{\phi}(\mathbf{x})$ can, for example, be a multivariate polynomial.

(2) The class of *composed functions:*

$$f(\mathbf{x}; \boldsymbol{\alpha}, \boldsymbol{\beta}_1, \boldsymbol{\beta}_2, \ldots, \boldsymbol{\beta}_K) = G[H_1(\mathbf{x}; \boldsymbol{\beta}_1), H_2(\mathbf{x}; \boldsymbol{\beta}_2), \ldots, H_K(\mathbf{x}; \boldsymbol{\beta}_K); \boldsymbol{\alpha}]. \tag{B.9}$$

For example,

$$f(\mathbf{x}; \boldsymbol{\alpha}, \boldsymbol{\beta}) = \alpha_1 H^3(\mathbf{x}; \boldsymbol{\beta}) + \alpha_2 H^2(\mathbf{x}; \boldsymbol{\beta}) + \alpha_3 H(\mathbf{x}; \boldsymbol{\beta}) + \alpha_4,$$

with

$$H(\mathbf{x}; \boldsymbol{\beta}) = (x_1 - \beta_1)^3 (x_2 - \beta_2)^3 (x_3 - \beta_3)^3 + \beta_4 x_1 + \beta_5 x_2 + \beta_6 x_3 + \beta_7.$$

This example defines a restricted class of 27th-order polynomials in three variables with 11 parameters; a fully general polynomial of that order in three variables would require 4060 coefficients.

The last example indicates, with perhaps an exaggerated case, the sense by which we mean efficient classes of functions; by choosing the composed function properly (a matter to be discussed later), one can potentially achieve considerable reduction in the number of parameters for which it is necessary to minimize the criterion functions and an extreme reduction in the complexity and storage requirements for the final approximation derived. The first class of functions, piecewise linear form functions, have this same quality; in many cases very complex functions can be approximated by piecewise polynomial functions defined by many fewer parameters than required to define a general polynomial for equally accurate approximation.

The first problem fits into the category of spline approximation if it is required that the functions be continuous; however, methods for efficient multivariate spline approximations on *general* subregions have received a minimal amount of attention in the literature. As far as this author knows, the problem of composed functions has not even been broached in any generality.

B.2 CONTINUOUS PIECEWISE LINEAR FORM APPROXIMATIONS

B.2.1 A Canonical Form

If the function $f(\mathbf{x})$ in Eq. (B.8a) is continuous and the functions $\boldsymbol{\alpha} \cdot \boldsymbol{\phi}(\mathbf{x})$ over each subregion X_i are nth-order polynomials, then the boundaries between regions are given by

$$\boldsymbol{\alpha}_i \cdot \boldsymbol{\phi}(\mathbf{x}) = \boldsymbol{\alpha}_j \cdot \boldsymbol{\phi}(\mathbf{x}) \qquad \text{(B.10)}$$

and are polynomials of order at most n.

If we are given samples as in Eq. (B.2), then the transformation

$$\mathbf{z} = \boldsymbol{\phi}(\mathbf{x}) \qquad \text{(B.11)}$$

gives samples

$$\mathbf{z}_i = \boldsymbol{\phi}(\mathbf{y}_i), \qquad i = 1, 2, \ldots, M; \qquad \text{(B.12)}$$

the redefined problem of finding the optimal piecewise *linear* function

$$f(\mathbf{z}; \boldsymbol{\alpha}_1, \ldots, \boldsymbol{\alpha}_R) = \begin{cases} \boldsymbol{\alpha}_1 \cdot \mathbf{z}, & \mathbf{z} \in Z_1 \\ \quad \vdots \\ \boldsymbol{\alpha}_R \cdot \mathbf{z}, & \mathbf{z} \in Z_R, \end{cases} \qquad \text{(B.13)}$$

given samples $\mathbf{z}_i$ defined by (B.12) and $F(\mathbf{z}_i) = F(\mathbf{x}_i)$ as the value to be approximated, is exactly equivalent to the original piecewise linear form problem.

The coefficients $\alpha_1, \ldots, \alpha_R$ are exactly the same, and the piecewise linear boundaries of the subregions $Z_1, \ldots, Z_R$ correspond directly to the piecewise linear form boundaries of $X_1, \ldots, X_R$; Eq. (B.10) yields a linear hyperplane in Z-space. We may hence consider only piecewise linear functions with applicability to piecewise linear form functions.

It is convenient to add a notational convention to this canonical form of the problem. Since any practical set of functions $\{\phi_i(\mathbf{x})\}$ will contain a constant function which is transformed into the constant term of the linear form by (B.12), we will use a vector $\mathbf{x} = (x_1, x_2, \ldots, x_n)$ and its *augmented* form: $\mathbf{x}' = (x_1, x_2, \ldots, x_n, 1)$. The standard function form is then

$$f(\mathbf{x}; \alpha_1, \ldots, \alpha_R) = \alpha_i \cdot \mathbf{x}' \quad \text{for} \quad \mathbf{x} \in X_i \tag{B.14}$$

and X-space is considered to be n-dimensional.

B.2.2 Specifying the Subregion

If an arbitrary set of hyperplanes is defined in X, they define a set of *elementary subregions* $E_1, E_2, \ldots, E_K$:

Given hyperplanes $\mathbf{v}_1 \cdot \mathbf{x}' = 0, \ldots, \mathbf{v}_K \cdot \mathbf{x}' = 0$, a subregion E is an *elementary subregion* relative to $\mathbf{v}_1, \mathbf{v}_2, \ldots, \mathbf{v}_K$ if for some fixed assignment of μ_i, $i = 1, 2, \ldots, K$, $\mu_i \in \{-1, +1\}$, $\mathbf{e}$ is an interior point of E if and only if

$$\mu_i \mathbf{v}_i \cdot \mathbf{e}' > 0, \quad i = 1, 2, \ldots, K. \tag{B.15}$$

Figure B.1 indicates the eleven elementary subregions for the four hyperplanes chosen. The definition above can be stated more informally: An elementary subregion is one bounded by the given hyperplanes, but which cannot be further subdivided by an existing hyperplane. It can be shown that elementary subregions are convex sets.

A given elementary subregion is defined by the K-tuple of values $\boldsymbol{\mu} = (\mu_1, \mu_2, \ldots, \mu_K)$. The sign of μ_i indicates on which side of the hyperplane $\mathbf{v}_i \cdot \mathbf{x}' = 0$ the subregion lies; for example, E_3 is on the positive side of $\mathbf{v}_1 \cdot \mathbf{x}' = 0$, the negative side of $\mathbf{v}_2 \cdot \mathbf{x}' = 0$, the negative side of $\mathbf{v}_3 \cdot \mathbf{x}' = 0$, and the positive side of $\mathbf{v}_4 \cdot \mathbf{x}' = 0$, i.e., $\boldsymbol{\mu} = (+1, -1, -1, +1)$ defines E_3. Computationally, it is easy to determine into which elementary subregion a point falls by examining the sign of the quantities $\mathbf{v}_i \cdot \mathbf{x}'$, $i = 1, 2, \ldots, K$.

More complex subregions are given by unions of the elementary subregions, as in Fig. B.2, e.g.,

$$X_1 = E_1 \cup E_2 \cup E_{10} \cup E_{11}.$$

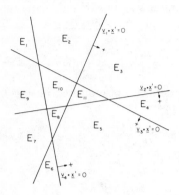

FIG. B.1 Elementary subregions.

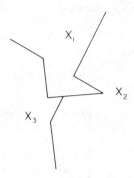

FIG. B.2 Unions of elementary subregions.

A continuous piecewise linear function can be defined over any set of such subregions; as an existence proof, one can simply note that the degenerate case $\alpha_1 = \alpha_2 = \cdots = \alpha_R$ is always continuous.

B.2.3 Continuous Piecewise Linear Transformations

When we require that the approximating function be continuous, there is an intimate interaction between the values of the parameters of the functions defined on the subregions and the boundaries of those subregions. Specifically, if regions X_i and X_j have a common boundary, then

$$\alpha_i \cdot \mathbf{x}' = \alpha_j \cdot \mathbf{x}' \tag{B.16}$$

must hold for $\mathbf{x}'$ on that boundary. Equation (B.16) can be written as

$$\mathbf{v}_{ij} \cdot \mathbf{x}' = 0, \tag{B.17a}$$

with

$$\mathbf{v}_{ij} = \alpha_i - \alpha_j. \tag{B.17b}$$

Alternatively, if we consider the boundaries given by (B.17a), Eq. (B.17b) implies a constraint on the parameters α_i. Let us consider both points of view.

Suppose we were given $\alpha_1, \alpha_2, \ldots, \alpha_R$. How might we define consistent subregions $X_1, X_2, \ldots, X_R$ such that $f(\mathbf{x})$ of Eq. (B.14) is continuous? Are these subregions uniquely determined?

Let us consider an example:

$$\begin{aligned}
\alpha_1 &= (1, 0, 1), & \alpha_3 &= (-1, 0, -1), \\
\alpha_2 &= (0, 1, 1), & \alpha_4 &= (0, -1, -1).
\end{aligned} \tag{B.18}$$

Boundaries of X_1, X_2, X_3, and X_4 are piecewise linear and, to preserve continuity, must be formed from hyperplanes given by (B.17):

$$\mathbf{v}_{12} = (1, -1, 0), \quad \mathbf{v}_{14} = (1, 1, 2), \quad \mathbf{v}_{24} = (0, 2, 2),$$
$$\mathbf{v}_{13} = (2, 0, 2), \quad \mathbf{v}_{23} = (1, 1, 2), \quad \mathbf{v}_{34} = (-1, 1, 0). \tag{B.19}$$

The six hyperplanes (in this case, lines) so defined are indicated in Fig. B.3.

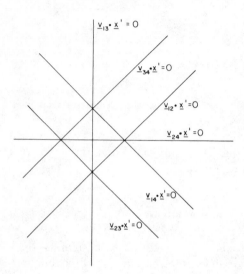

FIG. B.3 Potential boundaries to preserve continuity. Underscored symbols are vectors.

If we can partition the space into four subregions with boundaries formed from the indicated lines such that X_i is bounded only by planes $\mathbf{v}_{ij} \cdot \mathbf{x}' = 0$ or $\mathbf{v}_{ji} \cdot \mathbf{x}' = 0$ for any j, then $f(\mathbf{x})$ will be continuous as defined. The solid lines in Fig. B.4 indicate a consistent definition; for example, the boundary between X_1 and X_2 is $\mathbf{v}_{12} \cdot \mathbf{x} = 0$. It is immediately clear that this solution is not unique; Fig. B.5 indicates another valid partition. In two-space, this is

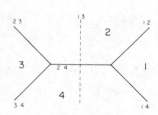

FIG. B.4 One consistent set of boundaries for the hyperplanes of Fig. B.3.

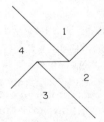

FIG. B.5 Another consistent set of boundaries derived from Fig. B.3.

an interesting visual puzzle; in higher dimensions, finding consistent bound-aries is a difficult topological problem. By using the concept of elementary subregions specified by binary variables μ_i as in (B.15), the problem can be approached by solving a set of logical equations and using the concepts of "minimal expressions" from switching theory [2]. We will not pursue this approach further in the present discussion.

Consider the inverse problem: Given hyperplanes defined by $v_1, v_2, \ldots, v_K$ and forming portions of boundaries, find $\alpha_1, \alpha_2, \ldots, \alpha_R$ so that $f(x)$ of Eq. (B.14) is consistent. The difficulties are similar. We must find a consistent assignment of an integer pair (i, j) to a vector v_k such that each hyperplane

$$v_k \cdot x' = 0 \qquad (B.20)$$

is a portion of the boundary between X_i and X_j. We then require that (B.16) hold for all x' such that (B.20) holds, and $f(x)$ will be continuous. The reader will readily agree that this latter approach is equal in complexity to the former approach.

B.2.4 A Simple Algorithm for Convex or Concave Functions

Suppose the function we are approximating is convex (or nearly so). There is an elegantly simple means for specifying a continuous convex function which avoids the problems of Section B.2.3; let

$$f(x; w_1, \ldots, w_R) = w_i \cdot x' \qquad \text{if } x \in X_i, \qquad (B.21a)$$

where

$$X_k = \{x \mid w_k \cdot x' \geq w_j \cdot x' \quad \text{for} \quad j = 1, 2, \ldots, R\}. \qquad (B.21b)$$

A point x is hence in the subregion X_k if $w_k \cdot x'$ is greater than or equal to $w_j \cdot x'$ for all j; the *value* of the function at x' is then given by $w_k \cdot x'$. The function defined by (B.21) must be continuous, since x' is only on a boundary between X_i and X_j if $w_i \cdot x' = w_j \cdot x'$, insuring continuity.

It is easy to show that $f(x)$ in (B.21) must be convex; a univariate func-tion so defined is illustrated in Fig. B.6(a). Concave functions can be defined by reversing the inequality in (B.21b).

If the family of functions $\mathscr{F}$ in (B.1), (B.4), and (B.5) is given by (B.21a) and (B.21b), then those equations may be minimized with respect to w_1, $w_2, \ldots, w_R$ by many possible search techniques with assurance of continuity.

Figure B.6b indicates the obvious fact that nonconvex functions can be defined on subregions defined by Eq. (B.21b). We use this fact to extend the approach to the approximation of more general functions.

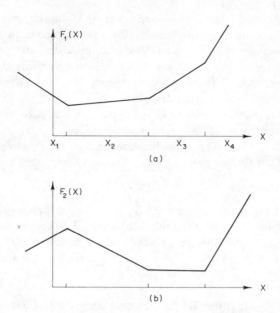

FIG. B.6 Piecewise linear functions: (a) convex; (b) nonconvex over the same regions.

B.2.5 Approaches to Continuous Piecewise Linear Approximation of General Functions

We noted in Section B.2.2 that elementary subregions could be used to construct more complex subregions, and, further, that elementary subregions formed convex sets. Since the subregions defined by (B.21b) are also convex sets, it is logical to use them to define elementary subregions, as in Fig. B.6a, but to define arbitrary continuous piecewise linear functions over those subregions, as in Fig. B.6b. By restricting $X_1, X_2, \ldots, X_R$ in (B.14) to elementary subregions, we do not reduce the generality of the approximation, but, as we shall see, we can obtain a computational algorithm for continuous piecewise linear approximation.

Let $X_1, X_2, \ldots, X_R$ be defined by $\mathbf{w}_1, \mathbf{w}_2, \ldots, \mathbf{w}_R$ as in (B.21b). Then potential boundaries are given by

$$\mathbf{v}_{ij} = \mathbf{w}_i - \mathbf{w}_j, \qquad 1 \le i, j \le R. \tag{B.22}$$

Let $\mathcal{O}$ be the set of integer pairs corresponding to operant boundaries:

$$\mathcal{O} = \{(i, j) \,|\, 1 \le i, j \le R; \quad \text{and} \quad X_i \quad \text{and} \quad X_j \tag{B.23}$$
$$\text{have a common boundary}\}.$$

(We shall discuss later how this set is determined from the $\mathbf{w}_i$.) Then, if

$f(\mathbf{x})$ given by (B.14) and (B.21b) is to be continuous, we require, for $(i, j) \in \mathcal{O}$,

$$\boldsymbol{\alpha}_i \cdot \mathbf{x}' = \boldsymbol{\alpha}_j \cdot \mathbf{x}' \tag{B.24a}$$

for all $\mathbf{x}'$ such that

$$\mathbf{v}_{ij} \cdot \mathbf{x}' = 0. \tag{B.24b}$$

This requirement is satisfied if and only if

$$\boldsymbol{\alpha}_i - \boldsymbol{\alpha}_j = k_{ij} \mathbf{v}_{ij} \tag{B.25}$$

for all $(i, j) \in \mathcal{O}$ and some constants k_{ij}. Equation (B.25) represents an under-determined set of equations with a small set of free parameters. Choosing the free parameters determines a particular continuous piecewise linear function with boundaries given by $\mathbf{w}_1, \ldots, \mathbf{w}_R$. Hence a direct search procedure over $\mathbf{w}_1, \ldots, \mathbf{w}_R$ and the free parameters of Eq. (B.25) will lead to the optimum approximation.

Let us discuss the determination of the set $\mathcal{O}$ specifying the operant boundaries. Because $X_1, X_2, \ldots, X_R$ have been defined by Eq. (B.21b), a potential boundary $\mathbf{v}_{ij} \cdot \mathbf{x}' = 0$, with $\mathbf{v}_{ij}$ given by (B.22), is operant if and only if $\mathbf{w}_i \cdot \mathbf{x}'$ and $\mathbf{w}_j \cdot \mathbf{x}'$ are greater than or equal to $\mathbf{w}_k \cdot \mathbf{x}'$ for all $k \neq i, j$ for at least one point $\mathbf{x}$ satisfying $\mathbf{v}_{ij} \cdot \mathbf{x}' = 0$; that is,

$$(i, j) \in \mathcal{O}$$

if and only if

$$\mathbf{w}_i \cdot \mathbf{x}' \geq \mathbf{w}_k \cdot \mathbf{x}' \qquad \text{for} \quad k \neq i, j, \tag{B.26a}$$

$$(\mathbf{w}_i - \mathbf{w}_j) \cdot \mathbf{x}' = 0, \tag{B.26b}$$

has a solution $\mathbf{x}'$. If (B.26b) is replaced by a pair of inequalities,

$$(\mathbf{w}_i - \mathbf{w}_j) \cdot \mathbf{x}' \leq 0, \qquad (\mathbf{w}_i - \mathbf{w}_j) \cdot \mathbf{x}' \geq 0, \tag{B.26c}$$

Eqs. (B.26a)–(B.26c) become a test for the consistency of a set of linear inequalities.† This can be tested, for example, by the familiar simplex algorithm of linear programming by minimizing $\sum_{i=1}^{n} x_i$ to obtain a particular feasible solution or an indication that none exists [40].

A procedure suggested by the above discussion is the following:

(1)   Choose $\mathbf{w}_1, \mathbf{w}_2, \ldots, \mathbf{w}_R$.
(2)   Find $\mathcal{O}$ through the use of Eq. (B.26).
(3)   Optimize over the free parameters of Eq. (B.25) to obtain the best approximation, given $\mathbf{w}_1, \ldots, \mathbf{w}_R$.

---

† Recall that $\mathbf{x}' = (x_1, \ldots, x_n, 1)$ so that $\mathbf{x}' = (0, \ldots, 0)$ is not an admissible solution.

(4)   Return to (1) if an acceptably small error in approximation has not been attained or if a test for the optimum value of a cost function is not passed.

The values for each iteration of the above procedure are chosen by appropriate direct search techniques based upon the values and success of the previous iterations. This is a computationally expensive procedure, justified in general only if the efficiency of the final decision is critical.

A much simpler approach, related to the composed functions discussed in Section B.3, is to form a linear sum of the convex functions of Section B.2.4; such a sum need not be convex. The coefficients of the sum form part of the parameters defining the function.

B.2.6   Indirect Imposition of Continuity

The methods discussed previously in this section aimed at insuring continuity through the reduction of the parameters through direct solution of the constraints imposed by continuity; the results of such methods are functions continuous within the numerical accuracy of the computations. In some applications, small discontinuities can be tolerated. The following definition is hence useful:

Suppose X and Y are metric spaces, $E \subset X$, $\mathbf{p} \in E$, $\beta > 0$, and f maps E into Y. Then f is said to be *quasi-continuous of bound β at* $\mathbf{p}$ if there exists a $\delta > 0$ such that

$$\|f(\mathbf{x}) - f(\mathbf{p})\|_Y < \beta \tag{B.27a}$$

for all points $\mathbf{x} \in E$ for which

$$\| \mathbf{x} - \mathbf{p} \|_X < \delta. \tag{B.27b}$$

If f is quasi-continuous of bound β at every point of E, then f is said to be *quasi-continuous of bound β on E.*

All discontinuities of a quasi-continuous function of bound β are clearly less than β. In practice, one would seek a quasi-continuous approximating function with an acceptably small bound β. If we developed a measure of quasi-continuity which was related to the bound β, we could use this as a constraint appended to the minimization of Eq. (B.1), (B.4), or (B.5). If $C(f)$ is such a measure, the constraint appended is

$$C(f) < B, \tag{B.28}$$

or, by the method of Lagrange multipliers, we may minimize

$$Q'(\boldsymbol{\alpha}, \mathbf{w}) = Q(\boldsymbol{\alpha}, \mathbf{w}) + \lambda C(\boldsymbol{\alpha}, \mathbf{w}), \tag{B.29}$$

where the function f is parametrized by Eqs. (B.21b) and (B.14) and where modifying the value of λ corresponds to modifying the value of B. This is a considerably simpler approach to formulate than that of the previous sections, but the former approach reduced the number of parameters by using the constraints relating them.

How might the measure of quasi-continuity $C(f)$ be defined? Let $\mathbf{y}_1$, $\mathbf{y}_2, \ldots, \mathbf{y}_M$ be, as before, samples in the domain of f. If $\mathbf{y}_i$ and $\mathbf{y}_j$ are close, i.e., if

$$d_{ij} = \|\mathbf{y}_i - \mathbf{y}_j\| \tag{B.30}$$

is small, then we want

$$d_{ij}^* = \|f(\mathbf{y}_i) - f(\mathbf{y}_j)\| \tag{B.31}$$

to be as small as possible so that the bound β in (B.27a) will be as small as possible. It is hence reasonable to choose

$$C(f) = \frac{\kappa}{M(M-1)} \sum_{i=1}^{M} \sum_{j>1} d_{ij}^* \mu(d_{ij}), \tag{B.32}$$

where $\mu(d_{ij})$ is a nonnegative, monotonically decreasing function for non-negative arguments, e.g.,

$$\mu(d_{ij}) = 1/d_{ij}^2, \tag{B.33}$$

and, for normalization,

$$\kappa = \left[\sum_{i=1}^{M} \sum_{j>i} \mu(d_{ij}) \right]^{-1}. \tag{B.34}$$

Equation (B.32) will tend to measure the change in the value of the function for small changes in the argument. With C as defined, minimizing Q' in (B.29) is a means of obtaining a quasi-continuous function minimizing Q. It is clear that, if $\mathbf{y}_1, \mathbf{y}_2, \ldots, \mathbf{y}_M$ do not change, and if $C(f)$ is to be computed repeatedly for different values of $f(\mathbf{y}_i; \boldsymbol{\alpha}, \mathbf{w})$, then it is best to store the pairs of indices (i, j) for which (B.33) is greater than some threshold, and to sum in (B.32) only over those pairs.

B.3 COMPOSED FUNCTIONS

B.3.1 A General Procedure

A composed function is expressed in the form

$$F(\mathbf{x}) = G[H_1(\mathbf{x}), H_2(\mathbf{x}), \ldots, H_K(\mathbf{x})], \tag{B.35}$$

where $H_i(\mathbf{x})$ may also be a composed function. If a function F can be represented by a composed function, that representation may be efficient (as in the example of Section B.1).

The most straightforward approach is to parameterize $G, H_1, H_2, \ldots H_K$ as in (B.9) and minimize (B.1), (B.4), or (B.5) with respect to all the parameters. If this procedure is to yield advantageous results, the class of parameterized functions must be efficient. If multivariate polynomials are used, the choosing of order of the polynomials or terms to be retained is generally pure guesswork, and the result is unlikely to be the most efficient decomposition. Multivariate piecewise linear form representation of $G, H_1, \ldots, H_K$ is advantageous in the sense that, while the number of subregions must be prespecified, the equivalent of choosing specific terms of a polynomials is not required; more simply, the procedure is considerably more efficient if the functions into which $f(\mathbf{x})$ is decomposed are efficient representations.

B.3.2 A Two-Stage Procedure

We will be concerned in the remainder of this section, however, with finding an efficient procedure for decomposition. To do so, we break the problem into a two-stage process:

(1) Given $H_i(\mathbf{x}; \boldsymbol{\beta}_i)$, $i = 1, 2, \ldots, K$, in parametrized form, find values of the parameters such that $G(H_1, H_2, \ldots, H_K)$ as a function of its arguments is as simple as possible.

(2) Given fixed functions $H_1, \ldots, H_K$, find $G(H_1, \ldots, H_K; \boldsymbol{\alpha})$ by minimizing (B.1), (B.4), or (B.5) with respect to $\boldsymbol{\alpha}$.

This process avoids the necessity of minimizing with respect to $\boldsymbol{\alpha}$ and $\boldsymbol{\beta}_1, \ldots, \boldsymbol{\beta}_K$ simultaneously and of having to choose the form of G before the H_i are fixed.

How might we choose $\boldsymbol{\beta}_1, \ldots, \boldsymbol{\beta}_K$ with no knowledge of the form of G except that it is continuous? For the sake of concreteness, let us consider the problem of Eqs. (B.2)–(B.4), approximation with $F(\mathbf{x})$ given only at sample points $\mathbf{y}_1, \mathbf{y}_2, \ldots, \mathbf{y}_M$. Then, once $\boldsymbol{\beta}_1, \ldots, \boldsymbol{\beta}_K$ are specified, the problem will be to minimize

$$Q(\boldsymbol{\alpha}) = \|\mathbf{F} - \mathbf{G}(\boldsymbol{\alpha})\|, \tag{B.36a}$$

where

$$\mathbf{G}(\boldsymbol{\alpha}) = [G(\mathbf{h}_1; \boldsymbol{\alpha}), G(\mathbf{h}_2; \boldsymbol{\alpha}), \ldots, G(\mathbf{h}_M; \boldsymbol{\alpha})], \tag{B.36b}$$

$$\mathbf{h}_i = [H_1(\mathbf{y}_i), H_2(\mathbf{y}_i), \ldots, H_K(\mathbf{y}_i)], \qquad i = 1, 2, \ldots, M. \tag{B.36c}$$

Equations (B.36a) and (B.36b) indicate that the problem, once the H_i are fixed, becomes a conventional approximation problem with samples in K-dimensional H-space given by (B.36c). (In general, K should be much less than the dimensionality of the original samples.) The result should be an approximation such that

$$F(\mathbf{y}_i) \approx G(\mathbf{h}_i), \qquad i = 1, 2, \ldots, M. \tag{B.37}$$

We wish to choose $\boldsymbol{\beta}_1, \ldots, \boldsymbol{\beta}_K$ so that the values of F in (B.37) can be approximated by a continuous function. We can draw on the results of Section B.2.6; Eq. (B.32) is a measure of quasi-continuity evaluated only at a set of sample points. For the present objective,

$$d_{ij}^* = |F(\mathbf{y}_i) - F(\mathbf{y}_j)| \tag{B.38a}$$

and

$$d_{ij} = \|\mathbf{h}_i - \mathbf{h}_j\|; \tag{B.38b}$$

that is, we measure the continuity of the function to be approximated by $G(H_1, \ldots, H_K)$ in the second step of the algorithm.

It is possible to motivate the choice of constant κ in (B.34) in terms of this application. Referring to (B.33), $\mu(kd_{ij}) = (1/k^2)\mu(d_{ij})$, and (B.32) is invariant to shrinkage of the space. Hence, modifications in the $\mathbf{h}_i$ which correspond to multiplication by a constant should not and will not affect the measure of quasi-continuity.

B.3.3 An Example of the Two-Stage Procedure

A general sixth-order polynomial in three variables has 84 terms. The coefficients of such a polynomial were chosen by a random number generator. Eighteen three-dimensional samples were similarly generated, each component from a uniform distribution on $[-1, 1]$, giving $\mathbf{y}_1, \mathbf{y}_2, \ldots, \mathbf{y}_{18}$. We obtained $F(\mathbf{y}_1), \ldots, F(\mathbf{y}_{18})$ by evaluating the randomly generated polynomial at each of the samples. No further use was made of the generated coefficients. We choose to attempt to approximate $F(\mathbf{x})$ by functions of the form†

$$F(x) = G[H(x)], \tag{B.39}$$

$$G(H; \boldsymbol{\alpha}) = \sum_{i=0}^{4} \alpha_i H^i, \tag{B.40}$$

$$H(\mathbf{x}; \boldsymbol{\beta}) = \beta_1 x_1^2 + \beta_2 x_2^2 + \beta_3 x_3^2 + \beta_4 x_1 + \beta_5 x_2 + \beta_6 x_3 + \beta_7. \tag{B.41}$$

The parameters $\boldsymbol{\beta}$ were chosen by minimizing (B.32) to obtain a local minimum

$$\boldsymbol{\beta} = (2.51, -2.03, 0.57, 1.20, 0.78, -0.907, 0.08).$$

† The order of $G(H)$ was chosen after H was specified.

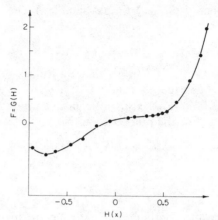

FIG. B.7 Decomposition by a two-stage algorithm.

The points on Fig. B.7 are a plot of $(\mathbf{h}_i, F(\mathbf{y}_i))$ for $i = 1, 2, \ldots, 18$. The solid curve is the polynomial of form (B.40) obtained by a fit which minimized the maximum error; the optimum coefficients were

$$\alpha = (2.69, 0.82, -1.50, 0.54, 0.09).$$

The resulting composed function in (B.39) gives an almost perfect approximation of the samples from the general sixth-order polynomial in three variables with a functional form which is much more efficiently evaluated and is specified by only 12 parameters.

SELECTED BIBLIOGRAPHY

1. Ahlberg, J. H., Nilson, E. N., and Walsh, J. L., "The Theory of Splines and Their Applications," Academic Press, New York, 1967.
2. Bartree, T. C., Lebow, I. L., and Reed, I. S., "Theory and Design of Digital Machines," McGraw-Hill, New York, 1962.
3. Birkhoff, G., and DeBoor, C. R., Piecewise Polynomial Interpolation and Approximation, *in* "Approximation of Functions" (H. L. Garabedian, ed.), pp. 164–190, Elsevier, Amsterdam, 1965.
4. Boehm, B. W., Tabular Representations of Multivariate Functions—with Applications to Topographic Modeling, Rand Corp., Santa Monica, California, Memo. RM 4636-PR, February 1967.
5. Boehm, B. W., and Rieber, J. E., A Compact Statistical Method of Topographic Representation, Rand Corp., Santa Monica, California, USAF Project Rand Memo RM-5081-PR.
6. Cantoni, A., Optimal Curve Fitting with Piecewise Linear Functions, *IEEE Trans. Comput.* **20**, 59–67 (1971).
7. Collins, D. C., Reduction of Dimensionality in Dynamic Programming via the Method of Diagonal Decomposition, *J. Math. Anal. Appl.* **30**, 223–234 (1970).

8. Collins, D. C., Dimensional Approximation in the Analysis and Control of Large Complex Systems, *Proc. Sys. Man, and Cybernetics Conf.: Joint Nat. Conf. on Major Systems, Anaheim, California, October 1971.*

9. Collins, D. C., and Angel, E., The Diagonal Decomposition Technique Applied to the Dynamic Programming Solution of Elliptic Partial Differential Equations, *J. Math. Anal. Appl.* **33**, 467–481 (1971).

10. Collins, D. C., and Lew, A., "Dimensional Approximation in Dynamic Programming by Structural Decomposition," *J. Math. Anal. Appl.* **30**, 375–384 (1970).

11. Comba, P. G., A Procedure for Detecting Intersections of Three-Dimensional Objects, *J. ACM* **15**, 354–366 (1968).

12. Coons, S. A., Surfaces for Computer-Aided Design of Space Forms, M.I.T., Cambridge, Massachusetts, MAC-TR-41, June 1967.

13. Davis, P. J., "Interpolation and Approximation," Wiley, New York, 1968.

14. DeBoor, C. R., and Rice, J. R., Least Square Cubic Spline Approximation: Variable Knots, Computer Science Dept., Purdue University, Lafayette, Indiana, Tech. Rept. 21, April 1968.

15. Esch, R. E., and Eastman, W. L., Computational Methods for Best Approximation, Sperry Rand, Sudbury, Massachusetts, Tech. Rept. SEG-TR-67-30, December 1967.

16. Ferguson, J., Basic Parametric Surface Equations for General Two-Dimensional Interpolation, Appl. Math. Dept., TRW Systems, Redondo Beach, California, No. 3122.3.245 (1968).

17. Fiacco, A. V., and McGormic, G. P. "Nonlinear Programming, Sequential Unconstrained Minimization Techniques," Wiley, New York, 1968.

18. Gordon, W. J., Spline-Blended Surface Interpolation through Curve Networks, Abstract 68T-68, *Notices Amer. Math. Soc.* **15**, (January 1968),

19. Gordon, W. J., Spline-Weighted Bivariate Interpolation through Curve Networks, Math. Dept., General Motors Defense Research Labs., Santa Barbara, California, GMR-758, April 1968.

20. Gordon, W. J., and Thomas, D. H., Computation of Cardinal Functions for Spline Interpolation, General Motors Defense Research Labs., Santa Barbara, California (1968).

21. Greville, T. N., Introduction to Spline Functions, *in* "Theory and Applications of Spline Functions," (T. N. Greville, ed.), Academic Press, New York, 1969.

22. Jordan, T. L., Smoothing and Multivariable Interpolation with Splines, Los Alamos Sci Lab., Los Alamos, New Mexico, LA-3137, 1964.

23. Kruskal, J. B., and Carroll, J. D., Geometrical Models and Badness-of-Fit Functions, *in* "Multivariate Analysis—II," (P. R. Krishnaiah, ed.), Academic Press, New York, 1969.

24. Künzi, H. P., Tzschach, H. G., and Zehnder, C. A., "Numerical Methods of Mathematical Optimization," Academic Press, New York, 1968.

25. Lawson, C. L., Recent Publications in Approximation Theory with Emphasis on Computer Applications, *Comput. Rev.* **9**, 691–699 (1968).

26. McMurty, G. J., Adaptive Optimization Procedures, *in* "Adaptive, Learning and Pattern Recognition Systems" (J. M. Mendel and K. S. Fu, eds.), Academic Press, New York, 1970.

27. Meisel, W. S., A Numerical Integration Formula Useful in Fourier Analysis, *Comm. ACM* **11**, 51 (1968).

28. Meisel, W. S., On the Design of Self-Programming Computers, *Amer. Soc. of Cybernetics Meet., Washington, D.C., October 1969.*

29. Meisel, W. S., The Efficient Representation of Functions in Pattern Classification and Feature Selection, *Proc. Sys. Man. and Cybernetics Conf.: Joint Nat. Conf. on Major Systems, Anaheim, California October 1971.*

30. Meisel, W. S., and Michalopoulos, D. A., A Partitioning Algorithm with Application in Pattern Classification, Piecewise-Constant Approximation, and the Optimization of Decision Trees (to be published).
31. Pavlidis, T., Piecewise Approximation of Functions of Two Variables and Its Application in Topographical Data Reduction, Princeton University, Princeton, New Jersey, Tech. Rept. No. 86, September 1970.
32. Pavlidis, T., A Simple Algorithm for Optimal Piecewise Approximation of Functions (to be published).
33. Schoenberg, I. J., (ed.), "Approximations with Special Emphasis on Spline Functions," Academic Press, New York, 1969.
34. Schultz, M. H., L^∞-Multivariate Approximation Theory, *SIAM J. Numer. Anal.* **6**, 161–183 (1969).
35. Schultz, M. H., L^2-Multivariate Approximation Theory, *SIAM J. Numer. Anal.* **6**, 184–209 (1969).
36. Schultz, M. H., L^2-Approximation Theory of Even Order Multivariate Splines, *SIAM J. Numer. Anal.* **6**, 467–475 (1969).
37. Schultz, M. H., Multivariate L-Spline Interpolation, *J. Approximation Theory* **2**, 127–135 (1969).
38. Schultz, M. H., and Varga, R. S., L-Splines, *Numer. Math.* **10**, 345–369 (1967).
39. Shisha, O., Monotone Approximation, *Pacific J. Math.* **15**, 667–671 (1965).
40. Simonnard, M., "Linear Programming," Prentice-Hall, Englewood Cliffs, New Jersey, 1966.

INDEX

Abend, K., 15
Absolute error correction algorithm, 68
Agrawala, A. K., 33, 44, 156
Aizerman, M. A., 98
Anticohesion, 154
Approximate risk, 55, 64ff
Approximation
   efficient, 91, 230–246
   integral-square, 85ff
   least-mean-square, 88ff
   weighted mean-square, 91ff
A priori probabilities, 24, 38, 44
Artificial intelligence, 3
Asymptotic convergence, 219–220, 225
Bashkirov, O. A., 98
Bellman, R. E., 13
Bhattacharyya distance, 183, 186
Binary variables, 79, 124, 214–215, 223
Binomial coefficient, 35, 78
Bonner, R. E., 147
Braverman, E. M., 98
Butler, G. A., 145, 184
Center adjustment algorithm, 146
Center-distance representation, 140–141,
      142, 147
Center-variance adjustment algorithm, 146
Chandrasekaran, B., 15, 23
Character recognition, 214
Chien, Y. T., 215
Cluster analysis, 138ff

Cluster seeking, 138
Cohesion, 154
Collins, D. C., 218
Composed functions, 178
Concave function, 122
Confusion region, 133
Convexity, 60
Cost function, 59ff
Covariance matrix, 42
Cover, T. M., 219
Curse of dimensionality, 12, 13, 42, 88, 186
Data analysis, 157
Data reduction, 3
Decision boundaries, 9, 16ff
Decision rule, 8, 9, 17ff, 23
Decomposition
   principle of, 166ff
   of probability density functions, 138
Design sets, 22–24
Dimensionality, 9, 12–15, 24–25
Direct methods, 28
Discriminant analysis, 163, 183, 202
Discriminant functions, 16ff, 18
Distance measures
   city-block, 145
   Euclidean, 9, 11–12, 123
Distortion-invariant feature extraction, 218
Divergence, 183, 186
Dot product, 48, 56
Dynamic programming, 164, 203, 216

Edge-weighted linear graph, 151
Edie, J., 146
Editing samples, 116
Electrocardiogram, 193, 218
Error correction method, 123
Estimation, unsupervised, 138
Factor analysis, 163, 196–197
False alarm, 40
Feasibility tests, 116
Feature ranking, 163–164, 199–202
Feature selection, 7, 24, 27–28, 162ff
Features, 7
Fisher discriminant, 183
Fischer, F. P., II, 172, 188
Fisher, R. A., 184
Fixed-increment algorithm, 68
Foley, D., 13, 14, 15
Fractional correction algorithm, 68, 70
Friedman, H. P., 146
Fu, K. S., 134, 201, 215
Fukunaga, K., 146, 197
Fuzzy sets, 21
Gaussian distribution, *see* Normal distribution
Global maximum, 50
Gose, E. L., 107, 108, 148, 203
Gradient, 47
Gradient technique, 48–50, 75
Gram–Schmidt orthonormalization, 86, 198
Graph-theoretic methods, 148–152
Grinold, R. C., 76
Groner, G. F., 55
Guard zone, 147
Hart, P. E., 219
Henrichon, E. G., Jr., 134, 201
Heuristic analysis, 216–219
Heydorn, R. P., 184
Highleyman, W. H., 23
Hill-climbing, 49
Histogram, 41–42, 103, 214
Ho, Y-C., 33, 44
Hoffman, R. L., 133
Hughes, G. F., 15, 24
Hyperplane, 56
Image processing, 163, 214
Implicit subclasses, 121
Independence of features, 214

Indirect methods, 28, 169ff
in clustering, 152
in optimization, 47ff
Inner product, *see* Dot product
Interset distances, 164, 179–183
Intraset distances, 179–183
Intrinsic dimensionality, 15, 162
Iterative adjustment of clusters, 145–146
K-nearest neighbor, 29–30
Kanal, L. N., 15, 23
Karhunen–Loève expansion, 164, 196–197, 202
Koford, J. S., 55
Koontz, W. L. G., 146, 197
Lagrange multipliers, 182
Layered networks, 125, 124–128, 169
Learning
decision-directed, 138, 155–156
with probabilistic teacher, 138, 156
without teacher, 138
unsupervised, 138ff, 155–156
Learning set, 22
Levy, D. M., 204
Likelihood, 40
Likelihood ratio, 215
Linear discriminant functions, 58, 92ff
Linear programming, 50, 70, 76, 131
Linear transformations, 169ff
Linguistic analysis, 216–219, 224
Local maximum, 50
Local minimum, 60
Localized distance, 164, 180–181, 188–189
Loss function, 39ff, 56, 59ff
Mangasarian, O. L., 131, 133
Many-at-a-time algorithm, 65, 68, 69, 75
Markovian dependence, 214
Martin, L. W., 35
Mean error, 55
Measurement space, 7–8
Measurement selection, 3
Meisel, W. S., 22, 95, 134, 174, 184
Michalopoulos, D. A., 134
Minimal spanning trees, 151
Minimax criterion, 44
Mixture distribution, 143
Mode, 143
Mode seeking, 144–145
Modified SPRT, 215
Moe, M. L., 133
Mucciardi, A. N., 107, 108, 148, 203

Multimodal distribution, 15
Multiple criteria, 166
Multivariate splines, *see* Piecewise linear
    function, Piecewise linear transfor-
    mations
Mutual information, 184
Nearest-neighbor technique, 29–30, 133
Nelson, G. D., 204
Neuron, 79
Neyman–Pearson criterion, 44
Nonconcave function, 122
Noninferior solutions, 166
Nonlinear mapping, 191, 206
Nonparametric methods, 28–29
Nonstationary pattern recognition,
    220–222, 225
Norm, Euclidean, 56, 105
Normal distribution, 42–43
Normalization, 9, 10, 106, 107, 169–170
Numerical taxonomy, 157
Nuisance samples, 117
One-at-a-time algorithm, 65, 68, 75
Orthonormality, 86–87
Owen, J., 134
Parametric methods, 28–29, 38ff
Parzen, E., 98, 103, 219
Parzen estimator, 91, 98
Parzen window, 98
Patrick, E. A., 172, 174, 184, 188, 218
Parameterized transformations, 169ff
Pattern classification, 8
Pattern classes, 9
Pattern space, 7, 9
    augmented, 63–64
Pavlidis, T., 217
Perceptrons, 124–128, 169
ϕ functions, 77, 92ff, 116
Piecewise linear clusters, 140
Piecewise linear decision boundary, 114,
    128
Piecewise linear discriminant function, 114,
    120ff
Piecewise linear functions, 116, 218
Piecewise linear potential function, 102
Polynomials, orthonormal, 228–229
Potential functions, 98ff
    generalized, 114–116
    polynomial, 108–114
    type 1, 106–107
    type 2, 106–107

Prediction, 5
Preprocessing, 7
Principal components analysis, 197
Probability densities, 21–22, 85ff
Prototype classification, 30–32, 123
Proximal surfaces, 141
Radar, 168
Random search, 51–53
Ranking formulas, 201, 202, 216
Ringwald, B. E., 157
Risk, 39ff, 44, 45
Rubin, J., 146
Sample space, augmented, 57–58
Samples, 2, 8
    labeled, 2, 8, 9, 33
    sheets of, 16
    subsets, 141–142
    unlabeled, 33, 138, 155
Schwarz inequality, 48
Sebestyen, G. S., 105–146
Sequential feature selection, 215–216, 224
Sequential probability ratio test, 215
Similarity matrix, 149–150
Size and shape parameters, 107–108
Skew, 109
Smith, F. W., 76, 94
Spanning tree, 151
Specht, D. F., 109, 110, 114
Speech processing, 214
Statistical decision theory, 39ff
Statistical formulation, 38ff
Stochastic approximation, 50, 87, 219–220,
    225
Structural analysis, 216–219, 224
Structure-preserving transformations,
    190–191, 206
Subset generation, 138
Successive dichotomy, 18–20, 87
Test sets, 22–24
Threshold elements, 78ff, 124, 127, 215
    variable-threshold, 80
Tou, J. T., 184
Training set, 22
Transformations
    custom, 193–199
    linear, 163
    nonlinear, 163, 172–179
    orthonormal, 163
    orthogonal, 170–172
    piecewise linear, 163, 174–178

Tree structure, 18, 51
  weight of, 151
Tsypkin, Ya. Z., 98
Vector, augmented, 57
Wald, A., 215

Watanbe, M. S., 154, 217
Weight space, 58
Weight vectors, 57
Zahn, C. T., 151, 152

4
– 5
C 6
D 7
E 8
F 9
G 0
H 1
I 2
J 3